Power on the Job

The Legal Rights of Working People

Michael Yates

South End Press   Boston, MA

Cover design by John Moss
Cover photograph by Rick Gerharter, Impact Visuals

Library of Congress Cataloging-in-Publication Data
Yates, Michael, 1946-
Power on the Job: the legal rights of working people/ Michael Yates.
p. cm.
Includes bibliographical references and index.
ISBN 0-89608-498-1 : $30.00. — ISBN 089608-497-3 (pbk.) : $16.00

1. Discrimination in employment—Law and legislation—United States. 2. Sex discrimination in employment—Law and legislation—United States. 3. Trade-unions—Law and legislation—United States. 4. Labor laws and legislation—United States. I. Title.
KF3464.Y38 1994
344.73\01133—dc20
[347.3041133]

94-32615
CIP

South End Press, 116 Saint Botolph St. Boston, MA 02115

99 98 97 96 95 94   1 2 3 4 5 6 7 8 9

To Karen, who brought me back to life.

Acknowledgements

I want to thank my editor, Carlos Suárez-Boulangger, and the other members of the South End Press collective for their friendly and professional assistance. The Press is a wonderful resource for working people. I also want to thank the Special Grants Committee of the University of Pittsburgh at Johnstown for a summer grant which allowed me to begin this book. Thanks again to Karen and our children, Tara, Thian, Rethe, and Zane, who have inspired me to try to make our world a better one. Thanks to all the working people I have taught and who have taught me. Finally, thanks to the good teachers I have had: Father Armand, Callistus, and Roderick at St. Vincent College and Earl Adams, Herbert Chesler, David Houston, and Arnold Katz at the University of Pittsburgh.

TABLE OF CONTENTS

Chapter 1

INTRODUCTION

I. The Working Life

Most of us spend our lives working for someone else. This is because we live in a capitalist economic system, one in which nearly all businesses are owned by a small minority of people. We must depend upon these owners to employ us if we are to live. So we work for newspaper companies, fast food restaurants, hospitals, public schools, and police departments. We do our work on assembly lines, in steel mills, in offices, in fields, on construction sites, and at home. No matter what the tools of our trade, we learn quickly that work is a heavy burden, fraught with dangers and disappointments. Each year, hundreds of thousands of us lose our jobs because our plants shut down or move or are sold. Millions of us experience layoffs, some short and some long. An estimated 150,000 of us are fired every year for no good reason. Perhaps our bosses did not like us; or our hair was too long; or we stayed home one too many days to tend to our sick children; or, and there is at least a one-in-twenty chance of this, we were fired for trying to organize a union.

Untold numbers of us will be exposed to dangerous chemicals and hazardous conditions at our places of employment. As a result, millions of us will suffer sickness and injury, and thousands will actually die, if not this year then some time in the future. If our pension funds are intact when we retire, and there is a good chance that they will not be, many of us will not live long enough or in health good enough to enjoy the fruits of our hard labors. My father is 72 years old. He worked for 44 years in a glass factory, under good union contracts. He retired ten years ago with a decent pension and full medical coverage. But in those ten years he has not drawn a single full breath because his lungs are full of glass dust, asbestos, and cigarette smoke.

Every year, a larger percentage of our labor force is made up of women and people of color. Work places an especially heavy burden upon these folks. Their employment prospects are dimmer and their pay is lower just because of their race or sex. They are harassed and intimidated by supervisors and coworkers, often with disgusting brutality and callousness. Racially and sexually motivated violence is common at the workplace. Even among the most highly paid workers, discrimination is a fact of life. Other things being equal, for example, black professional basketball players earn less than do white players, and female physicians earn less than males.[1]

All in all, the chances are very high that we will all be victims of at least one of the hazards inherent in the working life. Are there ways in which we can lower the odds against us? If something bad does happen to us, what should we do? This book details the legal rights of working people. It will explain your legal rights as workers and help you deal more effectively with the consequences of your employers' actions, or, better yet, help you prevent your employers from taking those actions in the first place. Here is a random sample of the kinds of questions which this book will help answer:

- What are our rights if we are fired? Can we collect unemployment compensation? Are we protected by any laws? Can we sue our employers to get our jobs back? Can we sue for backpay and for the pain and suffering caused by the discharge? Could we have done anything to protect ourselves while we were still employed?
- Can our employer force us to take a drug test? If we refuse to take one, can we be legally fired? Can we be made to take a lie detector test? Can we speak out in public about unsafe working conditions in our plant? Do we have any constitutional rights in our workplaces?
- Can our employers insist that we work overtime against our wills? Do we have to be paid overtime if we work more than eight hours in a day? Does every worker have to be paid at least the minimum wage?
- If we are injured at work, do we have the right to stay away from work until we are healed? Who is responsible to pay for our medical bills? If we are no longer able to do our former work because of injury at work, does our employer have to provide us with other work?
- Do we have the right to know the names and the physical and mental effects of the chemical substances used in our workplaces?

Can we refuse to work in an unsafe workplace? Can we get the government to come in to inspect our factory?

- Can we be refused a job because we are pregnant or might become pregnant? Do we have the right to paid or unpaid leave after our children are born?

- Does our employer have to give us warning that it is going to close or move our plant? If our plant does close, do we have any protections? Are there signs that will tell us our employer is planning to shut the plant?

- Can we be discriminated against because we are gay? Do gay people enjoy any civil rights?

- Do we have to be citizens of the United States to be entitled to our legal rights as workers? If we are in the country illegally, can we be fired if we try to form a union?

- What can we do if we are sexually harassed by our supervisors or by our coworkers? Is it legal for our male cowokers to decorate our office with pinups of naked women? Can a man be sexually harassed?

- If we suspect that we have been denied a promotion because we are black, what should we do? What exactly is meant by affirmative action?

- Can we be fired if we talk about joining a union at work? Can we pass out union authorization cards at work? Can our employer force us to attend anti-union meetings during work? After work?

- How can we tell if our employer has hired a union-busting company to defeat our union organizing attempt? Can we file unfair labor practice charges against the union buster as well as against our employer?

- Can our employer raise our wages or improve our benefits during a union organizing campaign?

- What should we do if our employer has committed unfair labor practices which have caused us to lose a union representation election?

- What should we do if our employer refuses to bargain with our union?

- Do our shop stewards have any special legal rights? Can we insist that our steward be present when we have trouble with our supervisors?

- How can we make our union more democratic? Does a union have any legal obligations to its members? Does a union have to take every grievance to arbitration?

This rather long list of questions does not begin to exhaust the many legal issues which routinely crop up in any workplace. This book will allow you to answer these and hundreds more, and also to know where to look or whom to ask to answer any questions this book does not cover.

II. This Book's Philosophy

Every book has a point of view or underlying philosophy. This book has several goals which express my particular point of view. First, I want readers to become knowledgeable about as many labor laws as possible since there is no telling which ones you will have to use. Most books on labor law concentrate on the law of union formation and collective bargaining. This law is obviously important, and I have devoted a lot of space to it. However, the vast majority of workers in the United States today are neither in unions nor trying to establish them. These workers have to be aware of their rights should they want to organize a union, but in the meantime there are numerous legal problems which they might face and have to confront. Second, the problems of women and minority workers are given a central focus in this book. This is not only because the majority of new entrants into the labor force will soon be neither white nor male.[2] It is also because discrimination against minorities and women is, in my view, the single most important barrier to the working-class unity necessary to turn this nation around. Working people are suffering the greatest decline in their living standards since the Great Depression.[3] Yet too many men and too many whites continue to see their female and minority coworkers as the source of their troubles instead of the actions of their employers and a government that to a large extent represents their employers' interests. It will simply be impossible to construct decent workplaces, organize democratic unions, and win good legal protections until racism and sexism are eradicated.

Third, this book emphasizes the need for solidarity among workers. A single worker can sometimes use the law effectively, but generally speaking the chances of winning a legal struggle are improved when workers act together. Obviously this is true if the issue is a strike or a boycott or the defiance of an injunction. But it is also true if the issue is the firing of a single worker or the sexual harassment of an individual woman. And it is certainly the case if the issue is the passage of better labor laws. Further, the legal rights which workers do have often require collective action to get them adequately enforced.

Fourth, I have tried to strike an honest balance between praise for and criticism of the labor movement. The labor movement in the United States has been the center of many heroic struggles without which every worker in the nation would be worse off than is now the case. Without the willingness of AFL and CIO unions to defy the laws, we would not enjoy the legal protections we have today. Yet, it must be admitted that the house of labor is not in very good shape today, and some of the blame for this must rest upon organized labor itself. Some unions are racist and sexist. Some are much too conservative. Some are corrupt. Some are not democratic. The internal problems of the labor movement must be confronted if we are to build a stronger and more democratic labor movement. Working people have as much right and as much need to know how to confront a union that is engaging in illegal behavior as they do an employer that is violating their rights.

Finally, I have tried to place the labor laws in their historical context. It is important for us to know how these laws came into being for two reasons. The manner in which a law is interpreted and enforced depends upon the circumstances in which it was enacted in the first place as well as upon current historical conditions. For example, a law passed when the labor movement is strong will be seen in an entirely different light than would the same legislation enacted when labor was weak. Further, the lessons of the past can help us to confront the future. We desperately need more and better legal protection. To get it will require complex political efforts which are more likely to be successful if we understand the efforts of the past.

III. How the Book is Organized

Each chapter begins with a story, based upon my own experiences or upon historical events, which will introduce the major topics of the chapter. I have done this so that the readers will see they are not alone, that people like themselves suffer injustices and fight against them. Hopefully then, the more formal statement of laws and legal principles which follows will be both more meaningful and easier to understand. Each of the following chapters ends with a list of questions and answers directly related to the issues discussed in the chapter and a short list of suggested readings. Footnotes are marked by raised superscripts in the text and are provided at the end of the book; Appendix I explains the case citations and provides information on researching labor law. A glossary of common labor law terms and a list of all of the cases cited in the book are included along with a collection of official forms and information sheets which may be of use to readers. I have assumed that the reader has no previous legal background. Everything that readers need to know to understand and to use the laws is explained in the text.

Chapter 2

DISCRIMINATION

I. Beep! Beep! Yale's Cheap

Yale University in New Haven, Connecticut is one of the country's elite educational institutions. Like other such schools, it supplies us with many of our political and business leaders. It is a wealthy school, with an enormous endowment, built by the contributions of the rich and famous. In 1984 and 1985 it was also the scene of one of the most important strikes since the great union organizing strikes of the 1930s.[1]

The strike by the 2,500 clerical workers at Yale showed the possibility of merging workplace and civil rights issues to the advantage of the workers at Yale and, if the lessons of the strike are learned by the labor movement, to the advantage of all workers. The union, Local 34 of the Federation of University Employees, became the bargaining agent for the workers (see Chapter Four for the legal aspects of union formation) in May 1983 after two previous unsuccessful attempts. The margin of victory was just 39 votes, but unions now win less than 10% of certification elections in units of more than 2,000 persons. In addition, Yale had waged a ruthless union-busting campaign with the help of two of the nation's top union-busting law firms (see Chapters Four and Five for a discussion on union busting).

The union organizing drive began as a series of lunch meetings between union sympathizers in the workforce and union organizers. The internal organizers became well-versed in building an organization and then fanned out over the entire university, talking to people about the issues and breaking down their fear of taking action and perhaps facing Yale's wrath for doing so. No one was asked to sign a union authorization card (necessary to get an election) until these issues had been thoroughly discussed and the workers knew what they were getting into. Then, after about a year, a "standing together" program was begun in which people would publicly proclaim their support for the union. Organizers asked, or often *pushed*, coworkers to sign the support statement. They realized that only if workers were willing to take risks and stand up for their beliefs would they have any chance of success. Four hundred people signed the statement, and it served as a great organizing tool. Workers could see that they were not alone and that together they might realize their goals.

Yale was a lousy employer, paying its clerical and technical workers less than the average for such workers in New Haven, itself one of the poorest cities in the United States. So, low salaries and crummy benefits were important issues for the workers. But, more significantly, the salaries within Yale were marked by considerable racial and sexual disparities. Women made up 82% of the full-time clerical and technical workforce and had greater average seniority than men but earned less money. Black workers, comprising 14% of the bargaining unit, made less than white workers. Black women had the highest average seniority but were the lowest-paid workers. The union made sex and race discrimination the major issue in both the organizing campaign and in the bargaining which followed the union's victory.

Further, the issue of "comparable worth" was central in the union's thinking.[2] In 1984 clerical workers at Yale made an average of $13,424 per year, while Yale truck drivers made $18,500. One year after being hired, a (female) lab assistant earned $10,208, but a (male) dishwasher earned $14,394. Women argued that the only reason for these differences was that the lower-paying jobs were held by women. The skills needed to do clerical and laboratory assistant work were at least as great as those required for truck driving and dishwashing. Jobs ought to be paid according to the skills required. When the skills of two different jobs in the same workplace were comparable (but different), the jobs ought to pay the same. The salaries of the women had to be raised up to those of the men. This argument had a powerful effect on the consciousness of the women who began to see it as a matter of simple justice. What is more, the men in the bargaining unit, to the extent that they did jobs in which women predominated, would also stand to gain, since it is the case that men earn less too when they work in "female" jobs. The truck drivers and dishwashers were not in the bargaining unit, but they did not have to feel threatened by the union's demand because it did not ask that their salaries be lowered.

After the union won the right to represent the workers, it requested that the university negotiate an agreement (see Chapter Five for the law of bargaining). The negotiations began in October 1983, but like a majority of employers today, Yale stonewalled and refused to bargain seriously. Yale could not imagine that it could be beaten by a group of secretaries. The disdain that Yale's managers felt for the women was well expressed by a top administrator who, when asked about comparable worth, said, "I wouldn't know about the comparable worth of a secretary to a truck driver seeing as how I've never held either job." Yale did not believe that the workers would go on strike. The union had won such a narrow victory, and besides these were women, naturally loyal to their benign employer and not used to taking aggressive actions. The rank-and-file knew, though, that their labor was critical to the functioning of the university. No college can operate for long without the work of the clerical staff. Exams and papers won't get typed, meetings and conferences won't be scheduled, students won't be registered, class rosters won't get delivered, etc. Without a doubt, the person most critical to the day-to-day functioning of any academic department is the department secretary.

The union organized continuously throughout the negotiations. All bargaining demands were fully debated and discussed with the members, and members were kept fully apprised of the progress of the negotiations. Most critically, the union began to build support both inside and outside of the university. Townspeople were natural allies; not only were they friends and relatives of union members, but they also harbored resentments at the rich and arrogant university in their midst. Within the university, the support of sister Local 35, made up of service and maintenance workers, was solicited, as was the support of faculty and students. Most support came from women, although Local 35's mostly male members were an honorable exception.

When it became apparent that Yale would not yield, the union took a strike vote, in April 1984. Fifteen hundred workers voted to go on strike, more than the number who had voted for the union in the representation election. The union gave the university one month to bargain seriously. The university did agree to some terms, which it would implement immediately: union security (see Chapter Five for details), health and safety, promotion and transfer, job descriptions and classifications, and the grievance procedure. The union bargained all summer over the money issues and discrimination, but to no avail. In September 1984, the workers took to the streets.

The clerical and technical workers conducted their strike with great intensity, employing a marvelous array of innovative tactics. The support-building paid off when members of Local 35 walked out in sympathy (see Chapter Six on the legality of sympathy strikes). The two strikes effectively crippled Yale's operations. Garbage piled up, and the cafeterias could not function properly. Some faculty began to hold classes away from the campus, and a lot of students began to boycott classes. The union held meetings not only among its own members but with numerous support groups to build solidarity. Mass rallies and civil disobedience which resulted in arrests gave the strike local and national publicity, and soon supporters from around the region and the country began to join the picketers. Picket signs carrying the slogan, "Beep! Beep! Yale's cheap," elicited a cacophony of car horns beeping. The strike generated much discussion, both within and outside of the college, about the general oppression of women and people of color. The Yale faculty, not known for its support of working people, nearly voted publicly in favor of binding arbitration to end the strike (see Chapter Five on arbitration).

Once the workers went on strike, they ran the risk of forfeiting control of the workplace to the university. To prevent this, they worked hard to maintain support by the teachers and students. This paid off when students would not use a cafeteria staffed by scabs (see Chapter Six on the hiring of replacement workers). They also began to contact their supervisors, taking them out to lunch and asking them what they were doing to end the strike. Then, when the university was about to close for the Christmas holidays, the union made a bold decision. The workers decided to unilaterally go back to work, while the bargaining continued. The benefits of this decision to the union were that the workers would regain control inside of their workplaces, they would earn money as would the Local 35 workers also on strike, and they would put tremendous pressure on Yale. The university could refuse to let them return to work. This is called a lockout (see Chapter Six on lockouts). If it did this, however, it would be hard-pressed to argue that it was truly concerned with the education of its students. Locked-out workers can usually collect unemployment compensation, which would have given the workers an additional strike benefit. So, Yale had little choice but to let them return to work, admitting, in effect, that the women were controlling the battlefield.

Facing the prospects of the resumption of the strike, further bad publicity, and continuous disruption, Yale finally caved in and signed a full agreement with Local 34 on January 25, 1985. While the issue of comparable worth was not directly addressed in the contract, the workers were able to win provisions which dealt with sexual and racial discrimination. Wages were increased by 35% over three years. Medical and dental benefits were greatly improved, and job security increased. The salary structure was reformed in such a way that longer-term employees, most of whom were women and many of whom were black women, received disproportionate wage increases. Women won the right to take maternity leave without breaking their seniority. But besides these gains, the women won respect from their employer, which would hesitate to take them on again. And they showed the labor movement how the joining of the civil rights agenda with union organizing can build a powerful movement, one capable of realizing the potential of both the labor and the civil rights laws.

Historical Background

The most important of our labor laws was enacted in 1935, the direct result of the labor unrest in the goods-producing industries such as auto, steel, rubber, glass, coal, and electronics. While both men and women and blacks and whites were organizing unions, the members of the new industrial unions were overwhelmingly male and white. Women played important support roles in the famous strikes which built the unions, but these roles were not played as wage workers. Blacks more often than women actually worked in the factories being organized and played crucial parts in the unions' successes. In neither case, however, did participation in organizing lead to power within the new unions.

The new law, the National Labor Relations Act (see Chapter Four), was silent on matters of race and sex. It simply granted workers the right to organize and join labor unions without employer interference and to bargain collectively with their employers. For the radical activists in the labor unions and in the political organizations such as the Communist Party, the law provided an unprecedented opportunity for working people to build a multiracial working-class movement of men and women. For a while, such a movement seemed to be a real possibility.[3] World War II saw the enormous influx of women into former male industrial strongholds and gave women the experience of the collective power of unions. Similarly, the war opened up jobs for blacks in these industries. At war's end, the union should have been poised to build upon the gains made during the late 1930s and early 1940s and extend their organizations into every workplace.[4]

Unfortunately, the unions did not move in a progressive direction after the war. They rejected the chance to organize women and black workers, and, in retrospect, sealed their fates when the goods-producing and heavily unionized industries began their long decline in the 1970s. When men returned from the war, the new unions did little to protect the women who had taken their place in the factories. Though many of the women wanted to remain in the paid labor force, the unions took the view that the jobs belonged to the men. The same was true for the less senior black workers. The CIO did begin a drive to organize black workers in the South, but this soon faltered. The progressive labor leaders who spearheaded this effort were purged from the labor movement, victims of the Cold War and the ambitious and conservative unionists who used the anti-radical hysteria sweeping the nation for their own ends.[5]

Thus did the possibility of a multiracial and nonsexist labor movement die. Women and black workers were left to fend for themselves, cut off from the labor movement. The National Labor Relations Act could have been used to increase their power, but it was not. The National Labor Relations Board did eventually rule that it was illegal for a union to discriminate against members on the basis of their race (and, by implication, their sex).[6] The trouble was that the unions did not use the Act to organize women and black workers. These oppressed groups were forced to organize as *women* and as *blacks* rather than as *workers*. Ultimately they helped to win important legal victories for themselves through the passage of the Civil Rights Acts. However, the labor movement was not in the forefront of the struggle for civil rights laws, nor did it fully embrace them once they were enacted. In fact, unions often found themselves to be defendants in lawsuits filed by women and people of color because they practiced sexism and racism. At best, the labor movement and the civil rights movement have had an uneasy alliance, to the detriment of both groups. The labor movement would not use the new laws to help to build a broader and more powerful movement, and the civil rights movement could not use the labor movement to improve its chances of enforcing and widening the coverage of the civil rights laws.[7]

II. The Civil Rights Laws

A. A Cautionary Note

In the Yale strike the clerical and technical workers fought against sexual and racial discrimination by organizing a union. Of course, they were able to do this because their fight had been preceded by the long struggle to win civil rights laws. However, they could have tried to redress at least some of their grievances directly through the civil rights laws themselves. It is illegal not to hire or promote a worker because of that worker's sex or race. Any employer practice which results in a disproportionate number of women or black workers in the lowest-paying jobs may be illegal. The same may be true if more senior women or workers of color earn less money than less senior white or male workers. A woman cannot ordinarily be paid less than a man for doing the same work. If an employer has a leave policy for workers disabled on the job, such a policy cannot exclude a pregnancy-related inability to work. It is illegal for an employer to sexually harass women on the job.

As we shall see, collective struggles by workers are more likely to be successful than individual efforts. The trouble with the civil rights laws which we are about to discuss is that complaints are usually brought by individual workers. It is possible for a group of employees to file a complaint, but even in such a case, it is difficult to organize around such a complaint, much less to sustain organization once the complaint has been filed. Once the complaint has been made, whether by a single worker or by a group of workers, it is taken over by a bureaucratic legal system, which operates with an enormous backlog of cases. It is possible for a worker to remove her case from this bureaucracy, but the burden and expense of this is placed squarely upon her shoulders.

On the other hand, a civil rights campaign waged as part of a union organizing effort can be waged collectively and controlled by the workers from beginning to end. This is not to say that the labor laws are not surrounded by impersonal bureaucracies or that workers will not often lose control of their struggles to these bureaucracies. It is only to say that the chances of success are greater when the struggle is by definition a collective one. In addition, a union, if it has the will, can more effectively fight a civil rights legal battle than can an individual employee or a group of workers. It already has lawyers and money, and it can use the solidarity of its members to put pressure on the administrative agencies and courts which are empowered to determine whether or not the laws have been violated.

B. The Major Civil Rights Laws

The civil rights laws of the United States make many types of workplace discrimination illegal. What follows is a brief introduction to the major laws:

1. The Civil Rights Acts of 1964, 1972, and 1991: These laws form the core of our anti-discrimination laws. Usually reference is simply made to Title VII of the Civil Rights Act of 1964, as amended. These statutes, enacted by the U.S. Congress, prohibit discrimination, by both employers and unions, against employees because of a worker's race, color, religion, sex, or national origin. These laws cover all private employers with at least 15 employees and all public employers irrespective of the number of employees. Employees working in other countries for either U.S. employers or foreign companies controlled by U.S. companies are covered by the Acts. Administration of the Civil Rights Acts is the duty of the federally-created Equal Employment Opportunity Commission (EEOC).

2. The Age Discrimination in Employment Act of 1967 (ADEA): This law makes it illegal to discriminate against workers because of their age. It covers only workers at least 40 years of age. To be covered, private employers must have at least 20 employees. Public employers are covered regardless of size. Employees of the U.S. Senate, the U.S. House of Representatives, and the executive branch of the federal government are not covered by the Act, but they are covered by the Government Employees Rights Act of 1991. The EEOC also administers the ADEA.

3. The Americans with Disabilities Act (Title I) of 1990: This law forbids discrimination against an employee based on the employee's disability. As we shall see, the Act defines disability broadly. Employees of the federal government are not covered, though they may be protected by the Rehabilitation Act of 1973. State and local government employees are covered by the Act, as are private sector workers who work for an employer with at least 15 employees. Again, this law is administered by the EEOC.

4. The Equal Pay Act of 1963: This Act requires employers to pay women the same rate of pay as men when they perform "equal" work. "Equal" is defined in fairly narrow terms, which means that the Act cannot be used to address the problem of occupational segregation by sex. For example, it cannot be used to fight for comparable worth. The Equal Pay Act is part of the Fair Labor Standards Act of 1938, and its coverage is basically the same. Nearly all employers, private and public, are covered, the only exceptions being certain small private businesses. Of all of the civil rights statutes, this one has the widest coverage, but it is probably of the least use in fighting discrimination. The Act used to be administered by the Department of Labor, but now the EEOC has been given this responsibility.

5. The Civil Rights Acts of 1866 and 1870: These laws were passed to statutorily support the Thirteenth and Fourteenth Amendments to the U.S. Constitution (see Chapter Eight for a discussion of constitutional protection of employees). Today these laws are part of the United States Code, which is the multi-volume compilation of all federal statutes. The Civil Rights Acts of 1866 and 1870 are Sections 1981 and 1983 of the Code and can be found in Volume 42.

Section 1981 gives all persons the same right to make contracts as white persons and guarantees that black persons will have the same benefits of all laws that secure persons and property as do white persons. The Supreme Court has interpreted Section 1981 as prohibiting racial discrimination in hiring.[8] Race has been interpreted to include ethnic groups, such as Hispanics, as well as black persons. It also has ruled that only hiring discrimination was illegal under Section 1981, but not other forms of racial discrimination in employment.[9] That is, discrimination in promotions would not violate Section 1981. Congress, however, has since amended Section 1981 to outlaw all forms of racial discrimination. Section 1981 does *not* prohibit discrimination on the basis of *sex.*

Section 1983 forbids all state and local governments (guarantee U.S. residents government) to deny any person protection guaranteed by the Constitution or by statutes. Therefore, Section 1983 makes both racial and sexual employment discrimination illegal. Coverage under Sections 1981 and 1983 is universal; there are no employer size limitations. No special agency oversees these laws, so enforcement is directly through the courts. There are a couple of advantages of using Sections 1981 and 1983 over the Civil Rights Act of 1964, and these will be mentioned as we proceed.

6. *The Constitution:* Chapter Eight of this book discusses the U.S. Constitution in some detail as it applies to employment. The Fifth and Fourteenth Amendments guarantee U.S. residents both equal protection of the laws and due process from the government at all levels. These protections have been interpreted by the courts to prohibit various types of discrimination, including, in some circumstances, discrimination on the basis of sexual preference, which is not prohibited by the federal Civil Rights Acts.

7. *The National Labor Relations Act of 1935:* This law, as amended, will be thoroughly examined in later chapters of this book. It is not ordinarily thought of as a civil rights law, though the right to form a labor union, which the Act protects, is an important civil right for all workers.[10] In addition, the courts have interpreted the Act to forbid a union to discriminate against employees that it represents on the basis of their race.[11] Presumably a union could not single out any group of workers which it represents for discrimination. A union has a "duty of fair representation" to all of the workers which it represents for purposes of collective bargaining. Remember, too, that unions are covered by the Civil Rights Acts.

8. *State and Local Civil Rights Laws:* Many states have their own civil rights laws. We cannot discuss them in this book, but it may be important for workers to be aware of them, because they may afford greater protection than the federal laws. For example, they may have greater coverage, either in terms of the number of employers or the number of employees covered. Or, they may protect categories of employees not protected by the federal laws. An example would be

a law that prohibits discrimination against employees on the basis of their marital status or sexual preference.[12]

9. The Immigration Reform and Control Act of 1986: This Act gives certain protections to immigrant workers, although these are of somewhat dubious worth. This law makes it illegal to discriminate in employment because of a worker's national origin or citizenship status. Employers are not allowed to knowingly hire illegal immigrants and must demand documents proving legal status from aliens. Employees are given some protection against the likelihood that employers will discriminate against "foreign-looking" persons. Employers cannot demand over-documentation from prospective employees; if they do, they are guilty of an unfair immigration-related employment practice. At this point, it is important to note that an employee need not be a citizen to be protected by the civil rights laws. For example, illegal immigrants are protected by the National Labor Relations Act.[13] An employer would violate this Act if it discharged such workers in the context of their engaging in activity protected by the Act (joining a labor union, etc.) on the grounds that the employees were in the country illegally. Note, too, that the Civil Rights Acts do not forbid discrimination on the basis of citizenship, although they do on the basis of national origin. The U.S. Constitution guarantees equal protection and due process to *all* persons in the nation, citizen or not.

10. Executive Order 11246: An Executive Order is an order issued by the president of the United States which has the force of law until Congress addresses the issue with which the Executive Order deals. Executive Order 11246 compels most businesses which deal with the federal government through contracts to operate their businesses in a nondiscriminatory manner. Companies which supply the federal government with goods and services and those which do construction work, including all of any company's subcontractors, must obey the Executive Order if they do more than a certain amount of business with the government. Such contractors cannot discriminate against their employees and job applicants on the basis of race, sex, color, religion, or national origin. They must tell all applicants that they will be hired on the basis of their qualifications, and they must notify the unions with which they deal of their nondiscriminatory practices. Larger contractors must put into place affirmative action programs (see below), which have the goal of balancing their workforces so that minorities and women are not under-represented. The law is enforced by the Office of Federal Contract Compliance Programs (OFCCP) within the Department of Labor. The OFCCP has the power to revoke a company's contracts and to refuse to readmit it as a contractor until it remedies its discriminatory practices.

With these summaries of the major civil rights laws in mind, let us examine each of the various forms of discrimination: by sex, by race, by national origin, by religion, by age, by citizenship, by disability, and by sexual orientation. After covering all of the groups, we will look at the procedures for bringing charges of discrimination and the remedies which are possible under the laws.

C. Discrimination by Sex

Women face a wide variety of discriminatory practices in their workplaces.[14] They are often paid less than men for the same work. They are segregated into certain types of occupations, which usually pay less than male-dominated occupations. Nearly all secretaries are (poorly paid) women, while very few women are (highly paid) plumbers. Many of the jobs which women do require skills comparable to those in jobs dominated by men, but women's skills are systematically devalued. Women are routinely not hired or denied promotions because they may or do have children or because it is assumed that they will leave their jobs if their husbands get job offers elsewhere. In situations in which the nature of the work may be dangerous to unborn fetuses, women have been denied access to jobs just because they might become pregnant. Finally, women are subjected to pervasive sexual harassment at work, not only by their supervisors but also by their male coworkers.

Let us look at the ways in which a woman might attack gender-based discrimination at work through the legal system, remembering from the discussion of the Yale strike the limitations of individual action. Much of what we say about sex discrimination applies as well to other forms of discrimination, and this will be noted when appropriate. We will look at four legal issues: equal pay for equal work, comparable worth, employment discrimination, and sexual harassment. We confine our discussion throughout to federal laws.

1. Equal Pay Act

The Equal Pay Act of 1963 guarantees women pay equality with men when they do equal work. This law is part of the Fair Labor Standards Act (see Chapter Ten), and it is, therefore, somewhat separate from the rest of civil rights legislation. Workers covered by the Fair Labor Standards Act are also covered by the Equal Pay Act. Coverage is not by the number of employees as in most civil rights legislation but by the monetary size of the business. Therefore, some small establishments are not covered, although they may be covered by state equal pay laws. Most public employees are covered by the Act.

While coverage under the Act is broad, discrimination is narrowly defined. To have a claim, a woman must compare herself to a man in the same firm. If a woman works at Sears, she cannot compare herself to a man working at Penneys. If she works at Sears Automotive, she probably cannot compare herself to a man working at Sears' Allstate Insurance Company. The man with whom the woman compares herself must do "equal" work. This means that the work done by the man and the woman must be equal in terms of the skill, effort, responsibility, and working conditions of the jobs actually performed. Skill, effort, and responsibility are given their ordinary meanings. The courts look only at objective considerations. For example, they will hold that lifting 200 pounds takes more effort than lifting 100 pounds or even 100 pounds twice. A job which requires a three-year apprenticeship will be considered more skilled than one which requires a one-year training program. A worker responsible for three other workers is in a job with more responsibility than one in which the worker is responsible for one other worker. Working conditions include surroundings and hazards. If I work on the second floor and you work on the first floor, our surroundings are not different, but if I come into contact with asbestos and you do not, they are different. If the noise levels in our workplaces are significantly different, then we have different conditions. It should be noted that the work does not have to be exactly equal, only *substantially* equal.[15] Minor differences do not make the work unequal.

Once it is established that the work is equal but the pay (in terms of rate of pay; actual earnings could be different if hours of work or the efficiency of the workers were different) is not, the employer can still prevail if one of the Act's exceptions applies. If the woman makes less than the man because of seniority, merit, piece rates, or some factor other than sex, no violation of the Act occurs. Assuming that a seniority system is not itself sex-biased, it can legally have the effect of paying a more senior man more than a less senior woman for the same work. If the piece rate for a job is 50 cents per unit, a man and a woman may earn different amounts of money, but this is not illegal so long as both the man and the woman are paid the same piece rate. Merit differences in pay are legal, but an employer must have reasonably objective standards for the awarding of merit raises. Factors other than sex might include the profitability of different departments; if the employer reaps a larger profit from the department in which the man works, it may be legal to pay the man a higher salary. If a man and a woman are both hired to be college teachers, the man may be offered a higher starting salary if he has more formal education or prior experience than does the woman. It is not legal to pay the woman less because it costs the employer more to hire women than men, perhaps because of higher insurance premiums. Nor is it legal to pay a woman less because she is more desperate for the job than is the man. In one case, a company was found to have violated the Act because it paid men more to work the night shift than it paid women. The fact that the reason for this was the unwillingness of men to work for less was irrelevant.[16]

2. Comparable Worth

The problem with the Equal Pay Act is that it does not explicitly address the fact that women typically are not employed in the same types of jobs as are men. The Act forbids an employer to pay a female secretary less than a male secretary in the same establishment, but this is of little value to women since almost no men work as secretaries. Similarly, since few women are plumbers, it is small consolation to know that a male plumber could not, other things being equal, be paid more than a female plumber. Women have correctly argued that many of the jobs which they do are "comparable" to those of men, though they are not "equal" in the sense required by the law.

To illustrate the idea of comparable worth, consider an example. A company hires a consultant to evaluate the jobs workers do in the company's plants. Job evaluators examine jobs so that the jobs can be ranked, which in turn will allow the company to assign appropriate rates of pay to them. Usually jobs are rated in terms of what are called "compensable factors," which are those factors inherent in a job which require the company to pay money to get people to perform. For example, a job may require physical dexterity, so this would be a compensable factor. Other compensable factors might be training time, education requirements, hazardous conditions, responsibility for equipment or other employees, etc. The compensable factors for each job are listed. Then, each compensable factor is weighted, according to its importance. For example, education requirements might count more for a job than physical dexterity. Points are next assigned to each factor with its weight, and the points are totaled. The more points a job is given, the higher it is rated and the more workers will be paid to do it.[17]

If the evaluation is done properly and fairly (meaning, for example, that compensable factors for jobs which women do, such as the tediousness of the work, are not given lower points than similar factors for work which men do, such as lifting weights), in many companies a lot of the jobs which women do will have roughly the same number of points as many of the jobs which men do. In the Yale strike, a job evaluation would probably have shown that a male truck driver's job got no more points than a secretary's job. Yet, the truck driver's pay was considerably higher than that of the secretary. The doctrine of comparable worth states that jobs equally evaluated should receive the same pay, other things being equal. Only if this were done could the segregation of women into certain types of work not also result in women systematically being underpaid. To proponents of comparable worth, the job segregation of women is clearly a violation of their civil rights; that is, it is a form of sex discrimination.

While the argument for comparable worth is sound, it has not been accepted by the courts. First of all, a comparable worth claim cannot be brought under the Equal Pay Act, because it is narrowly concerned with *equal* work, not comparable work.[18] If two jobs are of equal worth to the employer but they require different skills, they are not equal jobs under the Equal Pay Act. Comparable worth arguments have been brought under the Civil Rights Act, to be discussed shortly, but the courts have rejected them.[19] Employers argue that they pay women less than men for their jobs as a result of market forces. In other words, the Yale secretaries make less than the truck drivers because the conditions of supply and demand are different in the two markets. The courts have accepted this argument, rejecting the idea that the market conditions, themselves, are the result of sex stereotyping in the larger society. Some employers, especially in the public sector, have voluntarily agreed with unions of public employees to reevaluate jobs with an eye toward paying jobs according to their worth, but courts will not compel any employer to do so.[20]

The attitude of the courts on this issue is well summarized by the Seventh Circuit Court of Appeals:

> An employer (private or public) that simply pays the going wage in each of the different types of jobs in its establishment, and makes no effort to discourage women from applying for particular jobs, would justifiably be surprised to discover that it may be violating federal law because each wage rate and therefore the ratio between them have been found to be determined by cultural or psychological factors attributable to the history of male domination of society; that it has to hire a consultant to find out how it must, regardless of market conditions, change the wage it pays, in order to achieve equity between traditionally male and traditionally female jobs; and that it must pay back pay to boot.[21]

That employers might have had something to do with "the history of male domination of society" seems to have escaped the justices.

3. The Civil Rights Act of 1964

Title VII of the Civil Rights Act of 1964, as amended, prohibits employment discrimination on the basis of sex, as well as race, religion, color, and national origin. In this section, we will focus on sex discrimination, but most of what is said here applies as well to the other forms of discrimination covered by the Act. There are two types of discrimination which can be contested by employees under the Act: disparate treatment and disparate impact. Let us look at each type in turn.

Suppose that a woman applies for a job as a college teacher. She is told in her interview that she is not likely to be hired because the chairman of her department does not like women. She is not hired, and a man is. The employer's comments reflect an intent to discriminate; it does not want to hire her because she is a woman. This is illegal and is an example of disparate (unequal) treatment of women by the employer. Similarly, an employer cannot refuse to hire her on the grounds that she might become (or is) pregnant and will miss work. Nor could the employer charge female employees higher pension premiums than it charges men on the grounds that women live longer than men. Each woman must be treated as an individual; some women do not live longer than men. To charge a particular woman more is disparate treatment. Nor could men and women be required to pay the same premiums while women receive lower benefits, on the theory that since women as a class live longer than men, total benefits will be equal for men and women. This is also disparate treatment.[22]

In most cases, the employer will not make a statement that is overtly discriminatory. However, a woman might still be able to show disparate treatment. Suppose that as above a woman applies for a job as a teacher. She meets the stated qualifications for the job. She is rejected by the employer, and the employer continues to take applications or actually hires a man for the job. In such a situation, the woman can file a charge of sex discrimination against the employer, because she has established what the courts call a *prima facie* (she has given the courts reason to believe) case for finding that the employer has discriminated against her. Once she has done this, the burden shifts to the employer to demonstrate that it did not discriminate. The employer might try to show that she did not meet the qualifications for the job. Perhaps the job required previous teaching experience in the subject that she would be teaching, say history, but her experience was in teaching geography. Or, the employer could argue that she was not hired for a legitimate, nondiscriminatory reason, such as the fact that the person actually hired had clearly superior qualifications for the job. It would be advisable for the employer to make it clear in the job ad that it was looking for the best qualified person. Once the employer has given the court its reasons for rejecting the applicant, the applicant can try to convince the court that these reasons are pretextual and that the true reason was the sex of the applicant. Barring witnesses who could testify as to the motives of the employer, or clearcut proof that she was as qualified as the man who was hired, this may be difficult to do. In the end, it will be up to the court to decide; if the evidence is evenly balanced in the eyes of the court, the employer will win.[23]

Sometimes an employer establishes hiring (or promotion or salary increase) criteria which are not biased on their face but have the effect of excluding women (or any protected group) more than men. That is, the hiring criteria have a disparate *impact* on women. When there is a disparate impact, women can charge the employer with sex discrimination. However, the courts have established complex rules for such cases.

Consider again the hiring of women by a college. Suppose that women comprise 5% of the faculty and men 95%. Clearly there are many more male than female faculty. This fact alone does not show discrimination on the part of the college. Suppose, however, that the college requires a doctorate (Ph.D.) degree for each newly hired teacher. Suppose further that women comprise 30% of all persons with doctorates in the fields of study taught by the college. This means that you would expect that, if the college employed 200 teachers, roughly 60 of them should be women (30% of 200). The fact that only 5% of the teachers at the school are women strongly suggests that the employer has a bias against hiring women. If men and women were likely to be hired in proportion to their share of Ph.D. degrees, it is statistically very unlikely that a ratio of women to total faculty would be only one in 20 when the ratio of women Ph.D.'s to total Ph.D.'s is three in ten. In fact, statistical analysis shows that the odds are much less than one in 100 that the college's ratio of women to total faculty is due to mere coincidence. If women brought suit against the college for sex discrimination, a court might accept such statistical analysis as *prima facie* evidence of sex discrimination. The court will insist that the actual ratio of female to total employees be compared with a relevant comparison ratio. It would not be sufficient to argue that the college is biased against women because women make up say 40% of the local economy's labor force. The local economy's total labor force is not the group from which the college recruits teachers. Similarly, just because a much smaller percentage of a company's skilled jobs are held by women than men and a much higher proportion of women hold unskilled jobs is not by itself enough to infer a disparate impact.[24]

In another typical situation, the employer has a hiring requirement which is not overtly sexist. Suppose that the employer has a height requirement for a job. The height requirement excludes disproportionately more women from the job than men.[25] Such a disproportion could be used to establish a *prima facie* case of sex discrimination. The same reasoning could be applied to any job requirement. Employers sometimes require job applicants to take some type of examination or test and score above a certain number to qualify for a job. If disproportionately more women than men fail to achieve the minimum score, it can be argued that the test has a disparate impact on women and is therefore sex biased.

It is very important to note that when women allege that an employer's hiring practices have a disparate impact, they must be able to show that *specific* practices have a disparate impact, unless it is not possible to show which of several employer requirements is responsible for the disparate impact. Some courts have allowed a plaintiff to argue that an employer's entire hiring (or promotion) procedure, including subjective interviews, tests, a lack of uniform standards, etc. was biased. All that has to be shown in such cases is the disparate impact, that is, the fact that women are a disproportionately small share of employees.[26] Other courts, however, have insisted that the persons charging discrimination demonstrate which specific hiring (or promotion) practices cause the disparate impact. In one case, a federal appeals court rejected a disparate impact charge based on the argument that three of the employer's employment practices (tests, educational requirements, and subjective promotional decisions) together resulted in disparate impact. The court stated:

> The plaintiffs' initial burden included proof of a specific practice or set of practices resulting in a significant disparity....Statistical disparities between the relevant labor pool and [the employer's] work force are not sufficient. A plaintiff must offer evidence isolating and identifying the specific employment practices that are allegedly responsible for any statistical disparities.[27]

According to this court's reasoning, mere statistical disparities would never be sufficient to establish a *prima facie* case of disparate impact.

Once the *prima facie* case has been established, the employer can rebut it. This can be done in a number of ways. The employer might challenge the statistics of the plaintiff, arguing, for example, that the comparison group used was inappropriate or that the difference between the ratio of women to total employees in its workplace was not significantly different from that in a relevant comparison group. A second strategy for the defendant would be to argue that the job requirement in question was put in place because it was "job-related" and a matter of "business necessity." These are vague words and their meaning is not defined in the Act, so it is up to the courts to decide the merits of the defendant's arguments. A requirement can be shown to be job-related in several ways. First, a test given to job applicants can measure a person's ability to do the job in question. An example would be a typing test given to an applicant for a typing job. Or the test could approximate the content of the job. In a discrimination suit brought against the state of Maine, the state agreed to a physical agility test for state troopers which would rectify the contested low ratio of female to male troopers. Each person applying for a trooper job would be required to:

1. Push a standard-sized vehicle a distance of 12 feet on a level surface;
2. Rescue an injured child from a school bus;
3. Carry one end of a stretcher with a 175-pound mannequin a distance of 200 feet;
4. Climb a flatbed truck; and
5. Run 1.5 miles in a designated time.[28]

A second way to show that a test is job-related is to show that success on the test predicts success on the job. A test could be given to prospective employees but the test scores ignored in hiring. Then the performance of those hired is measured and correlated with their test scores. Or, actual employees could be given the test to see if it correlates with their performance. For example, a personality test might be used for prospective salespersons, in the belief that certain personality types make better salespersons. Employers would have to be cautious in using such tests because it might be difficult to prove that they correlate with the performance of the employee.[29] If a court has accepted a test as valid in one place, an employer in another place can use the same test in similar circumstances and be assured that it is valid.[30] The Civil Rights Act makes it illegal for an employer to adjust the test scores of job applicants because of their sex (or any other protected category, such as race or religion). If 50 points is the hiring cutoff score, the scores of female workers which are below 50 cannot be adjusted upward to account for any possible sex bias in the test.

The concept of business necessity is a narrow one. An employer cannot justify a sex-biased procedure simply because it is cheaper. A company which produced batteries refused to allow fertile women to work in areas of high lead concentration. There is good evidence that exposure to lead can harm an unborn fetus, and the inability of the company to sufficiently reduce or eliminate the lead exposure caused it to enact its policy. The company, in effect, argued that it could only operate its business to its satisfaction (hence, a business necessity) by excluding fertile women from jobs which would endanger their unborn children. In addition, no other, equally safe but less discriminatory, policy had been proposed in place of the one used. The Supreme Court rejected the company's argument, stating that it was up to the women to decide whether the risk to unborn children was worth taking. The company could not deny these jobs to employees solely on the basis of their sex.[31]

Sometimes an employer can justify sex discrimination on the grounds that sex is what the law calls a *"bona fide occupational qualification"*(BFOQ). For example, it is legal for an employer to insist that a man be hired to play a male role in a play or movie. In one case, the Supreme Court allowed the state of Alabama to restrict guard positions at male maximum security prisons to men. The justification here was that if women were hired as guards, the state could not guarantee the safety of the guards or the security of the prison.[32] As we shall see, the BFOQ exception is more commonly allowed with respect to age and religious discrimination. Race can *never* be used as a bona fide occupational qualification.

Once an employer has rebutted the charge of disparate impact discrimination, the burden is on the plaintiff to rebut the rebuttal. Obviously, the employer's statistical reasoning can be challenged just as the employer can challenge that of the person or group charging the discrimination. The government once sued the Teamsters Union and a trucking company for race discrimination. There were two types of driving jobs: city driving and line driving. The line-driving jobs involved driving between cities, while the city jobs involved driving only within the city. The former jobs were dominated by whites, to a much greater extent than could have been due to chance. The employer admitted discrimination before the passage of the Civil Rights Act, but said that it had hired fairly since then. The fact that the line-driving jobs were still dominated by whites was due, the company asserted, to the shrinking of the company's workforce. The implication was that since no additional new hiring was taking place, it was impossible for the workforce to reflect the company's nonracist policy. The government rebutted the employer's rebuttal by pointing out that, while the company's workforce was indeed shrinking, the company had actually hired hundreds of new drivers as a result of employee turnover. Nearly all of the new drivers were white.[33]

4. Sexual Harassment

It is a rare female employee who has not experienced sexist remarks or actions by supervisors and coworkers. Women are routinely propositioned by their bosses, often with the not so subtle implication that a refusal will harm the woman's work prospects. Even in a situation in which the supervisor is genuinely attracted to a woman subordinate, the woman may naturally feel awkward and uncomfortable about the inherent inequality of the relationship. What might seem to the male superior to be normal romancing (asking the woman out on a date, buying flowers, sending notes and letters) may be seen by the woman as harassment. Certainly a woman is not going to like unwanted physical contact or suggestive verbal comments.

While it is not at all uncommon for women to face overt sexual harassment at work, it is all but inevitable that they will experience sexist work environments. Men will tell sexist jokes in front of women without hesitation. They will make lewd remarks when a female coworker passes by, and they will plaster walls with pictures of unclad women. Bosses will call their secretaries "honey" and "doll." Women will hear references to their body parts, and men will use the word "bitch" with abandon. From a woman's perspective, it is an unusual workplace which does not have a "hostile" environment when it comes to sex.

The Civil Rights Act makes no reference to sexual harassment. It might be argued that, because men can be sexually harassed by women or by other men, sexual harassment is not sex discrimination. On the other hand, in a male-dominated society, it is inevitable that it will be women who are overwhelmingly the victims of sexual harassment. So, for all practical purposes, this is a form of sex discrimination. In 1980, the EEOC declared sexual harassment to be sex discrimination and actionable under the Civil Rights Act. The EEOC's guidelines are very useful in deciding whether or not sexual harassment is taking place:

> Unwelcome sexual advances, requests for sexual favors, and other verbal or physical conduct of a sexual nature constitute sexual harassment when (1) submission to such conduct is made either explicitly or implicitly a term or condition of employment, (2) submission to or rejection of such conduct by an individual is used as a basis for employment decisions affecting such individual, or (3) such conduct has the purpose or effect of unreasonably interfering with an individual's work performance or creating an intimidating, hostile, or offensive working environment.[34]

In 1986 the Supreme Court accepted the EEOC's guidelines and declared sexual harassment to be sex discrimination. It also held that an employee's participation in an employer's unwanted sexual advances could not be used as a defense against a sexual harassment charge.[35] An employer may be found not guilty of harassment, however, if it can convince the court that the advances were welcomed by the woman. In addition, an employer with a well-defined policy against sexual harassment and a fair and well-publicized procedure for dealing with it may be able to argue that a woman is bound to follow the company's procedure before filing suit. If a woman does not complain to the employer about harassment by a supervisor or by a coworker, the employer may not be liable because it cannot be expected to know about the harassment unless the woman tells the employer.[36]

It is crucial to understand that an employer which creates a hostile environment for women is also guilty of sexual harassment, even if no overt harassment takes place. In defining a hostile environment, the Supreme Court uses the "reasonable woman" standard. If a "reasonable woman" would think that a workplace environment was hostile to women, then the courts will agree. An employer cannot defend itself by arguing that sexist speech is protected by the First Amendment (see Chapter Eight). Nor does a woman have to show that she suffered serious mental health problems because of the harassment. In an important recent case, a supervisor made constant disparaging comments about the inferior abilities of women. He would ask women to feel what he had in his pockets or ask them to bend down to pick up a coin he had just dropped. He made comments about a woman's "race horse ass." The woman who brought sexual harassment charges against him testified about her extreme anxiety, fear, and inability to sleep. The Supreme Court ruled in her favor.[37]

Unions as well as employers must abide by the Civil Rights Act and most of the other statutes mentioned above. Unions cannot exclude women (or any other protected group) from membership or apprenticeship programs. Union hiring halls cannot refuse to refer women to jobs. Women members must have the same access as men to union offices. Both disparate treatment and disparate impact discrimination can and have been practiced by unions. The reader is referred to the discussion in Chapter Seven for more discussion of civil rights within unions.

D. Discrimination by Race

1. The Weber Case

The Kaiser Aluminum and Chemical Corporation employed various craft employees in its plants. To become a craft worker, an employee had to complete an in-plant training program. Prior to the installation of the in-house training program in 1974, the company usually hired outsiders already trained. Because of rampant racial discrimination in craft employment (discrimination practiced by both unions and employers), very few craft workers hired by the employer were black. In the Gramercy, Louisiana plant before 1974, a mere 1.83% of the craft workers were black, despite the fact that blacks comprised 39% of the local workforce. Of course, what was true at Kaiser was true across the nation. Black workers faced brutal discrimination, part of the oppression which black persons have endured since they first came to this country in bondage as slaves. You could walk into any factory from Maine to California, and if you saw black workers at all, you could be certain that you would see them in the most menial, dirty, or dangerous jobs. You might see black janitors and foundry workers, but you would not see black electricians and tool and die makers. And on construction sites, a black face would be as rare as a white face picking the crops on our farms. In towns and cities, blacks might be sanitation workers, but they would not be police or firefighters.

As we saw at the beginning of this chapter, the labor movement never fully embraced the civil rights of black workers, who were left to their own devices to improve their circumstances. The civil rights struggles of the 1950s and 1960s did not reinvigorate the labor movement, but it did give us the Civil Rights Act of 1964. Once the Act became law, black workers began to use it to desegregate workplaces and unions and to move up the wage scale. In those unions in which black workers had a solid presence, racist practices came under strong attack. Such was the case in the steelworkers' union. At Kaiser, the union, responding to pressure from black members, negotiated in 1974 an "affirmative action" plan to benefit black workers. The in-house craft training program was instituted, and workers were admitted to it with primary consideration given to the achieving of racial balance. Fifty percent of the admissions to the program were set aside for black workers until such time as black craft workers comprised the same ratio to total craft workers as the ratio of black workers to the total local labor force. Once this ratio was achieved, the set aside could be discontinued. As long as the training program was then operated on a nonracist basis, the balance between white and black workers would remain.

The affirmative action plan was voluntary; it was not mandated by the EEOC or by the courts as a result of a civil rights lawsuit. It did violate the union's usual commitment to the principle of seniority in that it would be the case that more senior white workers might not gain admittance to the program, at least until greater racial balance had been achieved. One such white worker, Brian Weber, charged, on behalf of similarly situated white employees, that the affirmative action plan violated the Civil Rights Act, which prohibits discrimination on the basis of race. He argued that the Act forbids discrimination against white as well as black workers. The affirmative action plan was "reverse discrimination."

The federal district court and the court of appeals agreed with Weber, but the Supreme Court reversed their decisions, holding that, under certain conditions, voluntary affirmative action plans, aimed at rectifying past racial (or sexual, etc.) discrimination, did not violate the statute.[38] The Court held that to take the wording of the Act literally and refuse to allow voluntary race-conscious plans would defeat the whole purpose of the Act, which was to bring discrimination to an end. Indeed, it is hard to see how the Kaiser plant's craft workforce would ever have achieved racial balance without such a plan. Without such plans, the Civil Rights Act would be, to a large extent, without meaning. The *Weber* decision was an important victory for civil rights.

2. Affirmative Action

There is a lot of confusion about affirmative action, so several points have to be made about it. First, the Civil Rights Act and similar legislation do not ever *require* affirmative action plans.[39] It is possible that the EEOC or the courts might order some type of affirmative action similar to that used at Kaiser to redress severe racial (or sexual, etc.) imbalances. Section 706 (g) of the Act gives the courts the power to "order such affirmative action as may be appropriate, which may include, but is not limited to ... any other equitable relief as the court deems appropriate." In one case, the Supreme Court upheld a court-ordered plan requiring the promotion of one black state trooper for each white trooper promoted until a racial balance in the workforce was achieved.[40] Courts do not order this type of affirmative action often; it is more likely that an employer will be ordered to develop a plan to actively recruit and train black workers (and this is the limit of most voluntary plans as well).

Second, while in *Weber* the Supreme Court ruled that the Civil Rights Act does not prohibit private parties from agreeing to the establishment of affirmative action plans such as the one at Kaiser, it also said that it would not accept *every* plan. And by extension, it would not approve *every* court-ordered plan. It is likely, however, that a private plan could be more extensive in attacking discrimination than could a court-ordered plan. In either case, the Supreme Court has established guidelines for acceptable affirmative actions: The actions taken must be part of a plan; the plan must be justified in terms of persistent and obvious racial (or sexual, etc.) imbalances; the plan must be temporary; and the plan must not unduly harm whites (or men, etc.). The harm done to Brian Weber (his inability to get into the craft training program when he wanted) is acceptable. He did not lose his job or have his pay lowered or even lose all opportunity to get into the program. By implication, a plan which gave a preference to black workers who scored lower on a qualifying test might be acceptable to the courts, as long as the above criteria are met. However, a plan which required the laying off or demotion of white workers (or men, etc.) would not be acceptable. It is important to note that we are not talking about court rulings that affirm that particular black workers were denied hiring or promotion. In that case, a court could order that a white worker be displaced, just as the NLRB might order a worker illegally fired to be reinstated even though this means the displacement of the worker who replaced her.[41]

3. Consent Decrees

An employer or a union facing a charge of racial (or sexual, etc.) discrimination can agree after the charge has been filed to end the discriminating behavior. That is, they can enter into what are called "consent decrees." As we shall see, when a charge of discrimination is filed with the EEOC, the EEOC must attempt to get the parties to reach a voluntary agreement. A consent decree is an agreement reached by the parties, with the aid of the EEOC, which is placed before a court for the court's approval. If the court approves the consent decree, it becomes enforceable by the court if its terms are violated. Like affirmative action plans, consent decrees can include race-conscious (or sex, etc.) remedies such as the quota device used at Kaiser Steel. In one case, the Supreme Court upheld an appeals court's approval of a consent decree entered into by the city of Cleveland and a group of minority firefighters.[42] The consent decree provided for racial preference in hiring, promotions, and assignments to rectify longstanding racial imbalances within the fire department.

In the Cleveland firefighters' case, the firefighters' union had opposed the consent decree. It argued that the decree would benefit persons who were not themselves victims of racial discrimination by the employer, and this is precluded by Section 706(g) of the Civil Rights Act. While the Supreme Court ruled that a court might not have the power to *order* such a remedy, it was lawful for private parties to *agree* to such a remedy. In a consent decree, the court agrees to enforce what the parties have accepted, but does not order them to do anything itself. As with affirmative action programs, however, the courts cannot enforce consent decrees which "unduly harm" whites (or men, etc.). Thus, the Supreme Court struck down a consent decree which would have resulted in less senior black employees being retained in a layoff over more senior white employees in violation of a seniority agreement.[43]

Unless and until there is a change in law or in facts (such as, for example, sufficient hiring of black workers to remedy the imbalance in the workforce which was the basis for the consent decree in the first place), a consent decree cannot be challenged by employer, union, or employees. This means that a consent decree entered into by an employer and black employees cannot be challenged by white employees after the court has approved it. The white employees must challenge the decree at the time of its making. White workers hired after the decree has been approved cannot challenge it on the grounds that they did not have a chance to object to it at the time of its making. The same would be true for men if this were a sex-based consent decree.[44]

4. Seniority Systems

At the time of the passage of the Civil Rights Act, unions were concerned that the Act would make collectively bargained seniority systems subject to legal challenge.[45] While a seniority system is an important protective device for employees, it certainly was the case that many seniority systems were discriminatory. Some contracts had separate seniority lines for white and black workers; these obviously were made with the intent to discriminate. Others were neutral on their face but had the effect of perpetuating discrimination. Consider a plant with several departments. Some departments, those with generally better jobs and working conditions, are predominantly white, while other departments, those with lousier jobs and poorer conditions, are predominantly black. Seniority is a determining factor in promotions and layoffs, but seniority is based on department. A high-seniority black worker who manages to get into a white department loses his departmental seniority and goes to the bottom of the seniority list in the new department. He will be laid off first if there is a reduction of personnel in the white department. Therefore, there is small incentive for the black employee to try to get into the white department. The departments remain segregated, and this segregation reinforced by the seniority system.

What does the law say about the racial effects of seniority systems? First, a seniority system which has a discriminatory *intent* is illegal and the courts will order it to be changed. Separate seniority lists based on race (or sex, etc.) are illegal. Second, seniority systems which have the effect of perpetuating past discrimination are *not* illegal unless it can be shown that there was an intent to discriminate. This is because Section 703(h) of the Civil Rights Act states:

> Notwithstanding any other provision of this title, it shall not be an unlawful employment practice for an employer to apply different

> standards of compensation, or different terms, conditions, or privileges of employment pursuant to a bona fide seniority or merit system...provided that such differences are not the result of an intention to discriminate.

Thus, departmental seniority systems such as the one described above are not, in and of themselves, illegal, and the courts will not order them to be abolished.

Third, if an employer assigns people to departments or job classifications on the basis of race (or sex, etc.), the employer is acting unlawfully. In one case, only whites were hired as long-distance truck drivers, while blacks were relegated to local driving. Job bidding was based upon departmental seniority, so that blacks could not bid into the higher-paying jobs. These black workers were entitled to relief under the Civil Rights Act.[46] They could be given their "rightful place" seniority in the higher-paying department, that is, the seniority they would have had had the employer not discriminated against them. The court ruled in a later case that it would only remedy such discrimination which had occurred after the passage of the Civil Rights Act.[47] In addition, the seniority system itself was not subject to legal challenge unless it could be shown that it was made with an intent to discriminate.

5. Sections 1981 and 1983

In addition to the Civil Rights Act, black employees and members of other ethnic groups can use the civil rights laws enacted after the Civil War. These are now titled Sections 1981 and 1983 of the United States Code. Section 1981 can be used *only* by black workers and other racial and ethnic minorities but not by women or any of the other groups protected by the Civil Rights Act. It covers all private employers, labor unions, and state and local governments. It is broader in coverage than the Civil Rights Act, which has minimal employer restrictions. Any type of employment discrimination can be challenged under this section, in hiring, pay, promotion opportunities, etc. A black worker does not have to file a complaint with the EEOC but can file a lawsuit directly in court. The suit must be filed within the time limit for the filing of personal injury suits, and this limit varies from state to state. If a worker has exceeded the limitation period for filing a complaint under the Civil Rights Act, she can still file a suit under Section 1981. Suits can be filed under both the Civil Rights Act and Section 1981 at the same time. One shortcoming of Section 1981 is that disparate impact charges can not be brought, only disparate treatment charges. Section 1983 prohibits both racial and sexual discrimination, but only by state and local government employers; private employers are not covered.[48]

E. Discrimination by Religion

The Civil Rights Act makes discrimination on the basis of religion by employers and unions illegal. Religion is broadly defined to include atheism and agnosticism, as well as personal faiths not affiliated with an organized church. The analysis of sex and race discrimination can be applied to discrimination by religion. For example, disparate treatment and disparate impact charges can be based upon religion; the procedures for establishing *prima facie* cases are exactly the same for religion as for sex and race. An employer in a town in which the workplace is predominantly Catholic would be subject to a disparate impact charge if its own workforce contained no or very few Catholics.

The Civil Rights Act does contain some unique features with respect to religious discrimination. First, religious organizations are permitted to insist that their employees be of their religion. Religious organizations include schools at all levels which are owned or operated by religious organizations. The employees need not perform religious functions. A Jewish school can insist that the teachers, as well as the secretaries and custodians, be Jewish. A Mormon Church can legally fire an employee because that employee is not Mormon. A newspaper which is essentially secular in its operations but which is owned by a religious organization can still insist that its employees uphold the church's religious precepts.[49] Of course, a nonreligious employer cannot compel its employees to engage in any type of religious practice or observance. Recently, some employers have hired consultants who attempt to motivate employees through so-called "new age" philosophies. Employers who have penalized employees for refusing to participate in such training programs on the grounds that they require employees to embrace religious precepts have found themselves subject to lawsuits. For example, some of these consultants preach that human beings are the center of the universe, a point of view in direct conflict with Christianity. A Christian worker might legitimately complain that, in effect, the employer that forced her to attend this consultant's sessions was compelling her to observe or embrace a religious belief.[50]

The second distinguishing feature of the law of religious discrimination is that not only can an employer not discriminate, but the employer is legally bound to try to accommodate the employee's religious practices and observances. Some religions require members to observe certain days of the week. This becomes a problem when the observance interferes with the employer's scheduling of workers. Suppose that a worker cannot work on Fridays because of her religion.

If the employer can accommodate this observance without incurring more than minimal cost, the employer must do so. For example, if the employer can make work assignments such that this worker does not have to work on Fridays, the employer must do this unless the employer would have to incur costs to do it. If the employer must hire a substitute worker, or pay another worker overtime, or force another worker to do the Friday work, the employer is *not* bound to accommodate the employee.[51]

The employer must solicit suggestions from the employee as to how the accommodation might take place. But, the employer is not bound to utilize the employee's suggestion in place of its own, provided only that the employer's accommodation is reasonable. In one case, a collective bargaining agreement allowed teachers to take three days off for religious observations and several days for personal reasons. The personal days could not be used for religious purposes. An employee who needed to have six days off for religious practices suggested that he be allowed to use the personal days for religious observations. He also suggested another alternative in which he would pay for the hiring of a substitute teacher at the substitute rate of pay and he would be paid his regular rate for the three days. The school board rejected his suggestions and instead insisted that he take three days of unpaid leave. The Supreme Court held that the employer's proposal was reasonable, and this ended the inquiry.[52] The fact that the employee's suggestions were also reasonable was not relevant.

F. Discrimination by National Origin

An employer who refuses to hire persons born in Mexico or any other country violates the Civil Rights Act. Discrimination by national origin could also be discrimination by race, color, or ethnicity. Most of what has been said about discrimination on the bases of sex and race applies as well to discrimination of individuals because of their national origin. For example, if an employer has a job requirement which excludes disproportionately persons of a certain national origin, the employer can be found guilty of discrimination unless the requirement can be justified as a business necessity. An example might be a requirement which excluded employees above a certain weight. This might exclude persons from certain countries if they tend to be heavier than persons of other national origins. It is important to note that the Civil Rights Act does not prohibit discrimination on the basis of citizenship. So, if the true reason the person born in Mexico was not hired is because that person was not a citizen, this would not violate the Civil Rights Act. The rights of aliens are discussed below.

A common type of discrimination is the requirement that a person be able to communicate effectively in English. Such a requirement would exclude many persons from other countries from employment. An employer would have to show that the job requires that the worker be able to communicate effectively in English. If this cannot be shown, the requirement is illegal. A person's accent is not sufficient reason to deny that person a job or a promotion. An employer may be able to insist that workers refrain from speaking their native language on the job if it can show that this is a business necessity.[53]

G. Discrimination by Age

Older workers often face discrimination. Employers may not want to hire them, because the employer thinks that they are less productive, they may demand higher salaries, they are more costly to insure, or they may not work long enough for the employer to recover any training costs which it has incurred. The same logic applies to promotions and transfers. An employer may want to shed itself of its older workers to cut costs. The Civil Rights Act does not make age discrimination illegal, but Congress has since enacted another law, the Age Discrimination in Employment Act of 1967 (ADEA).

The ADEA is administered by the EEOC, and it is similar in most respects to the Civil Rights Act. Both disparate treatment and disparate impact charges are possible. The Act protects workers 40 years of age and older. A 45-year-old who applies for a job and is rejected in favor of a younger worker can claim disparate treatment. The employer will then have to show that the younger worker was better qualified or provide some nondiscriminatory reason for its decision. An employer could argue that it paid a newly hired younger worker more than an older current employee because this was necessary to attract the younger worker to the job. Except in a situation in which the firm is under great financial stress, it is illegal to get rid of older employees just to save money. In disparate impact cases, employees must show that the entire protected group (workers 40 and older) are affected by the employer's practice and not just some part of the protected group (workers over 60, for example). Suppose that a fitness examination is given to all employees. Employees over 60 score low on the test and are excluded from certain jobs. Employees between 40 and 60 do as well as younger workers and are not excluded from these jobs. This could not be used as a proof of disparate impact.[54]

The law does allow age to be considered a *bona fide occupational qualification* (BFOQ) more easily than it does sex, but still this defense is relatively narrow. An employer has to show that most people in the protected category who would not qualify for a job because of some age limitation cannot do the job effectively. Alternatively, the employer has to show that some older workers cannot do the job effectively but that it is not possible to know which *specific* workers cannot. Effectiveness is most often judged in terms of the safety of coworkers and customers. A bus company had a policy of not hiring drivers over 35 years of age. It reasoned that new drivers would be assigned the most difficult and stressful routes, and that it would take the drivers ten years to master the driving. The employer was able to convince the court that driving skills diminish with age, so the hiring rule was justified.[55] Mandatory retirement ages are illegal under the Act (with the exception of certain highly paid executives) unless the employer can raise a *bona fide occupational qualification* (BFOQ) defence. An employer might successfully argue that airline pilots, police, or firefighters have to retire at a certain age, given the danger to others that an older worker might pose in such stressful and dangerous jobs.[56]

An important age discrimination issue involves various employee benefits such as health care, life insurance, and pensions. Older workers may be more costly for an employer to insure or obtain health care coverage for. Newly hired older employees may place a greater strain on pension funds. An employer cannot refuse to hire or to promote an older worker because the cost of that worker's benefits will be greater than those of younger workers. If benefit costs are equal, an employer cannot provide older workers with lower benefits or charge them more to participate in the benefit. An employer may not deny older workers access to benefits because of cost considerations.

On the other hand, if the employer can show that there are cost differentials in providing benefits for older and younger workers, an employer may make adjustments for this. It is legal for the employer to either provide a benefit so that the cost is the same for younger and older workers or charge the older employee more to keep the benefit equal. These adjustments can be made on a per benefit basis or on a benefit package basis. Here is an example from Michael Evan Gold's useful little book, *An Introduction to the Laws of Employment Discrimination*:

> Suppose an employer offers benefits X, Y, and Z, none of which is a pension plan, and the cost of each of these benefits is about the same. Suppose also that the extra costs for older workers would justify reducing each benefit by 10 percent. Because of the

workers' needs, the employer chooses not to reduce benefit X. The employer may reduce benefits Y and Z by 15 percent, or benefit Y by 20 percent and Z by 10 percent, or any combination adding up to the same total savings. [57]

The above considerations do not apply to pension plans. Pension plans may have minimum retirement ages, and an employer is free to stop paying into a plan when a worker reaches the plan's "normal" retirement age. An employee cannot be compelled to retire, however, at any age, presuming, of course, that the worker is still capable of performing the job. In one type of pension the employer (and perhaps the employee) contribute some fraction of wages to an individual retirement account. The managers of the plan then invest the monies in the workers' accounts. These are called *defined contribution* plans. Since by definition, these plans are no more costly for older workers, the employer can place no restrictions on the older workers' participation. Another type of plan is called a *defined benefit* plan; in these the benefit is defined and is usually based on years of service and wages in the year or years just prior to retirement. These plans may be more costly for older workers, because the employer may have to set more money aside to fund the plan per older worker than per younger worker. Under the Employee Retirement Income Security Act, pensions "vest" after five years of employment. This means that the employee is guaranteed to receive a pension even if she leaves this employer. Employers can refuse to allow employees hired within five years of a pension plan's normal retirement age to participate in it. If this age were 65, an employee hired at age 62 could be denied the right to be in the pension plan.

Employers sometimes offer employees incentives to retire early. Naturally they do this to save money. Are such incentives legal? They are if they are voluntary and not used as means to pressure older employees to retire. Employers often insist that employees accepting early retirement incentives sign a waiver giving up their right to sue the employer for age discrimination. Because some workers signed these waivers in ignorance or under duress, Congress established rules for such waivers. They must be voluntary; they must be part of a plan which provides the workers with benefits greater than they would normally be entitled to; they must make reference to the workers' rights under the ADEA; they must give employees an opportunity to back out; and they must advise the employees to consult their lawyers. [58]

H. Discrimination by Disability

It is often difficult for persons with physical or mental disabilities to obtain employment at all, let alone employment commensurate with their abilities. Despite the stories of courageous people overcoming the most terrible afflictions, people with disabilities make less money and suffer higher unemployment than do their counterparts.[59] During the 1980s, the disabled took matters into their own hands. Disability activists petitioned Congress, held rallies and demonstrations, occupied buildings, blocked traffic, and refused to attend classes. By militantly organizing, they caught the public's attention and forced the politicians to act. The result was the Americans with Disabilities Act of 1990 (ADA). Title I of the ADA, which went into effect in July 1992, prohibits discrimination in employment against persons with disabilities. The ADA is a complicated and comprehensive piece of legislation and too new to have generated many higher court decisions. We cannot do the Act justice here, but we can outline its basic provisions.

The ADA defines "persons with disabilities" very broadly; congressional supporters claimed that it protected the 43 million persons in this country with disabilities. Specifically, a person with a disability is one who has "(A) a physical or mental impairment that substantially limits one or more of the major life activities of such individual; (B) a record of such impairment; or (C) [been] regarded as having such an impairment." Major life activities include walking, breathing, seeing, hearing, talking, working, etc. Some conditions are specifically excluded from coverage, such as drug addiction and "homosexuality, bisexuality, transvestism, transsexualism, pedophilia, exhibitionism, voyeurism, sexual behavior disorders, compulsive gambling, kleptomania, [and] pyromania...."[60] Obesity, left-handedness, and other such physical characteristics are normally not considered disabilities. Persons who are in or have been in drug treatment programs are protected by the Act. Persons with a history of disability are covered, for example, a person with past bouts of tuberculosis. Persons with AIDS and related diseases are covered. Persons perceived as having disabilities are covered whether or not they are, in fact, disabled. A person cannot be discriminated against because she is associated with a disabled person.

An employer cannot discriminate against either current workers or job applicants because of their disabilities. The Act states: "No covered entity shall discriminate against a qualified individual with a disability because of the disability of such individual in regard to job application procedures, the hiring, advancement, or discharge of employees, employee compensation, job training, and other terms, conditions, and privileges of employment." Congress meant for this list to be interpreted broadly, so that an employer cannot discriminate in *any* aspect of employment. The one exception has to do with benefits such as health insurance. These can be limited according to risk, so that an employer could refuse benefits to persons with certain pre-existing conditions.

The term "qualified individual with a disability" is of great importance. An employee is qualified under the Act if that person "with or without reasonable accommodation, can perform the essential functions of the employment position that such individual holds or desires." This places an affirmative duty upon the employer to provide a disabled worker with reasonable accommodation to do the "essential functions" of the job. The essential functions of a job are those necessary for the job to be done. The law gives chief weight to the employer's own description of the job: "For the purposes of this title, consideration shall be given to the employer's judgment as to what functions of a job are essential, and if an employer has prepared a written description before advertising or interviewing applicants for the job, this description shall be considered evidence of the essential functions of the job."

If duties are peripheral to the essential functions of a job or if they take up a small fraction of the job's entire functions, they may not be considered essential. For example, suppose that a secretary in a firm has traditionally run errands for her boss. A disabled person who could not do this could not be denied this job, because the running of errands is not essential to the job. In one case, considered under the Rehabilitation Act of 1973 (which applies only to employees of the federal government and to certain private companies with federal government contracts), a nurse was denied reinstatement by a hospital after receiving drug rehabilitation. The reason the hospital gave was that one of the nurse's duties was to dispense drugs to patients. She successfully sued to get her job back by showing that the dispensing of drugs was not an essential aspect of her job, and that it was possible for the hospital to reasonably accommodate her by assigning someone else to dispense drugs or reassigning her to a job which did not require the dispensing of drugs.[61] On the other hand, most construction jobs require heavy lifting, so heavy lifting would be an essential function of the job. A worker with a bad back could probably be denied such a job, because she could not perform an essential function of the job.

No doubt, the concept of "reasonable accommodation" will generate a lot of litigation. The law refers specifically to the courts' standard in religious accommodation under the Civil Rights Act and declares this insufficient for the ADA. The law also provides examples of reasonable accommodation:

> The term "reasonable accommodation" may include: (A) making existing facilities used by employees readily accessible to and usable by individuals with disabilities; and (B) job restructuring, part-time and modified work schedules, reassignment to a vacant position, acquisition or modification of equipment or devices, appropriate adjustment or modification of examinations, training materials or policies, the provision of qualified readers or interpreters, and other similar accommodations for individuals with disabilities.

The extensive nature of this list makes it clear that Congress intended that employers spend money if necessary to avoid discrimination against disabled workers. Suppose that a worker's yearly pay is $30,000, but it will cost the employer $60,000 in equipment or hiring and scheduling costs to accommodate the worker. Unless the employer can show that this expenditure will be unduly burdensome in terms of the employer's *total* costs (and not simply the cost of this worker's salary), the courts might consider the $60,000 cost reasonable. Even in a situation in which the cost might be unreasonable, the disabled employee must be given an opportunity to pay the unreasonable part of the cost.

Several other features of the Americans with Disabilities Act deserve mention. First, an employer cannot ask questions of a job applicant about her disabilities. For example, an employer cannot say, "Do you have diabetes?" An employer can ask if the person can perform the job's duties. An applicant for a truck driving job can be asked if she has a driver's license, but she cannot be asked about her eyesight. Applicants cannot be required to take physical examinations until they have been tendered a job offer and then only if the examination is given to all employees (exceptions are made for jobs in which prehire examinations are mandated by law).

Second, a disabled employee must be told about the employer's duty to reasonably accommodate, but the employer does not have to make such accommodation until the employee requests it. The employer must consult with the employee about the accommodation, and the employee's suggestions must be given some weight by the employer.

Third, reasonable accommodation applies to all aspects of the workplace. If an employer takes employees to conferences away from the workplace, the employer must make sure that the disabled person can attend, too. If social activities are a regular part of the employment, the disabled person must be given an opportunity to participate as well.

Fourth, an employer cannot deny a disabled person a job because the employer thinks that the job might endanger the health of the disabled worker. There must be compelling evidence that the worker would be a danger to herself. This danger must be imminent, that is, it cannot be argued that the person might be endangered at some distant time in the future. It cannot be assumed, for example, that a person with high blood pressure cannot do stressful jobs on the grounds that this person will suffer harm at some future time. On the other hand, an employer would not have to offer a driving job to a narcoleptic. The law requires that more concern be given to the health and safety of coworkers and customers than to the presumed health and safety of the disabled person herself.

Fifth, collective bargaining agreements negotiated after the passage of the Act must conform to it. Collective bargaining provisions in conflict with the Act will not interfere with the Act's enforcement. Unions should make sure that their contract reinforces the Act's protections of the disabled and strengthens them if possible.

I. Discrimination by Sexual Preference

Although estimates vary, there are at least a few million gay and lesbian workers in the United States. One of the major shortcomings of the Civil Rights Act is that it does not prohibit discrimination against workers on the basis of their sexual preference. This means that it is perfectly legal for an employer to deny a worker a job, a promotion, a transfer, a pay raise because that worker is gay. This is a great injustice and should be immediately rectified. In addition, gay and lesbian workers cannot usually use their health and pension benefits on behalf of their partners as can married heterosexual couples.

Do gay workers have any legal protections? Yes, not many, but a few worth examining. First, gay public employees have some constitutional protection (see Chapter Eight). A public employee cannot be fired for speaking out on gay rights issues; this would violate the First Amendment. Nor could an employee be fired for living with a gay person; the First Amendment protects freedom of association. The Fifth and Fourteenth Amendments guarantee public employees due process from their employers. This means that a gay public worker could not be discharged without an investigation and a hearing and the right to present his side of the case. So far, the courts have been unwilling to extend to gay workers the "equal protection" guaranteed by the Fifth and Fourteenth Amendments (see Chapter Eight for details).[62] There is no good reason for this; it is the clear result of homophobia. When gay workers are granted this constitutional right, it will be illegal for public employers to discriminate *in any way* against their gay employees short of some *compelling* national interest, just as it is now unconstitutional for public employers to discriminate on the basis of race or sex.

No federal law protects gay workers in the private sector, but some state and local laws do. The National Gay and Lesbian Task Force estimates that there are at least 135 state and local civil rights laws and executive orders which offer some protection to gay persons, and some of these apply directly to private employment. Legislators in seven states (California, Connecticut, Hawaii, Massachusetts, New Jersey, Vermont, and Wisconsin) have enacted civil rights laws which include sexual orientation. Some public and private employers have allowed rights to accrue to the partners of gay employees, such as health coverage. Several cities have enacted such rights into law, including Berkeley, San Francisco, and Los Angeles in California and Madison in Wisconsin. These laws vary in content and coverage, and they are not a substitute for comprehensive federal legislation.[63]

While AIDS is a disease which has stricken people irrespective of their sexual orientation, it has devastated the gay male population. It is important to remember that AIDS is a disability under the Americans with Disabilities Act. It is illegal for an employer, within the confines of the ADA, to discriminate against a worker or job applicant with AIDS or any worker who is HIV positive. Similarly, a worker cannot be discriminated against because he or she is caring for a person with AIDS, although the ADA does not require an employer to make reasonable accommodations for such workers. If caring for someone with AIDS necessitates that I miss work frequently, I would still be subject to discharge for excessive absenteeism.[64]

One way that gay employees can gain legal protection is through a union contract.[65] Just as women have won contract provisions making sexual harassment a contract violation, gay unionists have won similar protection for sexual orientation. Needless to say, homophobia is common in many unions, but aggressive organization by gay workers and their allies can win contract protection. Some national unions have amended their own constitutions and bylaws to prohibit discrimination against gay members, and they have also committed themselves to include sexual orientation in nondiscrimination clauses which they negotiate in contracts with employers. This is one more area where unions can and should lead the way.

J. Discrimination by Citizenship

Anti-immigrant hysteria is sweeping the nation, especially in states in which there have been large influxes of immigrants from countries such as Mexico, Haiti, the nations of Central America, Africa, and East Asia.[66] Immigrants are unfairly accused of taking native jobs and overburdening various welfare programs. The great irony of this is that it is the actions of U.S. multinationals and the U.S. government which have driven people from their homelands in search of work and security.

Immigrants have begun to organize to protect themselves. Asian immigrants in New York City, who often work in subhuman conditions for wages well below the legal minimum, have formed independent labor unions to win better wages and working conditions, as have workers in other parts of the country. Some established unions have actively sought to organize immigrants, legal and illegal alike, not just at work but in their communities, as well.[67]

The labor laws offer scant protection to immigrants. As we shall see, they are covered by the National Labor Relations Act. Illegal immigrants cannot be threatened with deportation as a tactic to get them to vote against a union, nor can they be discharged for this reason. The Civil Rights Act does not prevent an employer from discriminating against a person because of his lack of citizenship, but this cannot be used as a subterfuge for discrimination on the basis of ethnicity or national origin. The Immigration Reform and Control Act prohibits employment discrimination against employees in the process of becoming citizens or those who have been granted amnesty under the Act. Finally, the Constitution protects aliens under the equal protection clause, providing important protection for public employees who are not citizens but who are in the country legally (see Chapter Eight).

III. Enforcement and Penalties

A. Introduction

The procedures which a worker must follow to enforce the laws against discrimination vary according to the law, but in most cases the employee will have to file a private suit. This means that the worker will have to find a lawyer willing to take the case. Given that a working person will probably not have enough money to pay the attorney, the attorney will have to agree to work on a "contingency fee" basis, collecting a percentage (usually 30% to 40%) of what the employee

ultimately is awarded. A civil rights case can go on for many years, and
the attorney may have to spend large sums of money to push the case
forward. Employers have numerous ways to delay a case, by, for
example, dragging their feet in providing information and documents
needed by the charging party.[68]

Given the long period of time between the filing of a charge and the
court award, it is difficult for a single worker or even a group of workers
to stay involved in the case and to put pressure on the employer to settle.
The case gets stuck in the legal system, from which the worker is far
removed. This is still another reason why labor unions should help workers
fight discrimination and make discrimination an organizing tool, as was
the case at Yale. Without constant collective efforts, the antidiscrimination
laws cannot be effectively enforced and expanded.

B. Filing Charges and Awards

If you believe that you have been the victim of discrimination by
your employer or by your union, what should you do? This depends
upon the nature of the discrimination and which of the laws you plan
to use. Let us summarize each of the laws discussed in this chapter.

1. The Equal Pay Act: It is part of the Fair Labor Standards Act, but,
unlike that Act, it is not enforced by the Department of Labor but by
the Equal Employment Opportunity Commission. However, the rules
of the Fair Labor Standards Act are used in EPA cases.[69] A woman has
two years from the time in which the discriminatory act began to file
a charge of equal pay discrimination, unless the employer's actions
are "willful," in which case she has three years to file. "Willful" means
that the employer "either knew or showed reckless disregard for the
matter of whether its conduct was prohibited by the statutes." This
may be difficult to show, so it is better to file the charge within two
years. Since EPA cases are difficult to win, a woman will usually file
both an EPA and a Civil Rights Act charge, since the disputed employer
practice may violate the latter if it does not violate the EPA.

Once a charge is filed by a woman with the EEOC, the EEOC will
meet with her to discuss the charges and help her to write up the
charges if the EEOC believes that they are warranted. Then the EEOC
decides whether or not to file charges. If the EEOC decides that a
charge of discrimination is not warranted, it issues a "right to sue"
letter to the woman, and she can sue the employer directly. If charges
are filed, the EEOC tries to conciliate the matter between the woman
and her employer. If the parties agree to a settlement, this is the end
of the matter. If conciliation fails, the EEOC can file suit on the woman's
behalf, but this is rare because the EEOC has neither the money nor
the personnel to do so. If the EEOC does not file suit, it issues a right
to sue letter. Often the EEOC does nothing at all after it gets a

complaint. The employee has the right to ask for a right to sue letter within 180 days after filing the initial charge. A worker who wants to sue immediately can ask for the letter, and the EEOC will usually comply.

The lawsuit will be filed in a federal district court, though decisions reached in this court can be appealed. If the woman wins, she will be awarded backpay, and her pay will be raised to that of the man with whom she compared herself. If she has compared herself to several men with different (but higher) wages, the court will require her employer to increase her pay either to that of the highest male wage or to an average of the several male wages. Under the Fair Labor Standards Act, the court can also award her "liquidated damages," which can be an amount up to the amount of backpay awarded. The amount of liquidated damages is up to the court, which may take into account the behavior of the employer, such as whether the employer had originally acted in good faith in setting pay rates. The woman may also recover attorney's fees. She cannot recover money for emotional distress, nor will the court award "punitive" damages, that is, money awarded to convince the employer not to break the law again.

2. The Civil Rights Act: This is also administered by the EEOC, but procedures are somewhat different than under the Equal Pay Act. Many states have agencies like the EEOC, often called Human Relations Commissions or Fair Employment Practices Agencies. Procedures differ according to whether the employee works in such a state or not. If the state does *not* have such an agency, the procedures are as described above under the Equal Pay Act, except that the initial complaint must be filed within 180 days of the act of discrimination, and the employee must file suit within 90 days of receiving a right to sue letter. If the state does have such an agency, the initial complaint must be filed with this agency first. A complaint can be filed with both the state agency and with the EEOC, but the EEOC will not act until the state agency acts. However, if the state agency has not acted within 60 days of the filing of the complaint, the worker can go directly to the EEOC. From this point, the procedures are as discussed above.

If the state does have an EEOC-like agency, the employee has 300 days from the date of the discriminatory act to file the complaint with the state agency. A person must be careful to file charges as soon as possible. The state agency has 60 days to investigate the case. If a worker waits for more than 240 days (300 minus 60) to file the charge, he may not be able to get the case before the EEOC on time. The local agency, if it has time, will investigate the case and try to get it resolved informally. An employee is best advised not to let this go on for more than the 60 days required by law before the EEOC can take the case. And, given the slowness of the EEOC and the few cases which it takes to court, a worker should probably ask for the right to sue letter immediately. He certainly should ask for the letter after the 180-day maximum.

Again, a lawsuit will be filed in a federal district court. (Remember that the parties can enter into a consent decree which they can put to the court for its approval.) The awards which the court can make depend upon whether the case is one of disparate impact or disparate treatment. In disparate treatment cases, the court can award backpay (minus any earnings in the meantime), promotion, reinstatement, hiring, "rightful place" seniority, attorney's and expert witness' fees, as well as affirmative actions. In disparate treatment cases, these awards are possible, plus additional awards in cases of "intentional" discrimination (see above). It is possible to receive compensatory and punitive damages to compensate for emotional distress and the denial of opportunities as well as to encourage the guilty party to obey the law in the future. There are limits placed on these awards for all but racial discrimination, the limits ranging from $50,000 to $300,000 depending upon the size of the employer. Where such damages are sought, the person making the charge can demand a trial by jury. Disparate impact complainants cannot insist on a jury trial.

3. Sections 1981 and 1983 of the U.S. Code: These laws are enforced directly in court through the filing of lawsuits by the alleged victim of discrimination. The time period within which a suit must be filed varies from state to state, but it is longer than that allowed by the Civil Rights Acts. The court can award a wide range of damages, and there are no limits on them.

4. Age Discrimination in Employment Act: The ADEA is also administered by the EEOC, and procedures under it are the same as for the Civil Rights Acts. Awards by the court cannot include compensatory or punitive damages, but they can include liquidated damages as under the Equal Pay Act.

5. Americans with Disabilities Act: Procedures and awards are the same here as with the Civil Rights Act. The EEOC once again administers the Act.

6. National Labor Relations Act: The full discussion of this law is in Chapters Four, Five, and Six.

7. Immigration Reform and Control Act: This law is administered by the Department of Justice. The Act created a Special Counsel for Immigration-Related Unfair Employment Practices to investigate complaints and to bring charges against employers. Either an individual or the Immigration and Naturalization Service of the Department of Justice may file a complaint. The Special Counsel's Office has 180 days to investigate the complaint. Then, 120 days after the complaint has been filed, the person is notified of her right to file a formal charge with an administrative law judge. Such a charge must be filed within 90 days of receipt of this notification.[70]

8. Executive Order 11246: Enforcement of this Order is in the hands of the Office of Federal Contract Compliance Programs, which investigates complaints and prosecutes them before an administrative law judge who sets remedies against employers who violate the order. The judge's decision is a recommendation to the Secretary of Labor. The secretary's ruling can be appealed to a federal court of appeals.

IV. Questions and Answers

Question 1: Suppose that a man quits a job or is fired. A woman is hired to replace him. Can she be paid less for the job which he had done?

She could be paid less for the same job only if the reason is one of the exceptions allowed under the Equal Pay Act— for example, if the man's higher pay was the result of a *bona fide* seniority system. Perhaps he had better job-related qualifications than she did.

Question 2: Does the Civil Rights Act require an employer to hire a minority job applicant over an equally qualified white applicant?

No. However, the minority applicant might still file a disparate treatment claim. It will probably be difficult for the minority candidate to show that he or she was exactly equally qualified. An employer can probably show some reason why it chose the white applicant, and it would be up to the court to determine if this reason is valid.

Question 3: What are some additional employer practices which might form the basis for a disparate impact discrimination claim?

A wide variety of employer practices have been challenged, including educational requirements, tests for job applicants, height and weight requirements, language requirements, questions about past criminal activities, arrest records, and residency requirements.[71] Suppose that an employer refuses to hire persons with arrest records. This may have a disparate impact upon groups with higher than average arrest records. The employer would have to show that this rule was job-related or a matter of business necessity. Or, suppose that a town will not hire persons who do not live in the city. But suppose that the town has no residents of a protected group, say African Americans. This rule will surely deny African Americans any chance to get a town job. The town would be hard-pressed to defend this practice under the Civil Rights Act.

Question 4: Can an employer be held liable for the sexual harassment of a female worker by a coworker or by a customer or by a coworker outside of the workplace?

Yes. However, as pointed out above, if the employer has a well-defined policy against sexual harassment and a good procedure for dealing with it, the woman may have to use this procedure before going to court. That is, her employer cannot be expected to be liable for the harassment without a chance to know and do something about it.

Question 5: Can an employer refuse to hire a white man because he is married to an Asian woman?

No. The employer's decision is motivated by the race of the man as well as that of the non-employee woman. The law forbids discrimination on the basis of race, white included.

Question 6: Can an employer insist on dress codes for employees?

Generally speaking, yes. However, an employer cannot insist that women dress in ways that might be considered sexually suggestive. The courts have upheld dress codes in which women are expected to dress differently than men. Dress codes could be racially biased or religiously discriminatory, depending upon whether the code singles out minorities of a religion for different treatment. An employer could not permit employees to wear baseball caps but refuse to allow a Jewish employee to wear a yarmulke.[72]

V. Selected Readings

1. Theresa Amott, *Caught in the Crisis: Women and the U.S. Economy Today* (New York: Monthly Review Press, 1993).

2. Camille Colatosti and Elaine Karg, *Stopping Sexual Harassment* (Detroit: The Labor Education and Research Project, 1992).

3. Paula England, *Comparable Worth: Theories and Evidence* (New York: Aldine De Gruyter, 1992).

4. Gertrude Ezorsky, *Racism and Justice: The Case for Affirmative Action* (Ithaca, N.Y.: Cornell University Press, 1991).

5. Michael Evan Gold, *An Introduction to the Law of Employment Discrimination* (Ithaca, N.Y.: ILR Press, 1993).

6. Herbert Hill and James E. Jones, Jr., *Race in America: The Struggle for Equality* (Madison, WI: The University of Wisconsin Press, 1993).

Chapter 3

ORGANIZING A UNION: HISTORY LESSONS

I. Eugene Debs and the Pullman Strike

Pullman, Illinois is a town just south of Chicago.[1] Like the little mining town in which I was born, Pullman was a company town, owned lock, stock, and barrel by the Pullman Palace Car Company. The Pullman Company was owned by George Pullman, a man who had risen from poor boy to rich capitalist, manufacturer of the famous sleeping cars which helped to revolutionize train travel. By 1894 he was one of the richest men in the United States, with wealth in excess of 25 million dollars. The Pullman Company had a virtual monopoly on the production, repair, and operation of the sleeping cars which could be found on most of the passenger trains in the country.

In 1880 Pullman began to purchase land on which he planned to build his main factories as well as what he conceived to be a model town. Eventually he bought 4,000 acres of land for $800,000, quite a bargain considering that this same land was valued at $5,000,000 in 1892, an increase of more than 600% in 12 years. The architect who designed his palatial Chicago mansion also designed his model town, which soon won praise from visitors and journalists as an outstanding example of corporate philanthropy. Visitors were impressed with its public buildings, clean streets, and neat employee housing. However, beneath the appearances George Pullman was a cold and calculating capitalist despot intent on controlling every aspect of his employees' lives. Pullman owned everything in the town, and he made a profit not only on his factories but also on the rents he charged for the workers' houses, the food sold at company stores, the rent on the churches, and on the fees he charged the citizens to use his library. Through a network of spies, he made sure that his worker serfs behaved in a manner which he deemed appropriate, sober and subservient, buying at his stores and renting his houses. Curiously, prices in Pullman were higher than in neighboring towns, but woe to the employee who shopped around.

While Mr. Pullman basked in the glow of the praise from outsiders, his workers saw things differently. As one employee put it, "We are born in a Pullman house, fed from the Pullman shop, taught in the Pullman school, catechized in the Pullman church, and when we die we shall be buried in the Pullman cemetery and go to the Pullman hell."[2] Such sentiments sharpened in 1893 when the Pullman Company introduced a series of drastic wage cuts, allegedly in response to deteriorating business conditions. Wages were cut by as much as 75%, but Pullman refused to cut the prices which his employees were forced to pay to live in Pullman. This meant that, after the deduction of rent, many workers were left with such a pittance that it was impossible for them to live without going into debt or leaving town. One worker had two cents left after payment of rent! Workers protested and implored Pullman to rescind the wage cuts or at least lower rents and prices, but Pullman responded with arrogance and contempt.

Pressed to the point of desperation, the Pullman workers began to form local unions of the new American Railway Union (ARU). The ARU was the brainchild of Eugene Victor Debs, its president and a long-time officer and organizer of one of the railroad craft unions known as Brotherhoods.[3] The Brotherhoods excluded unskilled workers from membership and operated exclusively on a craft basis. That is, there was one union for each of the railroad crafts, such as firemen, brakemen, shop workers, etc. Conservative in their outlook, the Brotherhoods were no match for the ruthless railroad barons of the day. The Brotherhoods often refused to honor each other's strikes or to participate in boycotts, and they did nothing to organize the thousands of unorganized workers in the biggest industry in the nation. Debs concluded from his experience that the only way to beat the railroads was to build a large industrial union of all railroad workers so that a strike could completely shut down the trains. The ARU was amazingly successful, winning a strike against the Great Northern Railroad not long after the union was founded. After this victory, membership rose dramatically, putting fear into the hearts of the owners.

The Pullman workers were hot to strike, but Debs and the other officers of the union urged caution, believing that the infant union was not ready to take on Pullman. If a strike against Pullman spread as other ARU members refused to work on trains which carried Pullman cars, the ARU would have to confront the power of all railroad capital and its business allies. The advice of Debs went unheeded, however, amid the union fervor of the long-suffering employees. They called a strike for May 12, 1894, but upon learning that Pullman planned to lock them out, left the plant one day early. The great strike had begun.

Within six weeks, the strike spread throughout the country as the national ARU agreed to support it by a boycott. Debs was a brilliant strike leader, and the strike and boycott struck a responsive chord among workers everywhere. Despite the best efforts of the owners—who fired workers by the thousands, hired thugs to beat up and intimidate strikers and supporters, and tried to provoke strikers into acts of violence—the strike was a tremendous success. As one writer put it, "There is little doubt that the ARU could have brought the railroads to their knees and caused them to pressure Pullman to negotiate or arbitrate, were it not for the intervention of the federal government."[4] Simply put, the strike and boycott stopped the trains and with this the flow of profits to the companies.

A labor struggle of the magnitude of the Pullman strike is no ordinary struggle. The Pullman strike challenged the dominance of the owners of the nation's means of production. A victory against the railroads would have given workers the confidence to challenge the owners' political power. The owners feared not just declining profits but the loss of their property. This they would not tolerate, so they turned to their ultimate ally, the federal government.

We like to believe that we live in a democracy, that we have government of the people, by the people, and for the people. Perhaps in a narrow sense there is some truth to this, but it has only rarely been true when it comes to the conflicts between workers and their employers. Most often the government, whether it be state or federal, has sided with the employers.[5] This is a fact of the greatest importance because the government has power much greater than that of any business. The government makes the laws and backs them up with armed might if necessary. This power was quickly made evident in the Pullman strike.

President Grover Cleveland acted decisively and in close cooperation with the railroad corporations to defeat the strike. The railroads had already hired goons and thugs to intimidate the strikers and act as provocateurs, destroying property so that the local police would arrest union supporters. Of course, the railroads fired thousands of workers who refused to handle Pullman cars. At that time it was legal to fire strikers and replace them with strikebreakers. As we shall see, it is still legal to replace strikers with scabs, although it is not legal to fire them, a difference which does not amount to much in practice. President Cleveland's attorney general, Richard Olney, appointed a special federal counsel to deal with the strike, one Edwin Walker, who had been a railroad attorney for 24 years. Olney then began to appoint U.S. deputy marshals to help the companies defeat the strike. Quite often these deputies were the very thugs hired as scabs by the corporations. These unsavory elements were actually given badges and guns and the power to arrest strikers and sympathizers. Deputies terrorized union supporters and committed numerous acts of violence. Some committed acts of such outrageousness that they themselves were arrested by Chicago police. To further weaken the strike, President Cleveland eventually sent federal troops to those areas where the strike was most successful. Before the strike was over, 12,000 troops were involved, more than one-half of the nation's entire standing army!

Readers should note carefully this use by the federal government of its "police power" to defeat a strike. An entire book could be written about the many times this power was used against workers.[6] It has seldom been used to protect working people, although it certainly could have been. This business bias of the government, federal, state, and local, is very difficult for workers to combat effectively because of the sheer physical power the state has at its command. Its use transforms a strike from a conflict between two private parties to one between working people and their own government. It puts workers in the position of "outlaws" and makes it hard for them to win public sympathy for their actions. In effect, it shields the actions of the employers from public scrutiny and confuses people as to the nature of the conflict. Unfortunately, it can be taken as a guarantee that the government will become involved in any serious labor dispute, almost always on the side of the employer. During the recent Pittston coal strike in southern Virginia, at one point some 90% of the state police were on duty protecting scab production and transport of the company's coal (see Chapter Six for details).

Injunctions

In conjunction with the use of federal deputies, the attorney general petitioned the federal courts to issue injunctions to stop the strike. Because the injunction is so important in labor law, it will be useful for us to discuss it in some detail at this point.[7] Deriving from the common law of England, an injunction is an order issued by a court demanding that certain parties stop doing certain things. Historically, courts issued injunctions only if there was an immediate danger to a person's physical property in a situation in which that person had no other legal recourse. For example, suppose that there is a tree on the border between your land and mine. You tell me that you are going to cut the tree down, but I claim that you cannot do this because the tree is on my property. To prevent you from cutting down the tree, I petition the court for an injunction prohibiting you from doing so. The injunction prevents you from taking a future action until we decide who owns the tree. If you had cut it down and it was on my property, I could have sued you, but the tree would have been lost. If you cut it down after the injunction has been issued, you are in contempt of the injunction and are liable to fine, imprisonment, or both, at the discretion of the judge (see Chapter Six). Special courts, called equity courts, oversaw the issuance of injunctions, but these have been abolished and today any court can issue injunctions.

Until the 1880s courts in the United States followed the English precedent of insisting upon probable or actual damage to real tangible property before issuing injunctions. This meant that the most common actions of labor unions—namely striking, picketing, and boycotting—if conducted peacefully, could not be subjected to injunctions. A strike may stop an employer from doing business, but it does not threaten to physically damage the employer's plant and equipment. During the 1880s, however, the courts began to develop the novel idea that the employer's property rights included the "right to do business" with its suppliers and customers. Therefore, whatever interfered with this "right" caused the employer to suffer damage to its property, that is, had exactly the same effect as would the workers intentionally setting fire to the employer's buildings.[8]

Once the courts had expanded the definition of property, the way was open for a direct attack upon labor unions, because it is certainly true that a successful strike will disrupt the employer's normal business relationships with customers and suppliers. Employers were quick to use this new weapon. All that they had to do was find a judge willing to issue an injunction against a labor action. This was not difficult to do since most judges were from the same social class as the employers and shared the same hostility toward labor unions.[9] The procedure was a simple one: Find a judge, petition for an injunction, and charge the union with contempt if the injunction was disobeyed. No formal hearing was necessary, and the union did not have to be notified in advance that the injunction was being sought. The union had no right to be in court to present arguments and witnesses against the injunction.

To make matters worse, the court was not limited as to the actions and persons it could enjoin (when a person faces an injunction, she is said to be "enjoined"). Courts routinely issued what were called "blanket" injunctions aimed at stopping virtually any person at any time and in any place from doing anything which would aid the union in a labor dispute. In the infamous *Red Jacket* injunction issued by Judge McClintic in 1922, the United Mine Workers union was barred from doing anything in the West Virginia coal fields:

- that will suppress or unduly limit the right of plaintiffs to employ nonunion labor, or that will prevent or restrain the rights of the plaintiffs from voluntarily contracting with their employees or will prevent or restrain their employers from voluntarily contracting with them;
- that will in any way interfere with or restrain free competition among those seeking employment;
- that will create and establish a monopoly of mine labor for the purpose of unreasonably increasing wages or the price of labor above what it should be under normal conditions; and
- to unionize the mines of plaintiffs by means of persuasion, threats, menaces, intimidation, force or violence...to break contracts or prevent employment or in any manner interfere with the lawful right of the plaintiffs to employ such laborers as they may choose, and to discharge them when and as they see fit, either with or without cause.[10]

During the 1922 railroad strike, a barber was found in contempt of an injunction for placing a sign in his shop stating that he would not cut the hair of scabs, as was the proprietor of a boarding house for refusing to let rooms to strikebreakers.[11]

On July 2, 1894, Judge William A. Woods issued an injunction forbidding the American Railway Union from "compelling or inducing, by threats, intimidations, persuasion, force or violence, railway employees to refuse or fail to perform their duties."[12] This injunction basically said that anything which Debs and the other strike leaders might do to push the strike forward would violate the injunction. The union was denied the use of the mails and the telegraphs, and when the strike did not end after the injunction was issued, Debs and others were charged with contempt. At the contempt hearing, Debs was sentenced to six months in prison, which he served at Woodstock jail, about 50 miles outside of Chicago. The injunctions, coupled with the aggressive use of federal troops, and the ruthlessness of the employers, crippled the strike and destroyed the union. The skilled workers returned to the conservative Brotherhoods, while the unskilled workers would wait many years before being able to unionize again. In 1895, the U.S. Supreme Court rejected Debs's appeal, giving its seal of approval to the blanket injunction.[13] Decade by decade, the use of injunctions in labor disputes became more common. During the 1920s, 2,130 labor injunctions were issued, covering 25% of all strikes conducted during the decade.[14]

Although the Pullman strike was defeated, Debs learned its lessons well. While in prison he developed a radical consciousness and determined that the entire capitalist system had to be overhauled. Within ten years, he helped to found the Socialist Party and the most militant industrial union of all time, the Industrial Workers of the World.

II. Some Historical Background

In an economic system such as our own, the land, raw materials, factory buildings, machinery, and equipment are in large part owned by a small number of private individuals. A congressional study done in 1983, for example, showed that an incredible 36% of all of the nation's wealth was owned by a mere 0.5% of all families.[15] Most people have little wealth, especially wealth in the form of capital such as business enterprises. This means that most of us will be unable to survive from what we own. Instead, we will have to sell our ability to work to those who own the capital. Since we must do this or starve, we are at a definite disadvantage with respect to the owners. To make matters worse, the owners have structured their workplaces in such a way as to make most of us replaceable. Most jobs do not require so much skill that only a few persons can do them; not many of us are indispensable. If I confront my employer with the ultimatum that I will leave unless I am paid substantially more money, my employer will urge me to leave.

When our country was young, not that many people were wage laborers, but this was no longer the case as industry began to develop and it became more difficult for a man to strike out on his own. And women were confined to wage labor right from the start, being for the most part considered the property of their fathers or husbands. A sizeable number of workers were slaves with no chance to be independent; even after slavery ended, they had almost no chance to avoid wage labor.

Workers were quick to realize their vulnerability as individuals facing their employers. To improve their lot, they began to form organizations of workers, originally called trade unions because the members followed some trade or craft, but eventually just called labor unions.[16] They reasoned that while a single worker could put but little pressure on an employer, a group of workers might be able to compel an employer to pay higher wages or shorten hours. The first workers to form unions were skilled workers, their skill giving them added leverage. A group of shoemakers in a city might, for example, club together and inform their employers that henceforth they would not work for anything less than certain sums of money and they would not work alongside of any worker not a member of their organization. If enough workers could be persuaded to join, their employers would be faced with the choice of paying the union scale or going out of business.

Naturally, the employers, or masters as they were often called, did not like these labor unions and organized to combat them. They pursued many avenues of confrontation, prominent among which was the law. As we shall see, the Constitution is silent on unions and on employer-employee relations. It might have been possible to get federal or state legislatures to enact statutes to curtail these upstart trade unions, but this was a cumbersome process, and one bound to lead to conflict in that the workers considered the government to be as much theirs as their employers'. Skilled workers who had recently fought to win the country's freedom from England were unlikely to tolerate the passage of a statute like England's Combination Act of 1790 which made membership in a union a crime.

The legal device chosen by employers to attack the workers was, therefore, neither the Constitution nor statute but the common law. The common law is the unwritten law made by judges, deriving originally from the common law of England, but adopted to changing conditions in the United States by our judges (see Chapter Nine for more details on the common law).[17] The first use of the common law in a dispute between workers and their employers occurred in 1806. The shoemakers of Philadelphia had formed an organization to compel the masters or owners of their shops to pay them certain minimum amounts for various types of work. They made up a list of "prices" and refused to work for any master who would not pay these prices or alongside any shoemaker who would work for less. To the workers, staunch supporters of the recent Revolutionary War, their union was seen to be a way for them to be free, for without sufficient income and independence, it was not possible to be a free citizen of the new republic. But to the masters the union was the very antithesis of freedom, a bold attempt to create a labor monopoly which would deprive the masters of their "freedom of trade" and the nonunion men of their freedom to work. In addition, it would injure the public by raising costs and prices and causing unemployment.

To put an end to the workers' bold disregard for the welfare of both the owners and the community, the masters charged the shoemakers with criminal conspiracy. Under the common law a conspiracy is a "combination of two or more persons, by some concerted action, to accomplish some criminal or unlawful purpose, or to accomplish some purpose not in itself unlawful or criminal, by criminal or unlawful means."[18] If, for example, a group of people meet and plan a murder, the meeting and planning are themselves criminal acts, that is, conspiracies. Of course, if they carry out their plans, they are also guilty of murder. The masters succeeded in getting the local law enforcement officers to so charge the men, and they were duly brought to trial. The prosecutor argued that the shoemakers were a "threat to liberty," that their union was evidence that they had conspired to harm their employers, the nonmembers, and the general public.[19]

It is not obvious that the actions of the shoemakers fit the definition of conspiracy. They had simply formed a union, refused to work for prices below those on their list, and put whatever pressure they could upon nonmembers and masters to abide by their scheme. None of these "means" seems to be illegal, nor does their "end" of attaining higher wages. In modern language they were trying to establish a "closed shop," in which none but members of the union could get employment. Naturally their ends conflicted with those of the masters and the nonmembers and conceivably with some segments of the public, but this did not make them criminal. The court, however, thought otherwise and found the workers guilty of conspiracy and made them pay a fine. The judge sided fully with the employers and condemned the union in the strongest language, suggesting that the shoemakers' union "threatened the survival of republican government."[20]

It is not too surprising that the shoemakers were found guilty. Judges were not popularly elected and were overwhelmingly recruited from the wealthier classes; they moved in the same circles as did the employers and shared their prejudices, prominent among which was the notion that anything which interfered with a "free" labor market was an evil to be condemned as both antisocial and a threat to economic growth. To make matters worse, the juries in the conspiracy trials were comprised of property owners, who alone had the right to serve on juries. This meant that workers were not tried by their peers and were therefore less likely to obtain justice. Between 1806 and 1842, there were at least 21 conspiracy trials, and workers lost most of them.[21] The conspiracy doctrine was dealt a blow in 1842 when the Supreme Court of Massachusetts held that the Boston Journeymen Bootmakers' Society was not guilty of a conspiracy when it struck an employer who had hired a nonmember. Chief Justice Shaw said that the mere formation of a union or a concerted refusal to work were not, in themselves, illegal, so no conspiracy could be charged.[22]

Shaw's ruling was a victory for workers, but a limited one, since it applied only to Massachusetts, and many more conspiracy charges were brought against unions after it. A few states enacted conspiracy statutes, strengthening the conspiracy doctrine, and judges used conspiracy language well into the twentieth century. The conspiracy doctrine went into decline after the Civil War, right at the time that the majority of people were becoming wage laborers and more general labor organization was taking place. In fact, it was not that big an issue among the workers themselves, although they did condemn it, even to the point of organizing mass demonstrations. As juries came to be made up of working people, employers hesitated to use the doctrine, fearing correctly that juries would refuse to convict. But what is important about the conspiracy doctrine is that it foretold the attitude of the courts toward labor organizing. Almost without exception, they were hostile to it, and they were willing to reshape the common law into an anti-union weapon of great power.

We will have occasion later in this book to examine one of these weapons, the at-will employment doctrine, a common law creation of the 1880s which is still alive (see Chapter Nine). There are many others, so it may be worth our while to look briefly at the historical record.

A good example of how the common law develops as well as of its general anti-labor bias is the invention of the tort of "inducing breach of contract."[23] A tort is a civil as opposed to a criminal wrong; the party claiming to be wronged can sue the party accused of doing something wrong for money damages. Tort law is often common law and changes as the judges see fit. The new tort of inducing breach of contract arose originally in a case in England involving an opera singer named Wagner. She had an agent named Lumley, but another agent named Gye got her to break her contract with Lumley and sing with him. Ordinarily Lumley would have sued the singer for breach of contract, but, probably because she had no money, he sued Gye instead for getting or "inducing" her to breach the contract. Lumley won the case, and thus was created a new tort. Employers put this new legal device to good use with the "yellow dog contract." This was an agreement that an employer, often a coal company in a small mining town with no other employment, required employees to sign to keep their jobs. In it they swore that they were not members of any labor union, nor would they become members while in the employ of this company.

Yellow dog contracts were common in many industries until the 1930s, when they were made illegal. Their purpose was not really to justify a discharge because of union membership; the at-will doctrine already gave the employer the right to fire a worker for any reason. Its purpose was to prevent a union from organizing workers. A union organizer who attempted to get workers who had signed the yellow dogs to join the union could be sued for inducing breach of contract. The existence of yellow dogs was sufficient grounds for a judge to issue an injunction against the organizing union. Now you might think that a yellow dog is not a contract at all, since true contracts cannot be signed under duress, which was certainly the case with the yellow dogs. Yet the U.S. Supreme Court held otherwise in the famous *Hitchman* decision of 1917, which declared that a yellow dog was a valid contract that a worker was free to sign or not.[24]

The common law of injunctions has already been discussed. The inclusion of the employer's "right to do business" in its property rights made any of a labor union's conventional tactics subject to injunction. If a union went on strike or set up pickets or urged people to boycott (refuse to buy or use) an employer's product, it would interfere with that employer's normal business relationships. This meant that it threatened the employer's property and could be enjoined. Judges took an especially dim view of picketing, many of them considering it to be illegal (a tort) in and of itself, meaning that picketing might be subject to a lawsuit for money damages as well as an injunction. Remember, too, that the injunction could be a blanket order, prohibiting any type of labor solidarity.

III. The State's Police Power

Throughout the period from the first conspiracy case to the Great Depression of the 1930s, the common law gave employers powerful weapons in their struggle against labor organizing. It is no wonder that only the most skilled workers, those upon whom the employers were dependent, had any success in forming labor unions. Yet the law was not the only weapon available. After the Civil War, the large corporations which formed and came to dominate the economy organized themselves politically and were able to exert great pressure upon all levels of government to do their bidding. Local police, state militia, and federal troops were often called upon to restore law and order during labor disputes, which is a polite way of saying that they broke strikes. It is difficult to discover a major strike during this period in which police of one kind or another were not involved. The railroad strikes of 1877, the Pullman strike, the Homestead steel strike and the great 1919 steel strike were defeated in large part by the government's use of its police power. Thousands of other labor actions met with police repression, and thousands of workers were arrested and sent to jail or fined. As one historian put it, "Between 1886 and 1930, the U.S. Army came close to being a national police force...In all, federal or state troops were employed in over 500 disputes between 1877 and 1903, or nearly one in every 60 strikes."[25]

So intertwined were the property rights of employers and the state's police power that local law enforcement officials who showed any sympathy toward strikers were often subjected to injunctions and arrests by their superiors. In Pennsylvania the notorious Coal and Iron Police, who ruled the coal towns with an iron fist, were created by act of the state legislature but hired by the coal companies. It is testimony to the great skill and bravery of the miners and their families that, despite these "pussyfoots," yellow dogs, company goons, and injunctions, they were able to form the United Mine Workers of America.

IV. Early Statute Law

Because the common law and the police power of the government were thoroughly biased in favor of employers, working people organized politically to get legislatures to enact statutes which would give them some rights. Despite the many roadblocks, workers were able to form national organizations like the American Federation of Labor and the Knights of Labor. Both succeeded during the 1880s in organizing hundreds of thousands of working people into labor unions. The Federation concentrating on skilled laborers, while the Knights were more inclusive. Both laid out political programs which included legal reforms, and some successes were achieved, especially at the state level.

Among the legislative goals of the new labor movement were a shorter work day, the abolition of sweatshop labor, the outlawing of payment to workers in scrip, restrictions on child labor, the prohibition of restrictions on union activity, the banning of yellow dog contracts, and limitations on the use of labor injunctions. Many laws were passed, but the courts invariably struck them down as unconstitutional. Judges took the view that among the rights guaranteed by the Fifth and Fourteenth Amendments to the Constitution was the right of a company to make whatever "contracts" with its employees that it could. The fact that workers were less powerful than their employers, usually huge corporations, meant nothing to the courts. They continued to rule as if the two parties to an employment bargain were equals. Or, if they admitted the obvious inequality, they simply stated that it was not within their power to do anything about it. Specifically, it was not a lawful use of the state's police power to enact legislation that interfered with the employers' right to get labor under whatever terms they were able. To put such laws into effect was to pass "class" legislation that benefited one group at the expense of another and therefore violated the Constitution's guarantee of equal protection. The fact that workers were unequally protected in the normal course of their economic life eluded the justices.[26]

It would take another book to detail all of the pro-labor laws which were struck down by the courts. Legal scholar William Forbath has calculated that by 1900 about 60 laws were invalidated:

> Between 1885 and 1900, one law proscribing tenement labor was struck down; none were upheld. Five prohibiting discrimination against union members were invalidated; none were upheld. Five regulating the weighing of coal at mines were voided; one was upheld. Four fixing the time of payment of wages were also voided; none were upheld. Finally, seven laws restricting labor injunctions were struck down or vitiated in explicitly constitutional terms; none were upheld or enforced. Although both state and federal constitutional standards were somewhat liberalized after the turn of the century, by 1920 courts had struck down roughly 300 labor laws.[27]

One statute which did pass constitutional muster was the Sherman Act of 1890. The remarkable growth of the economy after the Civil War witnessed the formation of gigantic corporations with unprecedented economic power. Through ruthless business practices and political chicanery, corporations such as Rockefeller's Standard Oil Company came to have near monopoly power in the production of basic goods. Farmers, small businessmen, and workers saw these "trusts" as threats to democracy and tried to bring them under the rule of law. The Sherman Act aimed to prevent "restraint of trade," that is, attempts by businesses to gain monopolies by restricting competition.

While the Act has never been effective in limiting the power of big business, it was utilized to wreak havoc upon the labor movement. One of the ways in which labor had managed to organize unions was through solidarity across craft and job boundaries. The 1880s were the heyday of the labor boycott and the sympathy strike. If, say, brewery workers in St. Louis were on strike to force their employer to recognize and bargain with their union, workers in St. Louis and perhaps throughout the country would refuse to buy the brewery's beer or patronize any saloon which sold it. Workers at other workplaces might strike in sympathy with the brewery workers, either by honoring their picket lines or refusing to work at their own premises. Such solidarity generally meant the difference between winning or losing a strike. Such actions were, it is true, often subject to injunctions, but they did not violate any statutes or generally make the workers liable to pay employers any money damages for loss of business caused by the solidarity. All of this changed drastically with the Sherman Act.

In the early 1900s the Hatmakers' Union tried to organize the workers at Loewe and Company, a hat manufacturer in Danbury, Connecticut, the one large company which had remained nonunion. To win recognition, the union waged a successful boycott, getting hat retailers and the public not to buy the company's hats. The company claimed that the boycott was a restraint of trade and violated the Sherman Act. It asked for the "treble damages" allowed by the Act. In 1908 the Supreme Court found the union guilty of a Sherman Act violation and fined the union's members large sums of money.[28] The fines bankrupted the union as well as many individual union members, some of whom were forced to sell their homes to pay the fines.

The "Danbury Hatters" decision was a landmark victory for employers because it made all similar boycotts statutorily illegal. A few years later the Supreme Court suggested that strikes too could be illegal under the Sherman Act.[29] An alleged Sherman Act violation was sufficient grounds for a labor injunction as well. Labor fought to have Congress exclude unions from Sherman Act prosecution, but it failed. In 1914, Congress enacted the Clayton Act, which contained provisions that appeared to exempt labor unions from anti-trust prosecution, but the Supreme Court quickly interpreted the new law so narrowly that Sherman Act prosecutions continued unabated until the 1930s.[30] We will look at the current liability of labor unions under the Sherman Act in Chapter Six.

V. Conclusion

Until the 1930s, when something of a revolution took place in labor law, workers trying to form unions came up against often insurmountable legal barriers. Not only were employers free to fire and blacklist them (give their names to other employers so that they could not get employment), but whatever workers did probably ran afoul of the law. Organizers and their supporters could be sued, enjoined, or jailed, often all three. Any success invited the local police, the state militia, special deputies, or federal troops into the fray on the side of their employers. Any legislative victories were soon nullified by the courts.

The terrible bias of the law did not go unchallenged. However, labor was not well positioned to bring about changes in the legal order of things. Skilled workers, separated by ethnic background from the rising numbers of unskilled laborers, made only sporadic efforts to organize them. Instead these skilled employees concentrated upon winning specific items from their own employers, such as higher wages and shorter hours, and too often saw the unskilled as competitors rather than allies.

The division of the working class by skill was only one such division. A division of great significance was by race. Skilled workers had, throughout the nineteenth century, thought of themselves consciously as white workers, and blacks were excluded by definition from their struggles. This made it impossible to forge the racial unity necessary for the formation of strong working-class organizations capable of challenging the power of the employers. Similarly, skilled workers thought of themselves as "men," again excluding women by definition. Yet women worked in factories in large numbers, and their inability to effectively organize ultimately weakened all of labor.[31]

To emancipate themselves from the shackles of the law, workers would have had to have formed strong political organizations, but the above divisions made this difficult, as did the strength of the two-party system which often siphoned off labor's best leaders.[32] A more subtle barrier to political power was the very success of the employers' legal victories. As employers were consistently able to get the government to intervene in labor disputes, either through the courts or the police, labor found itself cast in the role of "outlaw," because if it were to have any chance to defeat employers, it would have to break the law. The newspapers, themselves capitalist enterprises, never tired of depicting strikers as criminals and unrefined rabble. The notion that unions were criminal outfits and a danger to democracy (today the polite phrase is "special interests") embedded itself deep in the public mind, making it nearly impossible for labor to find allies among the middle classes.

The American Federation of Labor, representing the skilled workers, decided that it was impossible to fight against the law, that is, to organize politically like their counterparts in Europe. It therefore developed a strategy of "business unionism," relying upon economic power to confront capital and accepting the hostile legal climate as a fact of life. Rather than struggling directly against the law, it ingeniously tried to find common law arguments to support its own positions. Instead of a war against the labor injunction, for example, labor argued that employers ought to be subject to them as well. Instead of a labor political party, the AFL accepted the political system as it was and tried to get what it could by "rewarding labor's friends and punishing its enemies" with working-class votes regardless of party affiliation.[33]

Labor's strategy of accommodation to the status quo gradually hardened into an ideology opposed even to beneficial legal reform and rabid opposition to any group which took a more radical stance. AFL agents actually served as spies for the government against radical opponents of World War I. The AFL opposed federal unemployment benefits during the Great Depression, so strong was its distrust of the government.[34] However, it is one thing to distrust the government, and it is another not to see that political struggle is a necessary ingredient of labor power. The mass of unskilled, ethnically, racially, and sexually diverse workers could not be organized without it.

VI. Selected Readings

1. Jeremy Brecher, *Strike* (Boston: South End Press, 1972).

2. William Forbath, "The Shaping of the American Labor Movement," *Harvard Law Review* 102 (Jan. 1989), pp. 1111-1256.

3. Robert Justin Goldstein, *Political Repression in Modern America* (New York: Schenkman Publishing Co., Inc., 1978).

4. Christopher L. Tomlins, *The State and the Unions* (Cambridge: Cambridge University Press, 1985).

Chapter 4

ORGANIZING A UNION: THE CURRENT LAW

I. Mike and Jane Start a Union

Mike and Jane were custodians in the building where I work. Our employer is a large public university, although we work at a regional campus about 75 miles from the city in which the central unit of the university is located. Public employees now make up about one-fifth of the entire labor force or more than 20 million workers. In terms of working conditions and the relationships we have with our employers, we are not any different from workers in private businesses. Certainly this was true for Mike and Jane. We began to talk whenever one of them came into my office to clean or empty the waste baskets, and naturally, our discussions usually revolved around troubles on the job. Their pay was miserably low and their fringe benefits were substandard even within the university. The foreman was always changing their shifts and spying on them, threatening their job security if they did not do what he said. Some workers had cut special deals with the supervisors, and they got the best job assignments and shifts. Mike had been a union coal miner, so he was a little bolder than Jane at first, but gradually they both decided that it was time to do something about their situation. They began to talk about forming a union with the other janitors, with the women who cleaned the dormitories, and with the workers who maintained the buildings and grounds. I told them that I would help in any way I could.

At the time, there were 45 people working as maintenance and custodial employees. They could have tried to organize themselves as an independent union, but this would have been difficult. Organizing a union takes time, experience, and money, all of which were in short supply. We decided, therefore, to contact one of the large national unions to see if they had any interest in helping us. It is a sad fact that many unions in the United States have not acted aggressively to expand their memberships. In fact, this failure has been cited by some scholars as a major reason for the decline in union membership since the mid-1950s.[1] A couple of the unions we contacted showed no interest at all in a potentially small local which would not ship much dues money to the national treasury but which would require service from it nonetheless. However, one union was interested, the one which had already organized similar workers at the central campus. They were already bargaining with the university, so a small local would not present the same cost disadvantages as it might to another union. This union, the Service Employees International Union (SEIU), told us to set up a meeting away from the college so that union organizers could talk to the workers. A good attendance would show interest and build solidarity at the same time.

More than half of the workforce came to the first meeting, which we held in a motel a short distance from campus. The men and women there asked a lot of questions, and by the end of the meeting, we knew that a union was a real possibility. Our next step was to follow the procedures established by the labor laws to reach the point where we could get a secret ballot election in which the workers could vote to have a union. In the days of the Pullman strike discussed in the previous chapter, the only way in which workers could get an employer to deal with their union was to force it to do so, usually by striking, picketing, and boycotting the employer into submission. In some ways, this is the ideal way to form a strong union, because the heat of battle usually creates the greatest solidarity and the sharpest understanding of one's true interests. On the other hand, the hostility of employers and their allies in the courts and in the government made such struggles fraught with danger, and they usually ended in failure. Many labor leaders and their allies (but by no means all of them) believed that a large and powerful labor movement could only be built if employers could be legally compelled to recognize and to bargain with labor unions. As we shall see, such laws were finally enacted in the late 1920s and during the Great Depression of the 1930s, the direct result of massive struggle by working people to win basic civil rights. Because of these laws, and many others patterned after them, workers can now form a union without a strike, and they can legally force their employer to recognize and bargain with it.

The labor laws governing the formation of a union typically establish special boards to oversee this process. Our university is located in Pennsylvania, and we are employees of the state of Pennsylvania. In 1970, Pennsylvania passed a law, Act 195, through which public employees in the state won the right to organize unions and mandated that public employers deal with such unions. A state agency called the Pennsylvania Labor Relations Board (PLRB) was charged with overseeing the new law. One of the Board's duties is to conduct "representation elections" in which workers vote by secret ballot to form a union. Before a representation election can be held, the Board must have an indication that there is sufficient interest in a union among the workers to justify an election. This is ordinarily done in two steps. First, the workers constitute themselves as a "bargaining unit," that is, as a union which seeks to engage in collective bargaining with the employer. Most labor laws include provisions which place limitations upon the nature of these bargaining units, and it is up to the appropriate board to decide if a given unit is "appropriate" for collective bargaining. For example, supervisors are ordinarily excluded from bargaining units as are employees who have close family relationships with the owners of a company facing unionization. Initially it is up to the employees, themselves, to determine which jobs will be included in the bargaining unit. The custodial and maintenance workers at my school decided that their bargaining unit would consist of all full-time custodians and maintenance workers at our regional campus.

Second, most boards insist that 30% of the proposed bargaining unit sign union authorization cards. After our first meeting, the SEIU organizers passed out authorization cards and gave us extras for the people not at the meeting. That week, we put together a list of the people in the proposed bargaining unit and their addresses. At this point, the employer is under no obligation to provide such a list, and we did not ask for one because we were not ready for our campaign to be made public. This was somewhat naive on our part because the employer had spies at the meeting and knew all about it the day after it was held. We then mailed a letter to each worker, explained what was going on, summarized what had happened at the meeting, and urged that the enclosed authorization card be returned as soon as possible. I agreed that the cards be sent to me since I was in a less vulnerable position than were Jane and Mike. We said in the letter that the cards were confidential and would never be seen by the employer. This is generally true, but I learned later that under special circumstances the employer has a right to see them.[2]

We needed 13 cards (30% of 45), and we got them and a lot more within two weeks. Once the cards are signed, a union can petition the Labor Relations Board to conduct the representation election. The union did this, and the Board notified the employer of the petition. At this point, an employer has several options. The employer can agree to recognize the union, which will then be certified by the Board as the bargaining agent of the people in the bargaining unit. Or, the employer can consent to a representation election, in which case the Board will conduct the election. It is rare for an employer to choose either of these options. As we shall have ample opportunity to document, our labor laws, as currently enforced, allow an employer to use various delaying tactics to put off an election. Delay nearly always works to the employer's advantage, especially when used with other tactics, some allowed by the laws and others illegal but weakly penalized. The third option is for the employer to insist upon a formal hearing before an agent of the Board. At such a hearing, the employer can challenge the nature of the proposed bargaining unit, invoking either provisions of the law or past rulings of the Board or the courts.

As expected, the university requested a hearing, which was held in Pittsburgh. I was permitted to attend as a representative of the union. The meeting turned out to be a formality, because the university had no legal basis upon which to challenge the bargaining unit. Later, when the teachers at my college tried to unionize, the university successfully challenged our unit on the grounds that an appropriate unit could consist only of the teachers at *all* of the university's campuses. This argument was not available here, however, since the same jobs at the central campus were already unionized. Since the composition of the bargaining unit went unchallenged, the hearing officer, after consulting with both parties, set a date for the election, to be held about two months later.

Before the hearing, the university had begun to campaign actively against the union. This university is notoriously anti-union; it employs the law firm used by that vicious union buster and hypocritical philanthropist, Andrew Carnegie. It had not lost a union election in many years. Supervisors had begun to harass Mike, Jane, and other open union supporters. Mike's shift was changed, and his foreman was constantly spying on him, peering around corners to make sure that he was working, even in the middle of the night. Jane was threatened with job loss if she took too many sick days.

Once the election date was set, the university's campaign went into high gear. The university targeted women workers for the most severe abuse, calculating that they were more easily frightened. Women needed the jobs more than some of the men, who were already receiving pensions from previous employment. Some of the cleaning women in the dormitories had children and were sometimes a little late for work. Their foreman had not cared about this before, but now he used it as a way to threaten them. Vote for the union and you will lose this privilege. One night a woman called me at home, so upset that she started to cry. She wanted a union, but she desperately needed her job. I sympathized with her and told her that what her foreman was doing was clearly illegal and that we would begin to publicize it tomorrow. After about an hour, she had regained her courage. In the end, I think all the women voted for the union, shocking the employer who thought the women were the union's Achilles heel.

The labor laws now allow an employer great latitude in terms of the actions which it can take to combat a union. Almost any kind of speech, communicated to employees either verbally or in bulletins and letters, is legal as long as it does not threaten the workers or promise them benefits. Within limits, workers can be interrogated about unions by their employer.[3] Many employers hire "labor consultants" to run their anti-union campaigns. These consultants routinely violate the law, although the law is often so porous in this area that it is not always necessary to act illegally to defeat a union.

As the election date neared, the university's anti-union campaign intensified. The workers began to get letters at home badmouthing the union as an "outsider" that would interfere with the cordial relationship the university had always tried to maintain with its employees. Employees were reminded that they could always discuss problems directly with their supervisors and that a union could only complicate things with increased red tape and rules, many of which would ultimately be detrimental to the workers. And for all of this hassle they would have to pay high dues. Constant close scrutiny by the supervisors continued, along with the harassment of women. Two brothers, who ironically later became staunch union members, were promised promotions if they would criticize the union.

I had been using school copying machines to copy information favorable to unionization and distributing it to the workers. My dean ordered me to stop doing this. I told him that the university used these same machines to copy anti-union propaganda, so why could the union not do the same? He did not buy this argument, but I just kept on using the copiers anyway and nothing happened. About a week before the election, all of the employees were ordered to attend a meeting at the shift change. At this meeting, legal under the law, the administrator in charge of buildings and grounds attacked the union and predicted dire consequences if the union won. He gave special attention to me, calling me a troublemaker and a communist. This bit of redbaiting has been a common tactic of employers, one which aims to lump together union supporters with the official enemy of the nation. Unfortunately for the university, this nasty bit of union bashing backfired; the crude and mean-spirited style of the boss made the men and women angrier than ever.

On the day of the election excitement ran high. The Labor Relations Board had notices posted at the various workplaces on campus notifying the workers when and where the voting would take place. We had called union supporters to make sure that they would vote, especially those who were on vacation. A board agent arrived and set up a portable voting booth. Each side was allowed an observer who could challenge any voter the observer felt should not be voting. The employer had been ordered to provide a payroll for the payroll eligibility date established by the Board. This is usually the payroll for the period just preceding the date on which the Board ordered the election. To be eligible to vote, a person must usually be on the payroll on the payroll eligibility date and on the date of the election.[4] The employer must, within seven days after the Board has ordered the election and at least ten days before the election, also provide the union with a list of persons eligible to vote as of the payroll eligibility date.[5] Any person not on this list will be challenged by one of the observers.

Turnout at union representation elections is very high, in contrast to many political elections. Probably this is because working people know that a union election is more important to them than a typical election in which neither candidate is likely to represent their interests. In this election every person in the bargaining unit voted. In a large bargaining unit voting may be done at several sites and perhaps on more than one day. The ballot boxes will be sealed and the votes counted some time after the election. In our case, this was not necessary, and the votes were counted on the spot. The union won about 60% of the vote. After an election, the parties have seven days to file objections. These objections are normally claims that the other party committed "unfair labor practices" during the campaign or violated one of the procedural requirements of the law or of the Board. If no objections are filed, the Board certifies the union as the exclusive bargaining agent of the bargaining unit. The university filed no objections, and the Board duly certified the new SEIU local. Mike and Jane had won their union.

II. The Basic Labor Law Statutes

We have seen the great hostility of the common law and of the police power of the government toward labor organizations, and we have witnessed the heroic efforts of workers to form unions in the face of it. These struggles met with ferocious repression and often ended in defeat. However, they also put fear into the hearts of the capitalists and the politicians, and sometimes, when the political climate became more benign to labor, these fears led to a willingness to compromise. Labor had for years agitated for state and federal statutes which would guarantee to workers the right to form unions without employer interference. The courts struck down most of the few laws which were enacted, but when workers were well enough organized and employers most afraid, compromise laws were passed and upheld by the courts.

The most important federal labor laws were put into place during the Great Depression.[6] As the Depression deepened into the most profound crisis to ever strike capitalism, two things happened. First, the power of the capitalists, those who owned the mines, mills, and factories, decreased as the public began to see them as responsible for the crisis. The elaborate facade which they had established, through the media, the schools, the government, and their workplaces, to present to the public an aura of invincibility and power, collapsed along with the economy. It became politically acceptable to criticize business in a way that would not have been possible in a period of prosperity. This allowed for the successful campaigns of more populist and labor-oriented politicians, who began to gain significant power in state capitols and in the federal Congress. It was almost as if the Great Depression tore asunder the veil hiding the true nature of our economic system and exposed it for everyone to see. Congressional investigations uncovered staggering business and financial corruption as well as brutal corporate repression of workers and entire communities. These exposés left business reeling and without the ideological acquiescence by the majority of people upon which it normally depends.

Second, the power of working people increased dramatically. As workers recovered from the initial shock of the Great Depression, they became desperate and angry, ready to entertain thoughts and actions which would have been unusual in more normal times. Describing meetings of the unemployed organized by communists, radical union leader Len De Caux, observed, "Sometimes I'd hear a communist speaker say something so bitter and extreme I'd feel embarrassed. Then I'd look around at the unemployed audience— shabby clothes, expressions worried and sour. Faces would start to glow, heads to nod, hands to clap. They liked that stuff best of all."[7] The unemployed were the first to organize, forming councils to demand relief or jobs and to prevent poor people from being evicted from their homes. Then those still working, fed up with falling wages and crippling working conditions, organized, spontaneously striking and forming unions. More than at any time before, average working people were responsive to radical attacks upon the nature of the economic system and willing to take the risks necessary to get what they wanted.

Circumstances then existed which changed the balance of power. Capital could no longer rely upon brute force and a compliant government to bludgeon the labor movement. Its power had to be compromised or perhaps face more serious threats. Among the compromises achieved by workers through their collective strength were sweeping changes in the labor laws. Prior to the 1930s, the only federal labor law that guaranteed rights to workers was the Railway Labor Act, which will be discussed in the next section of this chapter, and which itself represented a compromise forced upon Congress by striking railroad workers. During the 1930s, however, more powerful laws were passed. In 1932, the Norris-LaGuardia Act (explained fully in Chapter Six) was enacted to greatly restrict the issuance of labor injunctions by the federal courts. The National Labor Relations Act (NLRA) was passed in 1935. By this Act, workers in most private workplaces won the rights to organize unions and force employers to recognize these unions and bargain collective agreements with them. That same year saw the enactment of legislation which secured old age pensions and unemployment compensation for workers. In 1938, Congress established a minimum wage, guaranteed overtime pay, and outlawed child labor in the Fair Labor Standards Act.

The original laws have been amended many times since their initial enactment. We are going to examine the laws as they currently exist, that is, as amended. Where it is important for readers to understand our labor laws better, the nature of the amendments and the political situation which made them possible will be explored. This is especially important in the case of the National Labor Relations Act (also known as the Wagner Act), since much of its progressive potential has been eroded by succeeding legislation. For example, the National Labor Relations Board (NLRB) was, at first, a strong proponent of the new unions, staffed by people with strong union sympathies. This opened it to attacks from conservatives and led to several congressional investigations. World War II strengthened the power of these conservatives, because they were able to portray strikes and radical labor politics as inimical to the war effort. After the war, employers went on the offensive, aided by the government's trumped up red scare. Unions were openly identified with communism, the new official enemy. In 1947, a set of sweeping amendments and revisions to the NLRA known as the Taft-Hartley laws were enacted, and much of the original promise of the Wagner Act was lost.

Please note that in the rest of this chapter, we will be looking at federal and state labor laws only in terms of their provisions with respect to workers organizing themselves into unions, and directly related topics.

III. The Railway Labor Act

The oldest federal labor law is the Railway Labor Act, passed in 1926.[8] It represents an approach to labor law which aims to place legal roadblocks to strikes. The Act does not make strikes illegal, but under its provisions, it is difficult for a union to conduct a successful strike, or, indeed, any strike at all. In 1926 and for at least 40 years before, the railroads were the most important industry in the nation. Not only did this industry directly and indirectly employ hundreds of thousands of workers, but it was the major mode of industrial transportation. Railroad strikes posed a threat to the profits of the railroads and all of the many corporations which depended upon them. Sympathy strikes could put tremendous pressure upon any business, as the Pullman strike demonstrated. The government, sharing the interests of the railway companies, determined, therefore, that railroad strikes could not be tolerated. The government and the corporations had a surprising ally in the Railroad Brotherhoods, the conservative and racist craft unions which had organized the skilled workers on the railroads and in the shops. The Brotherhoods refused to support the Pullman strike and often failed to honor each other's picket lines. Their lack of militancy made them acceptable to the owners, who would rather have dealt with them than with a more inclusive and radical union like Debs' American Railway Union.

To prevent strikes and to solidify the position of the conservative Brotherhoods, the federal government enacted a series of laws beginning in 1888. Each successive law involved the government more deeply in the relations between employers and their employees. For example, in 1916 the government enacted the Adamson Act, which mandated the eight-hour day on the railroads. During World War I, the federal government took over the ownership of the nation's railroads, and in order to avoid strikes which would impair the war effort, made significant wage and benefit concessions to railroad workers and accepted the unionization of the nonoperating and less-skilled workers. Union membership grew accordingly; by war's end, 80% to 90% of all railroad employees were in unions. When the war ended, the railroads were returned to private ownership, and the owners began an assault on the unions. This assault was aided by the fact that the government still regulated railroad labor relations and in 1922 issued a series of decisions which cut wages. These led to a bitter strike of the railroad shop workers, a strike defeated by the failure of the Brotherhoods to support it as well as by a series of sweeping injunctions. This strike renewed efforts to legislate an end to railroad strikes, and the result was the Railway Labor Act.

The Act specifically gives workers the right to organize into labor unions for purposes of collective bargaining. Originally the Act covered only workers on the nation's railroads, but a 1936 amendment also included airline employees. Note that we are talking about private sector employees. The air traffic controllers fired by President Reagan in 1982 were employed by the federal government, and as public employees were covered by special legislation. Under the Act, workers have the right to elect a union as their bargaining agent. A government agency, the National Mediation Board, has the power to conduct elections and determine appropriate bargaining units. The Act, itself, refers to "appropriate" crafts or classes of workers in connection with bargaining units, so the Board typically approves craft units or units of workers who do essentially the same type of work.

The Act also prohibits "interference, influence or coercion" of employees in the selection of their bargaining agent. However, it does not provide for any enforcement mechanism to prevent such activity. It makes no reference to "unfair labor practices," nor does it establish any board to determine if an employer has violated the law and what the penalty should be for a violation. Therefore, it has been up to the federal courts to protect the rights of workers specified in the Act. This is usually done by injunction. For example, the original Act did not specifically outlaw "company unions," organizations set up by the employers to avoid having to deal with real independent worker organizations. In an early decision under the Act, the Supreme Court upheld an injunction against a railroad which had established a company union on the grounds that this interfered with the workers' right to bargain through unions of their own choosing.[9] Similarly, if workers were fired in conjunction with an organizing drive, the union or the employees could seek an injunction to get the workers reinstated.

There are many other aspects of the Act which have had to be decided by the courts, but these will be discussed in later chapters. Also, the National Mediation Board has other duties besides resolving representation issues, but these too must be discussed later. We can mention here that the National Mediation Board has greater power in bargaining unit determination than does the National Labor Relations Board and most of the state boards which consider representation issues. For example, the Act makes little reference to bargaining units except for referral to "any craft or class of employees." It is up to the Board to decide if there is enough support for unionization to conduct an election; how, where, and when the election shall be conducted; and whether or not a union will be certified as bargaining agent. It does not have to hold representation hearings and can "regroup, amalgamate or splinter historic bargaining groups taking into account technological and functional changes, and its decision setting up a class for representation in a jurisdictional dispute is unreviewable by court."[10] The Board can certify a union in an election in which there is more than one union on the ballot even if "no union" gets more votes than the union with the most votes, as long as a majority of those who vote cast ballots in favor of unionization.

Do workers have to use the Board to determine who will represent them? Can they engage in an organizational strike to force the employer to recognize their union? The Act does not explicitly forbid or limit economic pressure to compel recognition. This is in contrast to the National Labor Relations Act, which prohibits organizational picketing (and, therefore, striking for all practical purposes) after 30 days. However, the entire philosophy of the Railway Labor Act is hostile to strikes. The first listed purpose of the Act is "To avoid any interruption to commerce or to the operation of any carrier engaged therein..." A federal court of appeals has ruled that a strike for union representation interferes with an administrative procedure set up by the Act, namely the duty of the National Mediation Board to oversee representation elections. The court upheld an injunction to end a representation strike and the accompanying picketing.[11]

IV. The National Labor Relations Act (Wagner Act)

A. Basic Provisions

The National Labor Relations Act (hereinafter NLRA) is the most comprehensive federal labor law. Originally called the Wagner Act after its chief sponsor, Senator Robert Wagner, it covers most workers engaged in "interstate commerce." Like the Railway Labor Act, it was enacted to reduce the incidence of striking, but unlike that Act, it does not place such severe roadblocks in the way of strikes. It does, however, specify a comprehensive procedure for the formation of a union, again through the method of secret ballot election.

Before looking at union organizing under the NLRA, we need to examine the Act's basic provisions, especially since we will refer to these many times in later chapters. Section 7 is the heart of the Act. It states:

> Employees shall have the right to self-organization, to form, join, or assist labor organizations, to bargain through representatives of their own choosing, and to engage in other concerted activities for the purpose of collective bargaining or other mutual aid or protection, and shall also have the right to refrain from any or all such activities.

Section 7 clearly says that employees have the right to organize unions to bargain with employers and to protect themselves. It also clearly implies that worker organizations are to be independent, that is, of the workers' "own choosing."

Section 8 contains both employer and union "unfair labor practices." These are actions by employers or by unions which violate the rights laid out in Section 7. It is interesting to note that the original Act had only employer unfair labor practices. The union unfair labor practices were added by later amendments, and, as we shall see, are both more numerous and more restrictive than those applicable to employers.

Section 3 establishes the National Labor Relations Board (hereinafter NLRB), a federal agency whose duty it is to administer the Act. Congress set up an independent board to do this because it felt that such a board would develop special expertise concerning the Act's provisions. This is in contrast to the Railway Labor Act under which workers must petition the courts to compel employers to obey it. The NLRB considers unfair labor practice charges and oversees and conducts representation elections. There are five members of the Board, appointed by the president for five-year terms. One member is designated by the president as the chairperson of the Board. Section 3 empowers the Board to establish whatever regional offices it may deem necessary. At present there are 34 regional offices. All representational and unfair labor practice matters begin at the regional offices, but are appealable to the NLRB. The Board does not have to meet as a whole; its powers can be delegated to any three members. Finally, Section 3 provides for an office of General Counsel. The General Counsel is appointed by the president for a term of four years. This office is only involved in unfair labor practice cases. It is the duty of the General Counsel to issue, investigate, and prosecute unfair labor practice charges. Thus, the General Counsel serves much like a district attorney in criminal cases.

Section 9 spells out the procedures to be followed in union representation elections. The NLRB has considerable freedom of action here, but it has made its own rules in areas not covered explicitly by the statute. Section 9 allows employees to petition the Board for a representation election and gives the Board the power to decide the appropriateness of any proposed bargaining unit. The union and the employer are free to agree to a representation election without a hearing as long as the election conforms with the Board's internal rules. No representation election can be held if one has been held within the past 12 months. Workers already represented by a union can use Board procedures to get rid of a union, that is, to "decertify" it.

Section 10 of the NLRA grants the Board great powers to prevent unfair labor practices. Let us take a typical case to illustrate the way in which an unfair labor practice would be processed. Suppose that during an election campaign a worker is fired for expressing sympathy for the union. The union and the employee must file an unfair labor practice complaint against the employer with the nearest regional office within six months of the alleged unfair practice. An employee at the regional office (a field examiner or an attorney) will be assigned to investigate the complaint.[12] The fired employee and possible supporting witnesses will probably be interviewed by the board agent, and a formal statement will be taken. The agent may conduct a preliminary investigation, interviewing persons who may be helpful in determining whether or not a formal unfair labor practice charge is warranted. The employer will be asked to give its views on the charge, but it is not bound to do so. The board employee then recommends to the director of the regional office whether or not to file the charge. A recommendation not to file a formal charge can be appealed to the Office of General Counsel, but fewer than 10% of such appeals win.[13] The charging party can withdraw a complaint which fails to get a positive recommendation. It is important to note the considerable power of the field examiner; if this person decides not to press a charge forward, it is, for all practical purposes, dead.

If a formal unfair labor practice charge is deemed meritorious, the regional director will notify the employer and perhaps propose a settlement. If the employer refuses, the regional director issues the formal complaint, which outlines in detail the basis of the charge. A hearing is then conducted before an administrative law judge, with the Office of General Counsel acting as prosecutor. Both the union and the employer are entitled to have attorneys present; in a case such as this one, the union's lawyer will help the Office of General Counsel attorney develop the case. Section 10 of the Act provides for a court-like hearing, with witnesses under oath, rules of evidence, transcripts, and so forth. Upon completion of the hearing, the attorneys will file written briefs for the administrative law judge to read. Finally, the judge makes a recommendation, either to dismiss or to sustain the unfair labor practice charge, and if the decision is to sustain, what the penalties should be. The judge's decision must be approved by the NLRB itself; any of the three parties to the case (the union, the employer, or the General Counsel) has the right to appeal the judge's ruling to the NLRB. The Board reviews the appeal documents and the materials from the original hearing but does not conduct its own hearing. The Board then issues its order.

The Act does not give the NLRB the power to enforce its own orders; only one of the 12 U.S. courts of appeals can do so. Let's say that the Board has ordered the fired employee to be reinstated with full backpay and benefits and no loss of seniority. If the employer does not comply, the NLRB can petition an appeals court to enforce the order. However, the employer can also file an exception to the Board's ruling to an appeals court. The court must do what the Board does when an administrative law judge's decision is appealed. The court might agree to enforce the Board's order, it may reverse the Board's ruling, or it may send the case back to the Board for a new ruling. If an appeal is based on a matter of fact, it has little chance of success, but if it is based upon interpretation of the Act, its chances are better. Most board decisions are upheld. The decision of the court of appeals may be appealed to the U.S. Supreme Court, but, unlike the court of appeals, the Supreme Court may and probably will refuse to accept a case. The Supreme Court usually only accepts cases in which the meaning of the law is not clear, perhaps one in which the courts of appeals have issued contradictory rulings. If the Supreme Court does accept an appeal, it does what the court of appeals and the NLRB did when they were faced with appeals. It reviews the record of the case and either sustains, reverses, or remands it back to the lower court.

B. Union Formation under the NLRA

Sections 3, 7, 8, 9, and 10 are the parts of the NLRA relevant to the formation of a labor union. The procedures are pretty much the same as those presented in the story which began this chapter. A group of workers decide to unionize. They carve out a proposed bargaining unit. They collect authorization cards, and when they get 30%, they can file for an election. If the employer refuses to recognize the union or to agree to a consent election, the regional office conducts a hearing. The regional office makes rulings on whether or not the employees are covered by the Act, the nature of the bargaining unit, and the validity of the cards. The decision of the regional office can be appealed to the NLRB but only on limited grounds. A board ruling cannot be appealed directly to the courts. The Office of General Counsel does not participate in representation matters.

Once an organizing campaign has begun, it is possible that the employer or the union may commit unfair labor practices. In connection with these, the key parts of the Act are Section 8(a)(1, 2, 3, and 4); Section 8(b)(1, 2, 4, and 7); and Section 8(c). The actual unfair labor practices are listed in Sections 8(a) and 8(b), but these must be interpreted in light of 8(c). 8(c) is the so-called employer "free speech" provision. It states:

> The expression of any views, argument, or opinion, or the dissemination thereof, whether in written, printed, graphic, or visual form, shall not constitute or be evidence of an unfair labor practice under any of the provisions of this Act, if such expression contains no threat of reprisal or force or promise of benefit.

This has come to mean that a clever employer, usually aided by a labor consultant, can say just about anything short of a direct threat without violating the law, including statements which demean unions or are not true. The Board sees union representation elections as analogous to political campaigns, in which the contestants battle it out verbally with no holds barred. Unfortunately for workers, this is a false analogy. If my candidate does not win an election, I am not subject to reprisals from the winner because I did not work for the winner. Workers are dependent upon work in a way unlike the outcome of a political election, and this gives any employer automatic power over employees. Statements which are not threatening in a political context take on a different meaning when uttered by the boss.[14]

Let's look at each of the pertinent parts of the Act. We will examine each part in the context of a union organizing campaign, but it is important to remember that they are relevant in many other contexts as well. Unfair labor practices can be committed at any time and not merely when workers are trying to form a union.

Section 8(a)(1) says it is an unfair labor practice for an employer "to interfere with, restrain, or coerce employees in the exercise of the rights guaranteed in section 7." This prohibits a wide range of employer actions aimed at defeating the union. An employer cannot threaten workers with loss of job or benefits or threaten to close the plant if the union wins. An employer cannot circulate anti-union petitions among the workers or promise benefits to defeat the union. An employer cannot engage in coercive interrogations of employees, spy on union meetings or pretend to spy (by pretending to take photographs of people entering the union hall, for example). An employer cannot conduct pre-election polls to determine union sentiment or pass out sample NLRB ballots with "No Union" marked unless it is clear that these come from the employer. An employer cannot refuse to allow workers to discuss the union in the workplace on the workers' own time, prevent the circulation of union literature or authorization cards in nonwork areas on the workers' own time, or prevent workers from wearing union buttons and insignia.[15] In 8(a)(1) cases it is not necessary for the union to show that the employers' actions were motivated by anti-union sentiment (or *animus*, to use the legal jargon). Of course, it is still up to the Board to determine if an unfair labor practice has been committed.

Section 8(a)(2) says that it is an unfair labor practice for an employer "to dominate or interfere with the formation or administration of any labor organization or contribute financial support to it: *Provided*, that subject to rules and regulations made and published by the Board pursuant to Section 6 [which gives the Board the power to make rules and regulations necessary to carry out the provisions of the Act], an employer shall not be prohibited from permitting employees to confer with him during working hours without loss of time or pay." This is an extremely important provision, and it is currently the source of great controversy.

Originally, this unfair labor practice was aimed at what were called "company unions." Company unions became common during the anti-union "open shop" movement of the 1920s. With help from the federal government, union membership grew rapidly during World War I. This help ended promptly after the war, and employers went back on the offensive to roll back the unions' gains. The employer attack took two forms. On the one hand, companies aggressively fired and blacklisted union sympathizers, using the courts to obtain a record number of injunctions and police, militia, and private thugs to teach workers the dangers of union organizing, picketing, and striking. On the other hand, however, employers began to use the techniques of "personnel management" to show workers that they did not really need a union. One of these techniques was the establishment of committees, or "unions," or "employee representation plans" to give workers a voice in their workplaces. These committees were set up, staffed, and financed by the employer, so they were not independent unions. They were meant to give employees the impression but not the reality of power and influence. Through them, employers hoped to increase productivity and hold unions at bay.[16]

Once the NLRA became law, many employers claimed that their workers were already represented by a union, so a certification election was not necessary. Other companies immediately established company unions to avoid union organizing. Section 8(a)(2) makes such company unions illegal. In such cases, the Board will order the company union to be disbanded, and the employer will be ordered to cease and desist from such activities. For a union to be certified by the Board, it must be a union of the workers' "own choosing," that is, it must be independent of the employer.

The careful reader may have noticed that company unions bear a striking resemblance to the "quality circles" and "teams" which are all the rage today and which President Clinton and his advisors have made one of the centerpieces of their plans to make the United States competitive with its economic rivals in Japan and Europe. Teams are a part of what has been called "total quality management" by its supporters and "management by stress" by its critics.[17] In return for promises, seldom kept, of job security and the right to participate in certain workplace decisions, workers are expected to cooperate with management to increase productivity. The basic unit in this scheme is the team, comprised of workers on a particular job and part of larger departmental and plant teams. Members of the team meet to discuss ways to improve productivity, raise the quality of the product, reduce absenteeism, and so forth. They may make suggestions to the management about these and other matters, which the management may implement or provide additional information about. For example, the employer may provide the teams with information concerning the introduction of a new technology and seek input from the teams.

Are these teams in violation of Section 8(a)(2)? In a nonunion setting, such as exists when workers are forming a union, the answer is almost certainly yes.[18] The NLRB uses a two-step approach to determine the legality of teams and all similar organizations. First, are the teams "labor organizations" within the meaning of Section 2(5) of the Act? A labor organization is defined as "any organization of any kind, or any agency or employee representation committee or plan, in which employees participate and which exists for the purpose, in whole or in part, of dealing with employers concerning grievances, labor disputes, wages, rates of pay, hours of employment or conditions of work." This is a very broad definition; it does not, for example, require that a labor organization bargain with the employer but only "deal" with it. Most quality circles, teams, action committees, or labor-management participation teams are labor organizations by the Act's definition. One exception might be a team which deals solely with matters of "inherent managerial prerogative," that is, matters about which, the Board has ruled, employers are not compelled to negotiate in a union setting. Suppose the teams discussed the selection of supervisors and the employer's cost of production accounts. Since these are examples of decisions over which the employer has absolute discretion, the team would not be defined as a labor organization.

Second, does the employer "dominate" the team? In a nonunion setting, it is difficult to imagine that this would not be the case, since one purpose of establishing the teams in the first place is to give workers the impression that they have some power at the workplace without actually ceding any to them. If the teams are started by the employer, if they are financed by the employer, if supervisors are team leaders or if the employer chooses the leaders, etc., then the teams are dominated by the employer and are illegal. The Board will order that the teams be disbanded, and the employer will be ordered to cease and desist from engaging in such illegal activity. It is not necessary that a union organizing drive be in progress either at the time the teams are started or afterward, although the presence of a union makes it more likely that an unfair labor practice charge will be filed in the first place. If a union loses a representation election when there are teams, the Board will order a new election after the teams are disbanded. Note that it is not necessary to show that the employer had an anti-union motive in setting up the teams.

If the employees are already organized in a union, the situation is different. The employer cannot introduce teams unless it bargains with the union. This is because teams are what is called a "mandatory" bargaining subject, and an employer cannot make unilateral changes in such subjects. In a union workplace, therefore, a union can simply say no to teams. Of course, some of the most obvious examples of "total quality management" can be found in union workplaces, but the unions have agreed to its implementation. Unions ought to be wary about teams.[19] The employer will use them to undermine the union, by, for example, beginning to deal with the teams rather than the union. This is illegal, but a union which has not been aggressive in limiting the role of the teams in establishing working conditions may find itself alienated from the rank-and-file. Because of the dangers inherent in the team concept, many unions have rejected them outright.

Several other types of employer activities are illegal under Section 8(a)(2). Under board rules, it is possible for more than one union to be on the ballot. In fact, a second union can get on the ballot by securing a single authorization card. In such a situation, an employer may prefer one union to another. It is illegal for the employer to actively aid one of the unions, with money, legal aid, information, or active encouragement. The employer *can* express its preference for one of the unions.[20]

Section 8(a)(3) makes it an unfair labor practice for an employer "by discrimination in regard to hire or tenure of employment or any term or condition of employment to encourage or discourage membership in any labor organization." Thus, an employer cannot fire a worker for signing an authorization card or supporting a union organization drive; an employer cannot refuse to rehire a legal striker if an opening is available; an employer cannot offer scabs special benefits such as "superseniority" (by adding years to the scab's actual time at work); an employer cannot demote workers or unreasonably change their work assignments because of their union activity; an employer cannot close a plant simply to prevent the workers from voting for a union; and an employer cannot refuse to hire job applicants because they are union members or sympathizers.[21]

Violations of Section 8(a)(3) are a little trickier than violations of Section 8(a)(1), though the two usually go together in that a violation of Section 8(a)(3) is also a violation of Section 8(a)(1). In an 8(a)(3) case, it is necessary to prove that the employer intended by its actions to discriminate "in regard to hire....to encourage or discourage membership in any labor organization." In some cases the actions are so destructive of workers' rights that the NLRB will infer intent from the action itself. Firing strikers would be a good example. In other situations, the Board will look at a range of circumstances to determine intent, such as the timing of a discharge, lack of proof for the employer's alleged reason for a discharge, failure to give an employee a warning for an alleged offense, or failure to discipline an employee prior to a union organizing drive for an alleged violation of rules. The difficulty with some Section 8(a)(3) charges is that there can be a "mixed motive." Suppose that a worker is an active union supporter, but that one day he threatens the foreman during a heated argument about a work assignment. He is summarily discharged. Was he fired for the threat or for the union activity? The Board will investigate and determine whether the union activity might have been a factor in the discharge. If it concludes that it might have been, the employer must prove that it was not, that the same action would have been taken in the absence of union activity.[22]

Section 8(a)(4) says that an employer cannot "discharge or otherwise discriminate against an employee because he has filed charges or given testimony under this Act." This is a straightforward provision which protects workers who are called to testify in unfair labor practice hearings. An employer cannot fire or demote or transfer a worker for doing so. Naturally, a violation of this section also violates Section 8(a)(1) and may violate Section 8(a)(3) as well.

Unions can also commit unfair labor practices during a union organization drive. The wording of Section 7 includes the phrase "the right to refrain from any or all such activities," and this phrase is important in interpreting the unfair labor practices listed in Section 8(b). Following our procedure above, let us look at the relevant unfair labor practices in turn.

Section 8(b)(1) makes it an unfair labor practice for a labor organization to "restrain or coerce (A) employees in the exercise guaranteed in section 7: *Provided,* that this paragraph shall not impair the right of a labor organization to prescribe its own rules with respect to the acquisition or retention of membership therein; or (B) an employer in the selection of his representatives for the purposes of collective bargaining or the adjustment of grievances." In some respects this section is the union counterpart to Section 8(a)(1). A union cannot threaten workers to get them to join the union or sign authorization cards; a union cannot tell workers that they will be fired if the union wins the election; a union cannot engage in mass picketing such that nonstriking employees cannot get into the plant; a union cannot threaten scabs during a strike; a union cannot harass or fine a member who gives testimony in an unfair labor practice hearing; a union cannot make a collective bargaining agreement with an employer if it loses a representation election; a union cannot try to force a single employer in a multi-employer bargaining situation to break away from the group and sign an individual agreement.[23]

The *proviso* in this section gives the union the right to make its own internal rules and regulations. However, these may come into conflict with the Section 7 phrase quoted above. In one case, a union had a rule which stated that a member of the union could not resign from the union during a strike. This rule allowed the union to discipline a member who crossed a picket line during a strike and returned to work. The discipline could take the form of a fine, which the union could collect in court if the member did not pay it. The Supreme Court struck down this union regulation because it violated employees' right not to engage in concerted activities such as a strike.[24] In another case, some union members had two jobs, one in grocery stores under union contract and one in nonunion stores. When the union began an organizing campaign at the nonunion stores, some of the members at these nonunion stores refused to support the campaign. The union sent all members letters which insisted that all members support the organizing drive. The nonunion stores and some of the union members filed unfair labor practice complaints against the union, alleging violation of Section 8(b)(1). Here the Board ruled in favor of the union, but the vote was not unanimous.[25]

In Section 8(b)(2) it is an unfair labor practice for a union "to cause or attempt to cause an employer to discriminate against an employee in violation of subsection 8(a)(3) or to discriminate against an employee with respect to whom membership in such organization has been denied or terminated on some ground other than his failure to tender the periodic dues and initiation fees uniformly required as a condition of acquiring or retaining membership." While this section refers mainly to practices of a union after it has been selected as bargaining agent, it would make illegal any attempt by the union to get the employer to discriminate against an employee for refusing to support the union, either during the representation campaign or afterward. We shall have occasion to examine Section 8(b)(2) in detail when we discuss the issue of union security.

Section 8(b)(4) is an extraordinarily complex provision best left to the chapter on strikes, picketing, boycotts, and injunctions. At this point, however, we can note that this is one of the most damaging of the Taft-Hartley additions to the original Wagner Act. It makes nearly all types of secondary pressures exerted by a union unfair labor practices. A "primary" activity is one in which employees confront their own employer. When workers strike against their own employer, they are engaging in a primary strike. When they picket their own employer, they are primary pickets. When they refuse to handle or buy their own employer's product, they are participating in a primary boycott. However, when their actions are aimed at other employers or other groups, they are utilizing secondary actions. There are many types of secondary activities, many of which we will look at in Chapter Six. A good example would occur when workers at a construction site refuse to work on materials delivered to the site from a plant struck by another group of employees. Another would be when unionized farm workers picket stores which sell a crop (e.g., lettuce) which the union is boycotting to put pressure on the lettuce growers with whom they have a primary dispute.

Historically, boycotts and sympathy strikes were important tactics used to force recalcitrant employers to recognize and bargain with labor unions. During the 1930s, for example, unionized truck drivers helped to organize nonunion construction sites by refusing to make deliveries to or accept deliveries from them. Section 8(b)(4) makes solidarity actions such as these unfair labor practices. What is worse, the NLRB must consider these to be especially serious violations of the Act and must, according to Section 10(l), seek an injunction from a federal court of appeals to stop them. Therefore, in an organizing drive, a union can avail itself of little in the way of strike, picket, or boycott support from other workers. It is not illegal for workers to honor a primary picket line, but, except in rare circumstances, the picket line itself cannot move to another workplace.

The NLRA encourages workers to attempt to form unions through the election procedures provided in the Act. However, it is not illegal for workers to use the traditional form of pressure by striking for a union. The right to strike is guaranteed in several parts of the Act. Section 13 states that "Nothing in this Act, except as specifically provided herein, shall be construed so as either to interfere with or impede or diminish in any way the right to strike, or to affect the limitations or qualifications on that right." Nonetheless, if workers strike and picket to force an employer to recognize their union, they may run afoul of Section 8(b)(7), a long and complicated provision which states that is an unfair labor practice for a union

> to picket or cause to be picketed, or threaten to picket or cause to be picketed, any employer where an object thereof is forcing or requiring an employer to recognize or bargain with a labor organization as the representative of his employees, or forcing or requiring the employees of an employer to accept or select such labor organization as their collective bargaining representative, unless such labor organization is currently certified as the representative of such employees: (A) where the employer has lawfully recognized in accordance with this Act any other labor organization and a question concerning representation may not appropriately be raised under Section 9(c) of this Act, (B) where within the preceding twelve months a valid election under section 9(c) of this Act has been conducted, or (C) where such picketing has been conducted without a petition under section 9(c) being filed within a reasonable period of time not to exceed thirty days from the commencement of such picketing: *Provided,* that when such a petition has been filed the Board shall forthwith, without regard

to the provisions of section 9(c)(1) or the absence of a showing of a substantial interest on the part of the labor organization, direct an election in such unit as the Board finds to be appropriate and shall certify the results thereof.

Subsection (C) is the critical part for our discussion. To force an employer to recognize a union without going the certification election route, it will surely be necessary for the union to strike and to picket. If the picketing carries on for more than 30 days (or fewer days if the Board concludes that a shorter period is "a reasonable period of time"), the union has committed an unfair labor practice and will be forced to stop the picketing.[26] The picketing does not have be done for 30 actual days; the 30 day period begins when the union begins the picketing. Furthermore, during the thirty-day period, the *employer* can file an election petition (called an RM petition), and the NLRB will conduct an expedited election if it determines that the union has committed an unfair labor practice. The bargaining unit and the date of the election are strictly up to the Board; no hearing need be held and the employer does not have to provide a list of employees with addresses. No authorization cards need be presented. This puts the union in the position of either having to have already gained the support of enough workers to win the election (in which case, it might just as well have used the election procedure) or facing a sure defeat in the expedited election. Plus, if the union should lose the election, it cannot get another one (or engage in organizational picketing) for another 12 months, as specified in Section 8(b)(7)(B). In other words, though it is not illegal to strike and picket for union recognition, the Act makes it difficult to legally do so.[27]

C. Penalties for Unfair Labor Practices

While unfair labor practices can be committed at any time, it is during an election campaign that they are most likely to occur. What penalties does the Act impose upon those who perpetrate unfair labor practices? The Board is given wide discretion to remedy unfair labor practices, as stated in Section 10(c):

If upon the preponderance of the testimony taken the Board shall be of the opinion that any person named in the complaint has engaged in or is engaging in any such unfair labor practice, then the Board shall state its findings of fact and shall issue and cause to be served on such person to cease and desist from such unfair labor practice, and to take such affirmative action including reinstatement of employees with or without backpay, as will effectuate the policies of this Act.

In an organizing campaign, an employer can harm both the union and individual workers. Suppose that the employer fires the leaders of the union movement. Obviously the workers fired have suffered harm. The penalties here would be obvious. The workers will be reinstated with backpay and the restoration of all benefits and seniority lost. The employer will also be required to post notices around the plant of the Board's order. This type of remedy is called a "make whole" because it puts the worker into the position he or she would have been in had the employer not committed the unfair labor practice, thus making the worker "whole." The Board will not impose any "punitive" remedy, that is, one beyond that required to make the worker whole. Employer scofflaws need not worry, therefore, that they will have to pay high fines for repeated violations of the Act. It is important to note that any earnings which the fired workers made between the time they were fired and the time they were reinstated will be deducted from the backpay award. Deductions are made on a quarterly basis to avoid gross unfairness to the harmed employee. Let us say that the fired worker is awarded backpay of $30,000 for the one year since she was illegally discharged. She managed to earn $25,000 in the meantime, but all of this was earned during the last quarter year before her reinstatement. The $30,000 is divided in four, and $7,500 is assessed to each quarter. Since she earned nothing during the first three quarters, she would get $7,500 for each of these three quarters, for a total of $22,500. She would get no backpay for the last quarter, and her total backpay would be $22,500 plus the interest that the IRS is currently using for tax refunds.

A union often loses an election because the employer has committed unfair labor practices. If the Board determines that this is the case, it will order one of two remedies. First, it can order a new election. This is the most common scenario. In some cases, the Board will give the union certain additional rights during the new campaign, such as the right to address the employees on company time, or it might impose more severe posting notices upon the employer, such as posting notice in a local newspaper.[28] Second, in extreme cases, where the employer has committed numerous, serious unfair labor practices, the Board may conclude that the employer has permanently tainted the election atmosphere so that a free election is no longer possible. Then, the Board can simply certify the union as the bargaining agent and order the employer to bargain with it. This is called a *Gissel* order after the name of the case in which the Supreme Court first upheld the Board's power to make such a remedy.[29] At present, the Board has to be shown that the union had an authorization card majority (a majority of the members of the bargaining unit have signed authorization cards) before it will issue a *Gissel* order, although one court of appeals has ruled that the Board has the power to issue a bargaining order even if the union has not achieved a card majority.[30]

D. If the Union Loses the Election

Several aspects of the NLRA come into play if the union loses a representation election. First, no union can get another representation election for at least one year. A union is free to seek voluntary recognition from the employer or to solicit new authorization cards, but any type of election (including a decertification election, to be discussed later) bars another election for one year. Organizational picketing and striking are illegal during this one-year period.

Second, nothing in the Act prevents the union from continuing to exist and to represent at least its members after the lost election. Unions typically view certification as bargaining agent as the ultimate end of a campaign, and have more or less disappeared from the workplace after losing elections. However, this is a counterproductive approach. Section 7 protects "concerted activity" for "other mutual aid or protection," and it is not necessary that workers either have a certified union or are trying to establish one to be protected. The Board and the courts have long held, for example, that workers in a nonunion setting and not attempting to form a union can engage in concerted activity. Suppose that a group of unorganized workers are unhappy that their workplace is bitterly cold. They complain to their supervisors, but to no avail. As a last resort, they walk off the job. In such a situation it would be an unfair labor practice [it would violate both Section 8(a)(1) and Section 8(a)(3)] for the employer to fire or otherwise discipline these workers.[31] If the union which had lost the election had stayed active and represented workers in a case like this, the result would be the same. This would be a good way to keep the union flame burning until another election is held. In fact, there are many other things which the defeated union could do. It can request that the employer bargain with it to establish terms and conditions of employment for its own members (it cannot claim to represent everyone unless it wins an election or the employer voluntarily recognizes it). If the employer refuses to bargain, the minority union can legally strike and picket. Individual workers can refuse to adjust their complaints or agree to wages and benefits with the employer unless the employer agrees to go through their union. The employer is not legally bound to bargain with a minority union, but it cannot discipline union members for asking it to bargain or, for that matter, for striking and picketing. An employer can recognize a minority union and negotiate with it to set wages, hours, and terms and conditions for the union's members. A minority union can also serve as an advocate for all workers in a wide variety of situations. A union could inform workers about their rights in the at-will exceptions described in Chapter Nine as well as in the areas of workers' compensation, health and safety, constitutional rights, and wages and hours laws.[32]

V. Organizing a Union Without the NLRB

Since the original Wagner Act was enacted, employers have learned how to use the law to make it difficult for a union to win a representation election. This difficulty has increased as the labor movement has weakened and the federal government has become more anti-labor. A union ordinarily benefits from a quick election. Sentiment for a union often builds quickly and emotionally, and it is best for the union to strike while the iron is hot. Delay works to the advantage of the employer, as the workers' passions cool and the gains that they were counting on recede into the future. The Act allows for considerable delay between the time the union petitions for an election and the time the election is actually held. Even if the bargaining unit is clear and every member has signed an authorization card, the employer can still request a hearing and an election. In Canada, by contrast, employers can be made to recognize unions on the basis of authorization cards alone.[33]

If the bargaining unit can be challenged, it may be many months or years before the Board makes a ruling. At my workplace, the employer was able to keep its challenge of proposed bargaining units for teachers going for several years. How can a union maintain a strong presence in the face of such delays?

During the campaign, the "free speech" proviso allows the employer to aggressively attack the union, using fear as an effective weapon. The penalties for employer unfair labor practices are not severe, and many employers see them as a necessary cost of avoiding unions. For this reason, along with the slowness with which unfair labor practices are processed by the NLRB, employers routinely commit unfair labor practices. Section 8(a)(1) and 8(a)(3) violations have skyrocketed over the past 20 years. Amazingly, today, one in ten union supporters is illegally fired during an organization campaign.[34] Even when some or all of them may get their jobs back, it is usually too late to help the union. Of course, the NLRB can issue a *Gissel* order if the employer's unfair labor practices are so severe that the Board concludes that the union's majority has been destroyed, but these are rare. The more likely scenario is for the Board to order another election, giving the employer the opportunity to do the same things all over again. That these tactics pay off for employers is shown by the sharp reduction in the percentage of NLRB elections won by unions. In 1950 unions won 74% of certification elections, but by 1990 the victory rate had fallen to 47.6%. In addition, the number of elections held has decreased by 50% since the 1960s.[35]

Compounding the inherent weaknesses in the Act was the rightward and anti-labor tilt taken by the Board during the Reagan/Bush years. Overtly anti-union members were appointed to the NLRB; recently one member was charged with an unfair labor practice by Board agents trying to form a union.[36] A string of decisions hostile to organized labor led some unions to the position that it might be better to forego using the Act at all. The United Food and Commercial Workers Union (UFCW) decided in 1987 to avoid the use of NLRB elections to organize workers.[37] Instead it focuses its attention on nonunion employers and organizes a "pressure campaign" against them, with the goal of either forcing them to recognize the union or go out of business. As union officer Joe Crump put it, "Organizing is war. The objective is to convince employers to do something that they do not want to do. That means a fight. If you don't have a war mentality, your chances of success are limited. Organizing without the NLRB means putting enough pressure on employers, costing them enough time, energy and money to either eliminate them or get them to surrender to the union. This is what the UFCW calls a pressure campaign."[38] First, the union does a power structure analysis, researching the employer to discover its weak points. Perhaps it can organize a campaign to get people to withdraw money from the banks which are the target company's lenders. Perhaps the target employer is vulnerable to bad publicity concerning its local environmental record. Perhaps it is violating some of the many laws with which any company must be in compliance, from overtime laws to workers' compensation. At the Delta Pride Catfish Company in Mississippi, the UFCW found out that hundreds of workers, past and present employees, had not been paid for all of the hours they had worked. The threat of a massive suit under the Fair Labor Standards Act (see Chapter Ten) was enough to get the company to voluntarily recognize the union.

A good tactic, especially when built upon rank-and-file community involvement, is a consumer boycott against the target company. This can be based upon all sorts of typical corporate behavior, from a grocery store short-weighing its food to the failure of an employer in a heavily black neighborhood to hire minority labor. A successful pressure campaign might drive a nonunion employer out of business, but this will do no harm to the union's image among other employers. Some of the nonunion's facilities may even be purchased by union companies.

It is possible to conduct representation elections without the NLRB, and such a strategy may fit nicely with a pressure campaign.[39] In a small town, for example, a union might try to organize the community, by conducting town meetings to discuss unionization of a key employer. At these meetings, the union can work with an organization rooted locally around concerns common to most citizens. Later, when union momentum is building, the union can get a prominent local person, such as a minister or local official, to agree to oversee a representation election, conducted just like the Board would conduct one. If the union wins, it next presses the employer to voluntarily recognize the victory and bargain with the union. Professional organizations like the American Arbitration Association will also conduct elections for a fee. Of course, the employer might not recognize the union on the basis of this type of election. However, the support organized during the community campaign may pay dividends during a succeeding official certification campaign or during a pressure campaign.

VI. Workers not Covered by the National Labor Relations Act

There are important groups of workers which are not protected by the National Labor Relations Act. Some of these are protected by other statutes, while others are not protected by any law. The Act, itself, excludes some workers, and the NLRB has excluded others by its own decrees. Let us look briefly at each group.

A. Railway and Airline Workers

These employees are covered by the Railway Labor Act, as we have already discussed.

B. Public Employees: Federal

Public employees are directly excluded from coverage under the NLRA. At the time of the Act's passage, there were not nearly as many employees of federal, state, and local governments as there are today, and there was no firm basis in the common law allowing for their unionization and collective bargaining. This does not mean that public employees did not try to organize, and, in fact, there were many strikes in the public sector. However, it was not until the 1960s that public sector workers, much more numerous and tired of seeing their wages and working conditions deteriorate, began to unionize in earnest. The willingness of large numbers of these workers to risk being fired for joining a union or striking eventually forced governments to enact legislation which afforded public employees some of the rights enjoyed by the private sector workers covered by the NLRA and the Railway Labor Act.[40]

Employees of the federal government are protected by Title VII of the Civil Service Reform Act of 1978 (CSRA), itself the end product of a series of Executive Orders issued by Presidents Kennedy, Nixon, and Ford. The rights given to federal employees under the CSRA are more narrowly defined than those granted by the National Labor Relations Act. Employees have the right "to form, join, or assist any labor organization, or to refrain from any such activity" and "to engage in collective bargaining with respect to conditions of employment through representatives chosen by employees under this chapter." Missing is any language about "concerted activities" for "mutual aid or protection." The Act strictly forbids strikes and excludes strikers from the definition of "employee." Strikers can therefore be fired, whereas under the NLRA, they can only be replaced and retain legal rights while on strike. Several important government agencies are excluded from coverage, including the FBI, the CIA, and the General Accounting Office. Striking unions are denied status as "labor organizations" under the Act. President Reagan seized upon these features of the law to quickly fire the striking air traffic controllers in 1982 and decertify their union.[41] It is important to note that a union of federal workers can compel the government agency whose workers it represents only to bargain about working conditions; wages and benefits are set by civil service regulations. Not all working conditions can be negotiated, including job classifications and conditions covered by other federal statutes. The Act spells out in detail certain "management rights" which are in the exclusive possession of the agency and its managers, further restricting the right of a union to bargain collectively. The president has the power to issue an order suspending all or part of the Act or to exclude any agency from its coverage if the president determines that this is in the national interest.

The CSRA establishes a Federal Labor Relations Authority, composed of three members, appointed by the president for five-year terms, to oversee the Act, and a General Counsel to investigate and prosecute unfair labor practices. The Authority has broad powers in deciding appropriate bargaining units and deciding what issues can be negotiated between unions and agencies. There are nine regional offices at which representation and unfair labor practice issues commence. Representation procedures are outlined in some detail in the Act, but basically the NLRB procedure is followed. A 30% show of interest is necessary before an election will be held, the Authority can hold hearings to determine the appropriateness of the unit, and the Authority conducts the election and certifies the winner as the exclusive representative of the members of the unit. Certification can be denied to any union "if the Authority determines that the labor organization is subject to corrupt influences or influences opposed to democratic principles." The Authority has the sole power to determine the appropriateness of bargaining units, and "shall determine any unit to be an appropriate unit only if the determination will ensure a clear and identifiable community of interest among the employees in the unit and will promote effective dealings with, and efficiency of the operations of, the agency involved." The Authority has the power to consolidate smaller units into larger ones at its discretion. Bargaining unit determinations are not subject to court appeal, although unfair labor practice awards can be appealed as in the NLRA.[42]

C. Public Employees: State and Local

At present, there are 35 states which grant public employees some statutory organizing and bargaining rights. There are several other states in which the state courts have given employees some of these same rights. A few states still do not permit public employers to engage in collective bargaining with unions, although collective bargaining has taken place in them. The great variability of state laws makes it impossible to examine them in depth in this book. State statutes are, for the most part, patterned after the National Labor Relations Act, although only nine states permit strikes under at least some conditions. Most states have boards similar to the NLRB which conduct representation elections and investigate and prosecute unfair labor practices. Many states have more than one public employee law. Pennsylvania has three: Act 111 covers police and firefighters (these cannot strike, but must use binding arbitration to settle disputes); Act 195 covers other public employees (some of these have the right to strike, but strikes can be readily enjoined); and Act 88 deals exclusively with teachers' strikes and places severe restrictions on them. Representation strikes and picketing are illegal or enjoinable even in those states which permit a limited right to strike. The story at the beginning of this chapter gives the reader a good feel for how most state public employee laws work in practice.[43]

D. Agricultural Employees

The workers who harvest our crops are among the most exploited in the nation. These largely minority and immigrant workers from Mexico, Central America, and the Caribbean earn the lowest wages and labor under the most horrible working conditions. Farm workers have waged heroic struggles to organize unions and gain basic human dignity, but their efforts have met largely with failure, victims of employer violence and police brutality. If any group of workers needs legal protection, it is farm workers.

Unfortunately, farm workers—those directly involved in agricultural production and fishing—are excluded from coverage under the National Labor Relations Act. Their exclusion reflected the power of southern congresspersons who could not imagine the unionization of the region's black field hands. Exclusion means that farm workers do not enjoy Section 7 rights. They can engage in concerted activity (i.e., form a union), but they can also be fired for doing so. They cannot compel an employer to bargain with any union which they do form. They are also not bound by the NLRA's prohibitions against organizational strikes and picketing and they can engage in prohibited secondary actions, but, without some basic legal protection, these may not be very useful.

In the absence of federal coverage, state law prevails, but only a few states have labor laws which specifically cover farm workers. California, the one state with a law similar to the NLRA, enacted in 1975 the Agricultural Labor Relations Act, complete with an Agricultural Labor Relations Board. This law provided the legal support to help the United Farm Workers Union to successfully organize thousands of farm workers into unions which began to negotiate collective bargaining agreements with the growers. It is not necessary to discuss this law in any detail because it is so similar to the NLRA, especially in its procedures for union certification. It does contain provisions for expedited elections to ensure that the migrant workers who make up the bulk of the harvest workforce get to vote in any election. Bargaining units are usually established by ranch, though "multiplant" units do occur. In recent years, conservative state governments have sharply reduced the Board's funding, which along with troubles within the union, has weakened the farm worker labor movement.[44]

Other states do have special farm worker labor laws, but none of these can compare with the California statute. Most of them make it illegal for farm workers to strike during the harvest. Naturally, a strike during harvest will have the best chance for success, so these provisions doom the unions to failure unless they are willing to break the law. Farm workers have pioneered the use of consumer boycotts to force recognition, and occasionally, as was the case in Ohio, they have won significant victories.[45]

E. Domestic Workers

If anything, the plight of domestic workers, those maids, cooks, chauffeurs, and governesses in household service, is worse than that of farm workers. They are not covered by the NLRA, and they are not protected by any state laws. This, along with their isolation at work, makes it hard for them to effectively organize. Note that employees of firms established to provide household services are most likely covered by the Act. For example, many companies now supply "maid" services. The employees of such companies are protected by the NLRA. The workers excluded are those who are hired directly by a household to work for that household. The nanny hired by President Clinton's recent attorney general nominee, Kimba Wood, would not be covered by the Act.[46]

F. Supervisors

The passage of the Wagner Act created great difficulties for foremen and supervisors because it took away from them the near dictatorial powers which they had enjoyed. They often saw themselves in the middle between newly aggressive workers and their own managers. In response, they began to form unions, demanding the same legal protection that workers now enjoyed. The NLRB and the courts made conflicting rulings concerning the Act's coverage of supervisors. Naturally businesses wanted them excluded, fearing a division in the managerial ranks if the lowest-level bosses joined a union. Congress accommodated employers in the 1947 Taft-Hartley Amendments to the Wagner Act. Supervisors are excluded by Section 2(11). Section 14(a) gives supervisors the right to join a union, but it also gives employers the power to refuse to deal with their unions.

The definition of "supervisor" in Section 2(11) is broad: "The term 'supervisor' means any individual having authority, in the interest of the employer, to hire, transfer, suspend, lay off, recall, promote, discharge, assign, reward, or discipline other employees, or responsibly to direct them, or to adjust their grievances, or effectively to recommend such action, if in connection with the foregoing the exercise of such authority is not of a merely routine or clerical nature, but requires the use of independent judgment." It is not the title of a person that matters but what the person does; some independent judgment is necessary before the NLRB will decide that a person is a supervisor. However, it is only necessary for a person to perform one of the duties enumerated to be declared a supervisor. It is possible that a person who does regular supervisory work but spends the majority of her time doing bargaining unit work will be defined a supervisor and denied the right to vote in any representation election.[47]

Two election campaign situations involving supervisors deserve attention. First, it is conceivable that some supervisors will support a union drive, either because they are or were union members or they think that a union will help them to get higher wages. Suppose that a supervisor advises employees to sign authorization cards. This would appear to violate Section 8(a)(1), but the NLRB may rule that it does not if the supervisor is speaking personally and not on behalf of the employer.[48] Second, it might be an employer unfair labor practice to discharge or discipline a supervisor during the campaign despite the supervisor's lack of statutory protection. An example would be the discharge of a foreman for refusing to illegally fire a union supporter.[49]

G. Family Members and Independent Contractors

An employer's spouse and children are not protected by the NLRA and must be excluded from any bargaining units. If my father owns a hardware store and I am one of 30 employees, I will be excluded from their bargaining unit. If I support the union, my father can legally fire me!

In most large cities today cab drivers are independent contractors. They lease or own their cabs and are responsible for gas, maintenance, and insurance. In such cases they are independent contractors and not employees under the Act. The Board often has to make judgment calls here because there is a lot of variation in terms of the control exercised by a so-called independent contractor. The more control a person has over the work and the product, the more likely he will be defined as an independent contractor. Sometimes employers will declare employees to be independent contractors to avoid unionization, but this is an unfair labor practice.[50]

H. Confidential Employees

Consider the personal secretary of the chief executive officer of a company. The company's secretarial staff has petitioned for a representation election. Since the CEO's secretary will have access to confidential information concerning the employer's campaign strategy, should this secretary be included in the bargaining unit? The NLRB has ruled that the answer is no. This secretary would be a "confidential employee," a type of employee excluded from the NLRA's coverage by board ruling rather than by statutory language. Confidential employees are narrowly defined; they must work in a confidential capacity for persons who are responsible for the employer's labor policies. The secretary to the head of labor relations would be confidential, but a person who occasionally typed labor relations related memos would not be a confidential employee.[51]

I. Managerial Employees

Some employees, while not supervisors, may be so closely allied with the management that they cannot be considered employees under the Act. Relatives other than spouses and children might be a good example. The chief accountant of a firm may not supervise anyone, but she clearly is a part of the management. Such employees are called "managerial employees," and the NLRB excludes them from coverage.

In a 1980 decision, *NLRB v. Yeshiva University,* the Supreme court greatly widened the definition of managerial employee.[52] The teachers at this university petitioned the NLRB for a representation election. The school claimed that the teachers were intimately involved in formulating the school's policies and were therefore managerial employees. They helped to decide which programs would be offered, which teachers would be hired, which teachers would be granted tenure, graduation requirements, etc. The University admitted that the Board of Trustees had final decision-making power and that the teachers gave advisory recommendations which occasionally were rejected. The Board ruled for the teachers, but the Supreme Court reversed in a five to our decision. The *Yeshiva* ruling had dealt a blow to the union movement at private colleges. In fact, teachers at some private schools have lost bargaining rights because of it. At Boston University, the teachers' union had already won important advisory powers through collective bargaining. However, after the *Yeshiva* ruling the employer refused to negotiate a new agreement on the grounds that the professors were now managerial employees. The employer won, and the teachers are now without a bargaining agent![53] While the *Yeshiva* decision does not directly affect public colleges, some public colleges have made similar arguments before state boards, fortunately without success so far.

J. Small Employers

The National Labor Relations Act (NLRA) covers workers in "interstate commerce." This means that the employer must engage in the purchase and/or sale of goods and/or services which move across state boundaries. The Board and the courts have defined interstate commerce so broadly that most private employers are covered. However, the NLRB had decided that employers must meet certain "volume of business" standards before it will take on a case brought by the firm's employees. For example, consider the employees of a small motel. The NLRB has set a volume of business standard for motels of $500,000 yearly volume of business. If the motel did not do this much business, its employees would not enjoy protection under the NLRA. They would be covered by any appropriate state law, but not many states have such laws for private sector employees, and those which do, do not offer protection equal to that of the NLRA. Employees of small businesses can thus be fired with impunity if they try to unionize.

VII. Questions and Answers

Question 1. What do union authorization cards say? Under what circumstances can an employer see them?

Union authorization or recognition cards (see Appendix 2) are of two types. Dual-purpose cards state that the signer wants an election to take place and wants to be represented by the union for purposes of collective bargaining. Single-purpose cards state that the signer seeks to have the union represent her for collective bargaining. Single-purpose cards are better for the union because the NLRB will use them to determine support in a case in which the union loses the election, the employer has committed grievous unfair labor practices, and the union asks for a bargaining order (a *Gissel* order) as opposed to a rerun election. The Board will not issue a bargaining order on the basis of dual-purpose cards, because it reasons that some employees may have signed them just to get an election rather than because they truly supported the union. A union organizer or supporter asking someone to sign a single-purpose card must make sure to tell him that he is signing the card to have the union represent him. If he is told that the only reason for signing the card is to get an election, the Board will not use the card as a basis for a bargaining order.

If a union loses an election in a situation in which the employer has committed serious unfair labor practices and the union asks for a bargaining order, the union will have to submit the authorization cards as evidence at the hearing. In this case, the employer will get to see the cards and will know who signed them. It is an unfair labor practice for the employer to discriminate against a worker for signing a card.[54]

Question 2. What factors are considered by the NLRB and other labor boards in determining the appropriateness of bargaining units?

The NLRA and other enabling statutes contain a variety of limitations on bargaining units. For example, under the NLRA supervisors cannot be in bargaining units with nonsupervisory employees. The same is true for managerial employees. In fact, as we have seen, neither of these groups is protected by the law at all. Professional employees cannot be in bargaining units with nonprofessional employees unless a majority of the professional employees agree to this. Plant guards and other security workers must be in separate bargaining units and cannot be mixed with other employees. Nor can guards be in a union which admits nonguards to membership. This does not mean that mixed units of guards and nonguards are illegal, but they will not be certified by the NLRB.

After considerable litigation, the NLRB established seven appropriate bargaining units in the health care industry. These are all registered nurses, all physicians, all other professionals, all technical employees, all skilled maintenance employees, all business office clerical employees, all guards, and all other nonprofessional employees.[55]

In deciding whether a particular bargaining unit is appropriate when the law offers no rules, the NLRB uses several factors. The history of organization among similar workers, the extent to which the workers in the proposed bargaining unit perform similar types of work, the extent to which the management of separate plants is integrated (in a case in which the decision is whether the unit should consist of workers in one plant or several plants), the location of the plants, and the extent of organization. This last one concerns single-plant versus multiple-plant units. Suppose that there are four plants of an employer which could form a bargaining unit. If the other factors favor a multiple-plant unit, the NLRA now mandates that the NLRB must rule for such a unit even if the union has successfully organized only one of the plants. If the Board concludes that a multiple-plant unit is not necessarily the best, it can weight in its decision the extent of organizing the union has already done.[56]

The NLRB has worked out special arrangements for special circumstances. Suppose that there are two groups of workers, group A and group B, and two unions, union X and union Y. Union X wants to represent only workers in group A, while union Y seeks to represent workers in both groups. The NLRB considers both units to be appropriate. On the ballot, group A workers will have the choice of voting for union X, union Y, or no union. Group B workers will choose between union Y and no union. If group A workers vote by majority to be represented by union X, then X will be certified by the Board as their union. If they do not, then their ballots are combined with those of group B to see if union Y will be selected as bargaining agent. Such a situation is called a *Globe* election after the case in which the NLRB first worked out this procedure.[57]

Sometimes a unit is composed of both skilled and semi- or unskilled workers. What if the skilled workers want to separate out from the larger unit and comprise a separate unit? This has become more difficult since a 1966 decision made by the NLRB.[58] For example, the Board will check to see if the skilled workers have maintained their identity and cohesion during the period in which they were included in the larger unit as well as the degree to which the skilled are integrated into the normal production processes at the plant.

The National Mediation Board makes bargaining unit determinations under the Railway Labor Act, but its rules are essentially similar to those of the National Labor Relations Board. Since the deregulation of the transportation industry, some rail and trucking operations have been integrated under one corporate roof. Trucking employees will only come under the jurisdiction of the Railway Labor Act if their labor is integrated into the operations of the railroad. Otherwise they will be governed by the NLRA.[59]

The laws which govern public employees may contain more specific rules which labor boards must consider in their determination of the appropriate bargaining unit. For example, Act 195 governing most public employees in Pennsylvania states that the Pennsylvania Labor Relations Board must avoid the overfragmentation of employees into separate units. Thus the teachers at branch campuses of two large universities were denied separate units in part on this basis. The Board felt that it would be too burdensome for the employer to potentially have to deal with a large number of bargaining units.[60]

Question 3. What are some examples of ways that an employer can delay a representation election?

One way an employer can delay an election is to challenge the union's proposed bargaining unit. Depending on the circumstances, this might allow the employer to delay an election for a long time. At my own workplace, our attempt to organize the teachers was delayed for several years as the university made one objection after another to the bargaining unit. A second technique is for the employer to file unfair labor practice charges against the union during the campaign period. The NLRB will not usually hold an election when there are pending unfair labor practice charges. If the employer is willing to spend the money, hearings before the Board and court appeals can take up many months or even years. Of course, at this point the union is free to strike to force the employer to recognize it.[61] The ability of employers to delay elections is one reason why some unions now refuse to use the Board at all in organizing campaigns. Legal reform to guarantee speedy elections is certainly warranted, as is recognition on the basis of authorization cards alone.

Question 4. What is an example of a legal anti-union letter sent to workers by an employer during an election campaign?

Section 8(c), the employer "free speech" provision of the NLRA, was added to the law to give employers greater ability to legally combat unions. A common tactic is to bombard employees and their families with letters attacking the union. These letters can legally contain exaggerations and outright false statements as long as the NLRB does not consider these to be coercive or to promise benefits. Here is a good example, found to be legal by the Board. Most workers would consider it to be threatening, but Board members do not come from the working class. The context of the letter is an attempt to unionize a restaurant. The owner owns another restaurant which is already organized.

Dear Fellow Employees:

1. As you know, there will be a Union election on July 9. At that election each of you will have the opportunity to vote to determine whether or not you want to be represented by the restaurant workers' union.

2. You are much luckier than the employees at Fiorello's, our restaurant on the west side. Some time ago those employees voted to be represented by the restaurant workers' union. They were led

down the primrose path by union promises of increased wage benefits. In fact, after the election the Union negotiated a contract with the restaurant management which, in my opinion, gave the employees at Fiorello's no more than they would have gotten had there been no union—and probably gave them less. In addition, I believe many of these employees will be hurt by the inflexibility of the Union contract.

3. On the other hand, you know from the experience of Fiorello's employees exactly the kind of contract the Union would negotiate if it became your collective bargaining representative. A contract which produces nothing more than you would expect to receive were there no union in the picture. For that, you are afforded the privilege of paying Union dues.

...

6. The restaurant does not want a union at Fiorello's! Our experience on the west side has shown that we can negotiate an agreement with the Union which does not cost us any more in wages and benefits than without the Union and may even cost less. But our experience on the west side has also shown us that the presence of the Union results in a tense working relationship with extreme disharmony among the employees.

This is a real cost to everyone. It can result in a loss of customers and a loss of income to our employees who serve those customers, as well as the restaurant itself. The Union benefits no one but itself.[62]

Question 5. Can labor consultants be charged with unfair labor practices?

Yes. If the consultant has been given control over supervisors in the anti-union campaign, then it is possible to charge the consultant directly with unfair labor practices.[63] However, the real culprit is the employer, so the charges are best filed against it. In any attempt to confront the consultant directly, it will be necessary to identify it. Businesses covered by the Landrum-Griffin Act of 1959 must report to the Secretary of Labor expenditures made to labor consultants, and the consultants must likewise report the terms of their contracts with employers. However, there are major loopholes in the provisions of the Act which make it unnecessary for most consultants to file. They only have to file if they speak directly to the employees, but most consultants use the employers' supervisors to do the dirty work. Further, attorneys who act as consultants may not have to file, because to do so would compromise the attorney-client privilege rule. Finally, the Department of Labor does not ordinarily check the accuracy of the reports which are filed. Fortunately for workers, the AFL-CIO keeps much better track of consultants. It publishes something called the *RUB*

Sheet (RUB stands for Report on Union-Busters) and tracks the activities of hundreds of union-busters. If you suspect that your employer is using a consultant, contact the AFL-CIO's Research Director at 815 16th St. NW, Washington, D.C. 20006. Some large unions also have materials on consultants and may run training seminars for workers. Check with your Central Labor Council.

Question 6. To what extent can an employer interrogate employees about their union sympathies?

The general rule now is that an employer may interrogate employees as long as the workers' rights under Section 7 are not violated. That is, the interrogation must not "coerce, restrain, or interfere with" the rights guaranteed under the NLRA. The Board will consider all of the circumstances of the case in making its decision. Did the employer use threatening language, such as suggesting that the employee could lose her job? Did the questioning take place in a hostile atmosphere, such as in a workplace where the employer had already been found guilty of unfair labor practices? Was the employee questioned in the plant manager's office or in the open with others present? Was it implied that the employee had to answer the questions? Etc.[64]

The employer may not poll the workers concerning their union sentiments. If a union requests that the employer recognize the union without a Board election, the employer may conduct a secret ballot election. Provided that a board election atmosphere is maintained, the parties are bound by the results of the election.[65]

An employer may not conduct surveillance of employees, by spying on them with cameras or taking down license numbers outside of places in which the workers are meeting. The employer cannot even give the impression that it is spying, when in fact it is not.[66]

Question 7. If the employer gives an anti-union speech at the workplace, does the union have the right to respond?

The employer has an absolute right to give such speeches during worktime and to make attendance mandatory. The exception is that no such speeches can be given by either side within 24 hours of the election. Elections will be set aside if the union loses and the employer has violated the twenty-four hour rule. Only speeches to mass audiences are prohibited; other forms of anti-union activities are permitted during the last 24 hours.

The union has no right to respond to a captive-audience speech on the employer's property or on company time. The NLRB does have the power to give union organizers access to the employees inside of the workplace in cases in which the employer has grossly violated the law. The employer may have so tainted the climate for a fair election that the Board feels that only drastic measures can give the union a fair chance to win the rerun election.[67]

Question 8. Do union organizers who are not employees have the right to be on the employer's property during the election campaign?

No, unless the Board concludes that to deny them access would violate the workers' Section 7 rights. Recently the Supreme Court denied a union the right to put leaflets on cars in a private parking lot, in circumstances in which it was extremely difficult for the union to reach the employees otherwise. This ruling effectively overturned previous more lenient rulings.[68] However, if the employees are practically confined to the employers' property (as in the case of migrant workers living in company housing or workers living in a company-owned unincorporated town), then the Board would give the organizers limited access to the employer's property to communicate with the workers.

Question 9. Are workers on layoff eligible to vote in a certification election? What about on a leave of absence?

This depends on the circumstances. An employee with a good chance of being recalled, such as one on temporary layoff with a definite recall date or one who has in the past been laid off and recalled, will have the right to vote. The union should urge all of the persons it thinks will vote for the union to vote and let the employer challenge the ballots. For those on leave, some rulings take the same approach as for those on layoff, while others presume that workers on leave are still employees eligible to vote unless they have resigned or been fired.[69]

Question 10. How are challenged ballots handled?

Ballots challenged by either side are separated from the other ballots. A two-envelope system is used. The secret ballot is placed inside of an unmarked envelope, and this envelope is placed inside of an envelop signed by the challenged employee. These ballots are considered only if they make a difference in the outcome. In this case, they are dealt with in a hearing in which the parties present evidence as to why they should or should not be counted, and the Board (regional office officer) makes a determination on a case-by-case basis.

Question 11. What are "runoff" elections?

In any election, whether for certification or decertification, 50% plus one of those casting valid ballots are needed for victory. This may not happen if there are more than two choices on the ballot. For example, suppose that there are three unions and "no union" as the choices, and the total votes for each choice are: union A-50 votes, union

B-40 votes, union C-30 votes, and no union-20 votes. There are 140 votes cast, but no party has the 71 votes needed to win. Therefore, there will be a runoff election between the two top vote getters, in this case, unions A and B. The winner of the runoff election will be the winner of the certification election.

Question 12. Who sits on the National Mediation Board established by the Railway Labor Act?

The NMB is made up of three members, no more than two of whom can come from the same political party, appointed by the president for three-year terms.

Question 13. Can a single employee engage in "concerted activity?"

Yes, if the worker is covered by a collective bargaining agreement. In the key case in this area, a worker refused to drive what he believed to be an unsafe truck. He was discharged for this. He could have filed a grievance under the contract, but instead he filed an unfair labor practice charge. The Supreme Court accepted the argument that, while he acted alone and did not discuss his situation with other workers, he, in effect, acted on behalf of all of the other workers covered by the agreement, which itself was the product of concerted activity.[70]

In a nonunion setting, the NLRB does not accept this logic. An employee fired for filing a safety complaint with a state occupational safety and health commission argued that he, too, was acting on behalf of other workers. That is, he was indirectly acting in concert with others, even though he had not discussed his problem with anyone else. This argument was rejected by the NLRB.[71] A worker in a nonunion setting must, therefore, discuss a problem with other employees, so that when she is disciplined, she can argue that she was engaged in concerted activity.

Question 14. Does the existence of a collective bargaining agreement bar a certification or decertification election?

If there exists a written and signed agreement between the parties, containing substantive provisions, and which is of a definite duration, the NLRB will bar any election for the length of the contract up to three years. If a contract does bar an election, another union can file for a certification election or employees may file for a decertification election, but they must do so in the period 60 to 90 days before the contract expires (90 to 120 days in the health care industry). Authorization cards can be circulated at any time, but, remember, they are only valid for one year. Also, if the original parties fail to reach a new agreement after the old one expires, the contract is not a bar to election.

Question 15. How does a decertification election work?

Such an election, in which employees attempt to rid themselves of an incumbent union, follows the same procedures as a certification election. First, there must be a 30% showing of interest. Second, another union may intervene and get its name on the ballot with a token showing of interest. This is a good idea if the workers intend to remain unionized. If no other union is on the ballot and "no union" wins, no new election may be held for 12 months, during which time the workers remain without a union. Third, the employer must not illegally interfere in the decertification process. This does not mean that the employer cannot actively campaign against the union or suggest to some employees the procedure for decertification. The employer cannot spearhead the drive or give material aid to the "no union" forces. Fourth, it takes a majority of votes cast voting for "no union" for the union to be decertified.[72]

While an employer cannot, itself, file a decertification petition, the employer can refuse to bargain with a union if it has a good-faith reason to believe that the union no longer represents the employees. This is somewhat risky, because the union may file an unfair labor practice charge for refusal to bargain. If the employer unilaterally changed wages and then lost the unfair labor practice charge, it would have to pay back wages and benefits. In such a situation, the employer can file for a representation election, called an "RM election."

Question 16. How long does it take for an unfair labor practice charge to be processed?

Too long, and this is one of the reasons why the labor law does not do justice to workers. Here are the average times:

- from making the charge to a regional officer filing a complaint: 45 days
- from charge to hearing: three to six weeks
- from hearing to decision at regional level: four months
- from regional decision to NLRB decision: one year
- from Board ruling to Appeals Court ruling: at least one year
- from Appeals Court to Supreme Court: at least one year[73]

While most cases are settled before any hearing occurs, it is not unusual for workers to be without justice for a very long time. An expedited procedure is badly needed.

Question 17. Which federal court of appeals has jurisdiction in an appeal from an NLRB decision?

The party making the appeal has a choice among three appeals courts: The circuit in which the unfair labor practice was committed, the circuit in which the employer or union does business, or the District of Columbia Circuit.

Question 18. How can a Board bargaining unit determination be appealed?

Bargaining unit determinations cannot be directly appealed, no doubt to prevent endless litigation before an election can take place. However, they can be indirectly appealed. Let's say that a unit has been established which the employer thinks is improper, perhaps because it contains employees the employer thinks should be excluded. If the union wins the election, the only alternative which the employer has is to refuse to bargain with it. The union will then file a Section 8(a)(5) refusal-to-bargain unfair labor practice. The employer can defend itself with the argument that the unit was improperly defined. Naturally the final determination will have to be made by the court of appeals, since the NLRB set up the unit in the first place.

Question 19. Are there any exceptions to the right of workers to wear union insignia?

In most cases workers have an absolute right to wear union buttons, hats, jackets, etc. to work. If the employer can show that the insignia create a safety hazard, it may be able to prohibit the wearing of some items. Or, if it can show that the wearing of insignia has created a workplace climate so hostile that production has been disrupted, it may again be able to refuse to allow the workers to wear them. In one case, after a bitter strike, in which union supporters fought with those opposed to the union, union supporters wore anti-scab buttons. These provoked physical violence, and the employer prohibited their display. The union filed an unfair labor practice charge, but the NLRB dismissed it. In such a situation, the employer will have to show that strife at work has occurred and production has been disrupted and not merely that production is likely to be affected.[74]

Question 20. Once a union has been established, can employees in the bargaining unit engage in concerted activity independent of the union?

No. In the leading case, black employees in the unit formed an organization to pressure the company and the union to improve its treatment of black workers. In opposition to the wishes of the union, the organization's members began to picket the employer. For this some of them were discharged. They filed unfair labor practice charges on the grounds that they were engaged in protected concerted activity. The Supreme Court disagreed, stating that the workers, once unionized, had to conduct their concerted actions through the bargaining agent.[75] This ruling is a blow to independent worker actions, but it is in line with the law's stress upon formal and bureaucratic employer-employee relationships.

Question 21. Are workers living illegally in the United States protected by the labor laws?

The case of immigrants has been dealt with in the context of discrimination law in Chapter Two, but here we can state that unless a group of workers is specifically excluded from coverage under the NLRA, they are protected. The term "employee" is defined in Section 2(3), and in connection with the rights of illegal immigrants, the Supreme Court has stated:

> The breadth of 2(3)'s definition is striking, the Act squarely applies to "any employee." The only limitations are specific exemptions.... Since undocumented aliens are not among the few groups of workers expressly exempted by Congress, they plainly come within the broad statutory definition of "employee."[76]

In a union organizing campaign, it would be illegal for an employer to threaten workers with deportation if the union were to win. It would also be illegal for a union to make such a threat if a worker refused to sign an authorization card. The NLRB has ordered new elections where the employer has made threats. If undocumented aliens are fired because of activities protected by Section 7 of the NLRA, the Board will not order them to be reinstated unless they are in a position to be legally hired by the employer. The Immigration Reform and Control Act of 1986 makes it illegal for an employer to knowingly hire an illegal immigrant, so the Board will not order such an employee to be reinstated. It is conceivable that the Board will order backpay, on the grounds that the employer should suffer a penalty for violating the Act, although there is judicial disagreement about this.[77]

Question 22. Are there situations in which an employer is required to recognize a union by collective bargaining agreement?

Two situations might arise in which this would be legal and not a violation of Sections 8(a)(2) and 8(b)(1). First, suppose that a company decides to move from one location to another. The workers at the original location are in a union, and the union has negotiated a clause which compels the employer to recognize the union at the new location. The NLRB will allow such agreements if the union can demonstrate that it has majority status at the new location. This might occur if the employer has also agreed to hire union members from other bargaining units at the new location.

Second, Section 8(f) of the NLRA specifically allows for "prehire" agreements in the construction industry, and these are legal whether or not the union can demonstrate that it has majority status at the construction site. Once an employer has signed a prehire agreement, it cannot reject it; it is good until it expires. However, a prehire agreement can be converted into a regular collective bargaining agreement only if the union wins a representation election. Should the union lose such an election, the prehire agreement is void, and no new election can be held for one year. If the union does not seek an election, the prehire agreement ends upon expiration, and the employer can make unilateral changes in wages, etc. without bargaining with the union. Therefore, it is wise for the union to seek majority status as soon as possible, even in situations in which it has had prehire agreements for many years.[78]

VIII. Selected Readings

1. Bruce Feldacker, *Labor Guide to Labor Law* (Englewood Cliffs, N.J.: Prentice Hall, 1990).

2. Matthew M. Franckiewicz, "How to Win NLRB Cases: Tips From a Former Insider," *Labor Law Journal* 44 (Jan. 1993), pp. 40-48.

3. Richard B, Freeman, "Unionism Comes to the Public Sector," *Journal of Economic Literature* 24 (March 1986), pp. 41-86.

4. Mike Parker and Jane Slaughter, *Choosing Sides: Labor and the Team Concept* (Boston: South End Press, 1988).

5. Paul Weiler, *Governing the Workplace: The Future of Labor and Employment Law* (Cambridge, MA: Harvard University Press, 1990).

Chapter 5

THE LAW OF COLLECTIVE BARGAINING

I. Bargaining in the 1980s: The Hormel Strike

The U.S. economy went into a tailspin in the early 1970s, marking the end of the great boom which followed World War II. As corporations lost market shares and profit margins plummeted, business leaders and their allies in government groped for ways to reverse the new and ominous trends. The strategy they eventually embraced can be best described as low-wage and anti-labor. Since unionized workers enjoyed the highest wages, benefits, and security, an attack upon organized labor was launched. The assault on the strongest segments of the working class was given a boost by the Reagan administration; its firing of the air traffic controllers served as a great symbolic victory for capital's hardline approach. Throughout the 1980s, one industry after another was rocked by plant closings, runaway shops, massive layoffs, the introduction of labor-saving technology, and the reorganization of work to eliminate skilled jobs and speed up the pace of labor.[1]

The meatpacking industry was no exception to these trends, but it was in this industry that some workers fought back in an epic confrontation with their employer.[2] A sketch of that struggle will provide us with a good introduction to the realities of collective bargaining law today, which are often a far cry from the niceties of the words of the statutes. Section 7 of the NLRA gives covered workers the right to bargain collectively with their employers through representatives of their own choosing. Section 8(a)(5) makes it an unfair labor practice for an employer to refuse to bargain in good faith (Section 8(b)(3) similarly requires unions to bargain in good faith). However, winning a decent agreement at the bargaining table demands more than just a good grasp of the law. And even with extraordinary efforts, the bargaining may end in failure. A union which wins a representation election has only about a 50% chance of forcing the employer to come to terms.[3]

The scene of this conflict was the industrial town of Austin, Minnesota, home of the Hormel Meatpacking Company. While the other major meatpackers faced declining profits in the late 1970s and early 1980s, Hormel's profits were robust. However, the company used the plight of its competitors to pressure its own workers into granting concessions. At the same time, it began to acquire plants in other communities and to layoff hundreds of workers in the Austin plant. The local union, Local P-9 of the United Packinghouse Workers, had come to be dominated by more senior and conservative "business unionists," comfortable with their privileged positions and suspicious of rank-and-file efforts which might have endangered the cozy relationship which they enjoyed with corporate management. The local was extremely cooperative with the company, granting it significant concessions in wages, bonuses, and production standards. Though employment dipped from a peak of about 5,000 to around 1,750, many new workers were hired between 1965 and 1970 to replace the older workers who retired early or transferred to other facilities. These younger workers were forced by their collective bargaining agreement to accept lower wages, worse safety conditions, and less desirable jobs and shifts than older workers, and this fueled deep resentment of both the company and the union.

In 1978, the company threatened to close the plant in Austin and build a new, ultramodern plant outside of town. In response the union signed a new agreement "that eliminated all incentive pay, raised productivity standards by 20%, froze wages for seven years, and banned all strikes for three years after the new plant opened." Compounding the workers' woes was the merger of their union into the United Food and Commercial Workers Union (UFCW). In the new union, packinghouse workers were a small minority, and the union's national leadership was intent on a policy of concessionary bargaining as the best way to cope with the deteriorating economic and political climate. These changes brought the anger of most of the younger and many of the older workers to a head, and a new, more militant cadre of union leaders were elected to office. These new officers and their supporters began to map out a strategy to revitalize their union and to stop the concessions. When the new plant opened in 1982, their efforts accelerated as working conditions deteriorated sharply.

After the new plant opened, Hormel's rivals began to slash wages by closing plants and reopening them on a nonunion basis, or by getting the union to grant wage concessions under the threat of shutting down the plants. Other competitors cut wages by filing for bankruptcy, taking advantage of a 1984 Supreme Court ruling that a company that has filed for bankruptcy could reject its collective bargaining agreement before going before the bankruptcy court. (This ruling was later overturned by Congress.)[4] Hormel got another plant to agree to mid-contract wage cuts (it took three votes and hundreds of layoffs) and then announced that it wanted wage concessions in Austin, as well. Local P-9 rejected the company's demands and began to organize an anti-concession movement within the local. The members agreed to hire Ray Rogers of Corporate Campaign, Inc. to spearhead a "corporate campaign" against Hormel. In such a campaign, union members pressure their company's chief financial backers (banks, insurance companies, etc.) through boycotts, picketing, and negative media publicity in order to put ultimate pressure upon their primary adversary. Union members would also forge alliances with other workers and other progressive groups to build a movement of mutual cooperation and solidarity.

Unbeknownst to the local's members, their agreement with Hormel had a "me too" clause in it, which basically said that Hormel workers would get the same wages and benefits as workers in the larger unionized meatpacking companies. When Oscar Mayer got wage concessions, Hormel demanded similar cuts. The company took its case to arbitration under the agreement and won not only a wage cut of 23% but an order for newer workers to pay back medical benefits which the company had allegedly overpaid. And in the meantime, the national union had agreed to wage concessions at Hormel plants, including Austin, whose members had just overwhelmingly rejected them. From this point, the local determined to fully support the corporate campaign, realizing that it faced not just a hostile corporation but a sellout national union as well.

The old collective bargaining agreement between Hormel and Local P-9 was due to expire in August 1985. The union wanted strong safety language and wage increases, while the company insisted on further concessions and a virtual gutting of the contract. A week before the contract expired, members voted 93% to 7% to strike. The national union approved the strike but forbade the union to use roving pickets (to picket other Hormel plants not on strike) and demanded that it abandon the corporate campaign. The strike began on August 17, 1985 and quickly developed into one of the most important labor-management confrontations of the decade.

Soon after the strike began, Local P-9 learned that labor law in this era of political reaction is as often an enemy as a friend. As a part of the corporate campaign, P-9ers and their supporters had organized a boycott against Hormel's chief financier and second largest stockholder, First Bank Systems. Picketers, leaflets, billboards, and advertisements urged people not to patronize the bank. Both Hormel and First Bank filed unfair labor practice charges against the local, arguing that the corporate campaign violated Section 8(b)(4)(B) of the National Labor Relations Act, which prohibits most secondary boycotts. First the administrative law judge at the NLRB regional office, then the Board itself, and finally the federal court of appeals agreed that the campaign against First Bank was a secondary boycott.[5] However, only the regional office's *preliminary* investigation really mattered. Once the investigator had reason to believe that a secondary boycott was taking place, he was bound by Section 10(l) to immediately seek a court injunction to stop it. In late September 1985, an injunction was issued which ordered the campaign against First Bank to end. This injunction was of importance to the national union as well as to the company. The UFCW was intent on destroying the independence of Local P-9, and it used the injunction to get the Minnesota State AFL-CIO to ban all P-9 literature at its meetings, on the grounds that such literature referred to First Bank and therefore violated the injunction.

Local P-9 believed that Hormel had begun to shift some of the work normally done in Austin to its other plants. In response, the local wanted to send roving pickets to these plants in the hope that union brothers and sisters would honor the picket lines. The legality of such picketing is questionable. Strictly informational picketing is allowed, that is, "picketing or other publicity for the purpose of truthfully advising the public (including customers) that an employer does not employ members of or have a contract with a labor organization" (Section 8(b)(7)(C)). However, if the picketing serves as a "signal" to employees not to cross the picket line, then it is not legal, because it then violates Section 8(b)(4)'s prohibition of secondary actions. Clearly in this case, the roving pickets wanted to signal Hormel employees not to go to work.[6]

The fact that the roving pickets were not informational pickets would not always mean that they were breaking the law. If union members at other Hormel plants were performing work normally done at the Austin plant, then these other plants were, in effect, "allies" of the Austin plant. This means that they were parties to the primary labor dispute between P-9 and Hormel. If this were the case, the picketing at these plants would be primary picketing and would be legal.[7] What is more, those who honored the picket lines could not be fired for so doing. Workers engaged in a legal primary strike (one against their own employer) cannot be fired, although they can be replaced. The difference, which will be explained in detail in the following chapter, is that workers replaced during a strike have certain recall rights when the strike is over. Workers who honor a primary picket line are called sympathy strikers, and they enjoy the same protection from firing as do the primary strikers themselves. Therefore, if the roving P-9 pickets were primary pickets, then the Hormel workers who honored their picket line could be replaced but not fired. It would eventually be up to the NLRB to decide whether the roving picketing was primary or secondary. The UFWC was not willing to let this happen, so it refused Local P-9 the right to use roving pickets.

Local members twice rejected the company's last offer by secret ballot, first in December 1985 and then in early January 1986. In response, the company stated that it would reopen the plant with replacements (scabs) on January 13, 1986. It advertised in the media for strikebreakers, and it tried to reopen the plant the following week. Massive picketing, demonstrations, and car blockades kept the plant closed, but these actions brought further legal troubles for the strikers. Under the Norris-LaGuardia Act of 1932, primary picketing cannot be wholly enjoined, but state courts are free to restrict picketing under a wide variety of circumstances.[8] Mass picketing prevents entry into and exit from a plant can be enjoined, whether it is peaceful or not. Mass picketing is also an unfair labor practice, violating Section 8(b)(1), because it violates the employees' right "not" to engage in concerted activities.[9] Minnesota courts had already placed severe restrictions on the picketing, including a prohibition of taking pictures of scab vehicles. The actions taken to keep the plant from reopening clearly violated the court orders and served as an excuse for more draconian measures.

Minnesota's "liberal" governor, Rudy Perpich, responded to the militancy of the P-9ers and their many allies by sending in the National Guard and the State Police. Over the next few days, the workers faced repression reminiscent of that suffered by the Pullman strikers. Police smashed car windows and dragged the drivers off to jail; hundreds of strikers and supporters were arrested and then mistreated in jail; and strike leaders were jailed on contempt charges. Local P-9 upped the ante, defying the national union by sending roving pickets to other Hormel plants. More than 500 sympathy strikers were summarily fired for honoring the P-9 picket lines. Rallies in support of the strike took place around the country, and numerous acts of civil disobedience resulted in more arrests and criminal charges. Had the national union supported these courageous acts, the strike might still have been won. Instead, in an act of duplicity which will forever shame the UFCW, the national placed the local in trusteeship, meaning that the national would now run the local directly (see Chapter Seven). Local officers were fired and evicted from union headquarters, new scab officers were installed, the national ordered the strike, as well as all boycott activities, ended and a new and wholly inadequate agreement was signed with the company. Many of the strikers were denied places on the recall list because of their strike activities and so permanently lost their jobs. In a final act of ignominy, national union officers sandblasted a mural painted on the wall of the union hall in support of the strike. No local workers would do the job.

II. The Laws of Collective Bargaining

A. Beginning the Bargaining

The labor relations laws of the United States regulate nearly every aspect of collective bargaining, from how the bargaining actually commences, to the process of bargaining, to the subject matter of bargaining, to the resolution of the bargaining. If a union wins a certification election and is certified by an appropriate board (e.g., the NLRB), the union must then notify the employer in writing that it wants to begin to negotiate a contract. There are no time constraints imposed upon the union in terms of how long it has to serve notice upon the employer.

If, on the other hand, there is a contract already in existence which is about to expire, and the union wants to negotiate a new one, the National Labor Relations Act (NLRA) places strict notice requirements upon the union. The union must notify the employer of its intent to negotiate at least 60 days prior to the expiration of the agreement (this 60 days does not include the day that the employer actually receives the notice). It must also notify the Federal Mediation and Conciliation Service (FMCS), a federal agency which offers mediation services to negotiators, 30 days before contract expiration. For an employer in the health care industry, the notice deadlines are 90 days to the employer and 60 days to the FMCS. The health care industry includes "any hospital, convalescent hospital, health maintenance organization, health clinic, nursing home, extended care facility, or other institution devoted to the care of sick, infirm, or aged persons." Further, in bargaining for a first contract, a health care union must give the FMCS 30 days notice of the existence of a dispute, and the FMCS must attempt to get the parties to resolve it. A health care union must also give the employer and the FMCS ten days notice before it can strike or do any kind of picketing. During all of these time periods, strikes are strictly prohibited. Employees who strike before the notice periods have tolled are denied protection under the NLRA and can be fired.

Employees not covered by the NLRA may also have notice requirements. Public employees may have more complex requirements, especially when the bargaining reaches an impasse or before they can legally strike. Some of these will be discussed in later sections of this chapter.

B. Good Faith Bargaining

Once the employer has been notified that the union wants to negotiate, it is the duty of both parties to bargain in "good faith." This duty is outlined in Section 8(a)(5) for employers and in Section 8(b)(3) for unions. Section 8(d) states:

> For the purposes of this section, to bargain collectively is the performance of the mutual obligation of the employer and the representative of the employees to meet at reasonable times and confer in good faith with respect to wages, hours, and terms and conditions of employment, or the negotiation of an agreement, or any question arising thereunder, and the execution of a written contract incorporating any agreement reached if requested by either party, but such obligation does not compel either party to agree to a proposal or require the making of a concession.

All of the passages dealing with bargaining are somewhat ambiguous, so it is up to the NLRB and the courts to spell out what "good-faith" bargaining means and how "wages, hours, and terms and conditions of employment" are to be defined. This is a complicated area of the labor law, but we can simplify it by taking a hypothetical situation in which a union has notified the employer that it wants to begin bargaining.

In order to negotiate effectively, a union must gather all sorts of information. Much of this information is held by the employer, but the employer is obligated to provide most of it to the union upon written request.[10] One of the first things a union should do, therefore, is ask the employer to supply it with information which the union believes will be necessary for the bargaining. The employer must provide the requested information within a reasonable period of time; failure to do so is an unfair labor practice. The information must be provided in the form in which the company has it. For example, suppose the union asks for a list of the hours worked by bargaining unit employees over the past year. If the employer has compiled such records, it must give them to the union. It could not give the union the employees' time cards, making the union calculate the hours. Unless the employer can show that a large amount of money is involved, it cannot charge the union for the information it provides. Once the union receives information, it can use what it learns from this to make additional requests. Information requests can be made at any time.

Among the types of information the union might find useful for collective bargaining, and which the employer must provide, are the following: accident records, company contracts (with subcontractors, for example), disciplinary records, equipment specifications, chemicals used by bargaining unit employees, health and safety records, job descriptions, payroll records, fringe benefits currently in effect, seniority lists, time-study records, the age and sex of each bargaining unit member, etc. The union must ask for specific records; it cannot just go on a fishing expedition.

Once the union has asked to meet and bargain with the employer, the employer must be willing to meet at regular times and at a mutually agreed upon place. The ground rules for the meetings must be established by the union and the employer. However, both parties are free to be represented by any persons they choose; the employer cannot refuse to bargain because it objects to one of the union's negotiators. Nor can either party insist that the meetings be open to the public or tape recorded.[11]

What does the law dictate that the negotiators do at the bargaining table? They must merely have the "intent" to reach agreement, but they do not actually have to agree to anything. The intent to reach agreement is ultimately judged by the NLRB and by the courts in cases in which the union files a Section 8(a)(5) unfair labor practice charge against the employer for bad-faith bargaining. Ordinarily, an employer might be found guilty of bad-faith bargaining if it does any of the following:

1. refuses to consider union proposals about such critical matters as seniority, grievance procedures, wages, etc. An employer which said that it did not believe in seniority and so could not consider a seniority proposal would be bargaining in bad faith.

2. refuses to offer counterproposals to union proposals. The essence of bargaining is the give-and-take of offers and counteroffers.

3. continually adds new demands or conditions once it appears that the sides are close to agreement.

4. takes items off the table after the parties have reached agreement on them.

5. refuses to reduce an agreement to writing.

6. tries to go around the union negotiators by negotiating directly with the members.

General Electric Company (GE) developed a bargaining strategy after World War II which came to be known as "Boulwarism" after its labor relations director, Lemuel Boulwar. GE would give the union its only proposal at the beginning of the bargaining and would not change it unless the union could show that it was not "objective." Then the company would aggressively market its proposal directly to the members through meetings, advertisements, and letters to the workers' homes. This "take it or leave it" approach combined with the end run around the union was found to be an unfair labor practice.[12] Usually the NLRB looks for a pattern of behavior made up of these practices, what is called a pattern of "surface bargaining," before it will conclude that the employer is bargaining in bad faith.

C. Bargaining Subjects

When a union meets with its members and asks them what items they would like to try to get into a new contract, it will get a long and varied list. Unfortunately, a union faces legal limits on just what it can insist that the employer consider at the negotiating table. The NLRA makes some subjects illegal, while the NLRB and the courts have divided bargaining subjects into those which are mandatory and those which are permissive. Let us look at each one in turn.

Three subjects are illegal and cannot be included in collective bargaining contracts. First, closed shops are illegal by implication of Section 8(b)(2). A closed shop is a form of union security agreement in which the employer agrees to hire only those persons who are already members of the union. Under this type of agreement, the union could force the employer to fire any nonmember.[13]

Second, union shops are illegal in what are known as "right-to-work" states (Section 14(b)). In a union shop each new employee must join the union within a certain number of days. There are 20 right-to-work states where union shops are illegal, most of them in the South and Southwest. More must be said about union shops. Many collective bargaining contracts have union shop clauses in them, but both an NLRA amendment and recent court decisions have weakened their impact. The 1974 amendments to the NLRA added Section 19, which exempts from union security agreements those persons whose religion makes it impermissible for them to join labor unions. In addition, the

Supreme Court has held that Sections 7, 8(b)(1), and 8(b)(2) make it illegal for a union to compel an employee to become a member of the union, contract language to the contrary notwithstanding.[14] All that a bargaining unit member has to do under a union shop agreement is pay the union's initiation fee and regular dues, but she does not have to become an actual member of the union. Further, upon demand, a nonmember may refuse to pay that part of the union dues which the union spends on matters not connected to the union's collective bargaining function.[15] This is a complex topic better dealt with in one of the questions at the end of the chapter, but we can note the harmful effect which these decisions have upon unions. Nonmembers are not subject to union discipline, such as a fine for crossing a picket line during a strike. The easier it is for a bargaining unit member to avoid the union's own bylaws and constitution, the weaker the union will be.

The third illegal bargaining subject is the hot-cargo agreement. This contract provision allows bargaining unit members to refuse to handle work in their plant which comes from a plant on strike. There are exceptions, but these will be discussed in the next chapter.

The parties must bargain (but remember, they do not have to reach agreement) about what are called *mandatory* bargaining subjects. The law makes no mention of mandatory subjects, but the NLRB has interpreted the statute to mean that it can declare some subjects mandatory and others *permissive*, the latter being those about which the union and the company can bargain but do not have to bargain.[16] That is, bargaining about such subjects is permitted but not mandated. The trouble is that there is no hard-and-fast rule for separating the two. For example, the wage rate for the jobs in the bargaining unit is a mandatory subject as are nearly all "bread and butter" issues such as vacations, holidays, pensions, health care, shift differentials, hours of work, etc. However, those issues which the Board and the courts believe are at the heart or core of managerial decision-making are very likely to be permissive. The subcontracting of bargaining unit work is a mandatory subject,[17] but most other subcontracting is permissive. The decision to close a plant is a permissive subject as are the choice of technology and the selection of supervisory personnel. As long as an employer can show a business necessity, as opposed to hostility toward the union, it can most likely shift bargaining unit work to another facility without negotiating with the union. The same is true for a partial plant closing, in which part of an operation is shut down while the rest of it remains open.[18]

If a subject is mandatory, a union can strike and picket to try to force the employer to agree to the union's proposal. However, a union can not legally strike and picket to compel acceptance of a permissive subject. To do so is an unfair labor practice, a violation of Section 8(b)(3) which prohibits bad-faith bargaining by unions. Suppose that the union and the employer have agreed to all mandatory bargaining subjects. Suppose further that the union has had to strike to win a contract. During the strike, the employer has, as is its legal right, hired permanent replacements for the strikers. The union demands that the replacements be released and the strikers returned to their jobs now that a settlement has been reached. The return of the strikers is called a strike settlement agreement. A strike settlement agreement is a permissive bargaining subject. This means that the union is powerless to strike and picket to enforce it. Therefore, it is critical that the union make such an agreement with the employer *before* it has settled all mandatory subjects. That way, it could strike over the unresolved mandatory subjects as a way to pressure the employer to accept the strike settlement agreement.[19]

The tendency of the current Board and courts is to narrow the range of mandatory bargaining subjects, denying unions the right to negotiate with employers over such important matters as the shutdown of allegedly unprofitable facilities or departments of a plant, the transfer of work to other places, or the introduction of new work processes and equipment. The only thing a union can do is to insist on bargaining over the *effects* of these managerial decisions. For example, a transfer of work will cause employees to lose their jobs. A union can demand that the employer negotiate severance pay for these workers or supplemental unemployment benefits, transfer rights, moving expenses, or early retirement, etc. And a union is free to legally strike if agreement on these issues cannot be reached. It would be much better if the union could force the employer to bargain over the decision itself in addition to the effects of these decisions. Suppose that an employer wants to close a plant. If it had to negotiate this decision, it would have to provide the union with information justifying its decision. The union would also have more time to develop a strategy to keep the plant open, including building community coalitions and lobbying politicians.

While the bargainers must negotiate about mandatory subjects, they do not, as we have seen, have to reach agreement. What happens if they do not reach agreement? The employer can declare that the negotiations are at an *impasse* and unilaterally impose its last offer. It is up to the NLRB to decide, on a case-by-case basis, however, whether or not an impasse exists. Let us say that the union and the employer have bargained long and hard over wages, but they have failed to come to terms. The employer says that they are at an impasse and puts its last wage offer into effect. The union will file a Section 8(a)(5) unfair labor practice charge accusing the employer of bad-faith bargaining. If the NLRB is convinced that, at this point, further bargaining would be fruitless, it will agree that there is an impasse and the employer's action in implementing its wage offer will stand. But if it says that an impasse does not exist, the employer will have to rescind its wage change and return to the table. The Board does not have strict rules to determine if an impasse exists, but there have been recent cases in which it has declared an impasse after only a few bargaining sessions.[20] Union negotiators should avoid uncompromising statements at the table, such as, "We will never agree to a wage freeze." Such statements make it more likely that the Board will conclude that the bargaining is at an impasse. It should be understood as well that any change in the circumstances surrounding the bargaining will probably break an impasse. If an impasse exists and the union then calls a strike (or the employer locks the workers out), the impasse is broken and the parties must renew the bargaining. In general, the duty to bargain is not affected by a strike or lockout.

D. Bargaining After the Agreement is Signed

Once a collective bargaining contract is signed, it is legally binding upon the union and the employer. Section 301 of the NLRA makes collective bargaining agreements enforceable in court. Should an employer unilaterally change any term of the contract, the union could sue it and force it to return to the original term. Of course, the union could also use the contract's grievance procedure to redress the wrong done to it by the employer's action. The employer is free to ask the union to agree to a change in the contract's language, and it probably can also threaten the union with a plant closing unless it agrees.[21] Nonetheless, it cannot simply make the change.

But what if the employer makes a change in a condition of employment which is not covered by the contract? Unless the union has clearly waived its right to do so, the employer must bargain with the union before it can impose any change in a mandatory bargaining subject. Suppose that the employer wants to begin drug testing of all bargaining unit employees, but the current agreement is silent on this matter. Drug testing of current employees (but not prospective employees) is a mandatory bargaining subject, so the employer would have to bargain with the union about its drug testing policy. Only if the bargaining reaches an impasse can the employer unilaterally put the drug testing into effect. Most likely the union could strike to try to prevent the employer from taking this action.

A union can waive its right to bargain over mandatory subjects not included in the contract by explicitly stated language in the contract. A contract clause which waives the union's right to bargain is called a "zipper clause." The NLRB usually demands that such clauses explicitly waive the union's bargaining rights concerning a particular subject; that is, it will not take literally a general zipper clause in which the union waives its right to negotiate all subjects not in the contract. A union can also waive bargaining rights by putting a subject on the table during negotiations but failing to win it in the contract. Consider a situation in which the union has proposed and aggressively tried to win a clause prohibiting employer discrimination against gay employees, but it fails to get this clause in the contract. After the contract is signed, the employer institutes a policy which overtly discriminates against gay employees. The union may not be able to force the employer to bargain about this since its failure to win it in the bargaining in the first place probably constitutes a bargaining waiver. The same would be true if the employer institutes a new policy concerning a mandatory bargaining subject but the union fails to request bargaining.[22]

E. Successorship

In these days of corporate takeovers and buyouts, workers often face a situation in which their plant is sold to another company. If this happens, what is the status of the collective agreement they had with the original owner? Does the new employer, called the "successor employer," have to honor the contract? Usually the answer is no. The union may have won a successorship clause in its agreement. Such a clause states that the employer will not sell the plant unless the buyer agrees to honor the agreement. If this is the case, the union has some real leverage. Should the employer sell the plant in violation of the successorship clause, the union can file a grievance and eventually sue the employer to force compliance. It can picket both employers and seek an injunction to prevent the sale. Note that the successorship clause must be specific and cannot simply say that the agreement is binding on any successor employer. The successor cannot be bound by the old agreement, because it was not a party to the original bargaining.

If there is not a successorship clause, the new employer can agree to the contract, but does not have to. Only if the successor's workforce is comprised of a majority of members of the old bargaining unit does the successor have to bargain with the union for *new* contract terms.[23] This gives the successor an easy way to avoid recognition of the union;

all it has to do is hire enough new employees to make the old employees a minority. (The Board will not, however, allow the employer to hire a token number of new employees as a start-up workforce as a ruse to avoid union recognition.) If the successor does hire enough old employees to require recognition, it is still free to set the initial wages, hours, and conditions from which the parties will bargain.

F. Penalties for Bad-Faith Bargaining

One of the weakest aspects of the NLRB's interpretation of the NLRA is its refusal to issue severe penalties for an employer's refusal to bargain. The Board has the power "to take such affirmative action...as will effectuate the policies of this Act." The Board does not order punitive damages (for example, an amount greater than the pay lost by an employee illegally discharged), but instead confines itself to "make-whole" remedies. As we have seen, these are remedies which put the aggrieved party back into the position in which she would have been had the party that has violated the Act not done so.

What is the appropriate make-whole remedy for employer bad-faith bargaining? The most common remedy is simply a board order that the employer return to the bargaining table and negotiate in good faith. This is a weak and ineffective penalty, because it does little immediate harm to the employer and, therefore, gives it little incentive to obey the law. It is no wonder that Section 8(a)(5) violations have skyrocketed, and unions, especially new ones, find it more difficult to win contracts without resorting to strikes, themselves hedged in by the laws and the courts. It is possible that the NLRB will ultimately obtain a court order to enforce its bargaining order and that the employer may eventually face contempt of court, leading to fines and/or imprisonment. This outcome is so rare, however, that employers have little reason to fear it.

Unions have argued before the Board that employers should be made to pay the union and the employees specific sums of money for bad-faith bargaining. Such a requirement was written into the national labor law reform bill which failed to pass Congress in 1978. Interestingly, such a possible penalty is part of California's Agricultural Labor Relations Act, which covers only that state's farm workers. Consider an example. A union has 50 contracts with employers similar to the one with which it is currently trying to negotiate a first contract. On average, it took the union 100 days to conclude bargaining and reach first agreement with the 50 employers under contract. On average, these 50 first agreements contained first-year wage and benefit increases of $1.50 per hour. The newest employer has a daily average of 1,000 employees, each of whom works an average of eight hours per day. This employer has been found guilty of refusing to bargain in good faith by the NLRB. Two hundred days have elapsed since the first day of bargaining. In this situation, the Board should order the employer to pay the workers what they could reasonably have expected to gain in wages and benefits had the employer obeyed the law. This would be 100 days (the 200 elapsed days minus the 100 days it normally takes the parties to reach agreement) times 1,000 employees times eight hours times $1.50, an amount equal to $1.2 million. Such a substantial penalty would make a lot of employers decide that it was cheaper to obey the law than to disregard it. It is a shame that the Board has concluded that it does not have the power to award such sums of money.[24] When an employer's behavior is bad enough, the Board might award legal fees to the union and force the employer to allow the union unusual access to the workplace to explain its bargaining proposals. Clearly, though, the rapid rise in employer refusal to bargain complaints indicates that this is not enough.

G. Mandatory Impasse Resolution

With two exceptions, the NLRA does not contain provisions which force the parties to try to resolve an impasse by particular methods. Section 206 of the Act gives the president of the United States the power to declare a strike by employees covered by the NLRA a "national emergency strike." This is a strike that "will, if permitted to continue, imperil the national health or safety." First, the president appoints a "board of inquiry," which investigates the strike and reports back to the president. Second, upon receipt of the report, the president can direct the Attorney General of the United States to petition any federal district court with jurisdiction over the parties to issue an injunction to stop the strike. Third, the court will in all likelihood issue the injunction, but the injunction is only in force for 80 days. Fourth, once the injunction is issued, the union and the employer must use the Federal Mediation and Conciliation Service (FMCS) to help them resolve the dispute. The parties are not bound to accept any settlement recommended by the FMCS. Fifth, the board of inquiry must be reconvened. Sixty days after the issuance of the injunction, the board reports to the president the status of the dispute, including the last offer of the employer, which the president then makes public. Within 15 days of this, the NLRB must conduct a secret ballot vote among the employees to see if they accept the employer's last offer. Once these results are counted, the Attorney General must ask the court to vacate the injunction. If the dispute has not been settled, the union is free to continue its strike. The president is empowered to ask Congress to step in and resolve the dispute through legislation. To date, no union has voted to accept the employer's final offer, and the president has not asked Congress to settle any strike. Nonetheless, it should be clear that the national emergency strike provisions of the Act give the president the power to stop any significant strike. Unions have defied the injunctions, but the legal consequences of defiance can be severe.[25]

The second situation in which a union can be compelled to try to break an impasse occurs in the health care industry. The director of the Federal Mediation and Conciliation Service is empowered to appoint a board of inquiry when he is of the opinion that "a threatened or actual strike or lockout affecting a health care institution will, if permitted to occur or to continue, substantially interrupt the delivery of health care in the locality concerned." This board will serve as a fact finder, investigating the dispute and making a recommendation for a resolution. The board must make its report within 15 days, and for these 15 days and an additional 15 days after it issues its report, "no change in the status quo in effect prior to the expiration of the contract in the case of negotiations for a contract renewal, or in effect prior to the time of the impasse in the case of an initial bargaining negotiation, except by agreement, shall be made by the parties to the controversy."

H. Administering and Enforcing Collective Bargaining Agreements

We have seen that the duty to bargain does not stop once a contract is signed. And once an agreement is reached, the law continues to surround the administration and the enforcement of the agreement. One of the union's major duties is to see to it that these are done effectively. In this section, we will consider several aspects of contract administration and enforcement: the rights of union shop stewards, the right of an employee to have a steward witness a meeting with a supervisor, the arbitration of labor disputes, and suits to enforce contract provisions.

A shop steward is the worker's representative at the workplace.[26] The union must make sure that the contract guarantees that a steward will be available at any time during the workday to handle complaints workers might have. While all workers have the right to engage in concerted activities, at least those not barred by the law or by the contract (such as a "no-strike" clause), shop stewards have been given greater protection by the NLRB. Even with a collective bargaining agreement in force, an employee is still considered the subordinate of the employer. An employee must ordinarily obey a direct command of the employer. If the command is in violation of the contract, the worker can file a grievance, but must still obey the order. Similarly, an employee can be disciplined for arguing with a supervisor or using strong language. Such is not the case for union stewards when they are acting in their official capacity. They are considered the *equals* of the employer and are free to defend employees and the contract with vigor. As the Supreme Court put it, the Act "gives a union license to use intemperate, abusive, or insulting language without fear of restraint or penalty if it believes such rhetoric to be an effective means to make its point."[27] This holds whenever a steward is investigating a grievance, requesting information, or in any way representing an employee. In addition, an employer cannot hold a steward to a higher standard of behavior or performance than any other employee. To do so is an unfair labor practice.

Since it is important that a steward be present at all times in the workplace, the union may try to get contract language that protect stewards against layoffs. Layoffs are usually regulated by seniority; the least senior worker is laid off first. To prevent stewards from being laid off, the contract may give them superseniority. This is legal, but only for union officials who are stewards or who perform steward-like duties. Other preferential benefits for stewards beyond superseniority are probably illegal. Unless the union could show, for example, that giving a steward preference for overtime assignments was necessary to ensure workers access to the stewards, such a clause would be illegal, a violation of the antidiscrimination prohibitions of Sections 8(a)(3) and 8(b)(2).[28]

One of a union steward's most important duties is to process grievances made by bargaining unit members against the employer. A steward is permitted by the law to actively solicit grievances and must be allowed to thoroughly investigate all grievances. In the absence of contract language permitting them to do so, the Board will allow stewards reasonable time to make investigations during regular work-time. An employee is required to participate in the employer's investigation of a grievance, but the steward's own investigation is privileged. The employer cannot question the steward about it or demand that the steward give the employer her notes. Section 9(a) of the NLRA gives an individual employee the right to discuss a grievance with the employer without a union representative being present. However, the employer cannot adjust the complaint unless the union has been given a chance "to be present at such adjustment."

In performing their duties, stewards have broad rights to ask the employer for information necessary to process grievances and to prepare for any upcoming negotiations. The right to information is broad, and, if asked, the employer must supply the information in appropriate form. Robert M. Schwartz, in his excellent booklet *The Legal Rights of Shop Stewards,* gives the following example:

> Employers must assemble relevant data and statistics. For example, in a grievance alleging sex discrimination in promotions, you can require the company to produce a list of women employees promoted in the past, along with the names of those denied promotions. When it comes to data, employers are *not* excused from compliance because of the size of the union's request.[29]

While it is ordinarily best to make requests for specific information (attendance records, disciplinary records, performance reviews, personnel files, etc.), the employer must also respond to general requests such as, "Please supply all documents or records which refer to or reflect the factors causing you to reject this grievance." About the only defense an employer can use to refuse to provide requested information is that of confidentiality. An employer might be able to argue that medical reports and employee aptitude test scores are confidential and cannot be released. To do this, the employer must have a policy of maintaining the privacy of these records, including not allowing supervisors to see them. In such a situation, the union should try to get the employee to agree to the release of the records, in which case the confidentiality defense will fail.

One of the most stressful events to which a worker can be subjected is an interrogation by a supervisor. Most workers would feel more comfortable in such a situation if they had a witness present, especially someone who could advise them. The NLRB does not give workers in a nonunion setting such a right, but in a union setting it does.[30] Under certain conditions, a worker has the right to have a union representative present during a meeting with a supervisor. This right is known as the "Weingarten right" after the case in which the NLRB first recognized it. To exercise this right, the employee must have reasonable cause to suspect that she may face some disciplinary action as the outcome of the meeting. Suppose that a worker is called into a supervisor's office. It becomes clear to the worker that the supervisor wants to discuss a fight in which the supervisor suspects the worker was involved. Since fighting may result in discipline, the worker should immediately ask for a representative to be present. She could request that another coworker be present, but it is best to ask for the shop steward on duty to attend the meeting. Note that the company is not obligated to inform a worker of her Weingarten rights.

Once the employee has requested the steward's presence, the employer can accede to the request, deny the request and stop the interview, or tell the employee that she can leave or have the interview without representation. The employer is free to conduct an investigation without the employee's cooperation, but the employer cannot refuse the steward's presence and still continue the interrogation without the worker's permission. The union representative cannot turn the meeting into a grievance settlement conference, but she can actively participate in the meeting. The steward can request to meet in private with the employee before the meeting continues. The steward can ask the employer to specify the purpose of the meeting, and the steward can advise the employee concerning how to answer questions, etc.

What happens in a situation in which a worker has been denied his Weingarten rights but has been disciplined by the employer? Let's say that the worker has been fired for coming to work intoxicated. At one time the NLRB would find an unfair labor practice for the denial of union representation *and* would also order the worker reinstated. Today the Board will let the discharge stand if the employer has credible evidence to support it.[31] This is a basic denial of due process rights, akin to letting the conviction of a poor person in a criminal trial stand when the person's right to a court-appointed attorney had been denied.

The work a shop steward does both administers and enforces the rights the workers have won in their contract. In addition to the rights which the steward enjoys, the Act gives workers further ways to enforce the agreement. Grievance procedures in collective bargaining agreements usually contain a series of steps ending in binding arbitration. If the union and the employer cannot resolve a grievance themselves, the union can force the employer into arbitration, and an outsider called an "arbitrator" will be selected to decide whether the grievance should be sustained or denied. If the employer refuses to go to arbitration, the union can sue the employer to force it to do so, since Section 301 of the NLRA makes collective bargaining contracts enforceable in state or federal court. In such a situation, the employer may claim that the dispute is not arbitrable under the grievance procedure. The Supreme Court has held that, unless they are expressly exempted from the arbitration clause, most contract provisions are arbitrable. Arbitration is considered by the law and by the courts as the preferred method for settling contract disputes, especially since most agreements contain "no-strike" clauses. The courts are also unlikely to overturn an arbitrator's award even if the judges would have ruled differently on the facts of the grievance. As long as the arbitrator's decision is plausibly consistent with the agreement, the courts will not substitute their judgments for that of the arbitrator. The union can also go into court to force an employer to abide by an arbitrator's decision.[32]

III. The Railway Labor Act

Most of what has been said about the law of collective bargaining under the National Labor Relations Act applies as well to the Railway Labor Act. The most significant differences concern mandatory impasse resolution. It is much more difficult for railway and airline workers to legally strike than for employees covered by the NLRA.

Let us say that a railroad and its employees have begun negotiations for a new collective bargaining agreement. They must notify the National Mediation Board (NMB), which must participate in the bargaining and try to facilitate an agreement. The parties are not bound by any recommendations of the NMB, but they must seek its services. If the two sides reach an impasse, the union is not free to strike as would be the case under the NLRA. Instead the NMB must propose arbitration to settle the impasse. This type of arbitration is called "interest" arbitration as opposed to the more common "grievance" arbitration. In the former, the arbitrator is asked to determine the terms and conditions of employment, while in the latter, the arbitrator merely determines how existing contract language and practices are to be interpreted.

The parties are free to reject arbitration of their dispute, but in that case, the NMB can advise the president of the United States that the dispute may create a transportation emergency (similar to the NLRA's national emergency discussed above). The president can next create a Presidential Emergency Board which will investigate the impasse and give a report to the president within 30 days. The report will recommend terms for the settlement of the dispute. While the Emergency Board is meeting and for 30 days after it makes its report, the union and the employer must maintain the status quo. The union cannot strike during this time; if it does, it will face injunctions. Sixty days after the Board has given its proposals to the parties, the union can legally strike. However, the U.S. Congress has the power to enforce Emergency Board recommendations or to make new ones. It does this by enacting a law which contains the terms of a new agreement.

Neither the president nor the Congress have been willing to tolerate railroad or airline strikes, including local disputes that do not create real emergencies. Legislation has become the typical means of resolving impasses. This has weakened the rail and air unions in two ways. First, it basically takes away the workers' right to strike, denying them their primary leverage over the employer as well as the solidarity which a strike can engender. Second, it has led the unions to become primarily lobbying organizations, relying far more on paid professionals in Washington than upon a committed and militant rank-and-file. Railroad and airline workers have become disgusted with this arrangement and have begun to form rank-and-file groups to resurrect their moribund unions.[33]

Under Railway Labor Act terminology, disputes over the initial terms of a contract are called "major" disputes. Disagreements over the meaning of existing contracts are called "minor" disputes. It is up to the courts to decide whether a dispute is major or minor. If a dispute is minor, the Act mandates that if the parties cannot voluntarily settle it, they must submit it to binding arbitration. The Act established the National Railroad Adjustment Board to arbitrate minor disputes. This Board is divided into four separate divisions, each dealing with a different occupational classification. If the Board deadlocks over a minor dispute (because it may have an even number of members, half from the employers and half from the unions), it tries to appoint a neutral arbitrator to resolve the disagreement. If it cannot choose an arbitrator, it can ask the NMB to choose one. If a grievance is before the Adjustment Board for one year without resolution, the parties are free to ask for the establishment of a special board of adjustment to make the binding ruling. For workers in the airline industry, the union and the airline must establish by their contract "system boards" to arbitrate minor disputes.

IV. Public Employees

The laws of collective bargaining for public employees differ in two important respects from those for private sector workers.[34] First, the scope of bargaining is narrower; that is, fewer subjects are mandatory. Federal government employees cannot bargain over wages, as these are set by law. Many statutes which permit collective bargaining by public employees list specific subjects which are the sole prerogative of the employer. Most agreements in the private sector contain "management rights" clauses which delineate those matters about which the employer is free to make decisions without bargaining with the union. Public employee labor laws often give public employers the statutory right to make certain decisions unilaterally. For example, Pennsylvania's Act 195 states:

> Public employers shall not be required to bargain over matters of inherent managerial policy, which shall include but shall not be limited to such areas of discretion or policy as the functions and programs of the public employer, standards of services, its overall budget, utilization of technology, the organizational structure and selection and direction of personnel. Public employers, however, shall be required to meet and discuss on policy matters affecting wages, hours and terms and conditions of employment as well as the impact thereon upon request by public employee representatives.

This provision has been the basis for declaring class size in schools and codes of conduct for teachers permissive rather than mandatory bargaining subjects.[35]

Second, public employee labor laws often mandate impasse resolution procedures and sharply curtail or forbid strikes altogether. Mediation is usually required, as well as fact-finding and arbitration. Fact-finding is a procedure in which a fact-finder is appointed by the state to investigate the dispute and make a recommendation for a settlement. When mediation and/or fact-finding fail to resolve the dispute, some type of arbitration is generally mandated. A single arbitrator or a panel of arbitrators is selected to conduct hearings and decide the terms of the agreement. The law may allow arbitrators to make any decision they believe to be fair. Alternately, the law may limit the decision arbitrators can make to either the union's or the employer's last offer. This latter system is called "final offer" arbitration, because the arbitrator can choose only one or the other final proposal.

V. Questions and Answers

Question 1: What should a union do if the company refuses to supply negotiators or stewards with requested information for bargaining or for processing grievances?

Ask for it again, and then file an unfair labor practice charge. Be sure to keep the members aware of the employer's actions.

Question 2: Can one union have persons from another union at its bargaining table?

Yes. The law specifies representatives of the union's own choosing. A union can have anyone it wants present at the table, and it is an unfair labor practice for the employer to insist that a specific person be present or that someone is unacceptable. The only exception might be if a member of the union team had threatened to physically assault someone on the other team (or actually done so).[36]

In a plant in which more than one union represents employees (for example, one union for maintenance and production workers and one for clerical workers), it can be a good idea to have members of each union on both bargaining committees. That way the company cannot pit one union against another by lying about what is going on at the bargaining table. This is also a good way to build solidarity.

Question 3: Can you give us a concrete example of "surface bargaining?"

An employer who has decided on a course of surface bargaining has already decided to subvert the law and get rid of the union. The most opportune time to do this is probably after the union has won a certification election, especially if the election was close. It is often the case that the employer has hired a consultant to run the bargaining charade. The following example is taken from Martin Jay Levitt's book, *Confessions of a Union Buster.*[37]

An Ohio nursing home lost a certification election after a long and brutal union-busting campaign run by Levitt. Rather than accept the union and negotiate in good faith, the employer kept the union-buster on to conduct the "bargaining." Levitt did not, as most union-busters do not, hesitate to break the law, because he knew that the law against bad-faith bargaining is poorly enforced and weakly punished. This was especially the case with the Reagan NLRB, which was staffed with people hostile to the very purpose of the law they were obligated to enforce.

. The bad-faith bargaining campaign began with a series of meetings with the supervisors, the persons who had been forcibly enlisted by the employer to try to stop the union in the first place. Playing upon their fears and anger at the union's victory, Levitt easily got them to cooperate in the bargaining fiasco. First, supervisors were ordered to run their departments strictly by the book and to never relate to their workers as human beings. Workers were denied any close personal contact with the patients, the one thing which they liked about their jobs. The workers had been told repeatedly that a union would make worklife subject to rigid contract rules, so now that the union had won, the employer instituted rigid rules. Second, workers were told that they would have to bargain for any benefits which they already enjoyed, and the employer began to (illegally) take away some benefits. Employees were told that the employer could not give the workers any wage or benefit increases because there was a union in place (this is not true if the union agrees to the increases or they are regularly scheduled raises). Third, each union stalwart was subjected to extremely tight supervision, given difficult assignments, and followed around and harassed by bosses in the hope that she would quit.

Fourth, Levitt delayed the first bargaining meeting as long as possible, by saying he had a tight schedule, by refusing to meet at a convenient place, and by insisting that the local union president be at the meeting. Fifth, the employer brought the supervisor of each local bargaining team member to the meetings to intimidate the workers. The employer then stalled the bargaining by refusing to discuss the union's proposals until it had a long time to study them and then repeatedly delayed bringing counterproposals. To give the appearance of real bargaining, the employer agreed to a few trivial items such as the union recognition clause, something which the law had already given the union. Sixth, at the workplace, Levitt organized a campaign of rumors, smearing the union with charges of autocracy and wanting a strike.

When the union could take no more of this, it took a strike vote, which the union-buster used to great advantage by playing up the vulnerability of the home's elderly patients. The employer put into effect a strike contingency plan aimed at intimidating and demoralizing the strikers. Help-wanted ads began to appear in the local papers; security was tightened and people were told that the strike would probably be violent; and the aged residents were assured that the employer would ensure their safety and well-being in the event of a strike. Finally, when the home opened a new medical center on the premises, it claimed that the center was a separate business, and it began to transfer union jobs into it. In this way the bargaining unit itself was decimated.

The union filed unfair labor practice charges, claiming Section 8(a)(5) violations for surface bargaining and Sections 8(a)(3) and (1) for the elimination of the union jobs. By this time, a year was almost up, and remember, a union's certification is only valid for a year. After a year workers can file a decertification petition, and this is what happened. The NLRB delayed the hearing on this petition until the unfair labor practice charges were decided. Incredibly, the Board found the employer not guilty of bad-faith bargaining, and although it ordered 18 workers reinstated with backpay (only one of them agreed to go back), it was too late for the union to get a contract. The union simply filed a "disclaimer of interest" and cut its losses by abandoning the struggle.[38] The facts of this case show clearly the inadequacy of the law, the enormous power of employers to deny workers their right to a contract, and the need for unions to develop effective counter-strategies.

Question 4: How can a union engage in bad-faith bargaining?

Naturally a union has a far greater stake in getting a contract than does the employer, so a union has no obvious reason to refuse to negotiate in good faith. A union could bargain in bad faith by ignoring the Act's notice requirements, by insisting upon bargaining on a permissive bargaining subject, by refusing to sign an agreement, and by insisting that independent firms sign off on the agreement reached between the union and a multi-employer bargaining unit.[39]

Question 5: Are closed shops good or bad for workers?

In some ways this question is irrelevant because closed shops are illegal. However, if we abstract from this fact, we can see that closed shops have good and bad features. On the plus side, they take the hiring decision away from the employer in the sense that it is difficult for the employer to hire workers with anti-union sentiments since all new hires must already be members of the union. On the negative side, a closed shop gives the union the power to discriminate against minority workers and women by just denying them membership or kicking them out of the union.

Question 6: Can a religious objector to union membership be made to contribute anything to the union in return for the services the union renders to every member of the bargaining unit?

Perhaps. However, a religious objector must be able to show membership in a religion which does have conscientious objection to union membership. A religious objector could, until recently, be made to contribute partial dues (that part used for bargaining purposes at least) to a charity selected from a list of charities contained in the bargaining agreement. The Sixth Circuit Federal Court of Appeals, however, has declared this provision of Section 19 of the NLRA unconstitutional under the First Amendment.[40]

Question 7: What are the details of the Supreme Court's prohibition of strict union shops?

A union shop requires all members of the bargaining unit to actually join the union within a certain number of days of hiring (or within a certain number of days from the signing of the agreement). The Supreme Court ruled that in a union shop context, Section 8(a)(3) requires only that each member of the bargaining unit tender dues to the union. If a worker refuses to join the union, he cannot be forced to join as long as he tenders the dues and any initiation fee. Further, he cannot be made to pay that part of the dues which go toward purposes other than collective bargaining. The union is not obligated to tell bargaining unit members about these rulings, but the union must abide by strict guidelines whenever someone insists upon paying only this part of the dues. Such a person is called a "financial core" member.

Suppose that a member of the bargaining unit insists upon financial core status. It is up to the union to provide this person with a breakdown of its expenditures. This is best done by an independent person such as a CPA, although if a dissenter files unfair labor practice charges against the union, the NLRB has the power to make this determination. The union can declare what percentage of the regular dues the financial core member must pay, but this must be "reasonable," and it is subject to challenge to the NLRB (and then the courts) by the financial core member. The union cannot deduct the entire dues and put the money in an escrow account until the appropriate percentage is determined by the Board or the courts. Escrow arrangements are possible, however, in the following situation: The union believes that 90% of the dues are used for bargaining functions, but it is only absolutely certain that 70% would be approved by the Board. In this case, it could collect 70% and put 20% in an interest-bearing escrow account pending Board determination.

Some of the expenditures which a financial core member can be made to pay are the costs of negotiating and administering the contract, the costs of filing and processing grievances, the costs of the union's conventions, the union's social activities (if nonmembers can participate), union publications (but not parts which, for example, support political positions or candidates the protester does not support), legal expenses incurred for services provided by the union to the financial core member or to this person's bargaining unit, etc. The Supreme Court has held that union organizing expenses *cannot* be charged to a financial core member because they are too far removed from the union's collective bargaining functions.[41] This is preposterous because a union will not long have a collective bargaining function if it cannot organize new workers.

This whole business gives right-wing groups like the National Right to Work Committee a good way to harass unions by encouraging anti-union members of bargaining units to ask for financial core status and force the union to spend money and time to show that its financial core dues are justifiable. At the least the Supreme Court ought to set some percentage of dues applicable to all situations, or the NLRA and the Railway Labor Act should be amended to do this.[42]

Question 8: What are the right-to-work states?

These are Alabama, Arizona, Arkansas, Florida, Georgia, Idaho, Iowa, Kansas, Louisiana, Mississippi, Nebraska, Nevada, North Carolina, North Dakota, South Carolina, South Dakota, Tennessee, Texas, Utah, Virginia, and Wyoming.

Question 9: What are some common mandatory bargaining subjects?

The following are mandatory subjects: wages, hours, discharge, paid holidays, paid vacation, duration of agreement, grievance procedure, layoff plan, reinstatement of economic strikers, change of payment from hourly base to salary base, union security and check-off of dues, work rules, merit wage increases, work schedule, lunch periods, rest periods, pension plan, retirement age, bonus payments, price of meals provided by the company, group insurance (health, accident, life), promotions, work assignments and transfers, no-strike clause, piece rates, stock-purchase plans, work loads, management-rights clause, discounts on company products, shift differentials, procedures for income tax withholding, severance pay, nondiscriminatory hiring hall, plant rules, safety, prohibition against supervisors doing unit work, superseniority for union stewards, check-off, seniority, layoffs, transfers, job-posting procedure, employee physical examination, profit-sharing plan, overtime pay, sick leave, subcontracting bargaining unit work, sexual harassment, nondiscrimination clauses, production ceiling imposed by union, most-favored-nation clause, and drug testing.

Question 10: What limits on subcontracting are mandatory bargaining subjects?

Besides prohibiting the subcontracting of bargaining unit work, about all that a union can propose is that the employer not use labor for subcontracting which does not receive "wages, hours, and conditions of employment established by labor unions having jurisdiction over the type of services performed." The union cannot insist that only certain workers (members of this or some specific union) do subcontracting work.[43]

Question 11: In determining that certain subjects are permissive, what is meant by "business necessity?"

The NLRB at present says that if labor costs are the major factor giving rise to an employer's decision, it must negotiate with the union about this decision. The idea here is that the union has some control over labor costs and could make concessions which would convince the employer not to make the decision. If labor costs are not determinative, "business necessity" simply means that the employer has decided to make the decision to increase profitability, to meet actions of competitors, to reduce costs, etc.[44]

Question 12: Are there any exceptions to the rule that a worker must obey an employer's order and then file a grievance?

About the only exception would be if an employee refuses an assignment which she believes is unsafe. In a union setting, the agreement may give the employee this right. In such a case, an employer disciplining a worker for refusing an unsafe assignment can be charged with an unfair labor practice. In both union and nonunion settings, Section 502 gives workers some protection by stating that refusals to do unsafe work, by one worker or several employees, are not strikes under the Act. A contractual no-strike clause does not deny Section 502 protection. However, under Section 502 the Supreme Court has ruled that to avoid discipline, the employees must have objective measurable proof that conditions are unsafe. This may be difficult in a situation where, say, a dangerous gas is present at the time of a worker's refusal but has dissipated by the time the employer disciplines the workers for refusing to work.[45] Finally in a nonunion setting or in a union setting where there is not a no-strike clause, safety strikes would be protected concerted activity under Section 7 of the NLRA.

Question 13: Can union officials other than stewards be given special contractual protection?

Yes, but only to a limited extent. On the surface, any benefit given to officers in a contract would seem to violate Sections 8(a)(3) and 8(b)(2) prohibiting any action by an employer which would either encourage or discourage union membership. Special benefits might be seen to encourage membership so that persons would then seek union leadership to get the benefits. However, the NLRB has held that in a case where union officers continue to receive benefits such as extended leaves of absence to perform union duties, the continuation of such benefits as pension credits and insurance while on leave may be necessary to get people to be union officers at all.[46] In other words, not allowing the benefits would discourage members from seeking leadership positions in the union.

Question 14: In a situation in which a bargaining unit member is asked to attend a meeting at which he has reason to expect discipline, what if no union steward is present? If stewards are present, can an employee request a specific steward?

It is the union's responsibility to make sure that a steward is present. If one is not, an employee should request that another employee be present at the meeting. An employee has the right to have a steward present, but not necessarily a particular one. If Department A's steward is at work and an employee in Department A is questioned by management, the employee cannot demand that another steward be present.[47]

Question 15: Our collective bargaining agreement has expired, and we are trying to negotiate a new one. Do the terms of the expired agreement remain in effect in the interim period?

With or without an agreement in effect, an employer in a unionized workplace generally cannot unilaterally change any wage, hour, or term and condition of employment which is a mandatory bargaining subject. Only when an impasse is reached can the employer unilaterally make the change. An exception involves matters of union security such as dues check-offs and union shop provisions, which do expire when the contract expires.

The grievance procedure of the old contract remains in effect, and grievances filed before expiration can still be brought to arbitration. Even grievances filed after expiration can be pushed to arbitration if the events giving rise to the grievance took place when the contract was still in effect.[48]

A union and an employer can agree to extend the old agreement, which guarantees that *all* of its terms must be honored, including a no-strike clause.

Question 16: How can collective bargaining address the problems of discrimination discussed in Chapter Two?

First of all, a union can be a major source of information to workers concerning all of their legal rights. Every local union should keep abreast of legal developments and make members aware of these through pamphlets, at union meetings, and through workshops and classes. Information learned through the union will be spread by members to their neighbors and friends, putting the union in a good light. Unions should encourage the formation of women and minority caucuses to ensure that the issues of race and sex are confronted directly within the union. Unions should also provide legal services to members who are contemplating discrimination lawsuits against an employer, or should at least help them to get the best legal advice available.

We saw in Chapter Two that the labor movement can grow through the use of racial and sexual issues to organize workers. It is possible to begin this process before the onset of any actual organizing drive. For example, the Service Employees International Union (SEIU) has provided valuable support to immigrants seeking to become citizens or to avoid deportation. It has obtained government grants to become the provider of English instruction to recently arrived immigrants. If these examples were extended a hundredfold, the labor movement would begin to regain its role as the leader of the entire working class.

In terms of bargaining issues, there are many ways in which discrimination can be faced. First, the contract can include explicit prohibitions against discrimination by race, sex, religion, age, handicap, national origin, etc. A union should definitely bargain for protection of groups not protected by the Civil Rights Acts. The most important protections would be for sexual preference, marital status, and political affiliation. Until, for example, gay workers are protected by law, a union contract might offer them the only protection they have against employer discrimination. This way, a member discriminated against by the employer could file a grievance and have the union take up her cause. The Supreme Court has ruled that a contractual remedy for discrimination does not bar the member from also pursuing a legal challenge through the Civil Rights Acts.[49] An arbitrator has the power to remedy discrimination through reinstatement, backpay, placing a person in her proper seniority position, abolition of a racist seniority system, etc. An arbitration ruling holds only for the contract which the arbitrator has been asked to interpret, so a favorable ruling won't benefit all employees in the discriminated-against class, as would a court ruling.

A union and an employer are free to make affirmative action agreements which have the purpose of eliminating past discrimination. Therefore, an agreement could be reached which gave preference to women entering apprenticeship programs until the share of women in the program was the same as it was in some reasonable reference group, such as the share of women in the employer's entire workforce or the share of women in a local labor market (see Chapter Two for further details). To avoid charges of "reverse discrimination" by white and/or male employees, such plans must not result in the layoff of senior white and/or male employees.

A collective bargaining agreement can provide for the setting aside of certain sums of money for "equity" adjustments to reduce pay gaps between women and men and minority and white employees which may have been due to past discrimination. A contract can include terms which directly help certain groups of workers. Examples would be pregnancy leaves and parental leaves during the first days or months of the newborn's life, childcare allowances or the provision of childcare on the employer's premises, flexible schedules to accommodate working mothers and fathers, provisions to accommodate religious practices, etc.

One topic that is becoming more common in contracts is sexual harassment.[50] Every contract should include strong language against sexual harassment. A broad no-discrimination clause includes sexual harassment, since this is a form of discrimination by sex, but a specific harassment clause is better. Language for the enforcement of the clause should also be in the agreement. It is better to have specific sexual harassment language in the agreement, which defines what sexual harassment is (with a broad definition to include both "quid pro quo" and "hostile environment" harassment (see Chapter Two), specifies that such harassment is grievable, and sets out specific enforcement language.

Question 17: Can a union offer any protection to workers against plant closings?

The decision to close a plant is a permissive bargaining item, so a union can only bargain about the effects of the closing. One thing a union can do is to negotiate a clause in which the employer has to give the union warning about the closing, not just of the entire plant but any part of it. The union could also negotiate a successorship clause in case the plant is closed. In addition, the union could try to negotiate a clause which compels the employer to offer to sell the plant to the employees or to the community.

Whether you are union or nonunion, you can organize the community around the issue of the plant closing. You might want to argue in favor of an employee buyout through something called an Employee Stock Option Plan (ESOP). There may be grassroots organizations in your area interested in this issue, such as the Steel Valley Authority in Homestead, Pennsylvania.

The Worker Adjustment and Retraining Notification Act (WARN) requires employers with at least 60 employees to notify the employees of a plant closing or mass layoff. WARN has many exceptions, however, and will get the workers some backpay, at best, if their employer violates it.

It is important to watch what your employer is doing so that you can get indications that it is contemplating a shutdown. Some of these indicators are plant closures or layoffs at other divisions, sudden turnover of management people, slowdowns in production, reductions in shifts, mergers, inadequate investment in plant and equipment, lack of repairs, loss of customers and contracts, the building of a new plant elsewhere, greater use of subcontracting, etc.[51]

VI. Selected Readings

1. Martin J. Levitt, *Confessions of a Union Buster* (New York: Crown Publishers, Inc., 1993).

2. Peter Rachleff, *Hard-Pressed in the Heartland: The Hormel Strike and the Future of the Labor Movement* (Boston: South End Press, 1993).

3. Robert M. Schwartz, *The Legal Rights of Shop Stewards* (Boston: Work Rights Press, 1988).

4. David P. Twomey, *Labor and Employment Law*, 9th edition (Cincinnati: South-Western Publishing Co., 1994).

Chapter 6

THE WEAPONS OF WAR: STRIKES, PICKETS, BOYCOTTS, AND INJUNCTIONS

I. The Pittston Strike

I was born in a small mining town situated along a bend in the Allegheny River in western Pennsylvania. Nearly every man in town worked in the mine, and everybody lived in company-owned houses and shopped at the company store. My grandmother had brought her two children there in the late 1930s to be near her family after her husband died. For a time, the three of them worked at the mine, too, unloading from trucks the dynamite which the miners bought to open up the seams of coal. It was a hard and not very happy life, shortened all too often by mine accidents and lung diseases.

What made life bearable was the sense of community found in all mining towns; people were brought together by the danger of their work and the poverty of their circumstances. A miner did not have to be told that he needed a union; he knew it as sure as he knew that his sons would never be Coal and Iron Police. Coal miners were hot for unions from the beginning, and they and their families built a legendary union by going to war with the coal operators.[1] By the end of World War II, most of the nation's miners were members of the United Mine Workers Union (UMW). They earned high wages and had good benefits, including comprehensive health care, not just for working miners but for those retired as well.

The economic crisis of the early 1970s did not spare the coal industry. Even before this, nonunion strip mines and rapid mechanization had depleted the UMW's membership, and internal corruption after the death of John L. Lewis had sapped the union of much of its fighting spirit. And while the rank-and-file had since reformed and rejuvenated the union, the coal operators saw the 1980s as providing them with the opportunity to destroy their union nemesis. They began to illegally close union mines and open nonunion pits, claiming that these were totally independent subsidiaries. Hard-pressed miners had little choice but to work nonunion, while the union tried to organize them again and file usually unsuccessful legal complaints against the companies. The sharp decline in union-mined coal put the union's welfare and pension funds in great jeopardy.

Traditionally the union had negotiated contracts with a multi-employer group of large coal companies called the Bituminous Coal Operators Association (BCOA). By 1980 it had become difficult to win new agreements without strikes, and by the late 1980s, some BCOA members were prepared to go it alone against the union, confident that they could defeat it. In 1988 the Pittston Coal Company seceded from the BCOA. It refused to ratify the 1988 UMW-BCOA agreement and demanded radical concessions from the union.[2] When the union's contract with Pittston expired, the union continued to work without a new contract, something it would not have done in the past. But with so many unemployed miners and with the union's strength in the industry eroded, it understood that a strike without massive preparations would end in disaster. However, the company refused to bargain in good faith, practically taunting the union to call a strike. The company then began to make unilateral changes in the terms and conditions of employment, emboldened by the fact that unfair labor practice charges would either fail or cost little.

The changes made by Pittston were sweeping and destructive:

> It refused to arbitrate grievances, terminated health- care benefits for some 1,400 retired widows and miners, many of whom were dying from black lung disease, and stopped paying royalties into the multi-employer health trust fund. Despite union concessions, including a no-strike promise at Pittston if the union had a labor dispute with the BCOA, the company refused to move, and in November 1988 presented the union with its final offer. This "last best offer" would mean the end of the union: it included complete freedom to subcontract work, mandatory overtime, compulsory work on Sunday, and massive cuts in health benefits, including those of retirees and widows.[3]

Despite the intervention of the governors of three states, the company would not yield, and finally, as pressure on the union mounted from angry miners, a strike began on April 5, 1989.

Pittston had done thorough strike preparation and immediately began to hire scabs with the help of the notorious union-busting private police company, Vance International. Vance imported goons and thugs who not only recruited strikebreakers but took them into the plant under armed guard. Vance agents also intimidated the strikers and their allies by flying helicopters over union homes and constantly taking pictures of strikers and supporters. In response to the union's campaign of nonviolent civil disobedience, which included mass picketing, miners sitting down in front of loaded coal trucks, and car caravans driving slowly on the mountain roads to slow down the coal trucks, the police and the courts were soon brought into the dispute.

Workers have a general legal right to picket their employer to further their ends in a labor dispute. Picketing on private property is normally not legal, but picketing on public property (along a highway or on a sidewalk, for example) is protected by the First Amendment to the U.S. Constitution.[4] It would be unconstitutional for a state or local government to enact a law banning all picketing on public property. In addition, the Norris-LaGuardia Act of 1932 prohibits federal courts from issuing injunctions to prohibit picketing,[5] and many states have similar laws. However, it is not usually illegal for states to enact laws restricting picketing, nor it is illegal for state courts to issue injunctions to restrict picketing. Certain types of picketing may also run afoul of the National Labor Relations Act.

To prevent the entry of scabs into the plant and the exit of coal from the plant, the union engaged in mass picketing and in various acts of civil disobedience. Both types of actions can be enjoined by state courts. We have learned that Section 7 of the National Labor Relations Act guarantees workers the right to engage in "concerted activities," among which would certainly be picketing in a labor dispute. And the courts have held that if an action by workers is protected by the NLRA, an employer must use the Act to combat the actions of the labor union. That is, the NLRA "preempts" any state laws.[6] This would seem to mean that the employer could not get a state court injunction to stop the picketing unless this was provided for in the NLRA. However, the courts have also carved out some exceptions to the preemption doctrine, and both mass picketing and criminal acts are exceptions which allow the employer to seek a state court injunction.[7] The same line of reasoning applies to the Norris-LaGuardia Act, which prohibits the issuance of injunctions in labor disputes. Therefore, both the mass picketing and the acts of civil disobedience could be enjoined. "Mass picketing is considered to be enjoinable because of its potential for producing violence, because it is inherently coercive, or because it amounts to a constructive seizure of the employer's property. Any of these characterizations permit state regulation under the preemption doctrine because of the strong state interest in protecting free access to private property."[8] If it comes to a choice between the rights of workers and "free access to private property," the latter will be given priority by the courts. State courts soon enjoined the mass picketing (placing limits on the number and location of the pickets).

There are a wide variety of criminal charges which may be brought against a union in a strike: aggravated assault, simple assault, reckless endangerment, terroristic threats, criminal coercion, arson, causing or risking catastrophe, criminal mischief, criminal trespass, obstructing administration of law, resisting arrest, riot, disorderly conduct (which could be applied to almost any picket line), harassment, obstructing highways, and interfering with railroad employees.[9] The courts began to enjoin the acts of civil disobedience and to arrest those who engaged in them or who disobeyed the injunctions. A nun was arrested for driving her car too slowly on the windy mountain roads, a tactic used by the union to impede the movement of coal trucks. Within a short period of time, hundreds of strikers and supporters were arrested, often treated roughly by the police. Fines against the union for contempt of the injunctions began to mount; by the end of the year, state court fines amounted to more than $1 *quadrillion* (or $1 million billion)!

Mass picketing also violates the NLRA's Section 8(b)(1) because it interferes with the rights of employees (in this case, the scabs) *not* to engage in protected activity. The union could have been charged with unfair labor practices, but the state court injunctions made this unnecessary. The union did, however, run afoul of the NLRA as a result of solidarity actions taken by miners at other mines. In sympathy with their Pittston brothers and sisters, miners across the coal fields began to set up picket lines which generated a rash of wildcat strikes. These strikes not only opened the local unions to suits for violation of contractual no-strike agreements (Section 301 of the Act makes collective bargaining agreements enforceable in court), but they were also illegal secondary actions which are unfair labor practices under Section 8(b)(4). Once the employers filed charges, NLRB agents did preliminary investigations to determine if there was reason to believe that Section 8(b)(4) violations were taking place. Upon finding this to be so, the NLRB *must* seek federal court injunctions to stop the actions. "Within a few months, the union was charged with scores of 8(b)(4) violations. Suits were also filed by employers against the union for losses suffered as a result of the wildcats. The union spent a small fortune defending itself in court."[10] Federal contempt fines began to mount, totalling some $25 million at year's end.

Naturally, in a situation in which workers and their union have been charged with criminal offenses and in which injunctions have been issued and defied, the police are going to be on hand to ensure "law and order." Such was the case at Pittston. "Hundreds of state police appeared to escort scabs to work and trucks to market. Throughout the strike, more than 60 percent of the state police were assigned to the strike; at one point, nine of every ten troopers were busy protecting Pittston coal. It was impossible to get a motel room in the area; all of the rooms were occupied by the police."[11] What clearer evidence of the anti-labor bias of the law could there be?

In response to Pittston's all-out war, the union, under the capable and imaginative leadership of Eddie Burke, devised a multifaceted plan, based upon solidarity and publicity. Picketers wore camouflage uniforms to avoid easy identification by police and company cameras and goons. The union established "Camp Solidarity" in the area as a place to receive support from sympathetic working people around the country. Thousands of people came to visit, to meet with the miners and their families, to see firsthand the gasping retirees, the police, and the company guards. Many brought food and money, and quite a few joined the picketing and got arrested. Support groups were formed around the country, and camouflaged miners began to appear with regularity at labor rallies and on the picket lines of other workers. The union had succeeded in turning the strike into a war of the entire working class against their employers. Unlike the Hormel strike, though, the Pittston workers had the unwavering support of their own union, and in the end, this made the difference.

Still, with all of the union's efforts, Pittston refused to settle. To keep up the strikers' morale and militancy and to keep the strike in the public's eye, Eddie Burke and his inner circle of advisors planned an audacious move. On September 17, 1989, "98 mine workers and a minister" invaded and occupied Pittston's main coal processing plant. This "sit-down" strike, supported by thousands of miners and sympathizers on the scene, electrified the workers and put the strike back on the front pages. Of course, an injunction was soon issued ordering the occupiers to leave, but the miners stayed on three hours after the deadline just to show their resolve. The occupation did not end the strike, but it made Pittston see that it could not break the union. Within a few months, the employer returned to the table and an agreement was reached, one which kept intact the union's major demands. The one unresolved issue is the payment of $64 million in state court fines; this matter is currently pending before the U.S. Supreme Court. Curiously, the father of the judge who levied the fines was defeated by a rank-and-file miner for his seat in the state legislature through a write-in campaign.

II. Strikes

A. Types of Strikes

The collective power working people possess is based upon their ability to disrupt the flow of production. Private employers can make money only if they can produce and sell their output, and they can do these things only if workers do their jobs. Public employers can produce public goods and services only if they have employees on hand to do the work. When workers collectively withhold their labor power, they engage in a strike. Historically the strike has been the most potent weapon wielded by working men and women in the war against capital. It is no wonder then that employers have tried to restrict the right of workers to strike, while at the same time fighting for their complete freedom to combat strikes. Today's strike labor law, like most of the rest of the law, reflects the balance of power between employers and workers. While employees have won important legal protection for their strikes, employers have succeeding in placing many restrictions upon the right to strike.

Before examining strike law, it will be useful to define the various types of strikes. A strike by workers against their own employer is a *primary* strike, for example, a strike by nurses against the hospital at which they work. The picket line they establish at their own worksite is a *primary* picket line. Primary strikes and primary picketing enjoy the most legal protection. A work stoppage aimed at putting pressure on an employer other than one's own is a *secondary* strike. Suppose that a telephone company has a primary dispute with its own employees. The telephone company uses supervisors or scabs to deliver materials to a construction site. Union workers at the construction site (employees of a contractor or subcontractor but not employees of the telephone company) refuse to install the equipment in solidarity with the employees of the telephone company. The construction site workers are *secondary* strikers. If the telephone company employees establish a picket line at the construction site, they are *secondary* pickets. Secondary actions by workers are almost always illegal and subject to heavy penalties.

Within the category of primary strikes there are two subcategories: economic strikes and unfair labor practice strikes. *Economic* strikes are those conducted for union recognition or for improved wages, hours, and terms and conditions of employment. When a collective bargaining agreement has expired and the negotiations for a new one have reached an impasse over, say, wages, the union may decide to strike to force the issue. This would be an economic strike. Suppose, however, that the union calls a strike because the employer has illegally fired a union worker. This would be an example of an *unfair labor practice* strike. Any time that an employer commits an unfair labor practice (as defined in the relevant statute) and the workers strike in response, they are unfair labor practice strikers. The labor law provides more protection to unfair labor practice strikers than to economic strikers.

Closely related to the legal concepts of primary and secondary strikes are *sympathy* strikes. Some sympathy strikes are akin to primary strikes in the sense that the sympathy strikers have the same legal protection as do primary strikers. Here are two examples of this type of sympathy strike. First, the production workers in a factory are on strike against their own employer. One or more clerical employees, not themselves on strike, refuse to cross the production workers' picket line. Second, a truck driver making deliveries to a plant notices that the workers in that plant are on strike and refuses to cross their picket line. In both of these cases, workers other than the primary strikers act in sympathy with them by honoring their picket lines. As we shall see, these sympathy strikers have the same legal status as the primary strikers themselves. However, sympathy actions can also be akin to secondary strikes. The construction workers who refused to handle the equipment delivered to their site by a struck employer engaged in secondary sympathy acts, as would workers or delivery drivers who honored any secondary picket line. Secondary sympathy strikers have no legal protection.

Four other types of strikes which deserve mention are wildcat strikes, sitdown strikes, jurisdictional strikes, and slowdowns. A *wildcat* strike is typically a strike in violation of a contractual no-strike clause. Such strikes are subject to severe legal penalties. In a *sitdown* strike the workers, in effect, occupy their workplace by refusing both to work and to leave the plant. This is what the Pittston miners did, and this is what workers in many industries did during the great organizing drives of the 1930s. Needless to say, sitdown strikes enjoy no legal protection. *Jurisdictional* strikes occur when one or more unions strike to try to force an employer to assign work to their members. These are most common in the construction industry. Finally, a *slowdown* involves a reduction in the pace of the work, so that less output is produced. It is not technically a strike, although its effects may be similar. One type of slowdown is *work-to-rule*, in which workers slow down production by obeying the letter of all work rules and regulations. For example, if city bus drivers scrupulously obeyed all traffic lights and safety rules, they would never get to their stops at the designated times.

B. The Right to Strike

A good argument can be made that the Constitution can be interpreted to protect the right of any workers to strike. An individual cannot be forced to work against her will, since such a situation involves either slavery or involuntary servitude, both of which are illegal under the Thirteenth Amendment. By this logic, a group effort to refuse to work could not be made illegal either, since the only difference is in the number of persons. However, the Supreme Court has refused to give constitutional protection to the right to strike. Therefore, statutes which restrict or deny the right to strike will most likely not be struck down on constitutional grounds, although the Court would no doubt have to strike down a statute which banned all strikes by private sector workers. Such a prohibition would be hard to square with the Thirteenth Amendment.[12]

Absent any statutory restrictions, denials, or protections, the right to strike would be a matter of the common law. Historically, the common law has been hostile to strikes but has not generally outlawed them *per se*, at least as far as private sector workers are concerned. For workers in the public sector, the situation is different. In many states, the courts have held that strikes by public employees are illegal if there is no law which explicitly either gives or denies public sector workers the right to strike. Courts have used a number of justifications for this holding, including the ability of public employees to deny residents access to essential public services and the right of the legislature alone to determine how much money will be spent for these services. The Supreme Court of California has ruled that absent statutory language, the common law must accommodate the right to strike by public employees in at least some circumstances.[13]

Workers in the private sector have important statutory protections of the right to strike. The least restrictive of these are in the National Labor Relations Act. This Act protects the right to strike in Sections 7, 8(b)(4)(b), 13, and 502. Section 7 gives employees the right to engage in concerted activities for purposes of collective bargaining or other mutual aid and protection. A strike is a form of concerted activity. Section 13 provides that "nothing in this Act, except as specifically provided for herein, shall be construed so as either to interfere with or impede or diminish in any way the right to strike, or to affect the limitations or qualifications on that right." Section 502 contains similar language.

When the NLRA refers to the right to strike, it excludes nearly all types of secondary strikes. Section 8(b)(4)(b), while it states that "Nothing contained in this clause (B) shall be construed to make unlawful, where not otherwise unlawful, any primary strike or any primary picketing," also prohibits secondary strikes. Workers who conduct secondary strikes or secondary picketing commit unfair labor practices. Once the employer has filed an unfair labor practice charge, the NLRB must give such a charge priority over all others. Further, once the initial investigator has concluded that there is good reason to believe that a violation has or is occurring (this will happen before a formal hearing), the Board is bound by Section 10(l) to seek a federal court injunction to stop the secondary action. The secondary strike may also be subject to an employer lawsuit under Section 303.

Though the right of most private sector workers to engage in a primary strike is protected by statute, both the NLRA and the Railway Labor Act place limits on this right. We have already seen that the NLRA gives the president the power to delay a primary strike for 80 days if the strike is declared by a federal court to be a "national emergency" strike. Similarly, the Railway Labor Act places many roadblocks in the way of primary strikes. One difference between the Railway Labor Act and the NLRA is that the former does not explicitly prohibit secondary actions. This does not necessarily mean that the courts will allow a rail union to use secondary pressure against an employer. Some courts have held that they cannot issue injunctions against secondary pressure because the Norris-LaGuardia Act prohibits them.[14] The NLRA specifically overrides the Norris-LaGuardia Act with respect to secondary actions, but the Railway Labor Act does not. Therefore, it would seem that unions could engage in secondary picketing and secondary boycotts without fear of injunctions. This is the view of some courts, but not all. A federal court of appeals has upheld an injunction against secondary pressure by a rail union, the Norris-LaGuardia Act notwithstanding, on the grounds that the target of the secondary pressure was not sufficiently involved in the primary labor dispute.[15]

Public employee labor law statutes always contain either restrictions or prohibitions of the right to strike. Federal government employees are forbidden to strike, and the penalties for doing so are severe: Strikes are unfair labor practices; striking employees will be legally fired, and a striking union will be decertified as bargaining agent. Strikers can also be prosecuted if they refuse an order to return to work.

The laws governing state and local government workers are too numerous to discuss in any detail. Ten states allow public employees a limited right to strike. Usually various conditions must be met before a strike can be called, such as mandatory mediation or fact-finding. No state allows all public employees to strike; police and firefighters are everywhere denied the right to strike. Where public employees cannot strike, it is typically the case that the law provides an alternative such as binding arbitration. In some states, this is "final offer" arbitration, in which the arbitrator must choose either the last proposal of the union or the last proposal of the employer, but no other position can be chosen by the arbitrator. The idea here is to encourage the parties to bargain seriously. If the union makes too high a wage demand, for example, it is likely that the arbitrator will choose the more "reasonable" proposal of the public employer. As is the case for federal employees, striking state and local public employees may face serious penalties if the strike is illegal.[16] In addition, even if the strike is legal, the statute will probably allow the employer to seek an injunction to stop the strike after a certain period of time or whenever the employer can convince the court that the strike poses a threat to public health or safety.

C. No-Strike Agreements

While the NLRA, the Railway Labor Act, and some public employee labor law statutes protect the right to strike, the parties to a collective bargaining agreement can voluntarily waive this right. Most agreements contain "no-strike" clauses, in which the union agrees not to strike during the term of the contract. Here is an example:

> Except as otherwise provided in this agreement, during the term of this agreement, the Union guarantees the Employer that there will be no authorized strike, work stoppage, or other concerted interference with normal operations by its employees.

Suppose that a disagreement arises over some managerial decision which a group of workers believes violates the contract. Rather than file a grievance, the workers walk off the job and other workers follow them. This is a wildcat strike, and it would breach the no-strike clause. In such a case the striking employees are subject to managerial discipline, including discharge. The employer does not have to go through any grievance procedure unless there is an explicit provision in the contract for employer grievances or a history of employer grievances.

In some contracts the union agrees to take specific actions in the event of wildcat strikes. Here is an example:

Should an unauthorized strike, stoppage, or other concerted interference with normal operations take place, the International Union shall in no event be liable, financially or otherwise, provided that the International Union within twenty-four (24) hours after actual receipt of notice in writing or by telegram from the Employer that a strike or work stoppage has commenced shall notify the Employer in writing that such strike, work stoppage or other concerted interference with normal operations is unauthorized and that a copy of such notice has been sent to the Local officers with instructions to bring it to the attention of the employees involved. The Local Union whose members are involved in such unauthorized actions shall not be held to its legal liability therefore, if any, provided it meets the following conditions. But in any event the Local Union agrees to: (a) Promptly post notices in conspicuous places at the affected plant and at the Local Union office stating that such action is unauthorized. (b) Promptly order its members to resume normal operations. The employees who instigate or participate in unauthorized strikes or stoppages in violation of this agreement shall be subject to discharge or discipline, in which event their recourse to the grievance and arbitration procedures shall be limited to the question of whether they did instigate or participate in such strike or concerted activity.

Such an agreement puts the union in a vulnerable position. If the international and the local fail to take the required actions, they open themselves up to a lawsuit for damages equivalent to the value of the production lost because of the wildcat strike under Section 301 of the NLRA. Remember that Section 301 makes collective bargaining agreements enforceable in court.

If the union has not agreed to a clause such as the one above, it cannot be sued for damages unless union officers actively participated in or actively condoned the work stoppage. For example, workers walk off of the job and go to the local union hall where they are given advice about how best to conduct the strike by local officers. Such actions would make the local liable for damages in a Section 301 suit. The individual union members who participated in the wildcat strike cannot be sued for damages, but they can be fired or otherwise disciplined.[17]

If a collective bargaining contract does not contain a no-strike clause, strikes during the term of the agreement may still be illegal. In a long series of decisions, the Supreme Court has held that arbitration is the preferred method of settling disputes over the meaning of collective bargaining agreements. If a dispute is or can be reasonably construed to be subject to the grievance and arbitration clauses of the contract, the parties must use this procedure. Let's say that a worker is disciplined by being suspended for three days for arguing with his supervisor. Under the contract he can file a grievance protesting the suspension, and this grievance could be carried to arbitration. The contract does not contain a no-strike agreement. In such a situation, if the employee's coworkers strike in protest of the suspension, they can be disciplined just as if there were a no-strike agreement. If the dispute is not subject to the grievance/arbitration clause of the contract, then the workers can strike without fear of being disciplined.[18]

The Norris-LaGuardia Act prohibits federal courts from issuing injunctions in labor disputes. As we have seen, the NLRA overrules Norris-LaGuardia in most secondary actions. This would appear to mean that no injunction could be issued in any primary strike irrespective of the strike's legal status. Wildcat strikes would appear not to be subject to injunction, though the strikers can be fired and the union may be subject to suit. However, in the *Boys Market* decision, the Supreme Court held that if a dispute is subject to the collective bargaining agreement's grievance/arbitration clause, a walkout over the dispute is subject to an injunction if the employer requests it.[19] This decision contradicts the clear language of Norris-LaGuardia, but it gives a good indication of how hostile the courts are to rank-and-file attempts to directly enforce their union contracts.

If an employer commits an unfair labor practice, employees may be free to strike, a no-strike clause notwithstanding. To forbid strikes to protest an employer's violation of the law would weaken the protection given to workers by Section 7 of the NLRA and would encourage employers to commit unfair labor practices. However, the NLRB has held that the unfair labor practice must be a "serious" one to justify a strike, and the union must not use an unfair labor practice as a pretext for what is basically a disagreement over wages, hours, or terms and conditions of employment.[20]

D. The Rights of Strikers

What can an employer do when it faces a legal primary strike? Assuming that it cannot get a *Boys Market* injunction, it is free to try to maintain production during the strike. It cannot fire the strikers; this would be an unfair labor practice. However, it can replace the strikers.[21] Replacements can be either temporary or permanent. Supervisors who remain inside of a power plant to do the work of striking utility workers would be temporary replacements. When the strike is over, the strikers will return to their old jobs, and the supervisors will resume their managerial work. Workers who answer want ads in a newspaper calling for new employees during a strike would be permanent replacements.

When the strike is over, all strikers who unconditionally agree to return to work are placed on a recall list. These former strikers must be offered any openings in the bargaining unit which exist at the time the strike ends and in the future. They need not be recalled in order of seniority, and they will lose their recall rights if they have found comparable employment or if they have engaged in violence on the picket line. The employer cannot cut special deals with permanent replacements such as giving them ten years of seniority or extra fringe benefits as inducements to scab.[22]

In practice, being permanently replaced is not much different than being fired. Strikers will be recalled only as openings appear. Further, if a strike drags on for one year, the replacements may file a petition to have the union decertified as bargaining agent. In the decertification election only the replacements will have the right to vote. In this era of widespread unemployment and poverty, employers may feel that they can risk or even encourage a strike, hire permanent replacements, wait a year, and have the union decertified. Such tactics became commonplace during the 1980s.

If a striking union, whose members have been permanently replaced, retains enough leverage to force the employer to settle, it will have to try to negotiate a strike settlement agreement in which the employer agrees to take back the striking workers and get rid of the replacements. However, unless the employer has made this possibility a part of the hiring arrangement with the replacements, the replacements may be able to file a state civil suit against the employer for breaching the hiring contract.[23]

The above analysis refers to what are termed "economic" strikers, that is, those on strike to secure better wages, hours, and terms and conditions of employment. Workers on strike to protest an employer's unfair labor practices are called "unfair labor practice" strikers. Unfair labor practice strikers cannot be permanently replaced, but they are subject to temporary replacement.

E. Lockouts

Occasionally an employer will refuse to allow workers to enter the plant. This is called a lockout, and it is done to put economic pressure upon the union to reach agreement on the employer's terms. Suppose a union strikes one employer in a multi-employer bargaining group. The other employers may lock out their workers to force all of the members of the bargaining unit to suffer the losses caused by the strike. Lockouts are legal, but locked out workers cannot be permanently replaced. The employer can use temporary replacements to maintain production, but when the lockout is over, the original members of the unit must be brought back.[24]

F. Sympathy Strikes

It is natural for a worker or a group of workers to be sympathetic to workers who are on strike and/or picketing. It is an article of faith among some people never to cross a picket line. When a group of workers in one workplace are on strike, it might seem to those in another plant that a sympathy strike against *their* employer might be a good way to show solidarity with the strikers. There have been a few occasions in our history when the workers in an entire city participated in a *general* strike, both in sympathy with some initial group of strikers and to further their own organizing, bargaining, and political objectives.[25]

The labor laws do not take kindly to group sympathy actions which result in the shutting down of a secondary employer. Recall the actions of the electrical workers who refused to install the equipment delivered to their worksite by the telephone company whose own employees were on strike. They were engaging in a sympathy action, but one which the NLRA considers to be secondary and therefore illegal. They violated Section 8(b)(4) of the Act and were subject to an automatic injunction mandated by Section 10(l).[26] Similarly, if steelworkers strike in sympathy with automobile workers, they are using an illegal secondary tactic. In addition, they would certainly be violating the no-strike clause in their agreement. In the former case, the employees were refusing to handle "struck work" or "hot cargo," namely the equipment delivered by the struck telephone company. With one exception, this is illegal and will result in an injunction under the NLRA (but not necessarily under the Railway Labor Act, as mentioned above). The exception can be illustrated by an example. Company A produces a part which is normally shipped to Company B, where the part is finished. Company A's workers call a strike. Company B then agrees to produce the part on its premises, that is, to do at its workplace the work normally done at Company A. Workers at Company B can legally refuse to handle the struck work, because their employer is in fact an "ally" of Company A; it has, by its actions, become a party to the strike. The sympathy action of B's workers cannot result in their firing, but, of course, they could be replaced, either temporarily or permanently.[27]

Different legal principles apply to situations in which individual workers honor picket lines. A production worker in a factory may refuse to cross the picket line set up by the factory's clerical employees, or a truck driver may refuse to make a delivery if it means driving the truck through a picket line. In these cases, the sympathy strikers (those who won't cross the picket lines) have the same legal protection as the workers who struck originally and are now picketing (or who have just put up a picket line). If the picketing is primary, the sympathy strikers can be replaced by their employer, but they cannot be fired. If the strike is a primary economic strike, the sympathizers can be permanently replaced; if it is a primary unfair labor practice strike, the sympathizers can only be temporarily replaced. However, if the picketing is secondary, the sympathizers can be fired, because there is no legal protection afforded to those who refuse to cross an illegal picket line. Sometimes, union members establish informational picket lines to inform the public of some anti-union practice of the employer, such as the use of nonunion labor or the payment of substandard wages. In most cases, an employer cannot fire a worker who refuses to cross an informational picket line. Again, workers who do so can be replaced.[28]

The legal status of sympathy actions can be affected by a collective bargaining agreement. First, it is illegal to include a "hot-cargo" clause in a contract, such that workers who refused to handle struck work could not be disciplined. Second, it is possible to contractually protect legal sympathy actions. It is important that such protection clearly prohibit the employer from replacing sympathy strikers. Language which says only that sympathy strikers cannot be disciplined is insufficient, because the NLRB holds that the replacement of sympathizers is not a form of discipline.[29] Third, a no-strike clause may prohibit sympathy actions. It can do this explicitly by including sympathy actions in its definition of a strike. Unfortunately, the NLRB and the courts today may conclude that a no-strike agreement which has *no* reference to sympathy actions may, nonetheless, outlaw them.[30]

A no-strike clause is intimately connected in the eyes of the Board and the courts with the contract's arbitration clause. When a union forgoes the right to strike, it agrees to use binding arbitration as the method for settling disputes over the meaning of the contract. Using this logic, any dispute, including a sympathy action, which could be settled by the arbitration procedure cannot legally be the cause of a strike. But how do we know that the no-strike clause parallels the arbitration clause? If the no-strike clause refers explicitly to arbitrable issues or if it is in the same article of the agreement, the Board and the courts will probably conclude that they cover the same issues and rule that a sympathy action is not covered by the no-strike agreement since it is not arbitrable. However, if the no-strike clause is separate from the arbitration clause, it might be held that it covers all strikes, whatever the issue. In this case, the sympathy actions would be covered by the no-strike agreement and would violate the contract. Here it is necessary for the union to negotiate language which explicitly protects sympathy actions.

For public employees, sympathy strikes will often be explicitly illegal under the relevant statutes. In Pennsylvania, for example, public employees are legally bound to cross the picket lines of striking public employees. In my own workplace, this would mean that if the janitors and maintenance employees are legally on strike and picketing, it would be unlawful for me as a teacher to not cross their line. If I refuse to cross, my employer can discipline me for my sympathy action.

III. Picketing

A. Types of Picketing

The most fundamental legal distinction between different types of picketing is between primary and secondary picketing. *Primary* pickets are picketing their own employer. This need not be only at their employer's premises. In certain situations, pickets may follow their employer's product and picket at another site, yet still remain primary pickets.[31] This may occur when striking truck drivers follow their employer's scab-driven trucks and picket them at an unloading dock at another worksite. Or it may occur when physical circumstances make it impossible for employees to picket their employer without at the same time picketing another employer. This is referred to as *common situs* picketing.

Secondary picketing takes place at the site of a secondary employer or other secondary party. For example, striking employees may picket the premises of one of their employer's suppliers or customers. With rare exception, secondary picketing is illegal under the NLRA. It is not illegal under the Railway Labor Act, but as we have seen, some courts may enjoin secondary railroad and airline picketing.

Before the passage of the NLRA, a union could usually win recognition only by forcing the employer to recognize it. This was often done by setting up an *organizational* picket line. Such picket lines are still used, but the NLRA places severe limits upon them. Since the persons engaged in organizational picketing are typically not employees of the picketed employer, they are called *stranger* pickets. Stranger pickets may also picket to advise the public about some anti-union practice of a certain employer. In this case they are using *informational* picketing.

Another distinction of great importance in the law of picketing is whether the picketing takes place on *public* or *private* property. Picketing on public streets enjoys much greater legal protection than does picketing on private property. Tricky questions arise when the property is private but has public characteristics, such as the parking lots and inside aisles of shopping malls.

B. The Legality of Picketing

1. Primary Picketing

Throughout the nineteenth and early twentieth centuries, the courts took a dim view of picketing. Picketing was seen as a coercive act which could be enjoined upon petition by the employer. Since picketing is a localized activity, it is in the province of state courts, and most states accepted the view that it was an unreasonable interference with an employer's right to do business.[32]

In the landmark ruling, *Thornhill v. Alabama*,[33] the Supreme Court struck down an Alabama law which prohibited all picketing. In this decision, the Court defended picketing as a form of speech protected by the First Amendment of the U.S. Constitution. This ruling is of some importance because it means that no state can completely ban all peaceful picketing by statute. Similarly, no state court can enjoin all peaceful picketing in a labor dispute. It should be noted that the picketing discussed here is picketing on public property; the law with respect to picketing on private property is a lot different.

Since *Thornhill*, the Supreme Court has had second thoughts about the constitutional sanctity of picketing. Statutes and injunction, *restricting* as opposed to banning peaceful picketing may pass constitutional muster. Here are some examples: First, state courts can enjoin all picketing if peaceful picketing is enmeshed in violence. Suppose that a union engages in acts of violence such as assaulting scabs, destroying the employer's property, and damaging the homes of nonunion workers. A court may rule that the picketing cannot be separated from these acts of violence and must be enjoined. Once the violence stops, the union can petition the court to lift the injunction.

Second, state courts can enjoin *mass* picketing, the purpose of which is to block all entrance to a plant. Mass picketing is not speech, the courts reason, but an act of aggression which does not have constitutional protection. States may not legislate unreasonable limitations on picketing, but courts may use injunctions to limit picketing.

Third, a state court may enjoin picketing if it holds that no labor dispute is involved. In one case a restaurant owner used nonunion labor to build his house. The union, therefore, picketed the restaurant. The Supreme Court upheld the injunction issued by the state court on the grounds that the union had no labor dispute with the restaurant. Fourth, an injunction may be issued if picketing interferes with employees' rights under some states' laws or with the employer's duties under state statute. A Virginia court enjoined organizational picketing of a nonunion shop because the state's right-to-work law gave workers the right not to join a union. An injunction against picketing also was allowed in a case in which an employer supplied nonunion peddlers with ice, contradicting an arrangement made by the union. The recalcitrant employer argued that such an agreement violated the state's antitrust law.[34]

Picketing on private property enjoys *no* constitutional protection. This is true even for such quasi-public spaces as parking lots and shopping malls. However, primary picketing and leafleting on private property may be legal under the National Labor Relations Act. Section 7 of the NLRA gives workers covered by the Act the right to use concerted action for collective bargaining or other mutual aid and protection. Picketing is a form of concerted action, so it is a protected activity. This creates no difficulty as far as picketing on public property is concerned, but a conflict arises if the picketing is on private (usually the employer's) property. The owner of private property has the right to deny access to it. But what if the denial of access to the property also denies workers their Section 7 rights? In such situations the Board and the courts have tried to reconcile the conflicting rights, although recently the scales have tipped in favor of the employer's property rights.

Suppose that a union wants to organize employees in a store located in a strip mall. To help them to do so, they place leaflets on the cars in the mall's parking lot. They are informed that the store, which owns part of the lot, does not allow any soliciting or distributing of literature. Security guards ask the organizers to leave, and the guards remove the leaflets. The union then uses a variety of means to contact the employees, including taking down license numbers and placing ads in a local newspaper. After several weeks the union is able to reach only about 20% of the employees. Believing that it will not have any chance to organize the workers unless it has access to the parking lot, it files an unfair labor practice charge against the employer. The Supreme Court held in a 1992 ruling that the employer's property rights were stronger in this situation than the employees' Section 7 rights.[35] This decision overturned a long series of NLRB and lower court rulings which had sought a fairer balance between property and Section 7 rights. Now, the only situations in which a union would win a case like this are if the employees actually live on the employer's property (as in the cases of migrant farm workers or lumberjacks) or if the employer allows other types of solicitation.

The above example involved a union-organizing attempt. If a union already represents the employees, picketing on private property is less likely to be illegal. Consider a restaurant on the twentieth floor of a skyscraper. The employees call an economic strike. The effectiveness of their strike will be greatly reduced if they are forced to picket on the sidewalks in front of the building. Therefore, they may be permitted to picket inside the building outside of their actual workplace. In these cases the Board and the courts try to accommodate the two conflicting rights "with as little destruction of one as is consistent with the maintenance of the other."[36]

2. Secondary Picketing

As we have seen, the Taft-Hartley Amendments to the National Labor Relations Act made a wide range of secondary labor disputes illegal and subject to automatic NLRB petition for injunction. The idea of the amendments is to deny a union the power to enmesh a third party in a labor dispute by putting economic pressure on it as a way of affecting the behavior of the primary employer. Taken literally, Sections 8(b)(4), 8(b)(7), and 8(e) would make it difficult to legally conduct any strike or picketing, because it is hard for a successful strike/picketing combination not to involve third parties. However, the language of the statute is not taken literally by the NLRB or by the courts, so not all secondary involvement in a labor dispute is illegal. We will look at some common situations, but the reader is cautioned that the law is complex and not every possibility is covered here.

Suppose a union sets up a picket line at the entrance to a factory. The picket line may be established by the factory's own workers, or it may be established by "strangers" such as members of a union that would like to organize these employees, or the stranger pickets may want to urge customers not to patronize this employer (this will most likely be part of an organizing campaign), or the stranger pickets may want to inform the public that this employer pays substandard wages. In each of these cases, the picketing is primary, because the employer being picketed is the one with which the union has the dispute. In each of these cases, people approaching the picket line (scabs, factory's employees, suppliers, and customers) may decide to honor it. Arguably, each person is in some sense secondary to the original dispute, and by ceasing, in effect, to do business with the picketed employer, forces the union to violate Section 8(b)(4).

In judging the legality of these primary picket lines, the basic rule is that as long as the *object* is primary, any secondary *effects* do not constitute a breach of the law. But this is not always the case, so let us look at the above examples in more detail:

a. The factory's own production workers are on a legal primary strike: Here the refusal of customers, suppliers, scabs, or other factory employees to cross the picket line does not constitute illegal secondary action. The striking union cannot be charged with an unfair labor practice, even though there are secondary effects of its picketing.

b. The factory workers above picket the premises of a customer or supplier of their employer: This is secondary picketing, it is illegal under Section 8(b)(4) and will result in an NLRB request for a federal court injunction. It should be noted here that any secondary action violating Section 8(b)(4) can also result in an employer-initiated damage suit under Section 303 of the NLRA. Naturally, such a suit would be filed by the damaged secondary employer. If, in the unfair labor practice hearing which may take place after the injunction is issued, the union is found guilty of an 8(b)(4) violation, the court hearing the Section 303 suit may take this as sufficient evidence of guilt. Then the only issue before the court will be the amount of the damages.[37]

c. Another union urges its members not to cross the factory workers' picket line: This union would be guilty of an unfair labor practice and subject to injunction.[38] Of course, the members of the secondary union may decide individually not to cross. As we have previously seen, though, such refusal may constitute a breach of the secondary employees' own no-strike clause.

d. The factory workers are not unionized, but stranger pickets have begun to patrol in front of the gate to force the employer to recognize the union as bargaining agent: Organizational picketing is no different from picketing to enforce a strike. It is primary, and the fact that others choose to honor it does not make the union guilty of an unfair labor practice. However, organizational picketing is, itself, restricted by law (Section 8(b)(7)), as we saw in Chapter Four. It is legal *if* no other union legally represents the employees or *if* no representation election has taken place within the past 12 months. But if it is legal, it can only be used for a maximum of 30 days, unless the union files for a certification election. Then the picketing can continue for more than 30 days. If the union wins the election, it can also continue the picketing. In any circumstance in which the organizational picketing is illegal, the union commits an unfair labor practice and is subject to injunction.

e. Strangers establish picket lines, carrying signs urging customers not to patronize this employer: While such picketing is legal, it is restricted by this language in Section 8(b)(7)(c): "unless an effect of such picketing is to induce any individual employed by any other person in the course of his employment not to pick up, deliver or transport any goods or not perform any services." If delivery drivers honor this picket line, the union is guilty of a violation and subject to injunction.[39] Note that if the employer were a retail store and retail customers honored the picket line, this would not cause the union to violate 8(b)(7)(c).

f. Strangers set up a picket line, carrying signs stating that the employer pays substandard wages: This picketing is legal, and secondary effects do not subject the union to an unfair labor practice charge. An exception would be if the true purpose of the picketing is to organize the employees, in which case the restrictions of Section 8(b)(7) apply. Therefore, it is important for the picketers not to give the employer any signs that the picketing is for recognition, such as telling a manager that the pickets would go away if the employer recognized the union.[40]

The above examples all refer to picketing. If the union engages in simply handing out leaflets, and if the leafleting is not disguised picketing, and if the leafleting is on public property, the union is free to directly involve most secondary parties. In the landmark *DeBartolo* ruling, the Supreme Court held that a construction union could urge through leaflets a total boycott of a shopping mall, despite the fact that its only dispute was with a single store in the mall which had used a nonunion construction company to do work for it.[41] The leafleting cannot be used with picketing, nor can it be directed at secondary employees. Otherwise, all secondary leafleting is legal as are all nonpicketing publicity such as billboards and radio or newspaper ads. Interestingly, this ruling was made after similar leafleting was declared illegal and enjoined in the Local P-9 strike described at the beginning of Chapter Five. Today, P-9's leafleting of First Bank would have been legal.

In all of the cases referred to so far, the primary employer was the sole occupant of the worksite. The law of picketing is more complicated if a workplace is occupied by more than one employer. Consider two examples. First, a construction site is utilized by the employees of several subcontractors, hired by the general contractor to perform the various types of work common to a construction project. A union representing employees of an electrical subcontractor calls a strike against the electrical subcontractor. There are several entrances to the site, and the union pickets all of them. As a consequence, all of the work on the project ceases as the workers of the other subcontractors honor the picket lines. By virtue of the nature of a construction site, this picketing is not only picketing of the primary employer but of the secondary employers as well. Is it legal? Yes, if there is only one entrance to the worksite or if the several entrances are used indiscriminately by all employees. No, if there are separate entrances or gates reserved for specific groups of employees. If the primary employer sets up a gate reserved for its employees and there are neutral gates for other employees, then under most circumstances the striking union must confine its picketing to the reserved gate.[42]

A second example is a union that represents workers on a ship. The ship is in dry dock for repair. The ship's employees call a strike and want to picket the ship. The dry dock's owner refuses to give the workers permission to picket on the dock next to the ship, so they picket the entrance to the dry dock. The picketing is aimed at the primary employer (the shipping company), but it is at a secondary site (the entrance to the dry dock). Is such picketing legal? Yes, but the NLRB has established four conditions which must be satisfied.[43] First, the picketing must be reasonably close to the premises of the primary employer. Second, the picket signs must clearly and specifically identify the primary employer as the target of the picketing. Third, the primary employer must be doing its normal business at the time of the picketing. Fourth, the primary employer must be present at the time of the picketing. There are some exceptions to these conditions. The primary employer cannot establish a gate in such a remote location that the picketing is inevitably ineffective in publicizing the union's dispute. If the neutral gates are regularly used by primary employees, they also become legal targets of the union's picketing.[44]

The rules for "common situs" picketing, picketing sites housing more than one employer, also apply to situations in which the primary employer moves around from site to site. For example, a trucking company's employees are on strike, and the company has hired scab drivers to make deliveries to its customers. The union can send picketers to follow the trucks, and they can picket the secondary employer while the trucks are making their deliveries, as long as the other conditions are satisfied.[45]

A twist on the above examples of secondary picketing occurs when there are secondary employers at the primary worksite. Consider the striking factory production workers. During the strike, the factory's owner hires a construction company to make certain repairs at the factory. The primary employer establishes a separate gate for use solely by the employees of the construction company. Can the striking factory workers picket this gate? No, if these three conditions are satisfied: (1)

A separate gate has been established for the outside contractor's workers and is appropriately identified; (2) the work being done is not related to the normal operations of the struck employer; and (3) the work is not such that it could only be done because of the strike.[46] Thus, a gate established for workers building a new maintenance shed at the factory could not be picketed, because new construction could have been done absent a strike and is not a part of normal business operations. But, a gate for workers doing routine repair work normally done by the striking workers could be picketed.

Suppose that a railroad makes deliveries along a right-of-way owned by the railroad. The tracks go onto the property owned by a company whose workers are on strike, through a gate which is part of a fence. The fence encloses both the struck employer's property and part of the railroad right-of-way. Striking employees picket the gate. The railroad company seeks an injunction, claiming a violation of Section 8(b)(4). Using the three criteria just discussed, the Supreme Court vacated the injunction upheld by the lower court. It argued that, despite the fact that the property picketed was owned by the secondary employer (the railroad), the picketing was lawful: "The legality of separate gate picketing depended upon the type of work done by the employees who used that gate; if the duties of those employees were connected with the normal operations of the employer, picketing directed at them was protected primary activity, but if their work was unrelated to the day-to-day operation of the employer's plant, the picketing was an unfair labor practice."[47]

3. Secondary Picketing Under the Railway Labor Act

We have already noted that the Railway Labor Act does not have a section like Section 8(b)(4) of the NLRA. Because of this and because of the Norris-LaGuardia Act's prohibition of federal court injunctions in labor disputes, some courts have held that railroad and airline unions are free to use secondary pressures without fear of statutory injunctions. However, all of the dispute resolution mechanisms of the Act must first be exhausted. Even then, some courts have justified injunctions on common law principles, on grounds that the union using secondary pressure did not "have a legitimate economic interest in influencing the policies of the employer against whom the pressure was exerted," or on grounds that the Act, itself, binds workers to "avoid conduct which might interrupt carrier services."[48]

4. Secondary Picketing by Public Employees

Secondary pressure could be utilized by public employees in a labor dispute. This pressure could be brought against either secondary public or private employers. For example, striking public school teachers might picket a private bus company which delivers students to the schools. Or, they might picket state office buildings. Are such tactics legal? Some public employee statutes explicitly forbid secondary pressures in language similar to that of the NLRA. In such situations, a board like the NLRB will probably be empowered to seek an injunction to stop the secondary pressure. Absent a statute, a court might still issue an injunction on common law principles. A difficulty arises when the public employees exert secondary pressure against a secondary private employer. In such a situation, neither the NLRA, which excludes public employees from coverage, nor the state statute, which excludes private employers from its coverage, will govern. Again, the injunction might be issued on common law grounds.[49]

IV. Boycotts

A. Types of Boycotts

A boycott can be defined as a "concerted refusal to do business with particular person or business in order to obtain concessions or to express displeasure with certain acts or practices of person or business."[50] Historically, boycotts have been an important organizing tool for unions. *Consumer* boycotts were used to force an employer to recognize a union rather than lose a lot of business. These boycotts could be aimed at a single product or an entire business. For example, the United Farm Workers Union once organized a boycott against the Gallo Winery. The union tried to strengthen the boycott by picketing stores that sold Gallo wines. The picketers in such a situation could urge customers of the store not to buy the wine, or they could urge customers not to patronize the store at all.[51] In both cases, the boycott is a *secondary* boycott, since the store is a secondary party to the primary labor dispute between the union and Gallo. The first case, however, is a *secondary* product boycott, because the picket signs are directed against the product.

Another type of boycott is a *labor* boycott. A refusal to handle struck work is such a boycott, and it is primary or secondary depending on whether the two employers involved are allies or not. If workers refused to work for an employer who had dealings with a struck employer, they would also be engaging in a secondary labor boycott. A union once struck a company which made printing presses. In solidarity with the striking workers, other workers refused to work for any company which used these printing presses.[52]

B. The Legality of Boycotts

As the careful reader might surmise, the legality of boycotts closely parallels the legality of picketing. Just as secondary picketing is usually illegal under the NLRA, so is secondary boycotting. There are three exceptions. First, in most cases, a secondary product boycott is legal, as is the picketing which accompanies it. That is, striking workers (and supporters) can picket outside of a store that sells their employer's product and urge customers not to buy that product. It would be illegal, however, to urge a total boycott of the store.[53] Also, a product boycott would be illegal if the store's only product was that produced by the striking worker's employer or if this product accounted for a large share of the store's business. In this case, the product boycott is, in effect, a boycott against the store.[54]

Second, any type of boycott by consumers can be urged if the union uses handbilling rather than picketing. This was the scenario in the *DeBartolo* decision discussed previously. A third exception involves the refusal to handle struck work where the two employers are allies.

A union covered by the NLRA which engages in an illegal secondary boycott commits an unfair labor practice and is subject to an injunction. The NLRB will seek an injunction prior to the unfair labor practice hearing. As is the case with secondary picketing, the secondary employer can file a damage suit under Section 303.

V. Injunctions

A. Introduction

We have already had numerous occasions to mention injunctions in this book. They have been the most powerful weapon used by employers against organized labor. The current law of injunctions is complex, so what follows is a bare bones account.[55]

The starting point for any discussion of labor injunction law is the Norris-LaGuardia Act of 1932. The purpose of this law was to help to redress the imbalance between the power of corporations and the power of employees by making it difficult for an employer involved in a labor dispute to obtain an injunction in federal court. The Act also made yellow dog contracts (see Chapter Three) unenforceable, gave those against whom injunctions were sought important procedural rights, outlawed blanket injunctions, and barred most anti-trust prosecutions against labor organizations.

One of the most important provisions of the Norris-LaGuardia Act is its broad definition of the term "labor dispute." Before the Act, courts had traditionally limited this term to disputes between employees and their own employer, that is, to primary disputes. The courts then felt free to enjoin or otherwise declare illegal all secondary disputes. The broad definition of labor dispute in the Act meant that the federal courts could not issue injunctions against unions that used secondary tactics such as secondary boycotts and picketing. It also led to the Supreme Court's anti-trust exemption of labor unions, as is explained in one of the questions at the end of this chapter. A number of states enacted "little" Norris-LaGuardia Acts, which restrict the issuance of injunctions by state courts.

It is important to note that, under the terms of the Norris-LaGuardia Act, the only situations in which a federal court can issue an injunction in a labor dispute are those involving fraud or violence. Picket line violence could be enjoined, but this could also be enjoined under common law principles by state courts. Presumably, a secondary boycott that used fraudulent statements about the employer could also be enjoined.

Before examining the many circumstances under which injunctions can be issued in labor disputes, let us briefly outline the procedural safeguards incorporated in the Act. First, a court can issue an injunction only after a hearing. The accused party must be notified and given an opportunity to participate. A five-day temporary restraining order can be issued without a hearing, but only if the judge can be convinced that "unless a temporary restraining order shall be issued without notice, a substantial and irreparable injury to complainant's property will be unavoidable." Second, the court has to be shown by the evidence that "unlawful acts have been threatened or will be committed unless restrained or have been committed and will be committed unless restrained." Third, there must be evidence of "irreparable injury" to the party seeking the injunction. Fourth, it must be shown that more damage will be done to the party seeking the injunction if it is not granted than to the other party if the injunction is granted. Fifth, the party seeking the injunction must not have an "adequate remedy at law." Sixth, the property of the party seeking the injunction must not be adequately protected by the appropriate public officers. Seventh, any injunction can be appealed to a higher court. Eighth, parties accused of contempt of court (for not obeying an injunction) have a right to a speedy trial. Ninth, a party accused of contempt can, under certain circumstances, petition to have the judge who issued the injunction removed from the contempt trial.

While the Norris-LaGuardia Act and its state counterparts were important victories for working people, legal developments since their passage have weakened their impact. The following represents a very incomplete list of situations in which injunctions can now be issued in labor disputes:

1. The Act has been held not to apply to public employment.[55] Therefore, a public employer will find it easier to obtain an injunction against public employees than will private employers. Since public employee strikes are illegal, most courts will issue injunctions against them, simply by virtue of their illegality. Some public employee labor laws explicitly state the conditions under which an injunction must or can be sought by a state board or by a public employer.

2. The Railway Labor Act mandates certain dispute resolution procedures, and the courts have held that failure to comply with these is grounds for an injunction, the Norris-LaGuardia Act notwithstanding. Injunctions have also been granted against secondary actions by railroad and airline unions, either on grounds that no "labor dispute" is in progress or on grounds that the party is not obeying some provision of the Act.[57] Remember, the Railway Labor Act contains no prohibition of secondary activities, so a good argument can be made that the Norris-LaGuardia Act prohibits injunctions to stop them.

3. Nothing in the Act prohibits state courts from issuing injunctions to limit picketing where there is violence or the threat of it or where mass picketing prevents entry into or exit from a workplace.

4. The NLRA as amended specifically voids the Norris-LaGuardia Act for all of the secondary labor disputes prohibited by Sections 8(b)(4), 8(b)(7), and 8(e). As we know, the NLRB *must* seek injunctions in such cases as soon as an unfair labor practice charge has been filed by the employer and the board investigator has good reason to believe that the alleged secondary action is taking place. It should be noted that the NLRB also has the power to seek an injunction to stop any employer unfair labor practice, but it seldom does.

5. The courts have further broadened the use of injunctions by allowing them to enforce arbitration clauses, despite the clear language of the Norris-LaGuardia Act. A strike over an issue which is arbitrable under a contract's arbitration clause can now be enjoined, whether or not there is an explicit no-strike clause. Fortunately, it is still the case that strikes over nonarbitrable issues cannot be enjoined.

6. The attorney general of the United States can seek an injunction when a strike has been declared by the president to be a national emergency strike.

7. As we saw in the discussion of picketing law, states can enact laws restricting peaceful picketing. These laws can then be enforced by injunctions in state courts.

VI. Conclusion

While the situation facing workers is not as one-sided as in the days of the Pullman strike, it is still the case that the labor laws favor employers by a wide margin. This is seen clearly in the P-9 and Pittston strikes. Radical changes in the law are needed, but unless working people are willing to do the kinds of things that their P-9 and Pittston sisters and brothers did, such changes will not happen.

VII. Questions and Answers

Question 1: What should workers know about the doctrine of "preemption?"

The doctrine of preemption states that federal law preempts or takes precedence over state law. The major application of this doctrine to labor law is with respect to the National Labor Relations Act. If conduct by an employer or by a union is either protected or prohibited by the NLRA, it cannot be regulated by the states.[58] For example, suppose that a state has a law against secondary picketing, and the affected employer can seek a state court injunction. Secondary picketing is clearly prohibited by the NLRA, so the affected employer must file an unfair labor practice charge with the NLRB if it hopes to get injunctive relief. If the state court did issue the injunction, the union could have it rescinded; in fact, it could get the NLRB to petition a federal court to enjoin the state court injunction. Ordinarily, an employer cannot go into state court to have peaceful picketing enjoined, since peaceful picketing is protected activity under Section 7 of the NLRA. However, as we have seen, mass or violent picketing can be enjoined.

A second area in which preemption may be important is a suit by an employee against an employer for a contract violation. The employee must use the contract's grievance procedure to contest the contract violation. In other words, the grievance procedure preempts the state court suit.[59]

If Congress intended that employer or union conduct not be regulated at all, but left to the economic strength of the parties, then states cannot regulate the conduct either. In one case, the city of Los Angeles ruled that it would not renew the franchise of a taxi company unless the company settled a labor dispute with the Teamsters Union. The Supreme Court held that the dispute had to be settled by the parties through the exercise of their economic power because this is what Congress intended.[60]

There are some exceptions to the preemption doctrine. A state suit against an employer for contract violation may be valid if the court does not have to interpret the collective bargaining agreement to settle the suit.[61] The NLRB is preempted by the federal courts in suits under Sections 301 and 303 of the NLRA, and these suits may also be brought in state court. Except for provisions in the Landrum-Griffin Act (see the next chapter), internal union affairs are not preempted. Also, an employer may, in some cases, seek a state court injunction to stop picketing on private property even if the picketing is permitted or prohibited under the NLRA. Suppose that a union is engaging in primary informational picketing on private property of the employer. If the employer asks the union to leave and the union does not file an unfair labor practice charge against the employer (so that the NLRB can rule on the legality of the picketing), the employer can seek a state court injunction.[62]

Question 2: Are work slowdowns illegal? Do they violate no-strike agreements?

Slowdowns are not illegal; they are a legitimate tactic a union can use to force concessions from an employer at the bargaining table. Under the preemption doctrine (see Question 1), states cannot make them illegal. However, depending upon the wording, they may violate a contractual no-strike agreement. This would ultimately be up to an arbitrator to decide.

Question 3: What happened to the Professional Air Traffic Controllers Organization (PATCO) strikers?

The federal air traffic controllers are employees of the federal government, and their relations with their employer are controlled by the Federal Labor-Management Relations Statute, part of the Civil Service Reform Act of 1978. Through their union, PATCO, they bargained terms and conditions of employment with the Federal Aviation Administration. When negotiations for a new contract reached an impasse in the summer of 1979, the union called a strike. As we know, this strike was illegal, and President Reagan ordered the strikers to go back to work. They did not, and he fired 11,000 of them, marking the beginning of his reign of terror against organized labor. In addition, the Federal Labor Relations Authority, using its power under the law, revoked the union's certification—in effect, decertifying it as the workers' bargaining agent. Civil and criminal contempt charges were filed against union members when they defied the injunctions issued to get the traffic controllers back to work.

The government blacklisted the striking workers and denied them the right to seek employment as federal air traffic controllers. President Clinton has since allowed most of them to apply for jobs. In addition, a new union has been certified as bargaining agent for the current controllers, most of whom were originally scabs. Organized labor missed an opportunity to build a movement of resistance to employer attacks by supporting the air traffic controllers through sympathy actions. The airlines could have been paralyzed by machinists' strikes alone, but the unions that could have made a difference did not have the courage to defy their own no-strike agreements.

Question 4: How do lawsuits under Section 303 of the NLRA work?

When a union violates the secondary boycott provisions of Section 8(b)(4) of the NLRA, the employer can go into state or federal court and file a suit for the monetary losses which it suffered as a result of the illegal boycott. The employer cannot seek an injunction; only the NLRB can do this. If the picketing is violent, the employer may be able to convince a state court to assess punitive damages in addition to the actual losses.

Question 5: What states allow public employees at least a limited right to strike?

Alaska, Hawaii, Idaho, Illinois, Minnesota, Montana, Oregon, Pennsylvania, Vermont, and Wisconsin. Also, as we have seen, some public employee strikes, not otherwise outlawed by statute, may not be illegal under the common law in California.[63]

Question 6: How can a union avoid the problem of an implied no-strike agreement?

This problem can be avoided if the union spells out in the agreement the right *to* strike for contract violations. Otherwise, it is hard to see how the courts, given past rulings, could not interpret an arbitration clause as an implied no-strike agreement.

Question 7: What type of dispute would not be subject to a typical contract's grievance procedure?

A political strike might be a good example. Suppose that the dockworkers' union in California wanted to show solidarity with the workers of Chile after the socialist president, Salvador Allende, was murdered by the military. Union workers, therefore, refuse to unload ships carrying Chilean cargo. This dispute is not between the union and the employers with whom it has signed an agreement. In such a case, the dispute could not be resolved through the grievance procedure. The importance of this is that such a strike will probably not violate a contractual no-strike agreement, unless that agreement specifically includes all sympathetic actions. In addition, such a strike is not subject to a *Boys Markets* injunction. However, a refusal to handle certain cargo may be ruled a secondary boycott and subject to a Section 303 damage suit.[64]

Question 8: Can an employer pay scabs wages higher than those paid to workers before the strike began?

The employer can pay replacements higher wages, but only wages equal to those in its last offer to the union. In general, the employer cannot discriminate in favor of scabs whether they be replacement workers or strikers who abandon the strike. An employer cannot agree to pay some benefit to which all strikers are entitled only to those who abandon the strike.[65]

Question 9: Can an economic strike also be an unfair labor practice strike?

Yes. A strike for higher wages becomes an unfair labor practice strike at the time the employer commits an unfair labor practice. Naturally, the regional office must decide that an unfair labor practice has been committed.

There is considerable advantage to a strike being declared an unfair labor practice strike. The employer cannot permanently replace unfair labor practice strikers, nor can sympathizers who refuse to cross the picket line be permanently replaced. A union involved in bargaining with an employer not bargaining in good faith can strike in response to this unfair labor practice. Once the employer has been found guilty of bad-faith bargaining, the striking workers cannot be permanently replaced.

Question 10: What is an example of an illegal secondary product boycott?

Secondary product boycotts are not prohibited by Section 8(b)(4) of the NLRA, with one exception. Suppose that workers are on strike against an insurance company. They picket the office of an insurance agent with signs urging customers not to buy policies issued by the struck company. But suppose also that this agent sells policies only of the struck company, that is, all of his business involves the struck company's products. Here the boycott, while ostensibly aimed at the primary employer's product, really amounts to an attempt to enforce a boycott against the secondary employer. The picket signs may say, "Do not buy policies from John Hancock," but when customers abide by the sign, they will not patronize the agent at all since he only sells John Hancock policies. Their signs might as well say, in the view of the court, "Do not patronize this agent."[66]

Question 11: How did the Norris-LaGuardia Act exempt unions from anti-trust prosecutions?

In Chapter Three we learned that unions were often prosecuted under the Sherman Act for restraint of trade and were assessed large fines when they lost their cases. By 1930 literally all secondary actions could be found to violate the Act. In 1914 Congress passed the Clayton Act, which organized labor believed exempted unions from anti-trust prosecutions. However, the Supreme Court ruled that the definition of labor dispute" in the Clayton Act only included primary disputes.[67] In the Norris-LaGuardia Act of 1932, Congress clearly defined labor dispute to include secondary disputes, but the Act says nothing about anti-trust laws.

In the lead case, the Anheuser-Busch brewery in St. Louis awarded some construction work to the machinists' union. The carpenters' union protested and organized a secondary boycott against the company's products. The government brought an anti-trust suit against the carpenters. The Supreme Court, however, ruled that the union was not guilty of a violation. The Court took the broad definition of labor dispute from Norris-LaGuardia, which includes secondary actions, and said that this was now the definition of labor dispute in the Clayton Act. Then it ruled that, since the Clayton Act states that any union action allowed by it cannot be prosecuted under the Sherman Act, secondary boycotts cannot violate the Sherman Act.[68]

There is one exception to the union anti-trust exemption. If a union colludes with an employer to restrain trade, the union can be in violation of the Sherman Act. The International Brotherhood of Electrical Workers Local 3 in New York City once had agreements with both electrical equipment manufacturers and electrical contractors such that no electrical equipment from outside of the city could be used in the city. The local was found to have colluded with the employers to keep outside companies from doing business in New York City, a clear restraint of trade. The local was found to be in violation of the Sherman Act.[69]

Question 12: What states have "little" Norris-LaGuardia Acts?

Arizona, Colorado, Hawaii, Idaho, Illinois, Massachusetts, Minnesota, Montana, New Jersey, New Mexico, New York, North Dakota, Oklahoma, Oregon, Pennsylvania, Rhode Island, Utah, Washington, Wisconsin, and Wyoming.

Question 13: What happens when a union violates an injunction?

The employer will notify the court that the injunction has been violated, or the court may take action on its own. The union or persons enjoined will be notified to appear in court to face charges of contempt. A hearing will be held before a judge, and the judge will decide if there is contempt. Then a penalty will be imposed. There are two types of contempt: civil and criminal. In civil contempt, the party found in contempt is threatened with certain actions (a fine and/or jail) unless the party obeys the injunction. If the party obeys, no penalty is actually imposed. In criminal contempt, the party found in contempt is punished for some past actions, and a penalty is imposed for this past action. In some criminal contempts (but not those arising from violations of NLRA-based injunctions) a jury trial is required. All injunctions (except temporary restraining orders) and contempts are appealable to the federal courts of appeals.

VIII. Selected Readings

1. Henry H. Perritt, Jr., *Labor Injunctions* (New York: John Wiley & Sons, 1986).

2. Michael D. Yates, "From the Coal Wars to the Pittston Strike," *Monthly Review* 42 (June 1990), pp. 25-39.

Chapter 7

THE DEMOCRATIC RIGHTS OF
UNION MEMBERS

I. Teamsters Take Back Their Union

Looked at narrowly, a union is an organization formed by working people to improve their work lives, through higher wages, more benefits, greater job security, and due process. However, a union *can* be much more than this. A union formed through collective struggle gives workers a feeling of power, and it teaches them more about the nature of our economic system than any formal education. It makes them a part of something larger than themselves, and this can be the first step toward an understanding that working people could change the entire society for the better.

For a union to be effective in either a narrow or a larger sense, it must act to further the interests of its members. To do this, it must be democratically organized. Power must flow from the bottom to the top; the leadership must be responsible to the members. Leaders must be democratically elected; every member must have the right to fully participate in all aspects of the union's work; collective bargaining must be conducted democratically; and the membership must have a say in the final content of the agreement. The union's participation in the larger political arena must be debated fully, and the actions it takes must be democratically decided.

The labor movement has not always lived up to these democratic ideals. Nowhere has this been more true than in the International Brotherhood of Teamsters, which until recently was both the largest and the most corrupt union in the nation. This was a union so openly corrupt that, prior to the election of Ron Carey as president in 1991, that five of its last six presidents either were indicted or went to jail, and the other one died before a similar fate befell him. Numerous large Teamsters locals were run by gangsters, and for years the gigantic Central States Pension Fund was one of the major "banks" of organized crime. This union was so bad that the AFL-CIO, not known for aggressive stands against corrupt affiliates, expelled it in 1957 and did not readmit it until 1987.[1]

Several examples will give the reader the flavor of corruption within the Teamsters. The Central States Pension Fund, upon which some 400,000 members and beneficiaries depend for retirement income, loaned billions of dollars to captains of organized crime to build casinos and hotels in Las Vegas and to finance various and sundry other criminal schemes. A large loan in Las Vegas was actually secured by $5 million in gambler's IOU's! It is estimated that the Fund lost some $385 million in loans never repaid or made at below-market interest rates. Local 560 in Union City, New Jersey was the personal fiefdom of the Provenzano family, itself associated with the Genovese organized crime family. The Provenzanos stole the money of the local's members for years. Professor Michael Goldberg, an expert on union democracy law, tells us, "During 1981, Tony Provenzano collected an officer's salary of $28,000 from his Teamsters Local 560 in Union City, New Jersey. In amount, Provenzano's salary was quite reasonable. Less reasonable was the fact that when he collected it, Provenzano was three years into the life sentence he was serving for ordering the murder of a political rival within his local."[2]

The national officers of the union were "elected" by delegates to the national convention of the union, but these delegates were, for the most part, appointed by the officials they were supposed to nominate and elect. Most officers of the union made exorbitant salaries, often drawing money from several union offices held simultaneously. The reform group, Teamsters for a Democratic Union (TDU), uncovered the salaries of Teamster officers and discovered scores of them making in excess of $100,000 per year. When Jackie Presser was appointed union president in 1983, he was knocking down $565,000 in annual salaries. The party held at the national convention to celebrate his ascension to the throne cost $647,960.

The corrupt and autocratic leadership of the union held the members in complete disdain. Here is a statement made by Weldon Mathis, secretary-treasurer of the union, to the 1990 Eastern Conference meeting:

> Our entire democratic system is a system of delegates making decisions for the masses. I am opposed to the membership vote

for the officers of this international union. I really am not concerned whether you agree with me or not. I'm telling you my position. I believe that the system that this international union has for electing officers of this international union is the best system there is.

Now I expect to read tomorrow or next week in TDU that Weldon Mathis is opposed to the members voting for the officers of this international union, and that doesn't bother me either.

What does bother me is the prospect of our members, without knowing who is qualified to do a job at the national level, without knowing whether our general president is qualified, without knowing whether any of the vice presidents who are now or will be in the future are qualified, because they don't know them. They are not acquainted with them. They don't deal with them. The delegates are the people that deal with the International officers of this union. You know who's best qualified to represent the members of this International.[3]

At the time that this statement was made, it was known both inside and outside of the union that organized crime bosses had in fact chosen three of the past four presidents of the union.

The rank-and-file suffered greatly from the corruption of their union. Honest union leaders, and there were many of them at the local level, were tainted by the image of the national union. Contract negotiations often resulted in "sweetheart" deals, in which employers paid money to union officers in return for agreeing to lower wages and benefits for the rank-and-file. For a national agreement, such as the one covering long-distance truck drivers, to be rejected by the members required a two-thirds vote, something nearly impossible to achieve. Once the legendary Jimmy Hoffa was sent to jail, the union fell into the hands of men who cared little about the members. While Hoffa was corrupt, he at least delivered better pay and benefits; his successors were more interested in making money and living the high life.

Corruption at the top of an organization breeds fear and cynicism at the bottom. It also breeds anger. Dissident groups had formed periodically to challenge the leadership, but they were usually defeated by a combination of lack of money, violence, and fear among potential supporters. The one exception was the Teamsters for a Democratic Union. Formed in the early 1970s by teamsters who came into the union from the radical political movements of the 1960s, TDU succeeded because its core members were not only incorruptible, but they also had a dedication to the labor movement based upon a vision of a just society. In other words, they had ideals, and they were committed to realizing them through the labor movement. TDU began patiently to organize, one person at a time through face-to-face meetings with union members all over the country.

TDU began to confront the union hierarchy on many fronts. Through its newspaper, *Convoy*, the new organization began to expose the corruption of the union to the rank-and-file. TDU researched the reports the union had to submit to the Department of Labor under the Landrum-Griffin Act and uncovered the bloated salaries of numerous officials and the millions of dollars spent on jet airplanes. It found many officials who did no work yet were paid salaries for several jobs. It agitated against ratification of the sellout contracts which the union had negotiated with the big trucking companies. It began to run candidates in local elections and managed to win a couple of them. It picketed union headquarters and the national convention. At great risk, TDU members made motions at these conventions, calling for direct election of officers, an increased strike fund, simple majority contract ratification, and other "radical" demands.

In 1979, TDU merged under the TDU name with another dissident group, PROD (Professional Drivers Council for Safety and Health), a Ralph Nader spinoff initially organized to fight for trucking safety, something woefully neglected by the union. PROD had become a full-fledged opposition organization, which in 1977 filed internal union charges against Frank Fitzsimmons, Hoffa's successor as president. Once the two groups combined, the pressure on the leadership increased and the TDU gained more visibility and credibility. Through news conferences and the dissemination to the media of information uncovering the inner workings of the union, TDU gained a national audience and presence. It could count on some money from progressives outside of the Teamsters along with dues from its members. TDU also caught the attention of the Association for Union Democracy (AUD), a nonprofit group led by a great champion of union democracy, Harold Benson. Working with TDU, the Association eventually helped to lay the groundwork for the lawsuit which eventually brought the control of the union by criminals and their union lackeys to an end.

Before TDU's rise to prominence, there were legal avenues which could have been taken to return the union to the members. However, these required that the federal government take action, and without the relentless pressure of TDU and its supporters, such action would not be taken. The Teamster hierarchy maintained cozy relationships with many politicians and actively campaigned for the anti-labor reactionaries Ronald Reagan and George Bush.

The National Labor Relations Act has two provisions which could be used by union members to make their union more responsive to their needs. Section 301 provides for lawsuits in state or federal court against labor organizations for contract violations. The Supreme Court has interpreted Section 301 to give a member of the bargaining unit the right to sue the union for failure to fairly represent her properly.[4] Ordinarily, such suits are filed in cases in which a union has refused to take up a worker's grievance, or failed to investigate a grievance properly, or refused to take a grievance to arbitration. The duty of fair representation also extends to the collective bargaining function of the union. An agreement that systematically discriminated against some category of workers (e.g., black employees) could be challenged by a Section 301 lawsuit.[5] It is conceivable that workers in corrupt Teamsters locals could have sued their unions for failing to represent them properly, by, for example, signing "sweetheart" deals with employers. The troubles with such suits are threefold: First, the workers must initiate the suits and pay the legal bills, which can be considerable. Second, the burden of proof is on the workers to demonstrate that the union failed in its duty to represent them fairly. The courts give unions a lot of leeway here, so this could be difficult to do. Third, the kind of massive corruption typical of the Teamsters probably cannot be dealt with effectively through Section 301 suits. If a union local were found guilty of a Section 301 violation in its bargaining, it is difficult to see what penalty the courts could provide that would rid the union of the underlying corruption. It can be noted here for future reference that when a union violates its duty of fair representation, it also commits an unfair labor practice, so a charge can be filed with the NLRB instead of a court.

Section 302 of the NLRA makes it illegal (in fact, it is a crime punishable by imprisonment) for an employer to make any payment to a union or its members and prohibits the union and its members from accepting such payments. There are a number of exceptions such as dues check-offs, welfare fund payments, regular wages paid to union officers who are also employees while they are performing union duties, etc.[6] However, monies extorted from an employer in return for labor peace would clearly violate Section 302, which is enforced through lawsuits filed by the U.S. Department of Justice. To the best of my knowledge, Section 302 has not been used to attack union corruption.

The Landrum-Griffin Act

A better legal vehicle for the maintenance of the rights of union members is the Labor-Management Reporting and Disclosure Act, better known as the Landrum-Griffin Act of 1959.[7] This law was enacted as the direct result of congressional investigations into labor union racketeering. Landrum-Griffin can be activated by individual lawsuits, or in the case of union election violations, by a complaint filed with the U.S. Department of Labor, which can then file a lawsuit on behalf of the union members. The Act has five sections or "Titles," each of which can be useful in ensuring that unions operate democratically.

Title I of Landrum-Griffin sets out a "Bill of Rights" for union members. (Note that this law covers only union members, while the NLRA covers all employees.) Union members are guaranteed equal rights and privileges within such organizations to nominate candidates, to vote in elections or referendums of the labor organization, to attend membership meetings, and to participate in the deliberations and voting upon the business of such meetings, subject to reasonable rules and regulations in such organizations' constitutions and bylaws.

Unions are not bound to grant any specific rights, but if they do, each member has an absolute right to exercise these rights. Title I also guarantees to every union member freedom of speech and assembly, including the right to speak freely at all union meetings. Unions cannot arbitrarily increase dues, since Title I provides for at least some democratic procedures in dues assessments. Of considerable importance, union members are guaranteed due process rights in any case of internal union discipline. Specifically: No member of any labor organization may be fined, suspended, expelled, or otherwise disciplined except for nonpayment of dues by such organization or by any officer thereof unless such member has been (A) served with written specific charges; (B) given a reasonable time to prepare his defence; (C) afforded a full and fair hearing.

Finally, every union is bound to make its members aware of their rights under the Act and to provide every member with a copy of the member's collective bargaining agreement.

Title II requires every union to adopt a constitution and bylaws and file these with the Secretary of Labor and make periodic reports concerning its internal operations and disbursements of funds. These reports are a matter of public record, kept in the public disclosure room (North 4677) in the Department of Labor building in Washington, D.C. It was here that TDU discovered the obscene salaries of so many of the Teamsters officers. As we saw in Chapter Five, employers have to file reports concerning their use of consultants, and the consultants must also file reports concerning their activities.

Title III limits the power of national unions to place their locals in trusteeship. Most union constitutions give the national union the power to take over the affairs of any local (put it in trusteeship) in certain situations. This would give the national a way to get rid of a corrupt local leadership; it would place the local in trusteeship and then appoint new officers, etc. However, a corrupt national union could also use trusteeship as a way to stifle dissent within the union by placing dissenting locals in trusteeship. Title III is aimed at the latter abuse. It provides:

> Trusteeships shall be established and administered by a labor organization over a subordinate body only in accordance with the constitution and bylaws of the organization which has assumed trusteeship over the subordinate body and for the purpose of correcting corruption or financial malpractice, assuring the performance of collective bargaining agreements or other duties of a bargaining representative, restoring democratic procedures, or otherwise carrying out the legitimate objects of such labor organization.

Trusteeships cannot normally be imposed for more than 18 months.

Title IV provides safeguards for the conduct of union elections. Unions cannot maintain unreasonable requirements for running for office, such as a requirement that all prospective office seekers must have attended a certain number of union meetings before the election. The union must treat all candidates for union office equally; it cannot deny one candidate access to the union's newspaper while giving it to another. Each candidate has the right to inspect the union's membership list within 30 days prior to the election. The union cannot refuse to distribute any candidate's literature, although the candidate can be required to pay for this distribution. Each union member must be notified of any election at least 15 days before the election day. Unions are required to conduct elections periodically: locals at least every three years, intermediate bodies every four years, and national unions every five years. All elections must be by secret ballot. The Act does not specify the method by which officers are to be elected. It does not require, for example, that national officers be elected by direct vote of the members; instead national officers may be elected by delegates to the national convention. A union is also free to have election rules of its own, so long as they do not violate the Act. The Supreme Court has ruled that it is lawful for a union to prohibit candidates to solicit or accept campaign funds or things or services of value from persons outside of the union.[8]

Title V of Landrum-Griffin lays out detailed "fiduciary" responsibilities of unions toward their members. Union officers must use the members' dues for the benefit of the members; they must not have conflicts of interest (by, say, having a financial interest in a company with which the union is negotiating); they must not loan money to union officers; they must not use union monies for their own benefit; they must not try to extort monies from employers. Importantly, certain persons, including convicted criminals, are not allowed to hold union office or act in any capacity with respect to the union except to be a union member, including convicted criminals, for up to 13 years.

Just this casual glance at Landrum-Griffin and minimum knowledge of the Teamsters will convince anyone that the union was in gross violation of the statute. Except for Title IV, which gives the Department of Labor exclusive jurisdiction to remedy post-election abuses, the Landrum-Griffin Act permits union members to file suits in federal (and, in some cases, state) courts against their union to force compliance. In Title IV cases, the Secretary of Labor has the power to overturn an election and order a new one under government supervision. In court suits to enforce the other Titles, the courts have broad powers to insure compliance. A judge could issue injunctions against the union and its officers ordering them to stop illegal practices. If deemed necessary, the court could appoint an outsider to put the union's house in order and could give the outsider whatever powers the judge felt were necessary to stop the abuses. The history of Landrum-Griffin cases, however, shows the courts to be usually unwilling to take such drastic measures.

State courts have long held powers to enforce Landrum-Griffin under the common law.[9] Before passage of Landrum-Griffin, there were cases in which, in response to civil suits filed by union members to enforce a union's own constitution or bylaws, courts ordered locals into trusteeship under court-appointed trustees. In fact, in 1957, 13 New York area teamsters filed suit against the union to stop Jimmy Hoffa from continuing gross violations of the union's constitution. This suit ultimately resulted in a consent decree (an agreement reached voluntarily by the plaintiffs and the union) which created a Board of Monitors "to serve as a watchdog and to recommend reforms necessary to permit a new convention, and a new election [Hoffa had rigged the previous one], to take place."[10] This Board lasted for three years but failed to reform the structure of the union. Without a mass rank-and-file movement to keep the heat on the union, Hoffa was able to defeat the Board with a combination of counter-suits, bribes, and intimidation.

In the early 1980s, the government, prodded by TDU and the Association for Union Democracy and embarrassed by the grossness of the union's corruption, decided to take decisive action against the entire union. The government utilized a relatively new law, not specifically a labor law but one aimed directly at racketeering and organized crime. This law is the Racketeer Influenced and Corrupt Organizations Act (RICO). As Attorney Goldberg informs us,

> ... a person violates the Act if he or she (a) uses income from a "pattern of racketeering activity" to acquire an interest in an "enterprise;" (b) acquires an interest in an enterprise through a pattern of racketeering activity; (c) conducts or participates in the operation of an enterprise through a pattern of racketeering activity; or (d) conspires to commit any of the foregoing violations.[11]

Under RICO a union is an "enterprise," so the Teamsters were covered by it. A "pattern of racketeering activity" consists of two or more of a wide range of illegal acts committed in the past ten years. The bribery, extortion, theft of union funds, murder, intimidation of union members, and the wholesale violation of the members' rights guaranteed by the union's own bylaws and constitution and by the Landrum-Griffin Act all qualified as patterns of racketeering activity. Not only were the actual gangsters who had infiltrated and controlled the union chargeable under the Act, but so also were the elected officials who had "aided and abetted" these criminals.

The powers given the courts under RICO are more sweeping than those under Landrum-Griffin, and the Act, itself, provided for triple damages to the victims of RICO violations.[12] A few RICO suits had been filed by the federal government against local unions, including Provenzano's notorious Local 560. These had some success, but in the case of the Teamsters, the corruption was so pervasive that it became apparent that no legal attack would work if it were confined to a few locals. The structure of the entire union had to be changed. In June of 1988, the U.S. Department of Justice filed a RICO suit against the whole union, after years of collecting damaging evidence against hundreds of union officials and members of organized crime. The union was accused of being a captive organization, controlled by organized crime. The suit asked the court to remove all union officers who had committed RICO offenses, to appoint a trustee to perform all of the duties of the union's General Executive Board, and to hold new elections for national officers. After a period of protracted negotiations, (the judge ordered that the accused would have to pay for their own defenses), the union reached a consent agreement in which it capitulated to all of the government's demands.

The consent agreement provided for the following: (1) The appointment by the court of three officers—an independent administrator, an investigative officer, and an elections officer; (2) The election of delegates to the national convention no longer than six months before the convention; (3) The secret ballot election by rank-and-file vote of the union's chief officers; (4) The appointment of a review board after the 1991 elections to investigate and punish corruption in the union; and (5) No union member could associate with organized crime figures.

This time, pushed by TDU and the Association for Union Democracy, the court-appointed officers did their jobs. They forced many officials to resign or face suits. They took control of the union's treasury and made sure that only proper expenditures were made (the officers were paid out of union funds, a nice irony—the union paying to have its own house put in order). Most important, the court agreed to the proposal put forward by the Association for Union Democracy for the conduct of the elections. Each local would hold secret ballot elections for the convention delegates, the number of delegates depending on the local's size. This meant that local union officers would not, as in the past, automatically go to the convention as delegates. Then at the convention, the elected delegates would vote by secret ballot to nominate the union's officers: the president, secretary-treasurer, 11 regional vice presidents, and five at-large vice presidents. To get nominated, a candidate had to get 5% of the appropriate delegate total. Any candidate who, before the convention, got 2.5% of the eligible voters for his or her office to sign a petition supporting candidacy would become an "accredited" candidate. An accredited candidate would have the right to inspect the union's membership and would be given a page allocation in the union's journal. Naturally, the union fought against these rules, again filing numerous countersuits against them. This time, however, the appeals courts rejected every union argument and threatened to hold some officials in contempt for filing frivolous suits.

Despite the unprecedented sweep of the RICO-based regulations placed upon the union, nothing would have changed if TDU and its allies had not created a climate in which candidates could come forward to take advantage of them. This is exactly what happened. Ron Carey, honest and militant president of a large New York United Postal Service (UPS) local, decided to run for president, and he put together a strong slate, including some TDU members and a few women as well. He hired Ron Burke, the man who directed the Pittston strike described in Chapter Six, as his campaign manager. Carey and Burke crisscrossed the country and, unlike their two insider rivals, ran a rank-and-file campaign. Carey received the support of the requisite number of delegates at the convention and won the election by a landslide. Since becoming president, Carey and his team have changed the union from top to bottom, selling off the jets, firing staffers, cleaning out corruption, winning good contracts, and organizing new members. There is still a long way to go, but now union members can say without shame that they are Teamsters.

II. Unions and Their Members

A. The Duty of Fair Representation

Once a union wins a certification election, it becomes the sole bargaining agent for all of the people in the bargaining unit. As such, the union assumes the duty to represent them. This duty applies to workers organized under the NLRA, the Railway Labor Act, and all of the public sector labor laws. What does this duty mean in practice? What exactly is a union bound to do for its members? The first cases to come before the courts involved unions which discriminated against black workers in their bargaining units. It was decided that a union must represent its unit members "fairly," and a union which discriminated on the basis of race violated this duty.[13] The NLRB now holds that it has the power to revoke the union's certification to penalize the union in such a case.[14] This is a powerful penalty, because it would allow the employer to refuse to bargain with a union. The NLRB also now views the violation of the duty of fair representation as an unfair labor practice, specifically a violation of Section 8(b)(1).[15] The union, in acting unfairly as sole bargaining agent, denies workers their rights under Section 7 of the NLRA.

A union which does not honor its duty of fair representation also violates Section 301 of the NLRA (assuming that the NLRA applies to this union).[16] This means that a member of the bargaining unit can sue the union in state or federal court. Suppose that I am a union dissident, highly critical of the union's operations. I am discharged for what I believe are unjust reasons. I file a grievance claiming that the employer violated the collective bargaining agreement by firing me without just cause. The union refuses to process and investigate my grievance and simply takes the employer's word that I was fired for just cause. I could file an unfair labor practice charge against the union, or I could file a civil suit against it. If I file a suit, I must file it within six months of the date the union notified me that it was not taking up my grievance. If the union does not notify me, I have six months from the date I could reasonably have expected to find this out, using normal diligence.[17]

The suit that I file should charge both the union and the employer. The employer has violated the agreement by firing me, and the union has breached its duty of fair representation by refusing to process my grievance. The court will have to determine first if the union has violated its duty to represent me fairly. No hard-and-fast rules can be given for how courts decide this, but I will have to convince the court that the union acted "arbitrarily, discriminatorily, or in bad faith."[18] In my case, the fact that I was a thorn in the union's side will weigh in my favor, as will the union's refusal even to process and investigate my grievance. Once the court has determined that the union has not fairly represented me, it will then decide whether or not the employer violated the contract. If it rules in my favor, the court will award me reinstatement with backpay. If, on the other hand, it rules that the employer did not violate the agreement, I have no recourse against the union, since, presumably, an arbitrator would have ruled against me anyway had the union done its job.

If I win, does the union have to pay any of the backpay awarded to me? It may. Initially, the courts were of the view that the employer must pay, because it was the employer who violated the contract. Now, however, the courts will apportion the award as follows: The employer is liable from the time of my discharge until the time an arbitrator would have reinstated me. The union is responsible for all the time after this.[19] This means that in a case which drags on for a long time, a union may have to bear the lion's share of the backpay award. Therefore, a union must be careful in processing grievances. This is especially the case since most duty of fair representation suits involve situations which are not as clear-cut as the one just described.

In one case, two truck drivers stayed the night in a motel. They turned in a room receipt for reimbursement to their employer. The receipt showed an amount greater than the price of the room. The employer discharged the drivers for filing a false voucher and for attempted theft of the difference. The drivers said that they paid the full amount for their rooms and suggested that the motel clerk must have tampered with the motel's records and stolen the money himself. The union told the drivers that it would investigate further, but it never did. The case went to arbitration. At the hearing, the drivers maintained their innocence, but the arbitration panel upheld their discharge. The workers filed a Section 301 suit against the employer and the union. As the case was being prepared, the motel clerk admitted that he had taken the money, not the drivers. The employer argued that, though the workers were innocent, an arbitration ruling was final, and this normally would be what the courts would rule, as we have seen. In this case, however, the employees had proven their innocence. This might have been discovered had the union bothered to investigate the grievance properly. Because the union did not do so, the court ruled that it had violated its duty of fair representation, and the drivers were ordered reinstated with backpay.[20] It is important to note that a union may not be at fault if it merely does a bad job in handling a grievance, although the courts of appeals are not of one voice in this matter. Some courts say that a union must exhibit some intentional misconduct to be guilty of not upholding its duty of fair representation. Other courts hold unions to a more demanding standard, and actions such as missing a filing deadline or failing to see the obvious relevance of a contract provision may lead to a finding of a union violation.[21]

The duty of fair representation applies to contract bargaining as well as grievance processing. A student of mine was an employee of a steel company, and he was represented by a local of the United Steel Workers union. He had a grievance pending arbitration which he had a good chance of winning, in which case he would collect a large amount of backpay. The plant was facing financial difficulties, and the company asked for concessions from the union at the bargaining table. One of the concessions was for the union to drop all of its grievances which were pending arbitration. In return for this and other concessions, the company would agree to keep the plant open. The union agreed to the concessions and so dropped my student's grievance. Naturally he was upset, and he asked me if he could file a charge against the union. He could have filed a Section 301 lawsuit against the union, claiming that it had failed to represent him fairly. He would have lost his suit. The union's obligation in bargaining is to act in the interest of the members of the bargaining unit. The Supreme Court has held that in bargaining the parties must have "wide latitude in their negotiations." Only if the union's bargaining is beyond a "wide range of reasonableness" and manifestly "irrational" or "arbitrary" will it be found to have breached its duty of fair representation.[22] Given the circumstances of a plant about to close, in which case all of the employees would lose their jobs, it was neither irrational nor arbitrary for the union to drop the grievances.

A union must act properly with respect to members of the bargaining unit at the arbitration hearing. Suppose that a union always uses an attorney to represent the grievant at the hearing. In a particular worker's case, however, the union refuses to use an attorney and assigns a union staffperson to the case. This might make the union susceptible to a duty of fair representation suit, if it could be shown that the staffperson was not as qualified as the attorney to defend the employee's rights. A union is not bound to use an attorney in all cases, but if it does in some but not in others, it could be asking for trouble.

It is possible that, if the union uses a staffperson, she may not be as well-versed in arbitration procedures as a labor lawyer would be. This would not make the union more liable to suit, because the courts recognize that a union is not bound to supply an attorney at all. A union staffperson will not be held to the same standard of performance as would be a lawyer.[23]

Sometimes a union can find itself in a difficult position in the handling of grievances. In one case, two workers were discharged for fighting. The union fought to have both workers reinstated, but the company would agree only to the reinstatement of the one the company believed did not instigate the fight. The union said both workers had to be reinstated, or none. The company stuck to its position, forcing the union to decide whether to push the discharges to arbitration. After a thorough investigation and a meeting of the local's membership, the union decided not to take either case to arbitration. The worker who would have been reinstated had the union agreed to the employer's offer filed a suit against the union. The court found in favor of the union, pointing out that the union's decision was neither arbitrary, discriminatory, nor in bad faith.[24] Its decision not to allow the company to make it choose between the two workers was not necessarily an illegal refusal not to take the cases to arbitration. In general, a union is not bound to take every grievance to arbitration or through all the steps of the grievance procedure except arbitration. On the other hand, it is bound to recognize all grievances and to investigate each one seriously.

B. More on the Landrum-Griffin Act

1. The Bill of Rights

If a union is to be a democratic organization, then members must be free to voice their opinions within the union. They must not be fearful that their union will seek to punish them if they are critical of the union's policies. Otherwise, a union just replicates the autocratic behavior of employers. The Act gives union members the greatest possible latitude to speak out. At a union meeting, a worker can pretty much say what she pleases, and the union cannot legally fine, suspend, or throw her out of the union. As labor lawyer Bruce Feldacker tells us, a member can make statements she knows to be untrue or comments which defame a union officer, and such speech is protected by the Act. A union can discipline members who urge workers to decertify the union or who urge workers to violate the contract.[25]

Under Landrum-Griffin, unions are free to establish their own internal rules and to enforce such rules through union discipline or court action in the case of a fine of a union member. But these rules cannot conflict with the law. Here are some examples:

1. A union can decide if and when to have union meetings. A union that holds infrequent meetings does not violate the Act.

2. A union is free to set its own dues structure. However, dues increases are subject to the Act's voting requirements spelled out in Section 101(a)(2). Also, it should be remembered that the NLRA makes the establishment of an "excessive or discriminatory" initiation fee by a union an unfair labor practice. A union could not have one initiation fee for women and another for men.

3. A union officer is free to employ nonelected staffpersons of his choice. Let's say that a new person has been elected union president, replacing an incumbent after a heated contest in which the old officer's policies were sharply criticized. The new president is free to discharge the incumbent's nonelected staff and choose new staffpersons more agreeable to the program of the new regime. It is not legal to discharge any elected officer or staffperson. To allow this would clearly undermine the democracy implied by elections.[26]

4. The union can demand that union members conform to certain standards of behavior. This is justifiable, especially in light of the inability of a union to force any bargaining unit member to become a union member, even under so-called union shop provisions. Remember the example from Chapter Four. A union begins a campaign to organize nonunion stores. Some of the union members in the nonunion stores refuse to participate in the union's organizing drive. The union is free to discipline these members.[27] Similarly, the union can discipline members who cross their own picket line during a strike. Remember, though, that a union cannot urge its members to engage in sympathy actions, despite the fact that individual members may be free to do so. Also, remember that the Supreme Court has held that a union rule which prohibited members from resigning during a strike is invalid, because it violates the employees' NLRA Section 7 right *not* to engage in concerted action.

5. A union is free to deny a person membership in the union, although this denial cannot be based upon characteristics protected by the Civil Rights Acts, such as age, race, sex, religion, etc.[28] If a union denies membership to a worker and the worker is willing to join, the union cannot then turn around and force the employee to pay dues as a financial core member. A person rejected as a member by the union becomes a legal free rider, represented by the union but not obligated to support it financially.[29]

We learned that a union cannot discipline its members unless it guarantees them certain due process rights. A union cannot make vague charges against a member; they must be specific. A member cannot be told that she engaged in behavior "unbecoming a union member" without being informed what this behavior was. A union member cannot be told today that her hearing is being held tomorrow. She must be given reasonable time to prepare his defense. Naturally, it is up to the courts to decide whether any specific time is reasonable. The worker must be given a full and fair hearing. This does not mean that the hearing must be administered by a neutral party. Most union charges against members are ultimately decided by other members of the union. A few unions, notably the United Auto Workers, have "Public Review Boards," neutral organizations to which an aggrieved member may appeal the final internal union decision.[30] Unions are certainly not required to have these. A member charged by the union does have the right to be represented at the hearing, though not necessarily by a lawyer, as well as the right to question all witnesses and to present her side of the story.

2. Union Elections

It was mentioned above that the Landrum-Griffin Act is enforced by individual (or group) lawsuits, except for Title IV, which regulates union elections. This is an important exception. In the 1970s the United Mine Workers Union underwent an intense internal struggle. The corrupt leadership of Tony Boyle, the successor to the great John L. Lewis, was challenged by former union officer Joseph "Jock" Yablonsky. An election for the presidency was held, but Boyle won. There was massive evidence of illegal procedures during the election, including open voting and fraud.[31] The insurgents challenged the election through complaints filed with the Secretary of Labor. The Department of Labor has complete control over what happens to such a challenge. Once workers have filed the complaint, they lose any control over the outcome. It is up to the Secretary of Labor to decide whether or not to file a court suit to overturn the election results. In the UMW case, the Secretary refused to act until after the Boyle-ordered murder of Yablonsky. Then, the Secretary ordered a new election, to be conducted with unprecedented scrutiny by the government. The Miners for Democracy movement ran Arnold Miller against Boyle, who had not yet been implicated in Yablonsky's murder. The government insisted that the campaign be run democratically and imposed some of the same rules that the court ordered in the Teamsters election. A government agent appeared at each place where voting took place to ensure secret balloting without intimidation. The Miller forces were permitted to have poll watchers at each site. The ballot boxes were handled as if they contained the gold in Fort Knox; they were never left out of the sight of the agent. As a result of this tight security, Boyle was easily defeated, and a new era of democracy began in the UMW. Unfortunately, the Department of Labor will not take such drastic measures often, irrespective of the need for them. If the Secretary of Labor decides that a new election is not needed, as he did in the unsuccessful bid by Edward Sadlowski to win control for the rank-and-file of the United Steelworkers Union, there are no further legal avenues available for the workers to pursue.

We noted above that Landrum-Griffin imposes certain reporting requirements upon both unions and employers. These are not too effective, but it is worth mentioning those imposed upon employers and consultants. Employers must make annual reports to the Secretary of Labor if they have made

> any agreement or arrangement with a labor relations consultant or other independent contractor or organization pursuant to which such person undertakes activities where an object thereof, directly or indirectly, is to persuade employees to exercise or not to exercise, or persuade employees as to the manner of exercising, the right to organize and bargain collectively through representatives of their own choosing, or undertakes to supply such employer with information concerning the activities of employees or a labor organization in connection with a labor dispute involving such employer, except such information for use solely in conjunction with an administrative or arbitral proceeding or a criminal or civil judicial proceeding.

Similarly, the consultants who undertake the activities described above have to file reports. Unions and their members have access to these reports, which might be valuable in identifying the consultant hired by their employer. Unfortunately, as we saw in Chapter Five, these reporting requirements are not all that useful.[32]

C. Unions and Civil Rights

We learned in Chapter Two that unions must obey the civil rights laws. It is sad but true that, 30 years after passage of the Civil Rights Act of 1964, unions often do not obey them. The biggest problems occur with respect to union treatment of women and persons of color. A look through the publications of the Association for Union Democracy presents a troubling picture of undemocratic unions refusing to open up their organizations to women and people of color. For example, in the mid-1960s the Department of Justice filed suit against Local 46 of the Ironworkers Union, and this case was taken over by the Equal Employment Opportunities Commission. (See Chapter Two for details of EEOC operations.) The EEOC caused the union to agree to a consent decree in which it committed itself to admit black workers into its previously segregated apprentice program and then into the union itself. A court-appointed monitor was to oversee the union's compliance with the decree. However, the monitor soon lost interest in the case, and today the situation is nearly as bad as it was when the original suit was filed. Black workers continued to file complaints with the NLRB because of the discriminatory operation of the union's hiring hall. The black workers who made it through the union-controlled apprenticeship program could not get the hiring hall to refer them to jobs. This is an unfair labor practice under the NLRA, but the NLRB has not taken action so far. Amazingly, the NLRB referred the workers to the Association for Union Democracy, which is now working with them to get some justice.[33]

What has been true for Local 46 is also true for hundreds of other locals in a wide variety of unions, and not just those in the construction trades, although these are notorious for their racist and sexist practices. Rank-and-file groups of women and workers of color are routinely harassed and intimidated by their unions. They are beaten up or threatened with harm, are placed under detective surveillance by their union, are cheated out of wages, are denied proper placement on seniority lists, are given excessive workloads, are given lousy work assignments. In some cases, shop stewards who support them are replaced. All of these actions are illegal; they either violate the unions' own constitutions and bylaws (in which case a worker might file a Section 301 suit or a civil suit against the union) or the NLRA (in which case an unfair labor practice charge might be filed) or the Landrum-Griffin Act (in which case a lawsuit might be filed). People of color and women workers who face such union problems will eventually have to get legal assistance. My best advice is to place a call to the Association for Union Democracy. See the questions and answers at the end of this chapter for further information. The laws can help, but good legal advice is necessary to know how to use them. The AUD can also provide assistance in helping rank-and-file groups to organize themselves more effectively.

D. A Few More Words on RICO

The RICO law is a powerful new weapon which can be used to clean up corrupt unions. While the Act does not specifically exclude private parties, such as union dissidents, from bringing suit under it, so far the government has initiated the legal proceedings against unions. For RICO to be used effectively to promote union democracy, it will be necessary for strong rank-and-file groups to be on hand to pressure the government to act in the interests of union members and for union members to take control of their unions once the courts have acted on RICO charges. Otherwise, nothing will change, even after RICO prosecutions. In addition, RICO charges might be filed against unions for actions in connection with normal union operations such as strikes, in situations in which violent acts take place. It might be the case that the NLRA would preempt RICO, but it is to be hoped that the courts would refrain from holding unions in violation of RICO unless corruption of the union has been demonstrated. In situations in which a union is abusing the rights of the members but is not infiltrated by organized crime, a vigorously enforced Landrum-Griffin Act could adequately redress the grievances of the members.

E. Conclusion

Books about labor law written from a labor perspective often give scant attention to problems of union democracy. The attitude seems to be that publicizing union corruption and autocracy gives aid and comfort to labor's enemies. The truth is just the opposite: ignoring the problem can only make it worse. In the best of circumstances, it is difficult to maintain democratic procedures and open debate in any organization. Those who attain power hate to give it up. Most unions, like most organizations, become more bureaucratic as they mature. The idealists who were their early leaders die; the problems they face become more complex and demand bureaucrats to deal with them; conditions move from one crisis to another, so that it appears that there is not time to debate things properly. The incumbents gradually convert the union into what has been dubbed a "one-party state." They structure the union so that it is very difficult for insurgents to defeat them. The United Auto Workers is often thought of as a democratic union; it is one of the few unions with a Public Review Board which acts as a supreme court for members brought up on charges by the union. Yet, the UAW's outgoing presidents have traditionally named their successors, much the same as do the outgoing presidents of

Mexico, a true one-party state nobody would mistake for a democracy. The UAW's incumbents' attitudes and actions toward the rank-and-file New Directions Movement should give pause to everyone concerned with union democracy.[34]

Most unions could use a dose of democracy, and some unions don't know the meaning of the word. The struggle for union democracy and the use of the laws (and the fight to get better ones) to strengthen it is at least as important as the fight for laws that will enable workers to organize unions more easily and negotiate good contracts. Large segments of organized labor were opposed to the use of RICO to end corruption in the Teamsters. Yet, without RICO, would it have been possible for Teamsters for a Democratic Union to accomplish this? And how many AFL-CIO leaders supported TDU in the first place?

III. Questions and Answers

Question 1: What can union members do if they believe that their pension fund is being mismanaged?

The management of pension funds is regulated by the Employee Retirement Income Security Act of 1974 (ERISA). ERISA is extremely complicated and has spawned literally thousands of articles in law reviews. However, it does place definite duties upon those who manage pension funds. In a typical case, a union fund is managed jointly by the employer and the union. In cases in which there are multiple employers, as in the construction industry, it is likely that top union officials will often be the chief trustees of the funds. Since these funds contain millions of dollars, they are a constant source of temptation to unscrupulous officials.

A detailed discussion of ERISA is beyond the scope of this book, but here we can note the main features of the law. First, ERISA provides that most pensions be "vested" after five years of work for one employer. A vested pension is one which is owned by the employee, and she is guaranteed some pension payment at retirement age whether or not she remains with this employer. Second, the Act requires that pension plans be adequately funded, with enough money set aside now to ensure that payments are made when employees retire. Third, certain types of pension plans, called "defined benefit plans," (see Chapter Two) are guaranteed by the federal government. Such plans are typically funded by employers and provide for specific (defined) benefits based usually upon years of service. In such a plan, a worker could calculate his pension benefits in advance, as opposed to a "defined contribution plan," in which the payments into the pension fund are defined and made in the name of the employee and then invested in stocks, bonds, etc. Defined benefit plans are guaranteed by the Pension Benefit Guarantee Corporation, which is funded by premiums paid by the pension plans and can also draw upon general federal government revenues.

Finally, ERISA requires that managers of a pension fund must do as would a "prudent man," that is, without taking undue risks and certainly without corruption. Either the Secretary of Labor or individual plan participants can petition a federal court for relief if a pension plan is being abused. The courts have broad enforcement powers and could order that the fund's trustees be removed and court-appointed trustees put in their place.[35]

Question 2: Does the Landrum-Griffin Act contain rules which define the method by which union officers are elected?

A typical union has three layers of authority: the national union, several intermediate bodies (councils or conferences of locals, for example), and local unions. Elections in local unions must be held at least every three years and must be by secret ballot of the members. In intermediate and national entities, elections must be held at least every four and five years, respectively. However, in these types of bodies, elections can be by vote of delegates. The delegates must be elected by secret ballot. These delegates are not required by the law to vote secretly; this depends upon the union's constitution and bylaws.

Question 3: Does Landrum-Griffin regulate the salaries of union officers?

No, these are completely controlled by the union's constitution and bylaws. However, union members have every right to enforce these, and to file suit against the union if they are violated.

Question 4: What information does a union have to file with the government under the Landrum-Griffin Act?

Here is a sampling of the information each labor organization must file with the Secretary of Labor:

1. A copy of its constitution and bylaws;

2. A report containing the union's name, addresses, name and title of each of its officers, initiation fees, dues, detailed statements of its rules and regulations for such things as qualifications for membership, discipline procedures, contract ratification procedures, strike authorization procedures, etc., and any changes in any of these items;

3. An annual financial report containing assets and liabilities, all receipts, all salaries in excess of $10,000, all loans to members, loans to any businesses, etc.

All of this information must be available to members. Members can file suit against their union if it refuses to make this available to them.

Question 5: What is the address of the Association for Union Democracy? What exactly does it do?

The AUD is located at 500 State St., Brooklyn, N.Y. 11217. Its phone number is (718) 855-6650. It is a nonprofit and nonpartisan organization devoted to the cause of union democracy. If you are having trouble with your union, you could not make a wiser move than to call or write the AUD. They can help you to organize a reform group, get proper legal help, learn about union democracy law, help you to prepare your case, etc. They also publish useful literature including the *Union Democracy Review* and numerous special reports, books, and pamphlets. They will also provide you with copies of Landrum-Griffin. I am a member, so if you contact them, tell them you learned about them through this book.

Question 6: Can unions make political contribution?

The NLRA in Section 313 prohibits unions from making direct contributions in "connection with any election to any political office." This includes primary elections and elections for the electoral college. Unions can establish political action committees funded by voluntary contributions from members or anyone else.

Question 7: What differences does it make if a bargaining unit member files a duty of fair representation charge with the NLRB or with a court?

One big difference is that an NLRB charge, if deemed meritorious (see Chapter Three), will be prosecuted by the General Council's office. This relieves the member of legal expenses, although it is possible that the member's own lawyer might participate in the hearing. In a court suit, the financial burden is squarely on the member. In both situations, the charge must be filed within six months of the violation.

The Board uses basically the same standards as the court, although the Board probably leans a little further toward giving a union the benefit of the doubt. Therefore, a member probably has a little better chance of prevailing in court than with the NLRB.[36]

Question 8: Are "financial core" bargaining unit members protected by Landrum-Griffin?

No, only full union members are protected. However, if a union arbitrarily denies a person membership, that person is still covered by the Act.

Question 9: Can a union exclude persons from running for office?

A union can exclude persons from membership, though not for any discriminatory reason such as race, sex, etc. A union generally cannot exclude members from holding office, but it can establish reasonable qualifications for office such as payment of dues on time. Attorney Bruce Feldacker advises union members to get the Department of Labor's pamphlet, "Electing Union Officers."[37]

The Landrum-Griffin Act prohibits certain persons from holding union office for periods of up to 13 years. These include "[any] person who is or has been a member of the Communist Party or who has been convicted of, or served any part of a prison term resulting from his conviction of, robbery, bribery, extortion, embezzlement, grand larceny, burglary, arson, violation of narcotics laws, murder, rape, assault with intent to kill, assault which inflicts grievous bodily injury, or a violation of Title II or III of this Act, or conspiracy to commit any such crimes." Presumably, a union could not exclude a person from running for office because of political affiliation except for membership in *the* Communist Party.

Question 10: Can union members petition a court for an injunction to prevent a union election from occurring?

No, Title IV allows complaints about election misconduct only through the Secretary of Labor and only *after* the election has taken place.

Question 11: Does a union have to allow rank-and-file ratification of collective bargaining agreements?

A union may have an internal provision for membership ratification, and if it does, members can sue to compel the union to obey it. But a union does not have to have such a rule.

Question 12: Can a union expel a member for attempting to get the union decertified?

Not only can a union expel a member for this, but it can also deny a member the right to speak about it at a union meeting. The NLRB has held that a union cannot fine a member for urging decertification.[38]

Question 13: Does a union member have to exhaust all internal union processes before filing a Landrum-Griffin charge against the union? What about a duty of fair representation charge? An NLRB unfair labor practice charge?

Many unions have procedures spelled out in their constitutions and bylaws for the handling of disputes between a member and the union. It is often, but not always, the case that the law or the courts in interpreting the law require a person to go through the union's internal procedure before filing a suit. The union constitution, itself, may require a member to exhaust all internal remedies before filing suit. The trouble is that this may take many months or even years, and a union facing a lawsuit has every incentive to delay internal hearings and appeals. Therefore, the law or the courts ordinarily set some time limit for internal proceedings, after which the member is free to sue whether or not the internal proceedings are finished. For Landrum-Griffin charges, this time period is four months, although the courts have the power to consider suits filed before four months. From a union member's point of view, it is wise to go through the union's internal procedures, making a complete record of everything that happens. If the member gets no satisfaction within four months and the prospects look dim for getting satisfaction in the near future, then it may be time to file a civil suit under Landrum-Griffin.

In duty of fair representation (Section 301) suits, the typical situation is the member's claim that a grievance hasn't been handled fairly by the union. Therefore, it is necessary that the employee file the grievance in the first place and pursue it through the grievance procedure. Then, when the union refuses to process the grievance further—for example, by refusing to take it to arbitration—the member has exhausted the contract's grievance mechanism and can file the suit. In another situation, the union may have constitutional or bylaw procedures through which a member can challenge the union's refusal to process the grievance. Or, the collective bargaining agreement may have an appeals right mechanism. A member may have to exhaust these appeals mechanisms if they could result in the reinstatement of the grievance. If they cannot, then a suit can be filed immediately.

In Section 8(b) charges filed against the union by a member, there are no exhaustion requirements. An unfair labor practice can be filed at any time within the six-month filing deadline.

Question 14: What are the advantages of a union "Public Review Board?"

Suppose that a union fines a member for behavior the union claims violates the union's constitution. The member objects to the fine, claiming that it was levied against her because she is a dissident in the union. She appeals the fine through the union's internal appeals procedure. There may be several levels in this appeals process; it may progress from the local union to the national union. In the end, however, the final disposition of the appeal will be made by people who are officers of the union. Of course, they may have a personal stake in denying the appeal. A Public Review Board consists of persons who are not members of the union, and the duties of the Board are to decide appeals from the final step in the union's internal appeals procedure. The advantages of such a Board are twofold: First, the member gets an appeal to persons who are likely to be more neutral than the union's officers, and second, the Board helps to reduce tension within the union. If the Board supports the union's original discipline, the union's officers do not have to take the heat for this decision. And if the Board supports the aggrieved member, this provides powerful evidence of the union's commitment to democratic procedures.

Question 15: Suppose that a union steward misses a contract deadline for processing a grievance. Does this give the grievant a foolproof argument in a duty of fair representation unfair labor practice or court suit?

No. If the steward can be shown to have missed the deadline intentionally, this would show a failure to represent the member. However, if the deadline is missed by accident or oversight, the union will probably not be found liable.

Question 16: Can an employee insist on having his own lawyer present at an arbitration hearing?

No. The contract and the union's certification as bargaining agent give the union the sole right to represent the member at the hearing. However, it is not unusual for the union to allow a private attorney at the hearing if the grievant requests it.

Question 17: How can a union avoid a duty of fair representation charge?

The best way is to investigate every grievance thoroughly and in a timely manner. The union should take every grievance seriously, listen carefully to the grievant's complaint, ask a lot of questions, keep careful notes of all meetings, follow as many leads as possible in investigating the grievance, and keep the member informed at all stages of the procedure. The union should have a grievance committee responsible for deciding whether to push the grievance forward, and an appeals procedure for the grievant would also be useful. A union should carefully train the representatives responsible for arbitrations; it is a good idea to engage in mock arbitrations before the real ones. Any doubts a union might have about processing a grievance should be decided in the member's favor.

IV. Selected Readings

1. H.W. Benson, *Democratic Rights for Union Members* (New York: Association for Union Democracy, 1979).

2. Kenneth C. Crowe, *Collision: How the Rank and File Took Back the Teamsters* (New York: Charles Scribner's Sons, 1993).

3. Michael J. Goldberg, "Cleaning Labor's House: Institutional Reform Litigation in the Labor Movement," *Duke Law Journal* (Sept. 1989), pp. 904-1011.

4. Jean T. McKelvey, editor, *The Changing Law of Fair Representation* (Ithaca, N.Y.: ILR Press, 1985).

Chapter 8

THE CONSTITUTION

I. Mr. Pickering's Letter

In the United States, the public school system is controlled by local government. In principle, local control gives the people control of what goes on in the schools that educate their children. In practice, however, this is seldom the case. Before the public schools were forced to racially integrate, black citizens had no say in school governance. The schools are run by Boards of Education elected by popular vote. This has meant that only those with the time and money to campaign for office have usually gotten elected. These Boards then select administrators to handle the day-to-day operations of the schools, creating a hierarchy pretty much immune to public accountability.

Within the schools, the teachers have historically had little power. The curriculum, the teaching load, the choice of textbooks, the methods of teaching, and so forth were either mandated by state school laws or dictated by the Boards and their administrators. Most teachers were poorly paid women, expected to do what they were told and to behave in ways deemed to be appropriate by the Board. It was not uncommon for school districts to require women to quit teaching when they married. All of this changed when teachers began their great union movement in the 1960s, but it is still the case that decision-making powers rest with the Boards, and it is still true that the average citizen exerts little influence upon school policy.

Marvin Pickering was a school teacher in a high school in Illinois.[1] A man of independent mind, he did not hesitate to criticize the Board of Education whenever it did something with which he did not agree. In 1961 the Board had asked residents to approve a bond issue of more than five million dollars to build two new schools. The citizens rejected a first request but approved a second one, and the schools were built. In 1964 the board put a tax increase before the voters to be used for educational purposes, but the board's request was twice turned down. The Board had engaged in active lobbying to get the tax hikes accepted, including letters to the local newspaper and to the voters. A letter attributed to the district's teachers' union supporting the tax increase also appeared in the newspaper.

It is in the context of autocratic public school administration that Pickering's case is instructive. After the voters defeated the board's tax proposal, Pickering wrote a letter to the local newspaper sharply criticizing the board. He accused it of mishandling the district's money, lavishly spending money on athletics while neglecting academics. He said, "To sod football fields on borrowed money and then not be able to pay teachers' salaries is getting the cart before the horse."

Further, he accused the board of strong-arming the teachers into supporting the tax increase. He said, "To illustrate further, do you know that the superintendent told the teachers, and I quote, 'Any teacher that opposes the referendum should be prepared for the consequences.' I think this gets at the reason we have problems passing bond issues. Threats take something away; these are insults to voters in a free society."

After his letter was published, the Board met and agreed to fire Pickering for writing it. The Board accused Pickering of making false accusations against board members, damaging their professional integrity. Further, the board said that Pickering's letter would disrupt school administration by fomenting "controversy, conflict and dissension" within the district. It would also disrupt faculty discipline.

Mr. Pickering filed a lawsuit in state court challenging his discharge on the grounds that it violated his free speech rights. The court ruled against him, refusing to consider his speech rights. When he took the job, the court reasoned, he had agreed not to openly criticize his employer. The state supreme court agreed with the lower court's decision, so Pickering petitioned the U.S. Supreme Court to hear his case.

II. The Constitution and the Rights of Workers

A. Introduction

In previous chapters we have seen that working people have won a wide range of statutory rights: the right to form a union; the right to bargain collectively with their employers; the right to strike and picket; and the right not to be discriminated against for their race, sex, religion, national origin, age, or disability. But what if a worker is not specifically protected by any statute? Do workers have rights not spelled out in any statute? There is no national law protecting gay workers. Do they have any rights? There are no statutes giving workers a general right to speak their minds in their workplaces. Are there circumstances in which they can do this?

There are two sources of potential nonstatutory worker rights. These are the Constitution and the common law, and these are the subjects of this and the following chapter. Typically, what protections the Constitution and the common law offer workers are individual protections rather than protections for groups or classes of workers. An individual employee will most likely have to act on his own behalf to get justice, although there is no reason why a worker cannot make his problem the focus of a larger group's concern.

B. The Nature of our Constitution

Our Constitution was written in 1787; since then the original document has been amended 26 times. While the Constitution is usually discussed in a reverential tone, it is well to remember that it was written by white men (no women or black persons), most of whom were merchants and large owners of land and slaves. These men constructed a document which has some universal appeal but which largely reflected their private interests.[2] The benefits that working people derived from the Constitution were the result of struggles. For example, working people supposedly have always had the same First Amendment right of free speech as everyone else. But in reality, in mining towns and industrial communities throughout the nation, a worker spoke up at her peril. The Industrial Workers of the World organizers had to be willing to be beaten and jailed to win the right to speak in public parks.[3] And, it took the Civil War to get the Constitution amended to end slavery and provide rights for black men and women. So, do not assume that your constitutional rights will automatically be upheld, either by the police or by the courts. On the other hand, do not ignore the Constitution; it can and has been used on occasion to empower working people.

The Constitution is the basic "law of the land." It does not lay out the laws in any great detail but instead spells out the basic rights of the people as well as the nature of our institutions of government and the principles by which these institutions are organized. For example, the

Constitution establishes a Congress to enact legislation and a Supreme Court to decide, among other things, whether the laws enacted are supported by the Constitution. The amendments are of special importance to working people, notably the first ten, which are called the "Bill of Rights." These and several related later amendments guarantee us specific rights with respect to our government. That is, they state that we can do certain things without government interference, or put another way, they prohibit the government from interfering with our guaranteed rights. Notice that the Constitution protects us from government restriction. It says nothing about restrictions placed upon us by private parties. For example, suppose that a person works for Wal-Mart at one of its many retail outlets. She is a strong supporter of gun control and talks about this issue with her coworkers. Her supervisor belongs to the National Rifle Association and does not approve of her point of view. He tells her to stop talking about gun control, and when she refuses, fires her. She can't believe this. What about "free speech?"

Unfortunately, her employer is not bound to respect her freedom of speech or any other right guaranteed by the Constitution because the Constitution only says that the government must respect her freedom of expression.

The Constitution says little about the relations between private parties. It is silent on the relationship between private employers and their employees. The Congress and state legislators may be free to regulate it by statute, and the common law may regulate it as well. But it is outside of the protection of the Constitution. The basic reason for this is that the framers of the Constitution did not want to restrict the powers of private business, as a matter of constitutional principle. Instead they were more comfortable leaving this power in the hands of the common law and Congress, knowing that our system of checks and balances would make it very difficult to unduly restrict the power of private businesses. Judges have historically been strong allies of business, which has given the common law a powerful business bias. Eventually, business came to be dominated by gigantic corporations. These corporations use their great wealth to control the legislators responsible for enacting laws which might protect workers. As we have seen, only in extraordinary times and with extraordinary efforts have working people been able to bend the courts and the lawmakers to their wills.

C. The First Amendment

In 1787 few people were employed by the government, but today public employment is widespread. There are more than three million federal government workers and some 14 million employees of state and local governments. A public employee enters into a special type of relationship with his employer because his employer is the government itself. Remember, the Constitution forbids the government from acting in ways which deny us our constitutional rights. This means that in public employment, the government cannot act as an employer so as to deny public employees their constitutional freedoms.

Perhaps the most famous of the amendments to our Constitution is the First Amendment. It says that "Congress shall make no law respecting an establishment of religion, or prohibiting the free exercise thereof; or abridging the freedom of speech, or of the press, or the right of the people peaceably to assemble, and to petition the Government for a redress of grievances." This amendment guarantees us, among other things, freedom of speech. This is one of our great rights, won through the struggles of thousands of forgotten people who insisted upon exercising it, often in the face of considerable private and public repression. During the "Little Steel" strike of 1937, the mayor of Braddock, Pennsylvania declared that Jesus Christ would not be allowed to give a pro-union speech in a public place in his town.[4] A lot of union organizers were arrested there and in towns across the country to prove otherwise.

Speech includes not just spoken words but written words and symbolic speech such as the wearing of arm bands or even the burning of the flag. Pickering's letter to the newspaper was clearly speech, and his employer was an agent of local government. Therefore, he argued that since the Board of Education fired him for writing the letter, it was unconstitutionally denying him his freedom of speech.

Before looking at the Supreme Court's decision in Pickering's case, we must note two things. First, the First Amendment mentions only Congress and not state and local governments. However, the Fourteenth Amendment, passed after the Civil War, states that "No State shall make or enforce any law which shall abridge the privileges or immunities of citizens of the United States; nor shall any State deprive any person of life, liberty, or property, without due process of law; nor deny to any person within its jurisdiction the equal protection of the laws." What this does is demand of the states the same respect for our rights as the first ten amendments demand of the federal government. Therefore, a school board can no more abridge the freedom of speech than can

Congress. Second, Mr. Pickering could make a constitutional claim only because he was a public employee. Had he worked for General Motors or another privately owned business, he could not have protested his discharge on constitutional grounds. This is something most people do not realize, but when workers go through a private factory gate, the Constitution must be left on the sidewalk.

The Supreme Court ruled in Mr. Pickering's favor, declaring that "Public school teachers may not constitutionally be compelled as a condition of retaining their employment, to relinquish the First Amendment rights that they would otherwise enjoy as citizens to comment on matters of public interest in connection with the operation of the public schools in which they work."[5] By implication, this would give free speech rights to all public employees. However, the Court did not make such speech rights absolute. Instead it established a "balancing test," in which it would weigh the speech rights of the public employee against the rights of the public employer to run its workplace efficiently. In other words, the speech of the workers must not interfere with the smooth functioning of the school or hospital or police department.

This balancing test approach is commonly used by the Supreme Court; its effect is to limit the rights of public employees because it allows for the possibility that the Court will give undue consideration to the "rights" of the employer. As we shall see, this has been the case with the current, ultraconservative High Court. In decisions after Pickering, the Supreme Court has upheld public employee speech rights in some cases but not in others. A black teacher's First Amendment rights were violated when she was fired for criticizing the racist practices of her employer. She made her comments in private to her supervisor, but the Court held that this did not make any difference.[6] In another case, a clerk in a county constable's office, on hearing about the attempted assassination of President Reagan, commented to a coworker that "If they go for him again, I hope they get him."[7] When told about her remark her boss fired her. Again, the Supreme Court held that her freedom of speech had been violated. Here, though, the Court based its decision upon the facts that her comments were made only to a coworker on the spur of the moment and she herself was not a law enforcement officer. Otherwise, the Court probably would have allowed her discharge to stand.

The following case demonstrates the limits which the courts might place upon the free speech rights of public employees. A woman was an assistant district attorney in Louisiana, and she had performed her job competently for five years. Her supervisor told her that she was being reassigned to different duties, and she protested. When told that her coworkers did not share the concerns she had raised about the office's personnel policies, she circulated a questionnaire to the other employees. This questionnaire asked what her coworkers thought about a variety of working conditions, including some aimed at throwing a bad light upon the district attorney. One of the questions asked if employees "had confidence in and would rely on the word" of their superiors. On the day the questionnaire was circulated, the woman was fired for insubordination. The Supreme Court refused to declare her discharge a violation of her First Amendment right of free speech.[8] The Court argued that she had distributed the petition mainly for her personal reasons (to prevent her reassignment) and to embarrass her boss. By circulating it during working hours, she had disrupted the work routine and potentially caused antagonisms and hostility in a small workplace in which the workers had to interact in a direct and personal way with their supervisors. While some of the questions implied wrongdoing on the part of the district attorney and this might have been of concern to those who had elected him, overall the Court felt that these considerations were outweighed by the employer's rights to discipline his subordinates and conduct business in an efficient manner.

When the courts rule that an employee's constitutional rights have been violated, they might not also rule that the employee be reinstated. In the *Pickering* case the Supreme Court remanded the case (sent it back) to the lower court for a ruling consistent with its decision.

D. The Fourth Amendment

The Fourth Amendment to the Constitution gives public employees potentially important protection, but as we shall see, the U.S. Supreme Court under Reagan and Bush has diluted its clear intent to the point of making it meaningless. The amendment says, "The right of the people to be secure in their persons, houses, papers, and effects, against unreasonable searches and seizures, shall not be violated, and no Warrants shall issue, but upon probable cause, supported by oath or affirmation, and particularly describing the place to be searched, and the persons or things to be seized." As with the First Amendment, public employees are protected, as employees, by this amendment.

Within the workplace, the most obvious application of the Fourth Amendment is drug testing. Everyone knows that drug use is rampant in the United States, and no wonder, given the stress of daily living in this most competitive of societies. Of course, drug use is often dangerous, both to the drug users and to society as a whole. No one wants to be robbed or killed by a desperate addict or transported in a plane piloted by someone who is drunk. There is no doubt that there is a drug problem and that public policies are needed to deal with it. Yet our own government's policies are questionable, to say the least. Instead of trying to eradicate the gross poverty and inequality which inevitably lead to drug use, and instead of trying to create a less stressful society where people do not need drugs to cope, our government has instead declared a "war on drugs." This war is aimed at those who use and distribute drugs, and denies that social conditions have anything to do with drug use. As in any war, civil liberties and basic democratic principles are discarded in the name of the government's right to protect the "national security."

One of the basic assumptions of the "war on drugs" is the need for and the right of employers to test their employees for drug use. Employers demand that workers give up their urine, blood, and hair follicles to be examined for signs of drug use. No matter that these tests yield many "false positives," are clear invasions of privacy, and cannot guarantee safety or whatever else it is that the employer wants. This is a war, and anything goes, most especially our freedoms. When we buy into this sort of thinking, we are agreeing that the end justifies any means, a dangerous proposition. As former Supreme Court Justice Thurgood Marshall said in an eloquent dissent, "History teaches that grave threats to liberty often come in times of urgency, when constitutional rights seem too extravagant to endure. The World War II relocation-camp cases, and the Red Scare and McCarthy-Era internal subversion cases, are only the most extreme reminders that when we allow fundamental freedoms to be sacrificed in the name of real or perceived exigency, we invariably come to regret it."[9]

Drug testing of employees is widespread today. A 1987 survey found that about 40% of companies test either current or prospective employees, and of the remaining businesses, more than half are seriously considering a drug testing program.[10] Of course, as we have learned, workers in the private sector enjoy no constitutional protection against actions by their employers, but what about public employees?

If we take the Fourth Amendment at face value, public employees would seem to enjoy considerable protection. Before their desks could be searched or their bodies probed for drugs, the government would have to have "probable cause" that something illegal is or is about to be occurring. "Mere suspicion or belief, unsupported by facts or circumstances, is insufficient."[11] Once probable cause has been established, the public employer would have to obtain a search-warrant from a justice or magistrate giving the employer permission to conduct the search. This would seem to mean that a public employer could not randomly search an employee's locker or desk or compel an employee to take a drug test. The Supreme Court has, on rare occasions, dispensed with the warrant and probable-cause requirements and applied a "balancing test." As Justice Harry Blackman put it, these could be dispensed with "when special needs, beyond the normal need for law enforcement, make the warrant-probable cause requirement impracticable."[12] It would seem that random searches could never be the subject of this exception.

Unfortunately for public employees (and for the public in general in contexts outside of the workplace), the Supreme Court has greatly widened the situations in which it applies a balancing test. It has given increasing weight to the public employer's right to conduct its business efficiently and to the government's "compelling need" to address certain social problems, such as drug use or violence in the schools. It has correspondingly given decreasing weight to the privacy rights of public employees. Most remarkably, it has uncritically accepted the government's arguments concerning its operations as employer and its definition of compelling needs. In other words, the government can say, without proof, that drug use in the workplace is widespread and very dangerous, and, therefore, the government has a compelling need to ensure that public employment be drug free and to conduct random drug searches to ensure that it is.

A wide range of intrusive actions by public employers has been given Court approval under the balancing principle over the past dozen years. In one case, a physician at a state hospital was accused of various improprieties, including the improper acquisition of equipment and the sexual harassment of employees under his supervision. While on administrative leave pending investigation of the charges against him, his employer searched his desk and seized personal items which were later used against him in his discharge hearing. This seizure took place without either probable cause or a warrant. The Supreme Court held that the seizure did not violate the Fourth Amendment, because the employer's right to operate its workplace without the undue burden which getting a warrant in every such case would entail outweighed the doctor's right to privacy in his personal papers.[13] Exactly what burden is placed upon the employer in a situation such as this is not clear, but as the dissenters in the case imply, a public employee's privacy rights are not held in high regard by the current Supreme Court.

Two 1989 cases further eroded the Fourth Amendment rights of public employees. In the first, the Federal Railroad Administration, which regulates the nation's railroads, issued a rule through the Secretary of Transportation mandating that railroad employers conduct blood and urine tests of all workers involved in certain train accidents. Another rule allowed but did not require the employers to conduct drug tests of workers who violated certain safety rules. The railworkers' unions filed suit in federal court claiming that such drug tests violated the Fourth Amendment.[14] Note that the rule mandates tests for *all* workers in certain situations whether or not there is any suspicion by the employer of drug use and without a warrant. This would appear to clearly violate the Amendment's probable cause requirement. In the second case,[15] the United States Custom Service ordered mandatory drug tests for all employees seeking transfers to positions involving the interdiction of drugs or who would handle firearms or classified documents. Again, the tests would be conducted without probable cause and without a warrant. In both cases, the Supreme Court said that the tests did not violate the Fourth Amendment, declaring that the government's compelling need to combat drug use justified the tests. So much for the right to privacy!

Lower court decisions after 1989 have not been encouraging.[16] Random drug testing has been allowed in so-called "safety sensitive" jobs such as piloting planes or trains and in law enforcement occupations such as police and prison guards. We have not reached the point yet where, say, public school teachers could be randomly drug tested, but we are not too far away from this. With most federal judges having been appointed by Presidents Reagan and Bush, public employees should look for further erosion of their constitutional rights.

E. The Fifth and Fourteenth Amendments

These two amendments are more complex than the First and the Fourth, but they have been of great importance in the history of labor law. Basically they say that the federal government (by the Fifth Amendment) and state and local governments (by the Fourteenth Amendment) must give all of the people "due process" and "equal protection." By due process we mean that people's rights will be protected through their right of access to certain legal procedures. For example, if I am accused of committing a crime, I have a right to a trial by jury of my peers. Similarly, the government could not take my property without cause and without paying me compensation. Due process rights apply to businesses, including corporations, as well as to individuals. Equal protection means that "no person or class of persons shall be denied the same protection of the laws which is enjoyed by other persons or other classes in like circumstances in their lives, liberty, property, and in their pursuit of happiness."[17]

In labor law, due process rights have been most important in determining the constitutionality of certain statutes, a topic which we will address later in this chapter. Equal protection, on the other hand, may be an important right of individuals. Equal protection guarantees that public employers cannot discriminate against public employees on the basis of race or sex. Like all of the rights protected by the Constitution, equal protection is not absolute. The courts may allow exceptions in special circumstances. Let us say that a government agency has set up a classification such that it treats people who are mentally retarded in a different manner than it treats other persons. The courts look at such classifications in terms of the notions of "suspect" and "quasi-suspect." If a classification is "suspect," then the government can use it only if it can show that there is a "compelling" reason for it. If a classification is "quasi-suspect," it can be used only if there is a "substantial" reason for it. If an employee can argue that discrimination by her public employer against her is suspect or quasi-suspect, then the courts might rule the discrimination unconstitutional.[18]

Classifications by race or by sex are suspect, so racial or sexual discrimination by a public employer is unconstitutional. The same is true for classifications by national origin and alienage (discrimination against noncitizens). Classifications by age and mental ability are not, however, suspect classifications, so a public employer may be able to discriminate against an older person without violating the equal protection clause (note that there may be statutory protection for older workers as well as for other groups whether in the suspect category or not).

Recent litigation has tried, unsuccessfully, to extend the list of suspect classifications to other groups of people. Probably the most important cases have involved the issue of sexual orientation. Can the government discriminate against gay employees without denying them equal protection? Right now the answer is yes. The United States Army did not violate the equal protection clause by discriminating against gay soldiers even if they had not engaged in homosexual acts.[19] A gay public employee may have a right to due process before being discharged, but this is a weaker right than would be guaranteed if sexual orientation were declared to be a suspect class. Given that gay persons have faced tremendous hostility and violence, that sexual preference is something over which a person has little control, and that sexual preference has little if anything to do with job performance, the courts should give it greater constitutional protection.

We discussed in Chapter Two the problem of discrimination against gay employees (and many other groups), but one final point can be made here. If a public employee merely speaks out against the treatment of gay persons, this speech would be protected by the First Amendment. It would be unconstitutional for the public employer to discriminate against the speaker.

F. The Thirteenth Amendment

The Thirteenth Amendment says that "Neither slavery nor involuntary servitude, except as a punishment for crime whereof the party shall have been duly convicted, shall exist within the United States, or any place subject to their jurisdiction." This amendment was enacted at the end of the Civil War to abolish slavery, but it also bans involuntary servitude. This means that a worker cannot be compelled to work against his will. A worker always has the right to quit, and this is true whether the employer is public or private, since involuntary servitude is abolished everywhere within the United States.

Can an individual's right to quit be extended to a group? Does the Constitution protect the right to strike? This would be a reasonable interpretation of the Amendment, but the courts have not thought so. As we have seen, there have been and are many restrictions placed by the laws upon strikes, and these restrictions have not been found to be unconstitutional. In fact, many workers are prohibited from striking at all.[20]

III. The Constitution and the Rights of Groups of Workers

The Constitution offers some protection for the actions and characteristics (such as race and sex) of individual workers, but the same cannot be said for actions taken by groups of workers. There is no general constitutional protection for strikes, pickets, or boycotts, the three most common collective actions taken by working people. The Supreme Court is willing to say, for example, that a public employer cannot fire a worker for the mere act of joining a union, but the Court will not say that a public employer must consider a grievance filed by one of its unionized employees. Similarly, the Court agrees that the Thirteenth Amendment prohibits involuntary servitude, but it does not agree that this amendment protects the right of a group of workers to strike.

While the Constitution offers no general protection to the actions of groups of workers, it may prohibit the government from enacting statutes which prohibit certain types of group actions. In 1939 the state of Alabama passed a law which banned all picketing and made it a criminal act. For participating in labor picketing, a worker named Byron Thornhill was arrested and sentenced to either a fine of $100 or three days in prison. The state supreme court upheld his conviction, but the Supreme Court overturned it in 1940 and declared the Alabama law unconstitutional. The Court ruled that picketing was a form of speech and was therefore protected by the Fourteenth and the First Amendments.[21] Any state statute which outlawed all picketing was, therefore, unconstitutional. Labor advocates hailed this as a landmark civil rights ruling, giving picketing the protection of speech. This was, as we have seen, in direct opposition to the way in which most courts had previously viewed picketing, and soon the Supreme Court, itself, backed away from its *Thornhill* decision. Since 1940, the Supreme Court has allowed the states to place many restrictions on peaceful picketing, although it is still unconstitutional for a state to ban all picketing.[22]

Similarly, a state law outlawing all strikes by private employees would not be constitutional. Consider, for example, the Sherman Antitrust Act, which we have seen was used by employers to attack unions. Employers argued that union actions such as boycotts restrained trade by keeping goods from being moved across state lines. Of course, any successful strike does just this. If automobile workers in Detroit shut down a GM plant with a strike, the cars produced in that plant will obviously not move out of the state. The Supreme Court would not conclude that a peaceful strike by employees against their own employers was a violation of the Sherman Act, however, because to do so would clearly run up against the Thirteenth Amendment.[23] Again, though, the courts have allowed great regulation of the right to strike, and in the case of public employees, have allowed both federal and state governments to prohibit them altogether. Federal government workers cannot legally strike. As the Air Traffic Controllers found out, striking is a sure way to lose one's job.

A third example concerns certain secondary labor activities. We know that most secondary actions are illegal and subject to severe penalties, but in a recent important ruling the Supreme Court held that at least one type of secondary activity enjoyed constitutional protection, although it did not say so directly. In this case, examined in Chapter Six, primary strikers passed out leaflets at a Florida shopping mall, urging people not to patronize the mall because they had a dispute with one of the mall's tenants. The Court held that to make this leafleting illegal would most likely be a violation of the First Amendment right of freedom of speech.[24]

The early labor statutes, such as the Norris-LaGuardia Act and the National Labor Relations Act, the two most important labor laws ever passed, had to pass constitutional muster.[25] Both laws were enacted in the 1930s during the Great Depression. Before this, Congress and state legislatures had passed a wide variety of laws aimed at protecting working people in one way or another. Invariably, the Supreme Court struck down these laws as unconstitutional. In some cases the Court held that Congress had no power to make such laws, implying that only the states could do so. But when the states did enact labor legislation, the Court ruled that these laws violated the employer's property rights because they denied employers the due process guaranteed by the Fifth and Fourteenth Amendments. By such logic the Court struck down child labor laws, laws which outlawed "yellow dog" contracts (these made the absence of union membership a condition of employment), laws which regulated the issuance of injunctions in labor disputes, laws which regulated the hours of work, and a wide variety of others.[26] Although popular and political pressures forced the Supreme Court to change its anti-labor ways in the 1930s and afterward, it still has the utmost respect for the "rights" of employers. It is certainly not the best vehicle a worker can use to address a wrong done to him by his employer.

IV. Questions and Answers

Question 1: Do "whistleblowers" have any constitutional protection?

Whistleblowers make the public aware of illegal or otherwise immoral behavior by their employers. Whistleblowers working in the private sector do not enjoy constitutional protection; however, whistleblowers in public employment do have constitutional rights. After all, Pickering was a whistleblower. I doubt that all whistleblowing would be protected by the First Amendment. A public employer might be able to argue that the whistleblowing greatly interfered with its right to efficiently manage the workplace. This would probably be a better defense in a situation in which the whistleblower was not in a position to have direct knowledge or expertise about the employer's wrongdoing.

Question 2: What happens after an employee wins constitutional protection? How, for example, could Pickering get his job back if his employer refused to reinstate him?

The Constitution does not contain an enforcement mechanism in cases such as this. Ordinarily, after the Court rules, it sends the case back to the lower court (remands the case) for a new ruling in accord with the law which it has laid down. Also, it is not uncommon for Congress to pass laws specifically to enforce constitutional rights. For example, Congress passed the nation's first Civil Rights Acts in 1866, 1870, and 1871 to give meaning to the recently enacted Thirteen, Fourteenth, and Fifteenth Amendments to the Constitution. These Acts and ones similar to them, such as the Civil Rights Acts of 1964 and 1972, not only give employees and other persons certain protection but they also include enforcement mechanisms such as the right to file suits or the declaration that violations of the Acts are crimes. Certainly a common law suit filed against an employer for wrongful discharge (see Chapter Nine) would be greatly strengthened by the fact that the discharge had been declared unconstitutional.

Question 3: What determines whether a law is unconstitutional?
The simplest answer to this question is to say that this is up to the nine justices on the Supreme Court. A law is unconstitutional if a majority of the justices declare it to be so. However, it is more complicated than this. Some justices say that they judge laws according to the intent of the "founding fathers" who wrote the Constitution. This ordinarily means that the justice is a conservative who will take an anti-labor point of view. Others say that the language of the Constitution must be judged in light of current social conditions. This more elastic view is more likely to result in opinions which respect the rights of workers, although this need not be the case.

It is important to understand that the Supreme Court is a political institution and is therefore influenced by the distribution of political power. A good example of this was the Court's deliberations on the constitutionality of the National Labor Relations Act.[27]   Given the previous history of labor legislation in the United States, it was a most remarkable piece of legislation. Employers assumed, with good reason, that the Court would promptly declare the law to be unconstitutional. The Court had struck down laws much less invasive of the rights of employers to conduct their labor relations in an unrestricted manner. It had agreed that industries such as steel were not really engaged in "interstate commerce" and could not be regulated by Congress. It had also agreed that the regulation of labor relations interfered unconstitutionally with the employer's property rights, which include the right to make whatever "contract" with its workers with which it could get the employees to agree.

Despite its previous decisions, the Supreme Court ruled that the National Labor Relations Act was constitutional. This decision can only be understood in the context of the tremendous political agitation of organized labor, especially the occupations of the nation's factories by workers conducting the famous "sitdown strikes." Had the Court held the new law unconstitutional, these strikes would have spread with who knew what consequences. The justices were not willing to risk the radicalization of the working class, so they ruled in its favor despite their past practices. This story tells us again that strong organization is the best way to pressure the Supreme Court. Even a Court comprised of reactionary justices is not immune to political reality.

V. Selected Readings

1. Richard C. Cortner, *The Jones & Laughlin Case* (New York: Alfred A. Knopf, 1970).

2. Jerry Fresia, *Toward an American Revolution: Exposing the Constitution and Other Illusions* (Boston: South End Press, 1988).

3. Jules Lobell, editor, *A Less Than Perfect Union: Alternative Perspectives on the U.S. Constitution* (New York: Monthly Review Press, 1988).

4. James Gray Pope, "Labor and the Constitution: From Abolition to Deindustrialization," *Texas Law Review* 65 (May 1987), pp. 1071-1136.

Chapter 9

AT-WILL EMPLOYMENT

I. My Brother Gets Fired

In February 1992 my brother was fired from his job as an optician at a Pearle Vision store in Butler, Pennsylvania. He had been a diligent employee for two years, working long hours, often without pay, not only making lenses and waiting on customers but also overseeing the bookkeeping and stocking operations. He had often been commended by the physician who owned the store, and he was a favorite with the customers who occasionally sent unsolicited letters praising his work. At the time of his discharge, he was earning about $25,000 per year with minimal fringe benefits. His wife was about to deliver their third child. They did not have any money to spare, but they were getting by.

As is common for most jobs these days, the work of an optician offers limited prospects. Most of the employers operate on a small scale with fewer than 20 employees, mostly women except for the opticians and perhaps an optometrist. There is a good deal of competition in the industry; there may be several stores selling eyeglasses in a single shopping mall. The key to a profitable operation is to pay low wages and to get as much work out of the employees as possible. There is considerable employee turnover, but this is not a major problem for employers because it is not difficult to train new employees to do the unskilled work of waiting on customers and fitting the glasses, and there is also a ready supply of opticians, either newly trained or looking for another job, to do the skilled work. All of these circumstances usually make for a poor work climate. People know that they can be easily replaced, so they are afraid to complain about low wages, long hours, and poor working conditions. Employers keep a vigilant watch over their workers, usually through a network of spies, who are employees promised benefits or promotions if they report to the boss any "disloyal comments" or talk about unionization by their coworkers. It is not uncommon for promises to be made to several employees, who then, in effect, spy on each other.

The owner of the store suspected that some workers were stealing supplies. In fact, about a year before his discharge, my brother had informed him that, after the departure of a former employee, a lot of stock was missing. The employer, probably on the advice of his lawyer, a man who had been snooping around the four stores owned by the physician, claiming to be the employer's accountant, decided to find out who was stealing from him by demanding that all employees submit to a lie detector test.

Several workers discussed the lie detector issue with my brother who advised them to refuse to take one. He told them that it was against the law for an employer to make the taking of a lie detector test a condition of employment.[1] A couple of them consulted lawyers who told them the same thing; they told my brother that they were going to refuse to take the test. As it turned out, however, all of them eventually agreed to take a polygraph examination. My brother was the only one to refuse. A short time later he was notified at the end of his workday that he was terminated. He went home in a state of shock.

No reason was given for his discharge by the store manager, but eventually the owner told my brother that he was fired for "willful misconduct," but on the advice of his attorney, the owner would not elaborate. My brother called him several times trying to get some explanation but was repeatedly given the run-around. He called me seeking advice. I had some ideas, but I consulted a labor attorney I knew to make sure I was on the right track. Together, we worked out a plan of attack.

First, my brother filed an unemployment compensation claim. The unemployment compensation system is controlled by federal law, first enacted during the Great Depression in 1935. The system is administered, however, by the states. It is financed by a percentage tax on the payrolls of employers. The tax rate depends upon how many successful claims are made by a particular employer's workers; the fewer the claims, the lower the rate. Not all workers who lose their jobs qualify for compensation. Today, in fact, only about 40% of all unemployed workers receive payments.[2] First-time job seekers and workers discharged for "good cause" do not qualify. Many public employees are not covered by the system. Other employees qualify according to how long they have worked for their employer, and the actual payments depend upon earnings in some prior time period. The best way to find out if you qualify is to file a claim. You can find out the location of the office nearest you by looking in the phone book under the "State Government" listings for something like the "Bureau of Employment Security."

Once a person files a claim, the employer has a right to contest it. Since the taxes that the employer pays depend upon the claims filed, the employer has an incentive to challenge claims. My brother's boss naturally challenged his claim, and a hearing was scheduled to determine if he was indeed fired for cause. In the meantime, the employer began to pressure my brother to agree not to take any legal action against him. He promised he would drop the unemployment compensation challenge and continue my brother's health insurance until his baby was born. To turn up the heat, he also claimed that he had two other employees willing to testify at the hearing that my brother had been using drugs on the day that he was fired! My brother made a careful record of these events as well as of his past work history. He found and filed the doctor's prescription for the bronchitis medication he had been taking, the so-called "drugs" he was accused of using. It is important for workers to keep a written record whenever they have problems at work. If you can, get a witness to sign your notes. Your records will be important in any legal proceedings.

My brother refused to agree to any deal, and as it turned out, his employer was bluffing about the drugs. He did not show up for the compensation hearing, and my brother was able to convince the case worker that he deserved to receive unemployment compensation. He began to get his weekly checks about two months after he was discharged. In Pennsylvania, payments are made for a maximum of 26 weeks, but the U.S. Congress extended benefits for a second 26 weeks because of the poor state of the national economy. The actual amount of money which a person collects in weekly benefits varies by state and by the amount of prior earnings, but on average, it equals about a third of pre-unemployment earnings.

In the meantime, my brother began several other actions. It is illegal under both federal and many state laws for an employer to make the taking of a lie detector test a condition of employment. The federal law is administered by the U.S. Department of Labor, so an employee has to contact the nearest office to file a complaint. In Pennsylvania it is a criminal offense to compel employees to take lie detector tests, which means that a complaint must be made to the district attorney. My brother filed both federal and state charges and waited for the appropriate offices to take action. He has had a long wait. After repeated calls, it became clear that no charges were going to be made against his employer. Perhaps the reason was the absence of a "smoking gun" such as a direct order to take the test; perhaps it was negligence. In any case, if the agency or office charged with enforcing the law will not take action, there is really nothing the employee can do.

We learned from our lawyer that it was possible that my brother's discharge may have violated the National Labor Relations Act; since he had discussed the lie detector tests with coworkers, he may have engaged in protected "concerted" activity.(See Chapter Four.)

II. At-Will Employment and Wrongful Discharge

A. The Common Law

The most important action taken by my brother was the filing of a lawsuit against his employer claiming that he was wrongfully discharged. Most workers in privately owned businesses are unaware that there is a good chance that they are "at-will" employees. This means that they are employed at the will of the employer and can be discharged for any reason or no reason at all.

The doctrine of at-will employment is part of what is called the common law. We had occasion to look briefly at the common law in Chapter Three, where we saw that the common law was historically biased against workers. The common law is defined as "the body of those principles and rules of action, relating to the government and security of persons and property, which derive their authority solely from usages and customs of immemorial antiquity, or from the judgments and decrees of the courts recognizing, affixing, and enforcing such usages and customs."[3] In the United States this common law was inherited from the British legal system. There, judges made decisions in cases brought before them without the benefit of written laws, or statutes, to guide them. Suppose, for example, that there were no written laws governing the legal relationships between two people living together as husband and wife but not formally married. The man abandons the woman, and she demands a part of the property they shared while they lived together. As such cases were brought before judges, they began to develop legal principles to deal with them. As these principles began to be followed by more and more judges, the concept of "common law" marriage took root.

In the United States, the common law is state law and therefore differs from state to state. It is important to understand that common law is made by judges; it is whatever they say it is. This means that it changes when they want it to change. If the way in which judges are placed into office changes so that the social-class backgrounds of the judges change, then it is certain that the common law will change. If the political climate in the state or in the nation changes, then the common law will probably change as well.

B. The Origins of the Doctrine of At-Will Employment

The common law doctrine of at-will employment was first used by judges in the 1870s.[4] Before that, employment contracts, including those without written agreements, were assumed to be of some duration. For example, farm laborers were hired for one year, so that the farmer could not discharge the worker after the harvest and the worker could not quit during the harvest. After the Civil War, however, the nature of our economy underwent a drastic change. Large plants using complex machinery began to replace small workshops, and unskilled labor began to replace skilled craftsmen. To extract as much profit as possible from the giant mills, their owners hired many more supervisors and engineers. To prevent this latter group from exercising power in the enterprise and to maintain the flexibility to meet changing market and technological developments, employers needed maximum control over their workers. This meant that contracts guaranteeing their employees at least some notice before being discharged were no longer tolerable. In 1877 an Albany, New York, lawyer named Horace Gray Wood wrote a book about employment law in which he argued in favor of at-will employment. The state courts were quick to change the common law, reflecting their subservience to the wishes of the manufacturers. Within 20 years, at-will employment was the law of the land. A Tennessee court put it bluntly: An employer can terminate employment "for good cause, for no cause, or even for cause morally wrong."[5]

At-will employment gives the employer tremendous power over the employees. A long-term employee, who has a great stake in keeping a job, can lose everything in an instant at the will of her boss. Under the at-will doctrine, a worker could be fired for asking for a raise, for being of the wrong religion, for refusing to have sex with the foreman, for joining a union, for doing or saying anything the employer did not like. A fired worker has no legal recourse. She could look for another job and hope for the best. There is no such thing as wrongful discharge.

C. Exceptions to the At-Will Doctrine

It is important for workers today to understand that at-will employment is still the law of the land. Ther are millions of employees who can be fired without just cause and who can do nothing legally about it. Recently a nurse in an Altoona, Pennsylvania hospital had to take a leave to receive treatment for cancer. She was informally promised that she could return to her old job when she had recovered. But when she did, her employer refused to reinstate her. She sued and lost. The court expressed sympathy for her situation but ruled that her employer's promise was not strong enough to outweigh the state's at-will employment assumption. It is estimated that at least 150,000 persons are discharged each year in the United States for reasons a reasonable person would consider unjust.[6]

While there is a good chance that any given worker could lose her job and be unable to do anything about it, the situation is not as bleak today as it once was. Employees now enjoy some statutory protection against unfair discharge, and state courts have begun to carve out some common law exceptions to the at-will rule. The statutory exceptions have been explained in detail earlier in this book, so it is sufficient just to list them now. It is illegal by statute for an employer to fire a worker for any of the following reasons: attempting to form or joining a labor union, being too old, being a member of a racial minority, being a woman, having a disability, being of a certain ethnic background or religion, and, as we have just seen, for refusing to take a lie detector test. If you suspect that you were fired for any of these reasons, read the relevant sections of this book.

As we said above, the common law changes as the times change, and the at-will doctrine is no exception. As federal and state statutes were enacted which protected workers from certain types of unjust discharges, state courts became more willing to consider other kinds of unfair firings. In 1959 a California court ruled that it was wrong for the Teamsters Union to fire one of its own employees because he refused to commit perjury on the union's behalf at a legislative hearing.[7] Another court declared it to be illegal for an employer to discharge a worker for refusing to participate in an illegal price-fixing scheme.[8] Similarly, courts held that employees were wrongfully discharged for serving on juries, filing workers' compensation claims, and "whistle-blowing," that is, reporting to the appropriate authorities that their employers had violated laws or were producing unsafe products.[9]

Situations such as these have come to be known as the "public policy" exception to at-will employment. The basic idea is fairly simple.

It is the public policy of the United States, as spelled out in the criminal law, that jurors and others giving testimony under oath must not commit perjury. Yet what would be the point of such a public policy if an employer could legally fire a worker who upheld this policy by refusing to lie under oath on the employer's behalf? Likewise, it is the public policy of all of the states, as reflected in their workers' compensation laws, that workers have the right to file compensation claims when they are injured at work. It would surely be strange if workers had such a right but their employers were free to fire them for exercising it. This "public policy" exception is the basis of the lawsuit my brother is now in the process of filing against his employer. There are both federal and state statutes prohibiting an employer from coercing a worker to take a polygraph test. Therefore, it violates public policy (as well as the statutes, themselves) for an employer to dismiss an employee for refusing to take one.

If you are fired for a reason similar to the ones described above, you can probably sue your employer. Most states have recognized the "public policy" exception, and even if your state has not, it might be ready for a change. The type of suit filed in such a case is called a civil suit, and what the employer is accused of doing is committing a "tort." A tort is a civil as opposed to a criminal wrong, and a worker sues his employer for money. You are accusing your employer of inflicting intentional harm upon you by causing you to lose your job. This is not a crime, and your employer will not go to jail for it. But you have a right to be "made whole" for the harm your employer has done to you. Thus, workers fired in violation of some public policy can sue for the earnings (wages and fringe benefits) they have lost. In addition, in this kind of case, a jury has the power to award the wrongfully discharged worker money for pain and suffering as well as punitive damages. For example, a jury might agree that my brother suffered considerable emotional stress when he was fired given that his wife was about to give birth to their third child. The fact that his employer also broke the federal and the state polygraph laws might justify the awarding of punitive damages, that is, a money penalty to ensure that the employer will not be likely to do the same thing again. Awards in such suits can be very large; a study of *all* wrongful dismissal jury trials in California between 1980 and 1986 found that the average punitive damages alone exceeded $500,000.[10]

There are two other common law exceptions to the at-will rule, not as generally accepted as the public policy exception and typically not as likely to result in a large settlement. The first of these is called the "malice and bad-faith" exception. It rests upon the notion that when a worker accepts employment, it is legitimate that she also assumes that she will be treated with good faith. Such an assumption is similar to the one which a tenant has when she rents an apartment and assumes that the landlord has made it habitable. The courts have come to recognize that the habitability of an apartment is implied by the lease and does not have to be explicitly stated. Suppose that a worker is fired right before she was to receive a commission for past work. Or, suppose a female employee is discharged for refusing her foreman's sexual advances. In a case in which I testified as an expert witness, a television reporter had made a contract with the station that when he retired, he would not go to work for a rival station. In return, he would be paid a sum of money each month for a period of years. He was fired, and as a result, the employer did not have to honor the contract. It is reasonable in all of these cases to argue that the employer violated the good-faith behavior implicit in the (unwritten) employment contract. As the Supreme Court of New Hampshire put it, "a termination by the employer of a contract of employment at will which is motivated by bad faith or malice or based on retaliation is not in the best interest of the economic system or the public good and constitutes a breach of the employment contract."[11]

An employee who claims that her discharge was the result of the employer's bad faith or malice will have a tougher case to win than one who makes a public policy claim. Not many states recognize this exception, and in states which do recognize it, employees may not be able to get money in excess of actual lost earnings.

The last common law exception to at-will employment is the "implicit contract" exception. Here, there is a claim that it was the intent of the employer not to fire workers except for just cause or there was an intent to employ the worker for at least some specified period of time. Some employees will, of course, have detailed written contracts which spell out the obligations of the employer. Such employees are not at-will employees in the first place. A good example would be professional athletes. When the Chicago Bulls contract with Michael Jordan to play for them for three years at several million dollars per year, they will have to pay him this money even if they "fire" him in the second year. Most workers, however, do not have written contracts. How, then, could there be an "implied contract?"

Some state courts, but by no means all, have found an implicit contract to apply in several situations.[12] Suppose an employee is hired with a yearly salary of $25,000, and this employment is renewable each year. The employee works under this arrangement for 15 years without a problem. In the first month of the 16th year, the employee is fired.

Some state courts would hold that the employer had broken the implied agreement to employ the worker for a full year. In other words, it was the intent of the parties that this be a yearly employment, the intent supported by the "yearly" salary and the long period of time over which this arrangement was used by the parties. An employee's claim in a case like this would be stronger if the employee had made some special sacrifice on behalf of the employer in order to take or to keep the job. If the worker had given up a better job to take this one or turned down a more desirable job or contributed money to the business or moved to a new location at the employer's request, it may be reasonable to imply from these "extra considerations" that the employment was not at-will but for some duration. Oral promises of lifetime or secure or permanent employment could support an implied contract claim.

Another variation of the implied contract exception can occur if the employer has instituted due process procedures. For example, suppose the employer has written an employee handbook which includes a formal or informal grievance procedure available to the employees. The implication of such a procedure is that workers cannot be fired except for cause, and a worker suddenly discharged could file a breach of contract suit against the employer for not being allowed to use the grievance procedure. As a result of successful suits filed by workers on the basis of promises made in company handbooks,[13] employers now usually include disclaimers in the handbooks. Here is a model disclaimer clause:

> This is not a contract of employment. Any individual may voluntarily leave employment upon proper notice, and may be terminated by the employer at any time and for any reason. Any oral or written statements or promises to the contrary are hereby expressly disavowed and should not be relied upon by any prospective or existing employee. The contents of this handbook are subject to change any time at the discretion of the employer.[14]

An employee facing such a disclaimer will probably not be able to file a successful breach of contract suit.

The "malice and good-faith" and the "implicit contract" exceptions to at-will employment are fundamentally different from the "public policy" exception. A discharged employee accusing an employer of violating a public policy is accusing the employer of committing a tort or civil wrong. Under tort law, the employee can win not only backpay but also large punitive and pain and suffering damages. The other two exceptions are covered by contract law. An employee sues the employer for breaking a contract. Here the damages are ordinarily confined to back wages; pain and suffering and punitive damages are not allowed. These cases are more difficult to win and are recognized by far fewer states than the public policy exception.

III. A Final Word

The weakening of the at-will employment rule over the last three decades has been a good thing for workers. The threat of a lawsuit and large awards make some employers more cautious about firing workers for no compelling reason, and this enhances the security of all workers. However, the victory is not as great as the reader might be imagining. Workers thinking about challenging their at-will status should be mindful of the following pitfalls. First, the burden of fighting an employer is upon the worker. The typical fired worker will not have a lot of money to pursue legal action against the employer, but the typical company will have plenty of money. This means that the worker will have to find an attorney willing to work on a "contingency fee" basis, that is, willing to pay the legal costs in return for a percentage of the award if the suit is successful. Since the legal costs may be high, lawyers will not usually take such cases unless they think there is a good chance of winning a significant amount of money. Because the amount of money sued for has to be based upon the actual earnings of the discharged worker, it is natural that lawyers will be more attracted to suits filed by higher-paid employees. In fact, most of the successful challenges to at-will employment have been mounted by managerial and professional employees, probably those workers who need protection from unjust discharge the least.

Second, though awards in some suits are very large, many are not, and when the lawyer's cut is subtracted, not much money is left for the worker who suffered the harm in the first place. In the previously cited California study, the fired employees received on average only 44% of the jury awards.[15] In another study of cases settled out of court, which happens in more than 90% of all cases, the employees received on average the grand sum of $18,000, while the attorneys got an average of $37,000. As is so often the case in lawsuits, the attorneys end up with most of the loot. In addition, a case may drag on for years, leaving the employee frustrated and angry.

Third, the lawsuits in at-will litigations are for money and not for reinstatement. A fired worker is not going to get her old job back. Of course, this is not necessarily a bad thing because a reinstated employee may face harsh treatment from an employer who has just had to pay her a lot of money. Nonetheless, a person might want the job back; it is no easy matter to find a job as good as the one you once had, especially if you had it for awhile. In a new job, a worker has to start at the bottom, learn the ropes all over again, and perhaps move to a new community away from family and friends.

Fourth, in these cases the fired worker is acting alone, isolated from his coworkers. We have a much better chance of winning justice at our places of work when we mount collective efforts against our employers. It is better for individual workers to have an organization, with supporters and resources, to back them up when they do battle with their employers. For example, workers in a unionized workplace are, by definition, not employees at will. Why? Because they have a collective bargaining agreement which states that employees cannot be fired (or demoted or reassigned to dangerous jobs or discriminated against in any other way) without "just cause." A discharged worker automatically has the right to file a grievance against the discharge, and the union is obligated to push the grievance forward. Ultimately an arbitrator can be called in to decide whether there was just cause for the dismissal. If the arbitrator decides that there is not, the worker will be automatically reinstated with full backpay and seniority. And the union will still be there to make sure that the reinstated worker is treated fairly once back on the job. The mere existence of the grievance procedure and the just cause provision makes it a lot less likely that the employer will unjustly fire a worker in the first place. My brother can sue his employer, and he may eventually win something. But he is acting alone, without support from coworkers and union. He may not be able to get current employees to testify on his behalf because they will fear reprisals. Had there been a union, the outcome would have been different.

IV. Questions and Answers

Question 1: Who qualifies for unemployment compensation?

Since the unemployment compensation system is run by the states, the answer will vary from state to state. Some workers are generally excluded from coverage, such as those employed in agriculture and domestic service. Others, such as railroad workers and employees of the federal government, may be covered by other systems. State and local government employees are covered in some states but not in others. Employers not covered by their state law may still elect coverage for their employees. No matter who your employer is, you should apply for compensation when you lose your job. Let the Bureau of Employment Security, or whatever the appropriate office is in your state, decide whether you qualify.

If you work in covered employment, you may still be ineligible for benefits. To qualify, you must have earnings above some minimal amount during four of the last five quarters (three-month periods). Again, the employment office will get the appropriate information from you and from your previous employers to see if you are eligible.

Finally, whether or not you qualify for compensation depends upon the reason why you are unemployed and whether or not you are now available for work. You cannot generally collect benefits if you are on strike, if you are collecting benefits from another state, or if you have recently exhausted a previous benefit claim. You cannot collect benefits if you voluntarily quit your job without good cause or if you have voluntarily retired. You cannot collect if your employer fired you for good cause such as willful misconduct.

Question 2: What should I do if my claim for unemployment benefits is turned down?

If you were turned down because you did not meet some requirement of the law such as you were in an uncovered type of employment or your past earnings were not large enough, there is not much you can do. However, if you quit your job or if you were fired, then you should probably appeal the decision. If you quit because your employer created intolerable working conditions for you, you still qualify for benefits. If your employer's claim that you were fired for good cause is false, you still qualify for benefits. In either case you will have to convince the referee who conducts the appeal hearing of the merits of your arguments. Make sure you have records such as letters or a log of phone calls and conversations which support your case. You can bring witnesses to the appeal hearing and an attorney as well. Make sure you know the appeals procedure for your state; ask the office for a copy of the appeals procedure. Most likely you will have 15 days from the date of the initial rejection of your claim to appeal. Be aware that if your claim was accepted, your employer can also appeal. You will be notified by mail of the date and time and place of the appeal hearing. You can request a delay of the hearing (and so can your employer), but you have to have a good reason. A request for a delay may or may not be granted.

The appeal hearing is conducted much like a hearing in a courtroom. Your employer has a right to be present, with an attorney, to call witnesses, to cross examine you and your witnesses, and to present documents into evidence. The appeal referee can also ask both parties questions.

The decision of the appeal referee can also be appealed, to a Board of Review, again within some maximum time period such as 15 days. The Board can simply review all of the relevant documents from the appeal hearing and make a decision, or it can conduct a hearing of its own (but no new evidence can be presented to the Board), or it can send the case back to a referee for reconsideration (for example, to receive new evidence). Either you or your employer can request that the case be sent back to a referee. Once the Board has made its decision, either party has 15 days to ask the Board to reconsider its ruling.

Once a Board decision has been made, either party can appeal this decision to the appropriate state court. If you do this, you will need an attorney.

Question 3: If I suspect that I am going to be fired, is there anything I can do to protect myself?

First, keep good records of all communications between yourself and your supervisors, including letters, conversations, phone calls, etc. If possible, get a witness for each communication, someone willing to verify what happened. Keep independent records of your work performance in case your employer argues that it was below average. Second, you may want to confront your employers directly to see if you can get them to say that your performance is satisfactory or that they do not plan to fire you. Of course, this can be risky, so use caution. Third, make sure that you discuss your situation with other employees. This might make it possible for you to file an unfair labor practice with the National Labor Relations Board or some similar state agency. For example, suppose that you have been complaining loudly about how cold it is at work. If you discuss the lack of heat with coworkers and you are then fired for complaining so much, you can probably file an unfair labor practice charge, which might get you reinstated with back pay. However, if you act alone and do not discuss your complaint with anyone else, you cannot file such a charge.

Question 4: How do I go about finding a good attorney to sue my former boss for wrongful discharge?

This can be a problem, especially in small towns, where no lawyer may be willing to take on a powerful employer. You might get recommendations from the American Civil Liberties Union or the National Lawyers Guild or the local American Bar Association. Shop around and be aggressive. You should ask a lot of questions from any attorney you are considering to represent you. Make him or her lay out a plan of attack and tell you honestly what your chances of success are. Be sure to get the fees worked out in advance. If the lawyer is going to work on a contingency fee basis, you should not have to put any or much money up front. Make sure you have agreed upon the attorney's percentage of any award. Set up a schedule of times for the lawyer to give you progress reports. If you are unhappy, let your lawyer know it. Do not be afraid to get another attorney if you find you cannot work with the one you have. Do not hesitate to ask the attorney how many wrongful discharge cases she has handled and what the outcomes were.

Question 5: I have been fired for publicly stating that my employer is dumping poisonous chemicals into the local river. What legal actions can I take against my employer?

You are what is called a "whistleblower." You have many possible legal protections, some by way of the common law and some by way of statute law. Your most likely common law protection is the public policy exception to the at-will employment rule. Your employer has probably violated both federal and state laws by its dumping. That is, there is a public policy against it, so your firing is a violation of public policy. Therefore, you can sue your employer for violating the public policy against illegal dumping. However, the court will have to be convinced that you were in a position to know that your employer was violating the law. For example, you will have a lot better chance of success if you were an environmental engineer with direct knowledge of your employer's waste disposal practices than if you were a production worker without such direct knowledge. If, to take another example, a worker claims that his employer's soon-to-be-marketed new drug is unsafe and is fired, he will be much more likely to win a suit if he was involved in the testing of the drug than if he had been a drug salesman.

You also may have statutory protection. There are many statutes which protect whistleblowers. Some of these laws apply to all workers and not just to whistleblowers. For example, if you ask the Occupational Safety and Health Administration to check into safety hazards at your workplace, it would be a violation of the Occupational Safety and Health Act for your employer to fire you. The same is true of many other statutes, including the National Labor Relations Act. Other statutes apply only to whistleblowers. At the federal level, the Whistleblower Protection Act of 1989 protects federal government employees against retaliatory discharges for whistleblowing. This Act protects only civil service employees, although similar legislation offers other federal workers, such as certain Defense Department workers, some protection as well.

Most states also have whistleblower laws, but these vary widely in terms of which workers are covered and which acts are protected. Some states have statutes which specifically protect public employees, while others have laws which cover all whistleblowers. Some state laws require the whistleblower to report the alleged wrongdoing to management first, while others insist that it be reported to some public body. Most states consider "violation of any federal or state rule or law" as the subject of whistleblowing, but some are more restrictive. Rhode Island's law includes only "violation of laws regarding toxic waste." There is great variation of remedy among the state statutes as well, ranging from simple reinstatement with backpay to these plus attorney's fees and fines levied upon guilty employers.[16]

A recent development in whistleblowing cases is for the employer to offer the whistleblower a cash settlement in return for a promise by the employee not to testify in any investigation of the employer's alleged wrongdoing and by the employer not to blacklist the worker for "causing trouble." Of course, if you agree to such a deal, you are letting the employer get away with the illegal actions which moved you to blow the whistle in the first place. Unfortunately, a lot of money may be hard to resist. Such deals ought to be made illegal, but to date, with the exception of the Nuclear Regulatory Commission, this is not the case.[17]

V. Selected Readings

1. Marvin J. Levine, "The Erosion of the Employment-At-Will Doctrine: Recent Developments," *Labor Law Journal* 45 (Feb. 1994), pp. 79-89.

2. Daniel P. Westman, *Whistleblowing: The Law of Retaliatory Discharge* (Washington, D.C.: BNA Books, 1991).

Chapter 10

HEALTH, SAFETY, WAGES, AND HOURS

I. The Clothes that We Wear

Not far from where I live, there is a block of fancy shops. People with money to spend flock there on the weekends to buy clothes at stores such as The Gap and Esprit. These companies have won a reputation as socially conscious businesses, donating large sums of money to environmental causes and instituting a wide variety of benefit programs for their employees. Esprit has taken a strong pro-choice stand for women, and its customers can buy its line of "socially and environmentally aware" clothing.[1] Another company, Levi Strauss & Company, prides itself not only on its many philanthropic endeavors but its above-average wages and benefits. As journalist Elizabeth Martinez put it:

> Levi Strauss makes grants to labor groups and community organizations around the country, and recently initiated a new grants program aimed at 20 foreign countries to fund entities that supposedly work on issues like social justice, combating racism, economic development. As an employer, its wage scale, vacation periods, and other benefits are often better than elsewhere in the garment industry.[2]

The public image of these corporations is one of "capitalism with a human face." Consumers can buy these products and investors can buy these stocks without guilt.

The clothing market is very competitive, so the "we are a socially conscious company" image can be seen as an advertising strategy aimed at convincing the marginal customer to buy Levi or Gap jeans rather than the close substitutes produced by other companies. That the image has little basis in reality can be seen if we look at the way these companies supply themselves with the final products they sell. One of Levi's most popular and heavily advertised products is "Dockers" pants. Originally, these pants were made in Honduras by women trained by the United States' Agency for International Development and paid much less than $1.00 per hour by their Honduran contractor. Later the contracting was shifted to Costa Rica to take advantage of still cheaper labor.[3]

While much of the contracting and subcontracting work critical to the profitability of the garment industry is done overseas, this is by no means always the case. There are thousands of contract shops in the United States, including subcontracting operations which farm out the work to women who do the sewing in their homes, often with the help of their young children. Ironically, the workers are often Hispanic women who did the same work in their homelands. For example, as the U.S.-sponsored war waged by the fascist government of El Salvador against its own people denied Salvadorans the ability to make a living, millions of them fled, often to the United States. Here they can be found in large numbers in Washington, D.C., New York, Los Angeles, and our other major cities doing our most onerous work.

Consider the cases of Elena and Phuong. (These names and the stories are fictitious, but the events are typical.) Elena migrated north from Guatemala, first to a refugee camp in Mexico, then into Mexico City, and finally into Los Angeles. She fled her rural village in Guatemala after army troops had defeated the guerrillas. The soldiers killed many villagers, including her husband and two of her children, to set an example for others. She has heard that the United States overthrew the only Guatemalan president who ever cared for the likes of her, but there are jobs in the North and she has other children to support. Although she lives in the city as an undocumented worker, she is working for a garment subcontractor.

Her workplace is a small and ugly store whose windows are covered with butcher paper. Inside, "she sits on a metal chair to which successive layers of cushioning have been added—a cloth, a thin pillow tied to the back, a little thicker one on the seat.... Her forefingers and thumbs are swollen out of proportion to the other fingers, and their heavily calloused skin is fissured with deep cracks."[4] She is not allowed to talk to her coworkers, nor can she go the bathroom. The room is poorly ventilated, and it is freezing in winter and sweltering in summer. Elena and the 30 other women who operate the sewing machines take work home every night. On a dress that sells for $100, she will earn $1.72. Her wage rate is seldom equal to the legal minimum of $4.25 per hour and has been as low as $1.00. She has gone weeks without getting paid at all; it is not uncommon for the contractors to declare bankruptcy, close shop without paying the employees, and then reopen under a different name at a new location.[5] There are 22,000 shops like Elena's in the United States and more than one million workers like her, illegally paid less than the minimum wage and laboring in unsafe working conditions.[6] It is not unusual for the workers to be literally locked into their workplaces. Journalist JoAnn Wypijewski tells us that "in New York City, locked exits is the second most common safety violation."[7] The Occupational Safety and Health Act of 1970 (OSHA) makes such abuses illegal, but the Act is poorly funded and enforced. In New York City, garment shops are a priority of the local OSHA office, but in 1993 it inspected a mere 118 of the city's more than 4,000 shops.[8] Terrible tragedies, like the Triangle Shirtwaist Company fire in 1911 and the Imperial Foods fire in 1992, are waiting to happen. In the latter fire, 25 workers were incinerated and 56 were injured, unable to exit the locked doors. When employees do file OSHA complaints, they are often illegally fired. OSHA seldom prosecutes employers for this, though the Act clearly makes it illegal to fire whistleblowers (see Chapter Nine). As two investigators put it,

> If they file on time [under OSHA, workers have only 30 days to file a complaint after they have been terminated for using the Act], workers must rely solely on the Labor Department to investigate and determine if discrimination has occurred. With no time restraints on evaluating the complaint, whistleblower cases languish in a bureaucratic black hole. Of over 5,000 cases found to have evidence of whistleblower discrimination by the Reagan and Bush Labor Departments, only eight were litigated on behalf of whistleblowers.[9]

Phuong's story is much like Elena's. She came to the United States after the war in Viet Nam, finally settling in New York City where she joined the ranks of Asian workers in the kitchen of a large restaurant. The work is hot and dangerous, the floors often slippery and wet. She had to pay a contractor to get the job, and one of many Asian gangs stands ready to intimidate the workers should they complain. Phuong works 60 to 70 hours a week without overtime pay, and her hourly wage is about half of the $4.25 legal minimum. She would like to get a green card and eventually become a citizen, but this will cost a lot more money than she can ever hope to accumulate. In the meantime, she keeps a wary eye out for the Immigration inspectors who will have her deported if they catch her.

One of Phuong's coworkers has told her about a local "workers' center." The Chinese Staff and Workers' Association is an organization helping Asian workers to organize within their communities to confront employers and any other issues important to them. The Association helped the workers at the Silver Palace restaurant, "Chinatown's most prestigious banquet restaurant." There the workers managed to form a union with the Association's help and against great odds. When the restaurant decided to drastically cut wages and replace full-time workers with part-timers, the union protested and the restaurant locked them out. The Association helped them to organize picket lines and to build coalitions with other progressive groups, which helped them to picket and to raise funds. They aggressively spotlighted their employer's violations of health and safety and wage and hours laws as well as those of most other restaurants. They declared Chinatown a "Disaster Zone for Workers." "Twice-daily pickets featured a mock coffin—a symbol of bad luck that resonated strongly in the Chinese community." The Association supported a boycott, filed NLRB charges, sued the restaurant in state court for stealing tips, and notified the IRS of the restaurant's tax evasion. After seven months of struggle, the employer capitulated and agreed to a new contract.[10] Phuong has heard from one of her relatives in California that the unions are not interested in Asian workers,[11] but this new grassroots organization looks like one that might help her and her coworkers confront her own employer.

II. The Fair Labor Standards Act

A. Introduction

During the Great Depression, a minor revolution took place within the field of conventional economics. Led by the great English economist John Maynard Keynes, the profession came to see that one reason why a capitalist economy might become mired in a depression is because the masses of people do not have enough money to spend to make it worthwhile for employers to produce a large quantity of goods and services. Such an idea, though not as elegantly formulated as the Keynesian theory, was common among working people and, in the heady days of the 1930s, won quite a few converts in Congress. If employers were forced legally to pay a minimum wage rate, the increase in incomes for those currently making less than this minimum would increase total spending in the economy and stimulate production and employment. Further, if employers had to pay a higher wage rate to workers when the workers labored for more than a certain number of hours in some period of time, they would find it more desirable to hire more workers and thus reduce unemployment. Finally, if the labor of children were restricted, then adults would have more jobs, since employers could not substitute cheaper children for them.

In 1938, Congress put these ideas into a statute, the Fair Labor Standards Act. This statute has been amended many times since 1938, and several companion statutes have also been enacted.[12] These amendments include:

- The Equal Pay Act (see Chapter Two)
- The Portal-to-Portal Pay Act, which regulates whether or not an employer has to pay an employee for activities before and after the employee's main work duties. For example, the requirement that a mining company pay its employees from the time they enter the mine to the time they leave it, that is, from portal to portal
- The Walsh-Healey Public Contracts Act, which regulates employment conditions under public contracts. Under this Act, employees must be paid the "prevailing minimum wage rate" as determined by the Secretary of Labor
- The McNamara-O'Hara Service Contract Act, an act similar to Walsh-Healey except that it covers employees working for contractors supplying the government with services as opposed to goods
- The Davis-Bacon Act, which requires the payment of "prevailing minimum wage rates" for workers employed by construction contractors, that is, those working on public buildings, and
- The Contract Work Hours and Safety Standards Act, which regulates employer practices in situations covering "mechanics and laborers employed on any public work for the federal government and employees performing services similar to those of mechanics and laborers in connection with the dredging or rock excavation in any river or harbor of the United States or the District of Columbia."

In what follows, we limit the discussion to the Fair Labor Standards Act.

B. Basic Provisions

1. Minimum Wages

All employees covered by the Act must be paid at least the minimum wage rate for all of their hours of work. The current minimum wage rate is $4.25 per hour. Three questions arise here: which employees are covered, what is counted as wages, and what are counted as hours of work. The Act's very broad coverage includes nearly all employees engaged in interstate commerce, either directly or indirectly (this means that they engage in production of goods and services destined for interstate commerce or work for firms that are local in scope but are part of businesses which themselves are engaged in interstate commerce). State and local government employees are also covered by the Act. However, there is a complicated list of exceptions to the minimum wage provision. Among the groups exempted from it are employees in certain amusement and recreational establishments, apprentices, domestic workers not covered by the Social Security Act, workers in gasoline stations which do less than $250,000 in annual sales, certain disabled workers, certain newspaper carriers, outside salespersons, professional, executive, and administrative personnel, certain retail establishment employees, seamen on foreign vessels, certain agricultural employees, and workers at small telephone exchanges.[13] A subminimum "training" wage may be paid to teenagers between 16 and 19 years of age for a period of 180 days but not for more than 90 days by any one employer. The training wage must be at least 85% of the regular minimum wage.

The minimum wage rate must be paid whether the employee is paid by the hour or on a piece rate basis. In the latter case, the weekly wage divided by the hours worked must equal the minimum wage rate. In either case, the wage is usually paid in money, but this is not always so. The minimum wage must be paid in cash or in "facilities furnished." Facilities furnished include meals furnished at employer restaurants or cafeterias, housing furnished for living purposes, fuel, utilities, and transportation during time which is not subject to the payment of the minimum wage. The employee must be aware that the facilities furnished are a part of the wage and must agree to this arrangement, and the facilities furnished must be customarily furnished by the employer.[14] Employees who regularly receive income in the form of tips can be paid less than the minimum wage, with the tips making up the difference. Today, an employer can take a tip credit of 50% of the minimum wage; that is, it can pay the worker one-half of the minimum wage.

In deciding the hours for which an employee must be paid the minimum wage, the courts (see section on enforcement) look at "whether the employer knew that the employee was engaged in such activity, whether the employee was specifically ordered to refrain from such activity, and whether the activity benefitted the employer."[15] Hours of work before and after what might be called "regular" work (as in the coal mining situation described above) are covered by the Portal-to-Portal Pay Act. Difficult cases arise when employees are on-call for their employer. It makes a difference whether the employee was "waiting to be engaged" or "engaged to wait." The later time is compensable while the former is not.[16]

2. Overtime

Covered employees must be paid at a rate one-and-one-half times their regular hourly rate of pay for all hours worked in excess of 40 hours per week. Note that an employer is not required to pay overtime for hours worked in excess of some amount per day. Therefore, an employee who works four ten-hour days in a week is not entitled to overtime pay. State and local government employees can be paid with compensatory or "comp" time from work instead of being paid in cash for overtime hours. However, there are maximum amounts of comp time that can be paid, and after these amounts have been reached, cash must be paid. Comp time must be paid the same as cash in the sense that one hour of overtime must be paid with one-and-one-half hours of comp time.

As with the minimum wage provision, some employees are exempt from the Act's overtime requirements. Most of these are the same as the minimum wage exemptions, although the overtime exceptions are both more numerous and complex. Executive, administrative, and managerial employees are exempt, as are outside salespersons and taxicab drivers.[17] However, an employer cannot simply declare that employees are managers, or administrators; their classification will depend on the actual work they perform.

Overtime is based upon the employee's regular rate of pay, so it is important to know what that regular rate is. This can be tricky if an employee is not paid on a strictly hourly basis for all of the hours she is compensated. Suppose that I get paid $3,000 in a particular month plus $1,000 in vacation pay or bonus pay. I worked 160 hours in the month. Should my regular rate of pay include the vacation or bonus pay? If it does, my regular rate of pay will be much larger than if it does not. These types of payments are not included in rate-of-pay calculations, but wages, salaries, commissions, piece rates, shift premiums, cost-of-living allowances, hazardous duty premiums, etc. are included.[18] Special provisions are made for employees whose workweek hours fluctuate above and below 40 hours per week if neither the employer nor the employees can control the number of hours worked.

3. Child Labor

The child labor provisions of the Act are the most complex of all. The major provisions are:[19]
  • Children under 14 are not allowed to work in any occupation or enterprise covered by the Act. There are some exceptions, includ-

ing actors and actresses, newspaper carriers, and some farm workers. Generally, this work must be done outside of school hours.

- Children between 14 and 16 cannot work in manufacturing or mining or as machine or motor vehicle operators. They also cannot work in construction, transportation, warehousing, or communications. There are, however, numerous exemptions and exceptions. A Department of Labor book, *Child Labor Regulations*, gives a list of permitted jobs for this group.
- Children between 16 and 18 cannot work at jobs declared to be "hazardous" by the Secretary of Labor. Some of these are mining, sawmilling, roofing, and excavation.

Child labor has become increasingly common in the United States, largely because the Act's child labor prohibitions are rarely enforced. A child must obtain a work permit to get employment, and an employer is bound to have a copy of it. Many employers don't bother with this requirement, and many do not hesitate to illegally hire children because they know that the Act will not be enforced against them. I once made a complaint to the Department of Labor, and I was told that nothing was likely to happen as a result of my complaint, and even if it was discovered that the employer had violated the law, nothing beyond a discussion with the employer was likely to take place.

C. Administration and Enforcement

The Fair Labor Standards Act is administered by the Department of Labor through its Wage and Hour Division. A typical case would begin with an employee or group of employees or any interested party making a complaint with the nearest office of the Wage and Hour Division. There are offices throughout the country and in all major cities. A complaint can be made by phone. The complaint will then be investigated by the office. Employers are required by the Act to keep records of the wages paid to and the hours worked by all employees. The Division and the courts do not look favorably upon employers without adequate records, so it is probably to the employee's advantage if the employer does not have such records because the employee's records might then be accepted. If an employer violation is found, the employer will be notified and an attempt will be made to get the employer to pay the monies owed. If no agreement can be reached, the Secretary of Labor can file a suit in federal court. The Secretary can also file a suit to obtain an injunction against the employer, and the court can order the employer to make whatever payments are due to the employee as a part of the injunction. The Secretary of Labor can seek an injunction barring the shipment of goods produced under conditions which violate the wage payment provisions of the Act. Such goods are called "hot goods." Such injunctions are rare, but a few of them have been issued in garment industry cases during the past two years.[20] The Secretary can file a suit without the permission of the aggrieved employee, and if the Secretary does this, the employee loses his right to file a private suit. In an injunction suit, the employee cannot collect the liquidated damages described below.

An alternative procedure is for an employee or a group of employees to file suit directly against the employer. Of course, the employees filing the suit will have to obtain an attorney and bear the legal fees. Such suits can be filed in either federal or state courts, although in a state court suit, the employee may have to show that the employer owes the employee more than some minimum amount of money, which varies from state to state. In the federal courts there are no minimums. The statute of limitations for either a Labor Department or an employee-initiated suit is two years unless the employer's violation of the Act is "willful," in which case the period for filing a suit is three years. A willful violation is one done with the full knowledge that the act is unlawful. Willful violators may also face criminal charges and be subject to fines and imprisonment, the latter for a second willful offense.

An employee who is successful in court will collect all lost wages and may collect an equal amount known as "liquidated damages." The amount of liquidated damages awarded to an employee may depend upon the employer's good faith in taking the illegal actions, its willfulness, its lack of adequate records, etc. An employee can also collect court costs and attorney's fees from the employer. It is important for all workers to keep accurate records of their pay and hours of work, because these may prove useful in any actions brought against their employers.

III. The Occupational Safety and Health Act

A. Introduction

During the 1960s coal miners in the Appalachian coalfields organized a movement to obtain compensation for black lung disease, a lung illness afflicting nearly all long-time miners. Through rallies, marches, demonstrations, and strikes, often in opposition to their own union, the rank-and-file succeeded in winning federal legislation (the Coal Mine Health and Safety Act and the Black Lung Benefits Act) creating a fund out of which black lung payments would be made.[21] Inspired by this victory, organized labor began to push for more general health and safety legislation.

Before passage of the Occupational Safety and Health Act in 1970, employees had limited legal protection in these areas. Unionized workers enjoyed some contractual protections, typically health insurance that would pay for medical care and perhaps replace some lost wages. Some agreements prohibited the use of certain chemicals or gave the union the right to know which chemicals were being used. Safety committees, mandatory use of safety equipment, paid union safety representatives, and the right to refuse to work in unsafe conditions were sometimes protected contractually. Of course, it is important for all unions to confront health and safety issues at the bargaining table. As we saw in Chapter Five, employers must provide most health and safety information requested by the union. This, along with recent scientific studies, can form the basis for a rank-and-file education campaign that can strengthen the union's bargaining position on these issues.

While only unionized workers benefit from contractual health and safety protection, all workers can use their state's workers' compensation laws. These statutes were enacted earlier in this century to provide income (for lost wages and medical bills) to both those workers injured on their jobs and those who had contracted occupational illnesses and diseases. Each workers' compensation law establishes an insurance scheme, usually administered by a private insurance company but in a few states by a public entity.

Employers pay an insurance premium into the insurance fund which is then the source of the payments to the distressed employees. The size of the premium is "experience-rated," meaning that it is lower the lower is the employer's incidence of occupational injuries and diseases. The workers' compensation statutes do not require that an employee be able to show that the employer was at fault for the injury or illness. In fact, a worker who has a pre-existing health problem can collect compensation if his current employment aggravates this condition. However, the statutes deny the employee the right to sue the employer for the injury or illness. In other words, workers' compensation is the exclusive remedy. This feature of the statutes, along with the rather small payments for serious impairments such as the loss of an eye or limb, was the main reason why employers supported them in the first place.

One trouble with the workers' compensation laws is that they do not place an affirmative duty upon employers to maintain workplaces which are both safe and not injurious to the health of the workers. This is what the Occupational Safety and Health Act purports to do, although it has not lived up to its promises to date. To make matters worse, most employees do not know the rights the Act gives them. Therefore, it is essential that we lay out its basic provisions.[22] Echoing the major theme of this book, this Act is best enforced through collective action. Unionized workers enjoy better protection than do their unorganized brothers and sisters.

B. Basic Provisions

The Act (usually called the OSH Act to distinguish it from the agency administering the Act) aims "to insure so far as possible every working man and woman in the nation safe and healthful working conditions and to preserve our human resources." The Act covers all private sector employees except domestic workers, but it does not include state and local public employees. (It does cover federal workers.) The lack of coverage for these public employees is a glaring weakness since nothing about public employment *per se* guarantees "safe and healthful working conditions." States are empowered to enact their own OSH Acts, and when these are at least as protective as the federal statute, much health and safety enforcement goes through them.

The OSH Act spells out rights for both employees and employers. Employees have the right to make a confidential complaint against their employer concerning safety and health hazards. They have the right to be told by their employer if they are being overexposed to dangerous materials and chemicals. (Many states have right-to-know laws which also give employees this right.) It is illegal for employers to discriminate against employees for using the Act. Employees have the right to have a representative take part in inspections of their workplaces conducted under the Act. Employers also have the right to participate in the inspections. They have the right to an opening conference, to seek a variance from any standards set under the Act, and to appeal any penalties assessed against them for violating the Act.[23] Initially the Act was interpreted to mean that an employer's premises could be inspected without notice. However, the Supreme Court held that an employer can demand a warrant before allowing an inspector onto its worksite.[24]

Three federal agencies were established by the OSH Act: the Occupational Safety and Health Administration (OSHA), the Occupational Safety and Health Review Commission (OSHRC), and the National Institute of Occupational Safety and Health. (NIOSH). All are within the Department of Labor and under the leadership of the Secretary of Labor. Offices are maintained throughout the country, so a worker can look under the federal government (Department of Labor) listings in the phone book for the nearest one.

The Occupational Safety and Health Administration is the major administrative agency. Its duties are to set health and safety standards (often on the basis of the research conducted by NIOSH) and to investigate and prosecute cases of noncompliance. OSHRC is independent of OSHA, and its job is to act as judge in appeals of enforcement actions taken by OSHA. OSHA has the authority to determine what the Act means in cases where there is some ambiguity. OSHRC cannot do this, although it can refuse to enforce an OSHA interpretation which it deems to be unreasonable.[25] Decisions made by the administrative agencies can be appealed to the appropriate federal court of appeals. Most OSHA investigations occur as a result of an employee complaint. However, OSHA can also target certain industries for inspections, and it can conduct random inspections. One of the most troublesome aspects of OSH Act enforcement is that most employers realize that the chances of their plants being inspected are not that great. There are simply too many plants and not enough inspectors. This is especially the case for the targeted and random inspections, but even the employee-initiated inspections are few enough in number. In his fine book *Dangerous Premises: An Insider's View of OSHA Enforcement*, Don J. Lofgren states:

> Unfortunately, some companies with the most hazardous working conditions operate year after year, in many cases for their entire business lives, without ever having a complaint filed against them. Typically, such companies are small and nonunionized, have mostly women and minority employees, and the working conditions exemplify management's attitudes toward its workers. The employees in such companies are usually ignorant of their rights under OSHA, and those few who are aware or their rights are reluctant to file a complaint for fear of losing their much-needed jobs.[26]

OSHA has the authority to set health and safety standards. For example, it can set the maximum amount of a particular chemical or particulate matter (e.g., cotton dust) that can be in a certain volume of air in a factory. OSHA can establish both temporary emergency and permanent standards. Temporary emergency standards can be set when there is a real and immanent danger to workers, but deaths or serious injuries do not have to occur in advance of the promulgation of the standard. Such a standard is valid for up to six months. Permanent standards must meet the condition that a significant risk exists in the absence of the standard. If, for example, OSHA sets a standard that implies that there is no safe exposure level for a chemical, then it must show that any exposure puts workers at significant risk. The Supreme Court invalidated an OSHA standard for exposure to the solvent benzene because it said that OSHA had failed to prove that its much lower exposure level put employees at significant risk.[27]

Conservative politicians and judges began to argue soon after the Act was passed that OSHA must use a "cost-benefit" analysis in making its standards. That is, a standard could be implemented only if the benefits to employees from it were greater than the costs to employers to abide by it. Given that the benefits are often difficult to quantify (for example, the number and value of the lives saved), they tend to be underestimated. This would be to the advantage of employers who could more easily combat strict standards. Fortunately, the Supreme Court rejected this approach to standard-setting. The Court pointed out that standards must meet only a "to the extent feasible, on the best available evidence" criterion and not a "benefits are greater than costs" criterion.[28] It is important to note that an employer has both a specific and a general duty to protect its employees. The specific duty is that which compels an employer to obey the specific standards which OSHA has established. Suppose that a specific OSHA standard is being met by an employer in a particular workplace operation. Yet the operation still subjects employees to a risk known by the employer, within the employer's control, and within the employer's ability to correct. The general duty clause (Section 5(a)(1)) makes the employer bound to eliminate the risk, its obeying of the specific duty notwithstanding.[29]

After OSHA promulgates a standard, it is possible for an employer to ask for a temporary or permanent exception or "variance" from it. A temporary variance can be issued for up to two years (one year plus two possible six-month renewals) if the employer shows that it cannot comply with the standard immediately. The employees must be notified of their employer's request, and the employer must also show that it is doing everything feasible to protect its employees. A request for a permanent variance must also be made known to employees, and they have a right to request a hearing to discuss the variance. The employer must be able to prove that its own standard, while not the same as the OSHA standard, is at least as effective in protecting the workers' health and safety. Both the workers and OSHA can, within six months of the granting of the variance, attempt to get it revoked.

C. Inspections and Records

The typical OSHA inspection is made after an employee has made a complaint against her employer.[30] The OSHA inspector first goes to the plant and contacts a representative of the employer such as the manager or superintendent. The inspector tells the employer why he is there and that the inspection consists of three phases: the opening conference, the walkaround, and the closing conference. The workers have a right to have a representative participate in each part of the inspection.

At the opening conference, the inspector will explain the law and the nature of the complaint, examine the employer's safety and health records, and discuss the employer's health and safety program. Under the OSH Act the employer must keep records of occupational injuries and illnesses. OSHA provides forms for employers to use, and these must be posted for the employees to see at least once a year. The inspector and employees (including their union) also have the right to see any other health and safety records the employer has voluntarily created.

The inspector next tours the workplace, usually accompanied by the employer and an employee representative. The inspector observes and notes any hazards he sees. As Don Lofgren tells us:

> The inspector notes whether machines are properly guarded, personal protective equipment is being used, ventilation appears adequate, and any other necessary items for controlling hazards are present or absent. The inspector usually conducts employee interviews, in private, to learn more about the company's safety and health program. Should noise or airborne contaminants need to be measured, arrangements for testing are made, often for a few days later.[31]

After the inspection, the inspector holds a closing conference-where he lays out the violations discovered to the employer and tells the employer about any citations that he is going to recommend. Serious violations will be assessed fines, the amount varying according to the nature of the violation, whether or not the violation is deemed to be willful, and whether the employer is a repeat offender. The inspector sets dates by which the violations must be corrected and notifies the employer about its appeal rights. The citations must be posted for three days or until the violation is corrected. Employers have 15 days to appeal the citations. Unfortunately, OSHA will usually meet with the employer before it hears an appeal and try to work out a compromise. During the Reagan/Bush era, this meant that fines would be greatly reduced, and the employer would agree to pay them, foregoing the appeal. If no settlement is reached, an OSHA administrative law judge hears the appeal. This decision is appealable to a federal court of appeal and to the Supreme Court. OSHA may also give the employer extra time to correct the problems, although employees can appeal this.

When an inspector observes a hazard, he will recommend some method for correcting it. There is a "hierarchy of controls," that is, a ranking in terms of which type of controls the inspectors prefer. *Engineering controls* are those which eliminate a hazard through physical means such as hoods for ventilation or machine guards. *Administrative controls* involve changing work schedules so that employee exposure is minimized. *Personal protective equipment* involves the use of respirators, earplugs, and other similar devices by employees to limit exposure.[32] Engineering controls are often the most effective, but these are most often resisted by employers because they ordinarily cost more money to use than do the other two controls.

D. Conclusion

The Fair Labor Standards Act and the OSH Act provide important protections for workers, but in practice these are not always realized. As we have seen, there are hundreds of thousands of employees illegally paid less than the minimum wage and denied overtime wages, and child labor prohibitions are routinely ignored. OSHA fines have been pitifully small, and throughout the past decade, OSHA has favored a policy of "forced consultation," in which it has put its main focus upon discussions of health and safety violations with employers but limited fines. It is necessary to use a policy of "enforcement through deterrence," one in which large fines are recommended by the inspectors and backed up by OSHA.[33] Once again, however, this is unlikely to happen unless there is a strong labor movement ready to demand it.

IV. Questions and Answers

Question 1: Can an hourly employee be paid less than the minimum wage for some hours of work and more than the minimum wage for other hours of work if the average hourly wage equals at least the minimum wage?

No. An hourly employee must be paid at least the minimum wage rate for each hour of work.

Question 2: Can discounts on purchases made by the employee from the employer be counted as part of the minimum wage?
No.

Question 3: Do states have minimum wage laws?
Yes, most states have minimum wage laws. The wage rate cannot be lower than the federal minimum, but it can be higher. Contact your state department of labor for more information.

Question 4: Can an employer deduct from an employee's paycheck a debt owed to the employer by the employee?
Yes. However, the deduction must not reduce the employee's wage rate below the minimum wage rate.

Question 5: What are the maximum amounts of "comp" time?
For public safety, emergency, and seasonal state and local public employees, the limit is 480 hours per year (320 hours of actual overtime work). For all other state and local public employees, the limit is 320 hours (240 hours of actual overtime work).

Question 6: How does a worker go about filing a workers' compensation claim?
(The following information is taken from the state of Pennsylvania. Time periods may be different in your state.) Notify your employer immediately of any work-related injury or illness. In the case of an occupational disease, you should consult your doctor first, making sure to give the doctor a complete work history. The OSH Act as well as state right-to-know laws give you the right to know what dangerous substances you have been exposed to, so contact OSHA if your employer has not or will not tell you. If possible, do not leave your workplace before giving notice to the employer of your injury. A coworker can give notice for you, but it is better if you do it. If you call the employer from home, be sure to tell the employer that you were injured at work. If you give notice within 21 days of the injury, you are eligible for compensation from the first day of your disability. If you give notice between 21 and 120 days, you will be eligible only from the day you gave notice. After 120 days, you lose your right to compensation.

Your employer must either pay you the mandated compensation (which varies from state to state—it equals two-thirds of gross pay, up to a maximum in Pennsylvania, for example) within 21 days of your notice or deny your claim. If your claim is denied or if 21 days pass without payment, you must contact a lawyer and file a formal claim. If your request for compensation is denied, you have three years to file a formal claim. Be sure to hire an attorney with experience in this area. Many lawyers will represent you on a contingency fee basis.

For two weeks after your injury, you must agree to be seen by a doctor on a list of doctors posted at your workplace by your employer (there must be at least five doctors on the list). If there is no list, you can choose your own doctor. After two weeks, you can use your doctor, but you must notify the employer of this. When the doctor says you are able to return to work, ask if there are any limitations on what you can do. Do not sign a "Final Settlement Receipt of Compensation" until you are completely recovered. Instead you can ask for a "Supplemental Agreement," which merely suspends benefits.

Great care must be taken in the area of workers' compensation, because employers will try to get you back to work before you should go back, or they might try to get you to see one of their specialists. In cases of permanent injury, they might try to get you to agree to a lump-sum payment. Consult your lawyer before agreeing to or signing anything. You can get a booklet about workers' compensation from many law offices that practice workers' compensation law. A good firm is Galfand, Berger, Lurie & March in Philadelphia. Call them at 1-800-222-8792.

Question 7: Is it possible to sue anyone for work-related injuries?
You can almost never sue the employer; the workers' compensation statutes preempt common law suits. A spouse cannot sue his wife's employer for what he has suffered (for example, loss of his wife's companionship) because of his wife's job-related injury or illness. A woman who suffers emotional distress because of sexual harassment cannot sue her employer on the grounds that her distress did not cause her to lose pay and, therefore, she could not recover money under workers' compensation.

If a third party (a coworker, a supplier, a customer) causes the work-related injury, the employee may file a common law suit for damages, including pain and suffering, against the third party. Such suits are difficult to win, because the third party may be able to successfully argue that the injured party contributed to the negligence which caused the injury or assumed the risk by taking the job in the first place.[34]

V. Selected Readings

1. Joseph E. Kalet, *Primer on Wage & Hour Laws* (Washington, D.C.: Bureau of National Affairs, Inc., 1990).

2. Don J. Lofgren, *Dangerous Premises: An Insider's View of OSHA Enforcement* (Ithaca, N.Y.: ILR Press, 1989).

3. Michael D. Yates, *Labor Law Handbook* (Boston: South End Press, 1987).

GLOSSARY OF LABOR LAW TERMS

ADMINISTRATIVE LAW JUDGE: A judge hearing cases for an administrative agency. An unfair labor practice hearing under the National Labor Relations Act is presided over by an administrative law judge, who makes a recommendation to the NLRB. Such a person used to be called a "hearing officer" or a "hearing examiner."

AFFIRMATIVE ACTION: An action taken by an employer or by a union or by both which aims to remedy some imbalance in the workforce. A policy which requires an employer to hire one black worker for every white worker hired until the ratio of black workers to total workers has reached some specified percentage is an example of an affirmative action program. These are usually undertaken voluntarily, but they can be ordered by a court.

AGE DISCRIMINATION IN EMPLOYMENT ACT OF 1967: Federal statute prohibiting discrimination against employees because of their age. The minimum age protected by the Act is 40.

AGENCY SHOP: A collective bargaining provision which states that every member of the bargaining unit must pay a dues equivalent to the union, though no member of the unit must actually join the union. Agency shops are illegal in right-to-work states.

AGRICULTURAL LABOR RELATIONS ACT OF 1975: California statute which gives farm workers the same protection as that enjoyed by most private sector workers under the National Labor Relations Act.

ALIEN: A person who is not a citizen of the United States. Aliens are covered by the National Labor Relations Act but not by the Civil Rights Acts.

ALLY EMPLOYER: An employer which allies itself with another employer involved in a labor dispute by, for example, performing work normally done by the employees of the employer involved in the dispute. The ally employer becomes a primary party to the labor dispute.

AMERICAN FEDERATION OF LABOR (AFL): A federation of craft unions formed in 1886. The AFL merged with industrial unions of the CIO in 1955 to form the AFL-CIO.

AMERICANS WITH DISABILITIES ACT OF 1990: Federal statute which, in Title I, makes it illegal for an employer or a union to discriminate against an employee because of that employee's disability.

ANTI-TRUST LAWS: Federal statutes aimed at preventing the formation of business monopolies but applicable in limited circumstances to actions taken by labor unions.

ARBITRATION: A dispute resolution technique in which a neutral party, called an arbitrator, resolves the dispute. Usually the decision of the arbitrator is binding on the parties.

ATTORNEY'S FEES: An award available, but not mandatory, to successful complainant under most of our labor laws. The losing party must pay the legal fees of the successful party.

AUTHORIZATION CARD: A card which, when signed by an employee, authorizes the union to represent that employee for purposes of collective bargaining. Under the NLRA, at least 30% of the bargaining unit must sign cards before the NLRB will conduct a representation election.

BACKPAY AWARD: A type of remedy in which a discharged or otherwise discriminated-against employee is awarded the pay lost due to the employer's and/or union's illegal actions.

BAD-FAITH BARGAINING: An unfair labor practice under the NLRA and similar statutes in which the employer or the union fails to demonstrate intent to reach agreement in collective bargaining.

BARGAINING UNIT: The group of employees established by the NLRB or similar board, after it has been petitioned by the employees for a representation election, for purposes of collective bargaining with the employer.

BENEFIT PLANS: Under the Employee Retirement Income Security Act, these include both pension and welfare (insurance, health, etc.) plans provided to employees.

BILL OF RIGHTS: The first ten amendments to the U.S. Constitution. The First, Fourth, and Fifth Amendments have important labor law implications. This is also the name given to Title I of the Landrum-Griffin Act, which spells out the rights of union members vis-à-vis their unions.

BLACKLIST: A list of "undesirable" workers produced by an employer, and then circulated to other employers with the purpose of making it difficult for the employees on the list to get employment. This would most likely be an unfair labor practice.

BLANKET INJUNCTION: An injunction forbiding any and all persons from participating in any way whatsoever in a labor dispute. The Norris-LaGuardia Act made this illegal.

BONA FIDE OCCUPATIONAL QUALIFICATION (BFOQ): An employer defense under the Civil Rights Act in which the employer argues that it is legal to discriminate against a protected group because it is necessary that employees possess a certain characteristic. For example, an acting company may insist that a male character in a play be played by a man. Sex, religion, and age may, in limited circumstances, be BFOQs, but race can never be one.

BONA FIDE SENIORITY SYSTEM: A seniority system regularly and uniformly used by an employer. Such a system does not violate the Civil Rights Act, even if it perpetuates past discrimination, as long as it was not established with the intent to discriminate.

BOYCOTT: A concerted refusal to purchase or transport or handle the product of an employer.

BOYS MARKET INJUNCTION: An injunction issued to stop a violation of a collective bargaining agreement. It will only be issued if the dispute is arbitrable under the collective agreement. This is an exception to the Norris-LaGuardia Act established by the Supreme Court.

BURDEN OF PROOF: In a legal dispute this is the requirement that a party prove something with evidence. The burden of proof may shift from one party to the other during the course of the trial or hearing.

BUSINESS NECESSITY: This is another employer defense under the Civil Rights Act. The employer argues that its discriminatory actions are matters of business necessity. For example, the employer might argue that if it hires employees who cannot speak decent English, it will go out of business. Such a defense is difficult to establish.

CAPTIVE-AUDIENCE SPEECH: An anti-union speech delivered by an employer to employees who are required to attend the meeting at which it is given. These are legal under the NLRA except in the period within 24 hours before the certification election date.

CERTIFICATION ELECTION: The secret-ballot election conducted by the NLRB or similar board in which the members of the bargaining unit vote to determine whether or not they will be represented by a union.

CIVIL RIGHTS ACTS OF 1866 AND 1870: Federal statutes enacted after the Civil War used to combat racial discrimination in employment. These are enforced directly through the courts and not through the EEOC.

CIVIL RIGHTS ACT OF 1964: The basic federal civil rights statute, amended in 1972 and 1991. It prohibits discrimination by employers and unions on the basis of race, color, sex, religion, and national origin.

CIVIL SERVICE REFORM ACT OF 1978: This federal statute contains the labor law affecting employees of the federal government. In terms of employee rights, it is much more restrictive than the NLRA.

CLOSED SHOP: A type of union security provision in a collective bargaining agreement in which the employer may employ only persons who are already members of the union. Closed shops are illegal under the NLRA and all similar statutes.

COLLECTIVE BARGAINING: The process by which an employer and a union attempt to reach agreement on wages, hours, and terms and conditions of employment.

COMMON LAW: This is judge-made law. When legal disputes arise between parties and no statutes apply, the judges have to decide who shall prevail. Their decisions form the common law.

COMMON SITUS PICKETING: Picketing that takes place at a site in which there is more than one employer. For example, if a union pickets a construction site where several contractors are working, it engages in common situs picketing.

COMPARABLE WORTH: This doctrine states that workers doing comparable, but not equal work, in terms of skill requirements, ought to be paid the same wage rate. This doctrine is not currently recognized by the courts.

COMPANY UNION: A labor organization formed, financed, and dominated by an employer. Company unions are illegal under the NLRA.

COMPENSATORY DAMAGES: Awards made by a court or a board which compensate the victim of an unfair labor practice or discrimination for lost earnings.

COMPLAINT: The initial charge filed by a party in an unfair labor practice case. A worker illegally fired by an employer for action protected by the NLRA would file a complaint at an NLRB regional office.

CONCERTED ACTIVITIES: Actions undertaken by a group of employees, for example, strikes, boycotts, and pickets. These are protected by the NLRA and similar statutes.

CONFIDENTIAL EMPLOYEES: Employees who have regular access to information related to the employer's labor relations policies and strategies. They are not protected by the NLRA.

CONGRESS OF INDUSTRIAL ORGANIZATIONS (CIO): A federation of industrial unions formed in 1935. It merged with the AFL in 1955 to form the AFL-CIO.

CONSENT DECREE: An agreement reached voluntarily by parties which is then submitted to a court for approval. The court issues the consent decree as a judgment of the court. Consent decrees have been important in civil rights law.

CONSPIRACY DOCTRINE: An early common law doctrine which declared that the activities of labor unions were criminal conspiracies. A conspiracy occurs when two or more people meet and plan to injure another person or persons.

CONSTITUTION: Our most fundamental set of legal principles. It lays out the rights of our people with respect to our government.

CONSULTANTS: Persons hired by employers to defeat unions in representation elections and collective bargaining.

CONTINGENCY FEE: An arrangement in which a lawyer agrees to take a case without payment from the client, but the client agrees to pay the attorney a share of any award won.

CONTRACT BAR: NLRB rule which prohibits a certification or decertification election during the term of a collective bargaining agreement. The limit is usually three years.

DECERTIFICATION ELECTION: An election under the NLRA and similar statutes in which employees decide whether or not to continue to be represented by their union.

DEFERRED BENEFIT PENSION PLAN: A pension plan in which the pension payment to the employee can be determined in advance according to some agreed-upon formula.

DEFERRED CONTRIBUTION PENSION PLAN: A pension plan in which employee and/or employer contributions are placed in a fund or funds (stocks, bonds, etc.). The pension payment cannot be determined in advance but depends upon how well the funds perform.

DEPARTMENT OF LABOR: Department in the Executive branch of the federal government which oversees many of our labor laws, including the Fair Labor Standards Act and parts of the Landrum-Griffin Act.

DISABILITY: According to the Americans with Disabilities Act, "(A) a physical or mental impairment that substantially limits one or more of the major life activities of [an] individual; (B) a record of such impairment; or (C) being regarded as having a disability."

DISCLAIMER OF INTEREST: An NLRB procedure by which a union abandons a bargaining unit. In a situation in which a union cannot win a collective bargaining agreement and members begin to resign, the union might decide to file a disclaimer of interest rather than wait for a decertification election.

DISPARATE IMPACT: Term used in discrimination cases to describe an employment practice which, while not discriminatory on its face, results in the disproportionate exclusion of some protected group. For example, a requirement that an employee must be at least six feet tall is not overtly sexist, but it would exclude most women from employment. Thus, it has a "disparate impact" upon women.

DISPARATE TREATMENT: Term used in discrimination cases to describe unequal treatment by an employer or a union of a protected group or a protected employee. An employee denied promotion because of his race suffers "disparate treatment."

DISTRICT COURTS: These are the first-level federal courts of general jurisdiction; that is, they are where most federal lawsuits are brought. There is at least one federal district court in each state.

DOUBLE-BREASTING: The employer practice of establishing nonunion subsidiaries and then transferring production to these from union plants.

DUE PROCESS OF LAW: The guarantee that every person will have access to a uniform and fair set of procedures when he or she goes into court or before an administrative agency. The Fifth and Fourteenth Amendments to the federal Constitution guarantee each of us due process of law in our dealings with the government.

DUTY OF FAIR REPRESENTATION: The duty of a union to represent each member of the bargaining unit fairly (without bias, malice, or bad faith) in bargaining, grievance handling, and arbitration.

ECONOMIC STRIKE: A strike over wages, hours, or terms and conditions of employment. Economic strikers can be permanently replaced, but they cannot be fired. They do have some recall rights.

EMPLOYEE RETIREMENT INCOME SECURITY ACT OF 1974 (ERISA): This federal statute regulates employee pension and welfare plans. It is administered by both the IRS and the Department of Labor.

EQUAL EMPLOYMENT OPPORTUNITY COMMISSION (EEOC): A five-member commission appointed by the president for five-year terms to administer the Civil Rights Act, the Equal Pay Act, the Age Discrimination in Employment Act, and the Americans with Disabilities Act.

EQUAL PAY ACT OF 1963: The federal statute guaranteeing that women doing the same work as men will receive the same wage rate. It is administered by the EEOC, but it is part of the Fair Labor Standards Act.

EXCELSIOR LIST: The list containing the addresses of bargaining unit members which the employer must supply to the union within seven days of the NLRB's setting of a date for a representation election.

EXECUTIVE ORDER 11246: This presidential order requires firms doing business with the federal government (federal contractors) to be equal opportunity (nondiscriminating) employers. Larger contractors must also implement affirmative action plans.

FACT-FINDING: A dispute resolution procedure in which a person called a fact-finder investigates the dispute (usually a bargaining impasse) and issues a report with recommendations for ending the dispute.

FAIR LABOR STANDARDS ACT OF 1938: This federal statute establishes the minimum wage and overtime pay and sets standards for the employment of children. It is administered by the Department of Labor.

FAMILY EMPLOYEES: Workers who are also members of the business owner's immediate family. They are not protected by the NLRA and similar statutes.

FEDERAL COURTS OF APPEALS: The decisions of the federal district courts as well as those of administrative agencies such as the NLRB can be appealed at these courts. The United States is divided into eleven "circuits," in each of which there is a federal court of appeals. There is also a circuit for the District of Columbia.

FEDERAL LABOR RELATIONS AUTHORITY: The agency administering the public employee provisions of the Civil Service Reform Act of 1978. It is similar to the NLRB, and it consists of three members appointed by the president for five-year terms.

FEDERAL MEDIATION AND CONCILIATION SERVICE: This organization was established by the Taft-Hartley Law of 1947 to mediate labor disputes. It must be notified by a party wishing to renegotiate a collective bargaining agreement at least 30 days (60 days in health care facilities) before the expiration of the agreement.

FIELD EXAMINER: This person typically conducts the preliminary investigation of an unfair labor practice charge under the NLRA.

FIFTH AND FOURTEENTH AMENDMENTS: These amendments to the federal Constitution guarantee the people equal protection of the law and due process of law.

FINAL OFFER ARBITRATION: A type of dispute resolution technique in which the arbitrator is constrained to impose either the union's last bargaining demand(s) or the employer's last offer.

FINANCIAL CORE MEMBER: A member of a bargaining unit who, under a union shop agreement, refuses to join the union and agrees to pay only that part of the union dues utilized for collective bargaining.

FIRST AMENDMENT: The First Amendment to the federal Constitution; it guarantees the people freedom of speech, assembly, and religion.

FOURTH AMENDMENT: The Fourth Amendment to the federal Constitution; it protects the people from unreasonable search and seizure by the government.

FREE SPEECH PROVISION: This is Section 8(c) of the NLRA. It guarantees employers and unions the right to vigorously campaign against each other in representation elections. An employer is free to say anything that does not promise benefits and is not coercive.

GENERAL COUNSEL: The person appointed by the president for a four-year term to prosecute unfair labor practice charges.

GISSEL ORDER: A bargaining order issued by the NLRB in a situation in which the union loses the election because of the employer's pervasive unfair labor practices. The Board concludes that the employer has so tainted the election environment that a rerun election could not be fairly conducted.

GLOBE ELECTION: An NLRB election procedure in a plant where there are more than two bargaining units, one of which includes the other, and more than one union is seeking to represent the workers in one of the units.

GOOD-FAITH BARGAINING: The NLRA requirement of Section 8a(5) by which the employer must face the union with the intent to reach agreement in collective bargaining.

GRIEVANCE PROCEDURE: The due process provisions of a collective bargaining agreement. The grievance procedure usually ends with binding arbitration of the grievance.

HIRING HALL: A collectively bargained arrangement by which the employer relinquishes to the union the decision as to which employees are hired. The union cannot discriminate against prospective employees who are not union members.

HOSTILE ENVIRONMENT: A workplace environment in which a "reasonable woman" would feel uncomfortable because of the demeaning treatment of female employees. The EEOC is now extending this concept to race and religion.

HOT CARGO CLAUSE: A collectively bargained agreement in which the employer agrees not to handle the product of a firm having a dispute with the union representing its employees. Hot-cargo clauses are illegal under Section 8(e) of the NLRA.

ILLEGAL IMMIGRANTS: Persons who come into the country without appropriate documents. They are protected by the NLRA, but they cannot be legally employed.

IMMIGRATION REFORM AND CONTROL ACT OF 1986: This federal statute regulates the employment of immigrants and establishes the obligations of employers with respect to immigrant workers.

IMPASSE: The point in collective bargaining at which it is not likely that the employer and the union will reach agreement. It is for the NLRB to decide in each particular case whether or not the parties are at an impasse.

IMPLIED CONTRACT EXCEPTION: One of the exceptions to the doctrine of at-will employment. The employee argues that she had an implied contract of employment through, for example, a verbal agreement or an employer handbook.

INDEPENDENT CONTRACTORS: Persons who independently contract out their labor services as opposed to selling their ability to work for a wage. They are not covered by the NLRA and similar statutes.

INDUCING BREACH OF CONTRACT: A common law tort in which a third party induces one of the parties to a contract to violate (or breach) it. This was used to justify injunctions against unions attempting to organize workers who had signed yellow dog contracts.

INFORMATIONAL PICKETING: Picketing aimed solely at informing the public about the activities of an employer, for example, that the employer uses nonunion labor.

INJUNCTION: A court order in which a party is ordered to stop doing something, such as picketing or striking. The issuance of injunctions by federal courts is regulated by the Norris-LaGuardia Act.

INTERSTATE COMMERCE: The movement of goods and services across state borders. Most businesses are engaged in interstate commerce and therefore must obey our federal labor laws.

INTRASTATE COMMERCE: Strictly local business; a business in intrastate commerce is not subject to federal labor laws.

JURISDICTIONAL STRIKE: A strike designed to compel an employer to assign work to one union rather than another. These are unfair labor practices under the NLRA.

LABOR-MANAGEMENT PARTICIPATION TEAM: An organization established by an employer (or by a union and an employer jointly) to promote higher productivity through greater worker participation in production decisions. These are often violations of Section 8A(2) of the NLRA. Teams and other such schemes are part of what critics call "management by stress."

LANDRUM-GRIFFIN ACT OF 1959: This federal statute amends the NLRA, and it also establishes rules which regulate the relationship between unions and their members.

LEAFLETING: The handing out of literature at or near a workplace. The person leafletting must not patrol back and forth or he will be considered to be a picket. Leafletting a secondary employer does not violate the NLRA.

LIQUIDATED DAMAGES: Compensation for damages awarded to employees whose employer "willfully" violated the Fair Labor Standards Act. It can be equal to the amount of the backpay award.

LOCKOUT: The employer's refusal to allow employees to enter the workplace. It is legal, but the employer cannot permanently replace the employees locked out.

MAINTENANCE OF MEMBERSHIP AGREEMENT: A type of union security, common in public employment, in which the employees who become members of the union must maintain their membership until the agreement expires.

MAJOR DISPUTE: Under the Railway Labor Act, a major dispute is one over initial wages, hours, and terms and conditions of employment.

MAKE-WHOLE REMEDY: A remedy which aims to put the employee back into the position in which she would have been had the employer not committed an unfair labor practice. Under the NLRA, this is the only type of remedy the NLRB will make. A backpay award would be an example.

MALICE AND BAD-FAITH EXCEPTION: An exception of the common law of at-will employment. The employee claims that his discharge was the result of the employer's malicious or bad-faith behavior. The assumption is that every employment relationship presumes good-faith behavior on the part of both parties. This exception is rarely upheld by the courts.

MANAGEMENT RIGHTS: The rights which employers claim are inherent in their management function. The NLRB holds that matters of inherent management rights are permissive bargaining subjects.

MANAGERIAL EMPLOYEES: Employees who, while not supervisors, are so closely aligned with the employer as to warrant their exclusion from bargaining units and their denial of NLRA protection.

MANDATORY BARGAINING SUBJECTS: Subjects about which the employer and the union are legally required to bargain with the intent of reaching agreement. Most wages, hours, and terms and conditions of employment are mandatory subjects, as long as they are not matters of inherent management right.

MASS PICKETING: Picketing by so many employees that it is not possible (or very difficult) for persons to enter or leave the plant. It is illegal under the NLRA and similar statutes.

MEDIATION: A type of dispute resolution procedure in which a third party, called a mediator, attempts, but cannot compel, the parties to reach agreement.

MINOR DISPUTE: Under the Railway Labor Act, this is a dispute over the meaning of a collective bargaining agreement.

MIXED-MOTIVE CASE: A case in which the employee claims an unfair labor practice, but the employer claims a legal reason for its action. For example, a worker who helps to organize the union is fired, but the employer claims that she was fired for excessive absenteeism. Similar cases arise under the Civil Rights Act.

MULTI-EMPLOYER BARGAINING UNIT: A unit in which the union negotiates with several employers.

NATIONAL EMERGENCY STRIKE: A strike which the president declares, under Title II of the amended NLRA, to be one that will endanger the nation's health or safety. An injunction will be issued to halt the strike for 80 days.

NATIONAL LABOR RELATIONS ACT OF 1935 (NLRA): The basic federal labor relations statute of the United States.

NATIONAL LABOR RELATIONS BOARD (NLRB): The administrative agency, comprised of five members appointed to five-year terms by the president, which administers the NLRA.

NATIONAL MEDIATION BOARD: Board made up of three members, appointed by the president for three-year terms, to administer the

Railway Labor Act. It does not have powers as extensive as those of the NLRB.

NATIONAL ORIGIN: A person's birthplace. It is a protected category under the Civil Rights Acts.

NATIONAL RAILROAD ADJUSTMENT BOARD: This Board, consisting of 34 members, half appointed by employers and half appointed by unions, resolves minor disputes under the Railway Labor Act.

NORRIS-LAGUARDIA ACT OF 1932: This federal statute sharply restricts the power of federal courts to issue injunctions in labor disputes. Many states have similar laws.

NO-STRIKE AGREEMENT: A collectively bargained agreement in which the union rescinds its right to strike during the time period covered by the agreement.

OCCUPATIONAL SAFETY AND HEALTH ACT OF 1970 (OSHA ACT): This federal statute gives workers the right to safe and healthy workplaces.

OCCUPATIONAL SAFETY AND HEALTH ADMINISTRATION (OSHA): The agency which administers the Occupational Safety and Health Act.

OCCUPATIONAL SAFETY AND HEALTH REVIEW COMMITTEE: This agency has the power to adjudicate disputes between employers and the Occupational Safety and Health Administration.

OFFICE OF FEDERAL CONTRACT COMPLIANCE PROGRAMS: This office in the Department of Labor oversees compliance under Executive Order 11246.

OPEN SHOP: A nonunion workplace or a unionized workplace where the union has been unable to win any form of union security.

ORGANIZATIONAL PICKETING: Picketing for the purpose of forcing an employer to recognize a union. It is strictly limited by Section 8(b)(7) of the NLRA.

ORGANIZATIONAL STRIKE: A strike designed to compel the employer to recognize the union. It is limited by Section 8(b)(7) of the NLRA.

PENSION PLAN: A fringe benefit which provides an employee with retirement income. Most of these are regulated by ERISA.

PERMANENT REPLACEMENTS: Workers hired in a permanent capacity to replace strikers.

PERMISSIVE BARGAINING SUBJECTS: Subjects about which the employer and the union are free to bargain, but neither party can be compelled to do so.

PICKETING: The act of patrolling in front of an employer's premises, usually carrying signs expressing the purpose of the picketing: a strike, an attempt to organize the workers, informing the public about some aspect of the employer's behavior, etc.

PLANT GUARDS: Employees providing security services to an employer. They are protected by the NLRA but must organize in separate bargaining units.

PREEMPTION: The doctrine which states that federal law takes precedence over state law.

PREHIRE AGREEMENT: A legal arrangement in the construction industry by which an employer agrees to recognize a union prior to the hiring of any employees.

PRESSURE CAMPAIGN: An organizing campaign designed to force the employer to recognize the union without an NLRB election.

PRIMA FACIE CASE: The presentation of enough evidence to a board or to a court to warrant a guilty verdict unless the evidence is sufficiently rebutted. It gives the board or the court reason to believe that a violation of the law has taken place.

PRIMARY PICKETING: Picketing aimed at the employer with which the union or group of employees has a dispute.

PRIVATE PROPERTY PICKETING: Picketing on an employer's property. This is ordinarily illegal.

PROFESSIONAL EMPLOYEES: These are employees whose work requires that they have taken some advanced course of studies or which requires that they do predominantly intellectual and varied work. Professional employees cannot, under the NLRA, be placed in a bargaining unit with nonprofessional employees unless a majority of the professional employees agree to this.

PUBLIC POLICY EXCEPTION: The most important exception to the common law of at-will employment. The discharged employee claims that his discharge violates some public policy. An employee fired for refusing to commit an illegal act or for whistleblowing might be able to make such a claim.

PUBLIC REVIEW BOARD: A board of neutrals established by a union to serve as the final appeal body for a union member who has a dispute with her union.

PUNITIVE DAMAGES: These are monetary damages awarded to a party over and above any make-whole award. Their purpose is to set an example and to convince the guilty party not to commit the wrongful action again. Such damages are not allowed under the NLRA.

QUALIFIED INDIVIDUAL WITH A DISABILITY: This defines a worker covered by the Americans with Disabilities Act. Basically it is an individual who can satisfactorily perform a job with or without employer accommodation.

QUALITY CIRCLES: A labor-management cooperation device in which groups of workers meet to discuss ways to improve the quality of the product or service.

RACKETEERING INFLUENCED AND CORRUPT ORGANIZATIONS ACT OF 1970 (RICO): The federal statute which has been used to attempt to reform corrupt labor unions such as the Teamsters.

RAILWAY LABOR ACT OF 1926: This federal statute regulates labor relations in the railroad and airline industries. It is somewhat similar to the NLRA and was the first federal statute to provide for the rights of employees to unionize and bargain collectively.

REASONABLE ACCOMMODATION: The requirement placed upon the employer by the American with Disabilities Act to help or accommodate disabled workers to perform a job.

REFUSAL TO BARGAIN: The unfair labor practice committed by an employer or by a union when it does not have the intent to reach agreement.

RELIGIOUS ACCOMMODATION: This requirement is placed upon employers by the Civil Rights Act. Employers must accommodate an employee's religious practices to the extent feasible without spending more than a minimal amount of money.

REPLACEMENT WORKERS: Workers hired as strikebreakers. A polite word for "scab."

REPRESENTATION ELECTION: An election conducted by the NLRB or a similar board in which members of the bargaining unit vote to determine whether or not they want to be represented by a union.

RESERVED GATE: A gate established by an employer at a multi-employer worksite to be used exclusively by that employer's workers.

REVERSE DISCRIMINATION: A claim made by members of a majority or dominant group that they are discriminated against to the advantage of underrepresented groups. For example, white males might argue that black men are given illegal preference over them in hiring.

RIGHT-TO-SUE LETTER: This letter is sent by the EEOC to the complaining party giving that party the right to pursue the complaint on his or her own through a civil lawsuit.

RIGHT TO WORK LAW: A state law making union shops illegal. A state in which there is such a law is a right-to-work state.

RM PETITION: A petition filed by the employer with the NLRB in which the employer seeks a representation election. These are allowed only under special circumstances.

RUNOFF ELECTION: A second certification election run after a first election has been conducted, but in the first election none of the parties won a majority of the votes cast. The top two vote-getters in the first election participate in the runoff election.

SCABS: The traditional epithet for replacement workers.

SECONDARY BOYCOTT: A boycott in which secondary parties (for example, customers, suppliers, other employees) refuse to purchase or deliver or work on the product of some primary employer.

SECONDARY PICKETING: Picketing aimed at secondary parties to a labor dispute.

SECRETARY OF LABOR: A member of the president's cabinet who oversees the enforcement of many of our labor laws.

SECTION 1981: This is the Civil Rights Act of 1866 as codified in the United States Code. Racial discrimination in employment is illegal under this statute.

SECTION 1983: This is the Civil Rights Act of 1870 as codified in the United States Code. Racial and sexual discrimination by state and local governments are illegal under this statute.

SENIORITY: The length of service of an employee.

SEXUAL HARASSMENT: A form of sex discrimination in which an employer either seeks sexual favors as a condition of employment or creates a workplace environment hostile to women (or men, though this is rare).

SEXUAL PREFERENCE: Personal choice in sexual partners. It is not a protected category under the federal Civil Rights Law.

SHERMAN ACT OF 1890: A federal statute which outlaws the restraint of trade. It can be applied to unions but only if they conspire with employers to restrain trade.

SHOP STEWARD: The unionized worker's shopfloor representative. She enjoys special protection under the NLRA.

SITDOWN STRIKE: A type of strike in which the workers occupy the workplace and refuse to work. This is an illegal strike and subject to injunction.

SLOWDOWN: A type of work stoppage in which the workers continue to work but at a slower pace. Working-to-rule would be a type of slowdown.

SOLE BARGAINING AGENT: The status of the union after it wins a representation election. The employer must negotiate with the union and not with individual employees or groups of employees.

SPECIAL COUNSEL FOR IMMIGRATION-RELATED UNFAIR LABOR PRACTICES: This office was established under the Immigration Reform and Control Act to investigate illegal employer treatment of immigrant workers.

STATUTES: Laws enacted by Congress or by state legislatures. They are written laws as opposed to the unwritten common law.

STRANGER PICKETING: Picketing of an employer by persons not employed by that employer.

SUBCONTRACTING: An employer's use of the services of another employer to have work done at the original employer's workplace rather than having its own employees do the work. Some subcontracting is a mandatory bargaining subject under the NLRA.

SUCCESSOR EMPLOYER: The employer which purchases or otherwise assumes control of another employer's business. Under some circumstances the successor must bargain with the union of the predecessor's employees.

SUCCESSORSHIP CLAUSE: A contract clause by which the employer is bound to sell the business only to a buyer willing to honor the collective bargaining agreement between the seller and the union representing its employees.

SUPERVISORS: Employees who oversee the work of other employees in such a way as to meet the definition of supervisors in Section 2(11) in the NLRA. Supervisors are not protected by the NLRA.

SUPREME COURT: The highest federal court. This court is the ultimate arbiter of the nation's laws.

SURFACE BARGAINING: An employer tactic whereby the employer gives the appearance of bargaining in good faith but does not have an intent to reach agreement. It is an unfair labor practice.

SUSPECT CLASS: A classification established by the Supreme Court in Fifth and Fourteenth Amendment "equal protection" cases. If an employee is in a suspect class, then a public employer would have to have a compelling reason to treat that employee in an unequal manner. So far, race, sex, and alienage are suspect classes.

SYMPATHY STRIKE: A type of worker solidarity in which workers refuse to cross a picket line or handle struck work. It also includes cases in which a group of workers strike their employer in sympathy with another group of striking workers.

TAFT-HARTLEY LAWS: These statutes, enacted in 1947, both amend and enlarge the National Labor Relations Act.

TEMPORARY REPLACEMENTS: Scabs who will be replaced by the strikers at the end of the strike or lockout. Often these are supervisors or other company personnel.

THIRTEENTH AMENDMENT: This Amendment prohibits slavery and involuntary servitude.

TORT: This is a civil (as opposed to a criminal) wrong, but it is not a breach of contract.

TRUSTEESHIP: An arrangement in which the national union takes over the running of a local union. This is regulated by the Landrum-Griffin Act.

UNEMPLOYMENT COMPENSATION: Monies received by workers who qualify under the state's unemployment compensation statute when they become unemployed.

UNFAIR LABOR PRACTICE: An act by an employer or by a union which violates Section 8 of the NLRA or the comparable section of some similar statute.

UNFAIR LABOR PRACTICE STRIKERS: Employees on strike in response to an employer's unfair labor practices. Unlike economic strikers, they cannot be permanently replaced.

UNION SECURITY CLAUSE: A provision in a labor agreement which secures the union by, for example, requiring each member of the bargaining unit to pay a dues equivalent or requiring the employer to deduct dues from paychecks and remit the money to the union.

UNION SHOP: A type of union security agreement in which each bargaining unit member must join the union within some specified period of time.

UNITED STATES CODE (USC): The bound volumes of all federal statutes.

VESTED PENSION: A pension whose accrued benefits are guaranteed to the employee. Vesting is regulated by ERISA.

WEINGARTEN RIGHTS: The rights of a unionized employee to have a shop steward present at a meeting with the employer, particularly when the employee has reason to believe that he will be disciplined.

WELFARE PLANS: Employee benefit plans other than pensions which are regulated by ERISA.

WHISTLEBLOWER: A person who makes others aware of some illegal or otherwise outrageous act of his or her employer. Whistleblowers may be protected by statutes or by the common law.

WILDCAT STRIKE: A strike not authorized by the union. The legality of such a strike depends upon the language of the contract.

WILLFUL VIOLATION: A violation of the law done with full knowledge that the act is unlawful. Such a violation may subject a party to substantial monetary liability.

WORK-TO-RULE: A type of strategy in which workers work exactly to the letter of their collective bargaining agreement and/or their statutory obligations. This results in a slowing down of the work.

WORKER ADJUSTMENT AND RETRAINING NOTIFICATION ACT OF 1988 (WARN): This federal statute mandates that certain employers provide at least 60 days notice before a plant closing or mass layoff.

YELLOW DOG CONTRACT: An agreement in which employees agree that they are not union members and will not become union members while working for the employer. These are now illegal.

ZIPPER CLAUSE: A contract clause in which the union agrees to forego bargaining for the duration of the agreement on issues not settled by that agreement.

INDEX OF CASES CITED

Castelli v. Douglas Aircraft Co., 752 F.2d 1480 (9th Cir. 1985).

Claude Everett Construction Co., 136 NLRB 321 (1962).

Clear Pine Moldings, 115 LRRM 1113 (1984).

Commonwealth v. Hunt, 4 Metcalf 111 (Mass. 1842).

Communication Workers, 124 LRRM 1009 (1986).

Communications Workers v. Beck, 487 U.S. 735 (1988).

Complete Auto Transit, Inc. v. Reis, 451 U.S. 401 (1981).

Connick v. Myers, 461 U.S. 138 (1983).

Coppage v. Kansas, 236 U.S. 1 (1915).

Corning Glass Works v. Brennan, 415 U.S. 972 (1974).

County of Washington v. Gunther, 452 U.S. 161 (1981).

County Sanitation District No. 2 of Los Angeles County v. Local 660, SEIU, 38 Cal. 564 (1985).

Dairylea Cooperative, Inc., 219 NLRB 656 (1975).

DeBartolo Corp. v. Florida Gulf Coast Building and Construction Trades Council, 108 S. Ct. 1392 (1988).

DelCostello v. Teamsters, 462 U.S. 151 (1987).

Department and Specialty Store Employees Union, Local 1265 v. Brown, 284 F.2d 619 (6th Cir. 1960).

Dothard v. Rawlinson, 433 U.S. 321 (1977).

Douds v. Metropolitan Federation, 75 Supp. 672 (S.D. of N.Y., 1948).

Dow Chemical Co., 244 NLRB 1060 (1979).

Dubuque Packing Co., Inc. and UFCWIU, Local 150A, 303 NLRB No.66 (1991).

Duldulao v. St. Mary Nazareth Hospital Center, 115 Ill.2d 482 (1987).

Duplex Printing Press Co. v. Deering, 254 U.S. 443 (1921).

Eastex, Inc. v. NLRB, 98 U.S. 2505 (1978).

Electrical Workers IUE Local 900 v. NLRB, 727 F. 2d 1184 (D.C. Cir. 1984).

Electrical Workers Local 761 v. NLRB (General Electric), 366 U.S. 667 (1961).

Electrical Workers Local 501 v. NLRB, 756 F.2d 888 (D.C. Cir. 1985).

Electromation, Inc., 309 NLRB No. 163 (1992).

Elevator Constructors Union Local 3, 129 LRRM 1066 (1988).

Ellis v. Brotherhood of Railway Clerks, 466 U.S. 435 (1984).

Emporium Capwell v. Western Addition Community Organization, 420 U.S. 50 (1975).

Engineers Limited Pipeline Co., 95 NLRB 281 (1982).

Ex-Cell-O Corp., 185 NLRB 20 (1970).

Excelsior Underwear, Inc., 156 NLRB 1235 (1966).

Indianapolis Power & Light Co., 291 NLRB No. 145 *(1988)*.

Industrial Union Department v. American Petroleum Institute, 448 U.S. 490 (1980).

Industrial Union of Marine Workers v. NLRB, 320 F.2d 615 (3d Cir. 1963).

J.P. Stevens, 102 LRRM 1039 (1979).

Jacksonville Bulk Terminals, Inc. v. International Longshoremen's Association, 457 U.S. 702 (1982).

John Deklewa & Sons, Inc., 282 NLRB No. 184 (1987).

Johnson v. Railway Agency, 421 U.S. 454 (1975).

Johnson's v. Uncle Ben's, Inc., 965 F.2d (5th Cir. 1992).

Kaiser Aluminum and Chemical Corp. v. Weber, 443 U.S. 193 (1979).

Lechmere, Inc. v. NLRB, 112 S. Ct. 841 (1992).

Letter Carriers v. Austin, 418 U.S. 264 (1974).

Lingle v. Norge Div. of Magic Chef, 108 S.Ct. 1877 (1988).

Local 93 Firefighters Union v. Cleveland, 478 U.S. 501 (1986).

Local 593, Amalgated Meat Cutters and Allied Workers of North America, 237 NLRB 1159 (1978).

Loewe v. Lawlor, 208 U.S. 274 (1908).

Los Angeles Dep't of Power and Light v. Manhart, 435 U.S. 702 (1978).

Mallinckrodt Chemical Works, 64 LRRM 1011 (1966).

Malta Construction Co., 120 LRRM 1209 (1985).

Marshall v. Barlow's, Inc., 436 U.S. 307 (1978).

Martin v. OSHRC, 111 S.Ct. 1171 (1991).

Martin v. Wilks, 490 U.S. 755 (1989).

Mastro Plastics Corp. v. NLRB, 350 U.S. 270 (1956).

McDonnell Douglas Corp. v. Green, 411 U.S. 792 (1972).

Meritor Savings Bank v. Vinson, 477 U.S. 57 (1986).

Meyers Industries, 268 NLRB 493 (1984).

Milwaukee Springs Div., Illinois Coil Spring Co., 115 LRRM 1065 (1984).

Miranda Fuel Co., 140 NLRB 181 (1962).

Mitchell v. Toledo Hospital, 964 F.2d 577 (6th Cir. 1992).

Monge v. Beebe Rubber Co., 114 N.H. 130 (1974).

Mormon Church v. Amos, 107 S.Ct. 2862 (1987).

National Treasury Employees Union v. Von Raab, 109 S.Ct. 1384 (1989).

National Woodwork Manufacturers Assn. v. NLRB, 386 U.S. 612 (1967).

NLRB v. Bildisco & Bildisco, 465 U.S. 513 (1984).

Rankin v. McPherson, 483 U.S. 378 (1987).

Republic Aviation Corp. v. NLRB, 324 U.S. 793 (1945).

Riley v. Letter Carriers' Local 380, 668 F.2d 224 (3d Cir. 1981).

Rossmore House, 269 NLRB 1176 (1984).

Sailor's Union of the Pacific (Moore Dry Dock), 92 NLRB No. 93, (1950).

San Diego Building Trades v. Garmon, 359 U.S. 236 (1959).

Sears, Roebuck & Co., 118 LRRM 1329 (1985).

Sears, Roebuck & Co. v. Carpenters, 436 U.S. 180 (1978).

Shultz v. Wheaton Glass Co., 421 F.2d 896 (3rd Cir. 1974).

Skinner v. Railway Labor Executives' Association, 109 S.Ct. 1402 (1989).

Spiegel Trucking Co., 92 LRRM 1604 (1985).

St. Francis College v. Al-Khazraji, 481 U.S. 604 (1987).

St. Francis Hospital I, 265 NLRB 1023 (1982).

Steele v. Louisville & N.R.R., 323 U.S. 192 (1944).

Steele v. Louisville and Nashville Railroad, 323 U.S. 92 (1944).

Struknes Construction Co., 165 NLRB 1062 (1967).

Summit Airlines, Inc. V. Teamsters Local 295, 628 F.2d 787 (2d Cir. 1980).

Sure-Tan, Inc. v. NLRB, 467 U.S. 883 (1984).

T.I.M.E.- D.C., Inc. v. United States, 431 U.S. 324 (1977).

Tameny v. Atlantic Richfield Co., 27 Cal. 3d 167 (1980).

Taracorp Industries, 117 LRRM 1497 (1984).

Tawas Tube Products, Inc., 58 LRRM 1330 (1965).

Teamsters Local 83, 96 LRRM 1165 (1977).

Teamsters Local 174 v. Lucas Flour Co., 369 U.S. 95 (1962).

Teamsters v. United States, 431 U.S. 324 (1977).

Texas & N.O.R.R. v. Railway Clerks, 281 U.S. 548 (1930).

Texas Department of Community Affairs v. Burdine, 450 U.S. 248 (1981).

Textile Workers of America v. Darlington Manufacturing Company, 380 U.S. 263 (1965).

Thornhill v. Alabama, 310 U.S. 88 (1940).

Trans World Airlines v. Hardison, 432 U.S. 63 (1977).

Trustees of Boston University, 281 NLRB No. 15 (1986).

U.S. v. Paradise, 480 U.S. 149 (1987).

U.S. v. Villages of Elmwood Park and Melrose Park, 43 FEP 995 (1987).

UAW v. General Dynamics Land Systems Division, 815 F.2d 1570 (D.C. Cir. 1987).

UAW v. Johnson Controls, Inc., 111 S. Ct. 1196 (1991).

Researching the Labor Law

Before reading this book, it will be useful for you to know a little bit about researching labor law. First of all, throughout the book, references will be made to the decisions made by administrative agencies and courts as they interpret the various labor law statutes. These decisions are printed and compiled in bound volumes called "Reporters." There are many Reporters, basically one for each type of court or administrative agency which makes decisions. The Reporters can be found in a courthouse library or in a law library at a university. By looking at a legal citation, you will know which Reporter to select to find the case in question. Let us look at some examples taken from the following chapters.

1. *Steele v. Louisville and N.R.R.*, 323 U.S. 192 (1944). The letters between the numbers "323" and "192" tell us the Reporter. The letters "U.S." tell us that this is a Reporter which publishes the decisions of the U.S. Supreme Court. The italicized words tell us the parties to this particular dispute, a person named Steele and a company called the Louisville and Nashville Railroad. The number "323" is the volume number of this set of Reports and the number "192" is the page number of this volume in which the decision begins. This case was decided by the Supreme Court in 1944. You would look on the library shelves for the set of bound volumes with "U.S." on their spines and take down Volume 323 to find the case.

2. *Mormon Church v. Amos*, 107 S.Ct. 2862 (1987). The letters "S.Ct." tell us that this is another Supreme Court Reporter. Reporters are published by private publishing companies, and more than one company might publish the reports of a particular court or administrative agency. In this Reporter, you would get Volume "107" and turn to page "2,862" for this 1987 Supreme Court decision.

3. *Pickering v. Board of Education*, 20 L Ed. 2d 811 (1968). The "L Ed." tells us that this is yet another Supreme Court Reporter; the letters stand for "Lawyers' Edition." The "2d" tells us that this is the second series of this Reporter; this term will appear on the spine of the bound volumes.

4. *Schultz v. Wheaton Glass Co.*, 421 F.2d 896 (3rd Cir. 1974). Here the "F.2d" tells us that this is the Reporter for the decisions of the U.S. Federal Courts of Appeal, the courts right below the Supreme Court. The United States is divided into 11 areas or "circuits," in each of which there is a Federal Court of Appeals. This case was heard by the Third Circuit. It is in the second (2d) series of the Reporter, Volume 421 and page 896. The Court of Appeals decided the case in 1974.

5. *Boyd v. Ozark Airlines*, 419 F. Supp. 1061 (E.D. Mo. 1976). The "F. Supp." tells us that this is the Reporter for the decisions of the Federal District Courts, the first level of federal courts, that is, the courts in which federal cases begin. States are divided into districts, and this case was heard by the Federal Court for the Eastern District of Missouri in 1976. The Volume is 419, and the page number is 1061.

6. *Monge v. Beebe Rubber Co.*, 114 N.H. 130 (1974). If a state's initials appear alone between the volume and page numbers, this is the Reporter of the supreme court of that state. In this case, we have the New Hampshire State Supreme Court Reporter. "PA" would show the Reporter for the Supreme Court of Pennsylvania, etc.

7. *Petermann v. Teamsters*, 174 Cal. App. 2d 184 (1959). States have first-level or district courts as well as appeals courts. Here the "Cal. App." tells us that this is the Reporter for the California Court of Appeals, second series.

8. *Struknes Construction Co.*, 165 NLRB 1062 (1967). Administrative agencies such as the National Labor Relations Board make legal decisions which are also published in Reporters. The term "NLRB" tells us that this case is in the National Labor Relations Board Reporter. The italicized terms give us the name of the party which brought the complaint before the Board, in this case, the Struknes Construction Company. The case is in Volume 165 on page 1,062; it was decided by the NLRB in 1967.

9. *Malta Construction Co.*, 120 LRRM 1209 (1985). This Reporter, published by the Bureau of National Affairs, reports cases involving the National Labor Relations Act, but it reports cases at all levels, from the NLRB to the Supreme Court. A university law library would have this useful Reporter. The term "LRRM" stands for "Labor Relations Reference Manual."

10. *Feldstein v. The Christian Science Monitor*, 30 FEP 1842 (1983). Discrimination or Fair Employment Practices cases at all levels are reported in the FEP or Fair Employment Practices Reporter.

There are many other Reporters, but the above will give you a good start in finding whatever case you might need. If you have problems, just ask the librarian for help.

A second aspect of researching the law is access to the relevant statutes. The basic federal statutes are available in a volume called *Federal Labor Laws*, which is available from West Publishing Co., 50 West Kellogg Blvd., St.Paul, MN 55102. Other good references are *The Developing Labor Law*, published by the Bureau of National Affairs, 2550 M St. N.W., Washington, D.C., 20037; and *Labor Law Course*, published by Commerce Clearing House, 4025 W. Peterson Ave., Chicago, IL 60646. All federal statutes can be found in the bound volumes of the U.S. Code, available in most libraries. State laws can be found in the relevant "Code" for your state. Ask your local librarian. If you are a state government employee, you might ask your local congressperson or state representative for help in getting you a copy of any state statute which you may need. If you are a federal government worker, you might write the National Federation of Federal Employees at 1016 16th St. N.W., Washington, D.C. 20036 for help with the statutes which affect federal government employees. When you have a question about the National Labor Relations Act, call the nearest regional office of the NLRB, which is probably located in the nearest big city. The same goes for civil rights questions; call the nearest EEOC office or state "Human Relations Commission." For laws administered by the Department of Labor, contact their nearest office. Be patient, but be persistent!

USEFUL FORMS AND CHARTS

To make this book as useful as possible, I have included some common labor law forms and posters. Some of them would be used if you were filing a labor law charge against your employer, while others must be posted by your employer at your workplace.

1. Union Authorization Cards:

These are samples of the cards needed to petition the NLRB or similar boards for an election.

_____ UNION AFL-CIO

I accept membership in _____ Union, AFL-CIO of my own free will and authorize this union to represent me in negotiations with my Employer about wages and all other conditions of employment.

NAME _____ DATE _____

SIGNATURE OF EMPLOYEE _____

ADDRESS _____

EMPLOYER _____ DEPARTMENT _____

SHIFT _____ JOB _____ RATE _____ WORKERS HOME TELEPHONE # _____

WITNESS _____

_____ UNION AUTHORIZATION CARD

WE BELIEVE THAT ONLY THROUGH COLLECTIVE BARGAINING CAN WE HAVE A VOICE IN OUR WORK PLACE, ACHIEVE FAIR TREATMENT FOR ALL, ESTABLISH JOB SECURITY AND FAIR BENEFITS, WAGES AND WORKING CONDITIONS. THEREFORE, THIS WILL AUTHORIZE THE _____ UNION, AFL-CIO TO REPRESENT ME IN COLLECTIVE BARGAINING WITH MY EMPLOYER.

PLEASE PRINT:

NAME _____

EMPLOYER NAME _____ DATE _____

ADDRESS _____

CITY _____ STATE _____ ZIP _____ PHONE _____

SHIFT _____ DEPARTMENT _____

SIGNATURE _____

NOTE: This authorization to be signed and dated in employee's own handwriting. Your right to sign this card is protected by Federal Law.

2. EEOC Intake Questionnaire:

This is the form you would fill out if you made a discrimination complaint under the Civil Rights Act, the Age Discrimination in Employment Act, the Equal Pay Act, or the American with Disabilities Act.

INTAKE QUESTIONNAIRE

This form is affected by the Privacy Act of 1974; see Privacy Act Statement on reverse before completing this form.

EEOC USE ONLY
Name (Intake Officer)

Please answer the following questions, telling us briefly why you have been discriminated against in employment. An officer of the EEOC will talk with you after you complete this form. (PLEASE PRINT)

NAME _____
    (First)   (Middle Name or Initial)   (Last)   TELEPHONE NO. _____
ADDRESS _____   (Include area code)

CITY _____   COUNTY _____

Please provide the name of an individual at a different address who is in the local area and who would know how to reach you.

NAME _____   STATE _____   ZIP CODE _____
    (First)   (Middle Name or Initial)   (Last)
ADDRESS _____   RELATIONSHIP _____

CITY _____   TELEPHONE NO. _____
    STATE _____   ZIP CODE _____   (Include area code)

What action was taken against you that you believe to be discriminatory? What harm, if any, was caused to you or others in your work situation as a result of that action? (If more space is required, use reverse.)

_____
_____
_____

Do you believe this action was taken against you because of: (Check the one(s) that apply and specify your race, sex, age, religion, ethnic identity or disability).

[ ] RACE   [ ] SEX   [ ] RELIGION   [ ] NATIONAL ORIGIN   [ ] AGE   [ ] COLOR   [ ] DISABILITY   [ ] RETALIATION
[ ] OTHER (Explain Briefly) _____

I WAS DISCRIMINATED AGAINST BY: (Check the one(s) that apply)

[ ] EMPLOYER   [ ] UNION (Give Local No.)   [ ] EMPLOYMENT AGENCY   [ ] OTHER (Specify)

NAME _____	NAME _____
ADDRESS _____	ADDRESS _____
CITY, STATE, ZIP CODE _____	CITY, STATE, ZIP CODE _____
APPROXIMATE NUMBER EMPLOYED BY THIS EMPLOYER	WHAT WAS THE MOST RECENT DATE THE HARM YOU ALLEGED TOOK PLACE?

Are you now employed by the Employer that harmed you? Answer below.

YES: I am employed in the position of	NO: I was not hired for the position of	OR: I was employed in the position of
since _____ (Date)	which I applied for on _____ (Date)	until I was ____ on ____ (Laid off, fired, etc.) (Date)

Normally, your identity will be disclosed to the organization which allegedly discriminated against you.

Do you [ ] CONSENT or [ ] NOT CONSENT to such disclosure?

Have you sought assistance in this matter from any Government agency, union, attorney, or any other source?

[ ] No   [ ] Yes _____
    (Name of source of assistance)

RESULT, IF ANY _____   (Date)

Have you filed an EEOC Charge in the past?   [ ] NO   [ ] YES (If answer is yes, complete below)

Approximate Date Filed _____   Organization Charged _____

SIGNATURE _____   EEOC Charge No. (If known) _____
    DATE _____

8/83:C:\PCWORK\VNT\EEOCFORM.283

3. Notice to Employees:

This is sent to be posted at your workplace once an election petition
has been filed.

NOTICE TO EMPLOYEES

FROM THE

National Labor Relations Board

A PETITION has been filed with this Federal agency seeking an election to determine whether certain
employees want to be represented by a union.

The case is being investigated and NO DETERMINATION HAS BEEN MADE AT THIS TIME by the National Labor
Relations Board. IF an election is held Notices of Election will be posted giving complete details for voting.

It was suggested that your employer post this notice so the National Labor Relations Board could inform you
of your basic rights under the National Labor Relations Act.

YOU HAVE THE RIGHT under Federal Law

- To self-organization
- To form, join, or assist labor organizations
- To bargain collectively through representatives of your own choosing
- To act together for the purposes of collective bargaining or other mutual aid or protection
- To refuse to do any or all of these things unless the union and employer, in a state where such agreements are permitted, enter into a lawful union security clause requiring employees to join the union.

It is possible that some of you will be voting in an employee representation election as a result of the request
for an election having been filed. While NO DETERMINATION HAS BEEN MADE AT THIS TIME, in the event
an election is held, the NATIONAL LABOR RELATIONS BOARD wants all eligible voters to be familiar with
their rights under the law IF it holds an election.

The Board applies rules which are intended to keep its elections fair and honest and which result in a free
choice. If agents of either Unions or Employers act in such a way as to interfere with your right to a free election,
the election can be set aside by the Board. Where appropriate the Board provides other remedies, such as
reinstatement for employees fired for exercising their rights, including backpay from the party responsible
for their discharge.

NOTE:

The following are
examples of conduct
which interfere with
the rights of employees
and may result in the
setting aside of
the election.

- Threatening loss of jobs or benefits by an Employer or a Union
- Promising or granting promotions, pay raises, or other benefits, to influence an employee's vote by a party capable of carrying out such promises
- An Employer firing employees to discourage or encourage union activity or a Union causing them to be fired to encourage union activity
- Making campaign speeches to assembled groups of employees on company time within the 24-hour period before the election
- Incitement by either an Employer or a Union of racial or religious prejudice by inflammatory appeals
- Threatening physical force or violence to employees by a Union or an Employer to influence their votes

Please be assured that IF AN ELECTION IS HELD every effort will be made to protect your right to a free
choice under the law. Improper conduct will not be permitted. All parties are expected to cooperate fully
with this agency in maintaining basic principles of a fair election as required by law. The National Labor
Relations Board as an agency of the United States Government does not endorse any choice in the election.

NATIONAL LABOR RELATIONS BOARD

an agency of the

UNITED STATES GOVERNMENT

THIS IS AN OFFICIAL GOVERNMENT NOTICE AND MUST NOT BE DEFACED BY ANYONE

65

4. Unfair Labor Practice Form:

This form begins the unfair labor practice procedure. You get this form from the NLRB regional office.

5. Sample NLRB ballot:

UNITED STATES OF AMERICA
National Labor Relations Board

OFFICIAL SECRET BALLOT
For certain employees of

Do you wish to be represented for purposes of collective bargaining by –

MARK AN "X" IN THE SQUARE OF YOUR CHOICE

YES | NO

DO NOT SIGN THIS BALLOT Fold and drop in ballot box.
If you spoil this ballot return it to the Board Agent for a new one.

6. NLRB Ballot Tally Sheet:

Used by the NLRB to tally the ballots in a certification election

---

FORM NLPB-760 (12-82)

UNITED STATES OF AMERICA
NATIONAL LABOR RELATIONS BOARD

Date Filed

Somewhere Industries, Inc.
Employer
and

A.B.C. Union, AFL-CIO

Case No. _14-RX-10632_ _July 12, 1991_

Date Issued _Oct 30 1991_

Type of Election
(Check one:)
☒ Stipulation
☐ Board Direction
☐ Consent Agreement
☐ RD Direction
Incumbent Union (Code)

(If applicable check either or both:)
☐ 8(b) (7)
☐ Mail Ballot

TALLY OF BALLOTS

The undersigned agent of the Regional Director certifies that the results of the tabulation of ballots cast in the election held in the above case, and concluded on the date indicated above, were as follows:

1. Approximate number of eligible voters .... _195_
2. Number of Void ballots .... _1_
3. Number of Votes cast for _Petitioner_ .... _98_
4. Number of Votes cast for _____
5. Number of Votes cast for _____
6. Number of Votes cast against participating labor organization(s) .... _86_
7. Number of Valid votes counted (sum of 3, 4, 5, and 6) .... _184_
8. Number of Challenged ballots .... _6_
9. Number of Valid votes counted plus challenged ballots (sum of 7 and 8) .... _190_
10. Challenges are (not) sufficient in number to affect the results of the election.
11. A majority of the valid votes counted plus challenged ballots (Item 9) has (not) been cast for _Petitioner_

For the Regional Director _Region 20 Sue Smith_

The undersigned acted as authorized observers in the counting and tabulating of ballots indicated above. We hereby certify that the counting and tabulating were fairly and accurately done, that the secrecy of the ballots was maintained, and that the results were as indicated above. We also acknowledge service of this tally.

For _Employer_ _Mr. Jones_

For _Petitioner_ _Mary Doe_

For _____

For _____

7. OSH Act Employee Rights:

This is a summary if your rights under the OSH Act

U.S. Department of Labor
Program Highlights

Fact Sheet No. OSHA 91-35

OSHA: Employee Workplace Rights and Responsibilities

The Occupational Safety and Health Act of 1970 (hereafter called the Act) created the Occupational Safety and Health Administration (OSHA) within the Department of Labor and encouraged employers and employees to reduce workplace hazards and to implement safety and health programs.

In doing so, employees were given many rights and responsibilities. They have the right to:

• review copies of appropriate standards, rules, regulations, and requirements that the employer should have available at the workplace.

• request information from the employer on safety and health hazards in the workplace, precautions that may be taken, and procedures to be followed if an employee is involved in an accident or is exposed to toxic substances.

• have access to relevant employee exposure and medical records.

• request the OSHA area director to conduct an inspection if they believe hazardous conditions or violations of standards exist in the workplace.

• have an authorized employee representative accompany the OSHA compliance officer during the inspection tour.

• respond to questions from the OSHA compliance officer, particularly if there is no authorized employee representative accompanying the compliance officer on the inspection "walkaround."

• observe any monitoring or measuring of hazardous materials and see the resulting records, as specified under the Act, and as required by OSHA standards.

• have an authorized representative, or themselves, review the Log and Summary of Occupational Injuries (OSHA No. 200) at a reasonable time and in a reasonable manner.

• object to the abatement period set by OSHA for correcting any violation in the citation issued to the employer by writing to the OSHA area director within 15 working days from the date the employer receives the citation.

• submit a written request to the National Institute for Occupational Safety and Health (NIOSH) for information on whether any substance in the workplace has potentially toxic effects in the concentration being used, and have names withheld from the employer, if that is requested.

• be notified by the employer if the employer applies for a variance from an OSHA standard, and testify at a variance hearing, and appeal the final decision.

• have names withheld from employer, upon request to OSHA, if a written and signed complaint is filed.

• be advised of OSHA actions regarding a complaint and request an informal review of any decision not to inspect or to issue a citation.

• file a discrimination complaint under Section 11(c) of the Act if punished for exercising the above rights or for refusing to work when faced with an imminent danger of death or serious injury and there is insufficient time for OSHA to inspect; or file a Section 405 reprisal complaint (under the Surface Transportation Assistance Act [STAA]).

Before OSHA issues, amends or deletes regulations, the agency publishes them in the Federal Register so that interested persons or groups may comment.

The employer has a legal obligation to inform employees of OSHA safety and health standards which may apply to their workplace. Upon request, the employer must make available copies of those standards and the OSHA law itself. If more information is needed about workplace hazards than the employer can supply, it can be obtained from the nearest OSHA area office.

Under the Act, employers have a general duty to provide work and a workplace free from recognized hazards. Citations may be issued by OSHA when violations of standards are found, and for violations of the general duty clause, even if no OSHA standard applies to the particular hazard.

The employer also must display in a prominent place the official OSHA poster which describes rights and responsibilities under OSHA's law.

This is one of a series of fact sheets highlighting U.S. Department of Labor programs. It is intended as a general description only and does not carry the force of legal opinion.

8. Family and Medical Leave Act:

This document outlines your rights under this act, which is not covered in this book.

Your Rights
Under The
Family and Medical Leave Act of 1993

FMLA requires covered employers to provide up to 12 weeks of unpaid, job-protected leave to "eligible" employees for certain family and medical reasons. Employees are eligible if they have worked for a covered employer for at least one year, and for 1,250 hours over the previous 12 months, and if there are at least 50 employees within 75 miles.

Reasons For Taking Leave:

Unpaid leave must be granted for *any* of the following reasons:

- to care for the employee's child after birth, or placement for adoption or foster care;
- to care for the employee's spouse, son or daughter, or parent, who has a serious health condition; or
- for a serious health condition that makes the employee unable to perform the employee's job.

At the employee's or employer's option, certain kinds of *paid* leave may be substituted for unpaid leave.

Advance Notice and Medical Certification:

The employee may be required to provide advance leave notice and medical certification. Taking of leave may be denied if requirements are not met.

- The employee ordinarily must provide 30 days advance notice when the leave is "foreseeable."
- An employer may require medical certification to support a request for leave because of a serious health condition, and may require second or third opinions (at the employer's expense) and a fitness for duty report to return to work.

Job Benefits and Protection:

- For the duration of FMLA leave, the employer must maintain the employee's health coverage under any "group health plan."

- Upon return from FMLA leave, most employees must be restored to their original or equivalent positions with equivalent pay, benefits, and other employment terms.
- The use of FMLA leave cannot result in the loss of any employment benefit that accrued prior to the start of an employee's leave.

Unlawful Acts By Employers:

FMLA makes it unlawful for any employer to:

- interfere with, restrain, or deny the exercise of any right provided under FMLA:
- discharge or discriminate against any person for opposing any practice made unlawful by FMLA or for involvement in any proceeding under or relating to FMLA.

Enforcement:

- The U.S. Department of Labor is authorized to investigate and resolve complaints of violations.
- An eligible employee may bring a civil action against an employer for violations.

FMLA does not affect any Federal or State law prohibiting discrimination, or supersede any State or local law or collective bargaining agreement which provides greater family or medical leave rights.

For Additional Information:

Contact the nearest office of the Wage and Hour Division, listed in most telephone directories under U.S. Government, Department of Labor.

U.S. Department of Labor
Employment Standards Administration
Wage and Hour Division
Washington, D.C. 20210

WH Publication 1420
June 1993

NOTES

CHAPTER ONE: INTRODUCTION

1. Lawrence Kahn and Peter Sherer, "Racial Differences in Professional Basketball Players' Compensation," *Journal of Labor Economics* 6 (January 1988), pp. 40-61.

2. Lawrence Mishel and Ruy A. Texeira, *The Myth of the Coming Labor Shortage* (Washington, D.C.: Economic Policy Institute, 1991), pp. 31-33.

3. See Michael D. Yates, *Longer Hours, Fewer Jobs: Employment and Unemployment in the United States* (New York: Monthly Review Press, 1994).

CHAPTER TWO: DISCRIMINATION

1. This discussion of the Yale strike is based upon the following sources: Teresa Amott and Julie Matthaei, "Comparable Worth, Incomparable Pay," *Radical America* 18 (September-October 1984), pp. 21-30; Aldo Cupo et. al., "Beep, Beep, Yale's Cheap," *Radical America* 18 (September-October 1984), pp. 7-20; and Toni Gilpin et. al., *On Strike for Respect: The Clerical and Technical Workers' Strike at Yale University* (Chicago: C.H. Kerr, 1988).

2. The issue of comparable worth is dealt with in great detail in Paula England, *Comparable Worth: Theories and Evidence* (New York: Aldine De Gruyter, 1992).

3. See David Milton, *The Politics of U.S. Labor: From the Great Depression to the New Deal* (New York: Monthly Review Press, 1982).

4. See Kim Moody, *An Injury to All: The Decline of American Unionism* (New York: Verso, 1988), pp. 17-70.

5. Good sources are Ann Fagen Ginger and David Christiano, editors, *The Cold War Against Labor*, 2 vols. (Berkeley: Meiklejohn Civil Liberties Institute, 1987); and Steve Rosswurm, editor, *The CIO'S Left-Led Unions* (New Brunswick, N.J.: Rutgers University Press, 1992).

6. *Steele v. Louisville & N.R.R.*, 323 U.S. 192 (1944); *Ford Motor Co. v. Huffman*, 345 U.S. 330 (1953).

7. See Herbert Hill, "Black Workers, Organized Labor, and Title VII of the 1964 Civil Rights Act: Legislative History and Litigation Record," in Herbert Hill and James E. Jones, Jr., editors, *Race in America: The Struggle for Equality* (Madison, WI: The University of Wisconsin Press, 1993).

8. *Johnson v. Railway Agency*, 421 U.S. 454 (1975); *St. Francis College v. Al-Khazraji*, 481 U.S. 604 (1987).

9. *Patterson v. McLean Credit Union*, 491 U.S. 164 (1989).

10. Jerome Auerbach, *Labor and Liberty: The LaFollette Committee & the New Deal* (New York: The Bobbs-Merrill Co., Inc, 1966).

11. See note 6 above.

12. On state civil rights laws, see Commerce Clearing House, *Employment Practices Decisions* (New York: Commerce Clearing House, various years); Commerce Clearing House, *Guidebook to Fair Employment Practices* (Chicago: Commerce Clearing House, various years).

13. *Sure-Tan, Inc. v. NLRB*, 467 U.S. 883 (1984). See also Christine Neylon O'Brien, "Reinstatement and Back Pay for Undocumented Workers to Remedy Employer Unfair Practices," *Labor Law Journal* 40 (April 1989), pp. 208-215.

14. See Teresa Amott, *Caught in the Crisis: Women and the U.S. Economy Today* (New York: Monthly Review Press, 1993); Donald Tomaskovic-Devey, *Gender & Racial Inequality at Work* (Ithaca, N.Y.: ILR Press, 1993).

15. *Shultz v. Wheaton Glass Co.*, 421 F.2d 896 (3rd Cir. 1974).

16. *Corning Glass Works v. Brennan*, 415 U.S. 972 (1974).

17. England, *Comparable Worth: Theories and Evidence*, pp. 189-224; Ronald G. Ehrenberg and Robert S. Smith, *Modern Labor Economics*, 4th edition. (New York: Harper Collins Publishers, 1991), pp. 575-578.

18. England, *Comparable Worth: Theories and Evidence*, pp. 227-228.

19. *County of Washington v. Gunther*, 452 U.S. 161 (1981).

20. *UAW v. State of Michigan*, 886 F.2d 766 (6th Cir. 1989).

21. *American Nurses Association v. State of Illinois*, 783 F.2d 716 (7th Cir. 1986), at 720.

22. *Los Angeles Department of Power and Light v. Manhart*, 435 U.S. 702 (1978); *Arizona Governing Committee for Tax Deferral v. Norris*, 463 U.S. 1073 (1983).

23. *McDonnell Douglas Corp. v. Green*, 411 U.S. 792 (1972); *Texas Department of Community Affairs v. Burdine*, 450 U.S. 248 (1981); *Postal Services v. Aikens*, 460 U.S. 711 (1983); *Mitchell v. Toledo Hospital*, 964 F.2d 577 (6th Cir. 1992).

24. *Griggs v. Duke Power Company*, 401 U.S. 424 (1971); *Wards Cove Packing v. Atonio*, 490 U.S. 642 (1989). Parts of the *Wards Cove* decision were overturned by Congress in the Civil Rights Act of 1991.

25. *Boyd v. Ozark Airlines*, 419 F. Supp. 1061 (E.D. Mo. 1976).

26. *Wards Cove Packing v. Atonio*, 490 U.S. 642 (1989).

27. *Johnson's v. Uncle Ben's, Inc.*, 965 F.2d (5th Cir. 1992) at 1367. See Catherine Connolly, "The Plaintiff's Burden Under the Particularity Requirement of Title VII," *Labor Law Journal* 44 (Dec. 1993), pp. 771-778.

28. *United States v. State of Maine*, CA-83-0195P, May 26, 1983, cited in David P. Twomey, *Labor and Employment Law*, Ninth Ed. (Cincinnati, OH: South-Western Publishing Co., 1994), p. 478.

29. See Twomey, *Labor and Employment Law*, pp. 477-479; *Albemarle Paper Co. v. Moody*, 422 U.S. 405 (1975).

30. *Friend v. Leidinager*, 588 F.2d 61 (4th Cir. 1978).

31. *UAW v. Johnson Controls, Inc.*, 111 S. Ct. 1196 (1991).

32. *Dothard v. Rawlinson*, 433 U.S. 321 (1977).

33. *Teamsters v. United States*, 431 U.S. 324 (1977).

34. See Camille Colatosti and Elissa Karg, *Stopping Sexual Harassment* (Detroit: The Labor Education and Research Project, 1992), p. 9.

35. *Meritor Savings Bank v. Vinson*, 477 U.S. 57 (1986).

36. *Yates v. Avco Corporation*, 819 F.2d 630 (6th Cir. 1987).

37. *Harris v. Forklift Systems, Inc.*, 114 S.Ct. 367 (1993).

38. *Kaiser Aluminum and Chemical Corp. v. Weber*, 443 U.S. 193 (1979).

39. See Michael Evan Gold, *An Introduction to the Laws of Employment Discrimination* (Ithaca, N.Y.: ILR Press, 1993), pp.15-16; Gertrude Ezorsky, *Racism and Justice: The Case for Affirmative Action* (Ithaca, N.Y.: Cornell University Press, 1991); John A. Gray, "Preferential Affirmative Action in Employment," *Labor Law Journal* 43 (Jan. 1992), pp. 23-30.

40. *U.S. v. Paradise*, 480 U.S. 149 (1987).

41. See the discussion in Bruce Feldacker, *Labor Guide to Labor Law* (Englewood Cliffs, N.J.: Prentice Hall, 1990), pp. 387-398.

42. *Local 93 Firefighters Union v. Cleveland*, 478 U.S. 501 (1986).

43. *Firefighters Local Union v. Stotts*, 467 U.S. 561 (1984); *Wygant v. Jackson Board of Education*, 476 U.S. 267 (1986).

44. *Martin v. Wilks*, 490 U.S. 755 (1989). This decision was overridden by the Civil Rights Act of 1991.

45. See Hill, "Black Workers, Organized Labor, and Title VII of the 1964 Civil Rights Act."

46. *Franks v. Bowman Transportation Co., Inc.*, 424 U.S. 747 (1976).

47. *T.I.M.E.-D.C., Inc. v. United States*, 431 U.S. 324 (1977).

48. See Feldacker, *Labor Guide to Labor Law*, pp. 392-394.

49. *Feldstein v. The Christian Science Monitor*, 30 FEP 1842 (1983); *Mormon Church v. Amos*, 107 S.Ct. 2862 (1987).

50. See Charles E. Mitchell, "New Age Training Programs: In Violation of Religious Discrimination Laws?," *Labor Law Journal* 41 (July 1990), pp. 410-416.

51. *Trans World Airlines v. Hardison*, 432 U.S. 63 (1977). See also Douglas Massengill and Donald J. Petersen, "Job Requirements and Religious Practices: Conflict and Accommodation," *Labor Law Journal* 39 (July 1988), pp. 402-410.

52. *Ansonia Board of Education v. Philbrook*, 479 U.S. 60 (1986).

53. *Fragante v. City and County of Honolulu*, 888 F.2d 591 (9th Cir. 1989). Recently the Supreme Court made a ruling which makes it easier for employers to establish "English Only" rules as matters of business necessity: *Garcia v. Spun Steak Co.* 998 F.2d 1480 (9th Cir. 1993); Cert. denied 62 USLW 3839 (1994).

54. See Gold, *An Introduction to the Laws of Employment Discrimination*, p. 43. See also Durwood Ruegger, "A Twenty- Year History and Review of the ADEA," *Labor Law Journal* 40 (Jan. 1989), pp. 31-36.

55. *Hodgson v. Greyhound Lines, Inc.*, 499 F.2d 859 (7th Cir. 1974).

56. *Western Airlines v. Criswell*, 472 U.S. 400 (1985).

57. Gold, *An Introduction to the Laws of Employment Discrimination*, p. 37.

58. Ibid., pp. 38-39.

59. Barbara L. Wolfe, "How the Disabled Fare in the Labor Market," *Monthly Labor Review* 103 (Sept. 1980), pp. 48-52.

60. Lawrence P. Postol and David D. Kadue, "An Employer's Guide to the Americans with Disabilities Act," *Labor Law Journal* 42 (June 1991), p. 324. See also Gold, *An Introduction to the Law of Employment Discrimination,* pp. 46-63.

61. *Wallace v. Veterans Administration,* 683 F. Supp 758 (D.Kan. 1988).

62. See Francisco Hernandez, "Homosexuals in Public Service: A New Suspect Class," *Labor Law Journal* 42 (Dec. 1991), pp. 800-806.

63. See National Gay & Lesbian Task Force, "Lesbian & Gay Civil Rights in the U.S.," pamphlet (Washington, D.C.: NGLTF, Oct. 1992).

64. Gold, *An Introduction to the Laws of Employment Discrimination,* p. 62.

65. See Miriam Frank and Desma Holcomb, *Pride at Work: Organizing for Lesbian and Gay Rights in Unions* (New York: Lesbian and Gay Labor Network, 1990).

66. See, for example, Tina Plaza, "Let's See Some Papers," *The Progressive* 47 (April 1983), pp. 18-23.

67. See "Mexican Drywallers Movement Stops Southern California's Construction Industry," *Labor Notes* (Sept. 1992), p. 1.

68. See Lewis M. Steel, "Why Attorneys Won't Take Civil Rights Cases," *The Nation* 236 (March 26, 1983), pp. 302 ff.

69. Joseph E. Kalet, *Primer on Wages & Hours Laws* (Washington, D.C.: Bureau of National Affairs, 1990), pp. 64-74.

70. Immigration and Naturalization Service, *Handbook for Employers* (Washington, D.C.: Government Printing Office, 1991).

71. *Gregory v. Litton Systems Inc.,* 472 F.2d 631 (9th Cir. 1972); *U.S. v. Villages of Elmwood Park and Melrose Park,* 43 FEP 995 (1987).

72. See Feldacker, *Labor Guide to Labor Law,* p. 374.

CHAPTER THREE: ORGANIZING A UNION: HISTORY LESSONS

1. This section is drawn from Rev. William H. Carwardine, *The Pullman Strike* (Chicago: Charles H. Kerr & Company, 1973); and Jeremy Brecher, *Strike* (Boston: South End Press, 1972), pp. 78-96.

2. Ray Ginger, *The Bending Cross: A Biography of Eugene Victor Debs* (New Brunswick, N.J.: Rutgers University Press, 1949), p. 110. On Debs, see also Nick Salvatore, *Eugene V. Debs: Citizen and Socialist* (Urbana, Ill.: University of Illinois Press, 1982).

3. See sources in note 2 above.

4. Virgil A. Vogel, "Introduction" to William H. Carwardine, *The Pullman Strike,* p. xx.

5. See Robert Justin Goldstein, *Political Repression in Modern America* (New York: Schenkman Publishing Co., Inc., 1978).

6. An exceptional article is William Forbath, "The Shaping of the American Labor Movement," *Harvard Law Review* 102 (Jan. 1989), pp. 1111-1256.

7. For all you might ever want to know about labor injunctions and then some, see Henry H. Peritt, Jr., *Labor Injunctions* (New York: John Wiley & Sons, 1986).

8. See Haggai Hurvitz, "American Labor Law and the Doctrine of Entrepreneurial Property Rights: Boycotts, Courts, and the Juridical Reorientation of 1886-1895." *Industrial Relations Law Journal* 8 (1986), pp. 307-361.

9. See Christopher L. Tomlins, *The State and the Unions* (Cambridge, England: Cambridge University Press, 1985).

10. Peter Graham Fish, "Red Jacket Revisited: The Case that Unraveled John J. Parker's Supreme Court Appointment," *Law and History Review* 5 (Spring 1987), pp. 51-104.

11. Forbath, "The Shaping of the American Labor Movement," p. 1185.

12. Vogel, "Introduction," p. xxiv.

13. *In re Debs*, 158 U.S. 164 (1895).

14. Forbath, "The Shaping of the American Labor Movement," Appendix B.

15. Jerry Kloby, "The Growing Divide: Class Polarization in the 1980s," *Monthly Review* 39 (Sept. 1987), pp. 1-8.

16. See the multivolume history: Philip S. Foner, *History of the Labor Movement in the United States* (New York: International Publishers, 1947-1965).

17. See Charles O. Gregory and Harold A. Katz, *Labor and the Law* (New York: W.W. Norton & Co., 1979), especially Chapters 1-6.

18. *Black's Law Dictionary*, 5th edition (St. Paul, Minnesota: West Publishing Co., 1979), p. 280.

19. Tomlin, *The State and the Unions*, p. 37.

20. Ibid., p. 37.

21. Marjorie S. Turner, *The Early American Labor Conspiracy Cases* (San Diego: San Diego State College Press, 1967).

22. *Commonwealth v. Hunt*, 4 Metcalf 111 (Mass. 1842). Here the Reporter "Metcalf" is the name of the actual person who made the report. This case was decided before the modern reporting system began.

23. Gregory and Katz, *Labor and the Law*, pp. 93-95.

24. *Hitchman Coal Co. v. Mitchell*, 245 U.S. 229 (1917).

25. Forbath, "The Shaping of the American Labor Movement," pp. 1194-1195.

26. Among many relevant cases, see *Coppage v. Kansas*, 236 U.S. 1 (1915).

27. Forbath, "The Shaping of the American Labor Movement," p. 1133.

28. *Loewe v. Lawlor*, 208 U.S. 274 (1908).

29. *United Leather Workers v. Herkel & Meisel Trunk Co.*, 265 U.S. 457 (1924).

30. See the discussion and citations in Gregory and Katz, *Labor and the Law*, Chapter 7.

31. See the chapters on race and sex in Moody, *An Injury to All*.

32. David Montgomery, *Beyond Equality: Labor and the Radical Republicans* (New York: Vintage, 1967).

33. Forbath, "The Shaping of the American Labor Movement," pp. 1203-1214.

34. Goldstein, *Political Repression in Modern America*, p. 124; and Michael Rogin, "Voluntarism: the Political Functions of an Anti-Political Doctrine," *The Industrial and Labor Relations Review* 15 (July 1962), pp. 521-535.

CHAPTER FOUR: ORGANIZING A UNION: THE CURRENT LAW

1. Michael Goldfield, *The Decline of Organized Labor in the United States* (Chicago: University of Chicago Press, 1987).

2. Feldacker, *Labor Guide to Labor Law*, p. 73.

3. *Rossmore House*, 269 NLRB 1176 (1984).

4. Feldacker, *Labor Guide to Labor Law*, p. 61.

5. *Excelsior Underwear, Inc.*, 156 NLRB 1235 (1966).

6. See Irving Bernstein, *Turbulent Years: A History of the American Worker* (Boston: Houghton Mifflin, 1971).

7. Len DeCaux, *Labor Radical* (Boston: Beacon Press, 1970), p. 163.

8. See Laurence Scott Jackson, "Railway Labor Legislation 1888 to 1930: A Legal History of Congressional Railway Labor Relations Policy," *Rutgers Law Journal* 20 (Winter 1989), pp. 317-391; Dennis A. Arouca and Henry H. Perritt, Jr., "Transportation Labor Regulation: Is the Railway Labor Act or the National Labor Relations Act the Better Statutory Vehicle?," *Labor Law Journal* 36 (March 1985), pp. 145-172.

9. *Texas & N.O.R.R. v. Railway Clerks*, 281 U.S. 548 (1930).

10. 45 U.S.C.A. 152, Note 105 (1988).

11. *Summit Airlines, Inc. V. Teamsters Local 295*, 628 F.2d 787 (2d Cir. 1980).

12. A useful article on what really goes on at the regional office when a worker files a complaint is Matthew M. Franckiewicz, "How to Win NLRB Cases: Tips from a Former Insider," *Labor Law Journal* 44 (Jan. 1993), pp. 40-48.

13. See Feldacker, *Labor Guide to Labor Law*, pp. 25-34.

14. For a good discussion of this and many other issues, see Paul Weiler, "Promises to Keep: Securing Workers' Rights to Self-Organization under the NLRA," *Harvard Law Review* 102 (Jan. 1989), pp. 1111-1256.

15. There are literally hundreds of cases which could be cited here. The interested reader is referred to Raymond L. Hilgert and Sterling H. Schoen, *Cases in Collective Bargaining and Industrial Relations* (Homewood, Ill.: Irwin, 1992). See also *Struknes Construction Co.*, 165 NLRB 1062 (1967) [on employer polls]; *Malta Construction Co.*, 120 LRRM 1209 (1985) [on union insignia]; *Eastex, Inc. v. NLRB*, 98 U.S. 2505 (1978) [on distributing literature].

16. David Brody, *Steelworkers in America: The Nonunion Era* (New York: Harper and Row, 1969).

17. Mike Parker and Jane Slaughter, *Choosing Sides: Labor and the Team Concept* (Boston: South End Press, 1988), especially pp. 48-60.

18. *Electromation, Inc.*, 309 NLRB No. 163 (1992). See also Ellis Boal, "Employee 'Cooperation' Plans Still Illegal," *Labor Notes* (Feb. 1993), p. 3.

19. Mike Parker, *Inside the Circle: A Union Guide to QWL* (Boston: South End Press, 1985).

20. *Spiegel Trucking Co.*, 92 LRRM 1604 (1985).

21. Again, there are hundreds of cases. See Schoen and Hilgert, *Cases in Collective Bargaining and Labor Relations*. Also, *Textile Workers of America v. Darlington Manufacturing Company*, 380 U.S. 263 (1965) [plant closing]; *NLRB v. Erie Resistor Corp.*, 373 U.S. 221 (1963) [special benefits for scabs].

22. *Wright Line*, 251 NLRB 1083 (1980).

23. See Schoen and Hilgert, *Cases in Labor Relations and Collective Bargaining.* Also, *I.L.G.W.U. and Bernard Altman*, 366 U.S. 731 (1961) [agreement with a minority union]; *Carnegie-Illinois Steel Corporation v. United Steelworkers of America*, 353 Pa. 420 (1946) [mass picketing]; *Clear Pine Moldings*, 115 LRRM 1113 (1984) [threats to scabs].

24. *Pattern Makers League v. NLRB*, 473 U.S. 95 (1985).

25. *Local 593, Amalgamated Meat Cutters and Allied Workers of North America*, 237 NLRB 1159 (1978).

26. *NLRB v. Teamsters, Local 239*, 289 F.2d 41 (2nd Cir. 1961); *Department and Specialty Store Employees Union, Local 1265 v. Brown*, 284 F.2d 619 (9th Cir. 1960).

27. See Feldacker, *Labor Guide to Labor Law*, p. 124.

28. *J.P. Stevens*, 102 LRRM 1039 (1979).

29. *NLRB v. Gissel Packing Co.*, 395 U.S. 575 (1969).

30. *United Dairy Farmers Cooperative Association v. NLRB*, 633 F. 2d 1054 (3rd Cir. 1980).

31. *NLRB v. Washington Aluminum*, 370 U.S. 9 (1962).

32. Clyde Summers, "Unions Without Majorities: A Black Hole?," *Chicago-Kent Law Review* 66 (1990), pp. 531-548.

33. See Weiler, "Promises to Keep...", pp. 1816-1819; Paul Weiler, *Governing the Workplace: The Future of Labor and Employment Law* (Cambridge, MA.: Harvard University Press, 1990), pp. 254-261.

34. Weiler, *Governing the Workplace*, p. 112.

35. Joe Crump, "The Pressure's On: Organizing Without the NLRB," *Labor Research Review* 18, p. 33.

36. Reported in *Labor Notes* (Feb. 1993), p. 4.

37. Crump, "The Pressure's On...," pp. 33-44.

38. Ibid., pp. 36-37.

39. Ashley Adams, "Winning Union Recognition Without the NLRB," *Labor Notes* (Feb. 1993), p. 12.

40. See Richard B. Freeman, "Unionism Comes to the Public Sector," *Journal of Economic Literature* 24 (March 1986), pp. 41-86.

41. *Professional Air Traffic Controllers Organization v. FLRA*, 110 LRRM 2676 (1982).

42. See Henry H. Robinson, *Negotiability in the Federal Sector* (Ithaca, N.Y.: ILR Press, 1981), pp. 9-10.

43. Pennsylvania School Board Association, Inc., *Act 195: A Complete Guide to Pennsylvania Public Employee Relations Act of 1970* (Harrisburg, Pa.: Pennsylvania School Boards Association, Inc., 1983).

44. Karen S. Koziara, "Agricultural Labor Relations Laws in Four States: A Comparison," *Monthly Labor Review* 100 (May 1974), 14-18.

45. See Jim Terry, "Campbell Soup in Hot Water with Organized Labor: Farmworkers Seek to Boycott America's Favorite Soups," *Business and Society Review* (Summer 1983), pp. 37-41. Interested readers should consult the January issue of the magazine, *Clearinghouse Review*, for a summary of recent developments in agricultural labor law.

46. See Suzanne Goldberg, "In Pursuit of Workplace Rights: Household Workers and Conflicting Laws," *Yale Journal of Law and Feminism* 3 (Fall 1990), pp. 63-104; Martha F. Davis, "Domestic Workers: Out of the Shadows," *Human Rights* 20 (Spring 1993), p. 14.

47. See Feldacker, *Labor Guide to Labor Law*, pp. 51-52. The Supreme Court recently made it easier for employers to argue that certain nurses are supervisors. *NLRB v. Health Care and Retirement Corporation of America*, 62 USLW 4397 (1994).

48. Ibid., pp. 73-74.

49. Ibid., p. 113.

50. Clyde Scott and Robert Culpepper, "Independent Contractors or Employees: The View from the National Labor Relations Board," *Labor Law Journal* 44 (July 1993), pp. 395-407.

51. *NLRB v. Hendricks County Rural Electric Membership Corp.*, 454 U.S. 170 (1981).

52. *NLRB v. Yeshiva University*, 444 U.S. 672 (1980).

53. *Trustees of Boston University*, 281 NLRB No. 15 (1986).

54. See footnote 2 above.

55. *American Hospital Association v. NLRB*, 111 S. Ct. 1539 (1991).

56. See Feldacker, *Labor Guide to Labor Law*, pp. 39-48.

57. *Globe Machine and Stamping Co.*, 3 NLRB No. 25 (1937).

58. *Mallinckrodt Chemical Works*, 64 LRRM 1011 (1966).

59. See Arouca and Perritt, "Transportation Labor Relations...," pp. 166-170.

60. *In the Matter of the Employees of University of Pittsburgh of the Commonwealth System of Higher Education*, Pennsylvania Labor Relations Board, Case No. PERA-R-2626-C (1973).

61. See, for example, *NLRB v. W.C. McQuaide, Inc.*, 552 F. 2d 519 (1977).

62. *Cafe Tartuffo, Inc.*, 261 NLRB 281 (1982).

63. *St. Francis Hospital I*, 265 NLRB 1023 (1982).

64. See footnote 3 above.

65. See footnote 15 above.

66. See Feldacker, *Labor Guide to Labor Law*, pp. 86-87.

67. See footnote 28 above.

68. *Lechmere, Inc. v. NLRB*, 112 S. Ct. 841 (1992). See also, Jerry M. Hunter, "Current Issues Before the NLRB General Counsel," *Labor Law Developments 1993* 39 (1993), Ch. 2, pp. 2- 13.

69. See Feldacker, *Labor Guide to Labor Law*, pp. 62-64.

70. *NLRB v. City Disposal Systems, Inc.*, 465 U.S. 822 (1984).

71. *Meyers Industries*, 268 NLRB 493 (1984).

72. See Robert Lewis, "Union Decertification: A New Look at Management's Role," *Labor Law Journal* 37 (Feb. 1981), pp. 115- 122.

73. Feldacker, *Labor Guide to Labor Law*, p. 25. For a good example of delay and the hardship it causes workers, see Calvin G. Zon, "Labor Law Reform: We Won't Wait any Longer," *United Mine Workers Journal* 105 (May-June 1994), pp. 4-9.

74. *Republic Aviation Corp. v. NLRB*, 324 U.S. 793 (1945).

75. *Emporium Capwell v. Western Addition Community Organization*, 420 U.S. 50 (1975).

76. *Sure-Tan, Inc. v. NLRB.*

77. See Chapter Two, footnote 13.

78. On prehire agreements, see *John Deklewa & Sons, Inc.*, 282 NLRB No. 184 (1987). See also Arthur B. Shostak, *Robust Unionism: Innovations in the Labor Movement* (Ithaca, N.Y.: ILR Press, 1991), pp. 125-130 for how some unions have responded to the *Deklewa* decision.

CHAPTER FIVE: THE LAW OF COLLECTIVE BARGAINING

1. See Moody, *An Injury to All*, pp. 95-126.

2. Most of this section on the Hormel strike relies upon Peter Rachleff's fine firsthand account of it: Peter Rachleff, *Hard-Pressed in the Heartland: The Hormel Strike and the Future of the Labor Movement* (Boston: South End Press, 1993).

3. Weiler, *Governing the Workplace*, p. 106.

4. *NLRB v. Bildisco & Bildisco*, 465 U.S. 513 (1984). This decision was overturned by law. See 11 USC Section 101 et seq (Supp. 1978). Today a bankruptcy court cannot allow a company to ignore a collective bargaining agreement without first insisting that the company bargain with the union. And even then, the court must conclude that the proposed modifications of the agreement are necessary for the survival of the business.

5. *United Food and Commercial Workers Local P-9*, 123 LRRM 1225 (1986).

6. See *NLRB v. Electrical Workers Local 265*, 602 F.2d 1091 (8th Cir. 1979).

7. *Douds v. Metropolitan Federation*, 75 Supp. 672 (S.D. of N.Y., 1948).

8. See Perritt, *Labor Injunctions*, pp. 82-91.

9. See Chapter Four, footnote 23.

10. Robert M. Schwartz, *The Legal Rights of Union Stewards* (Boston: Work Rights Press, 1988). You can order this very useful book from the publisher at 310 Franklin St., Boston, Mass. 02110.

11. *Communication Workers*, 124 LRRM 1009 (1986).

12. *General Electric Co.*, 57 LRRM 1491 (1964).

13. See *Engineers Limited Pipeline Co.*, 95 NLRB 176 (1951).

14. *NLRB v. General Motors Corp.*, 373 U.S. 734 (1963).

15. *Communication Workers v. Beck*, 487 U.S. 735 (1988).

16. *NLRB v. Wooster Division of Borg-Warner Corp.*, 356 U.S. 342 (1958).

17. *Fibreboard Paper Products Corp. v. NLRB*, 379 U.S. 203 (1964).

18. *First National Maintenance Corp. v. NLRB*, 452 U.S. 666 (1981); *Dubuque Packing Co., Inc. and UFCWIU, Local 150A*, 303 NLRB No. 66 (1991).

19. Feldacker, *Labor Guide to Labor Law*, p. 153.

20. *Milwaukee Springs Div., Illinois Coil Spring Co.*, 115 LRRM 1065 (1984).

21. Ibid.; *NLRB v. C&C Plywood Corp.*, 385 U.S. 421 (1967).

22. *GTE Automatic Electric, Inc.*, 110 LRRM 1193 (1982).

23. *NLRB v. Burns International Security Services, Inc.*, 406 U.S. 272 (1972); *Fall River Dyeing & Finishing Corp. v. NLRB*, 107 U.S. 2225 (1987).

24. *Ex-Cell-O Corp.*, 185 NLRB 20 (1970).

25. See Perritt, *Labor Injunctions*, pp. 501-546, and the many citations listed therein.

26. See Schwartz, *The Legal Rights of Shop Stewards.*

27. *Letter Carriers v. Austin*, 418 U.S. 264 (1974).

28. See *Dairylea Cooperative, Inc.*, 219 NLRB 656 (1975); *Gulton Electro-Voice*, 112 LRRM 1361 (1983), enforced *Electrical Workers IUE Local 900 v. NLRB*, 727 F. 2d 1184 (D.C. Cir. 1984); *BASF Wyandotte Corp.*, 274 NLRB 978 (1985).

29. Schwartz, *The Legal Rights of Shop Stewards*, p. 55.

30. *NLRB v. J. Weingarten, Inc.*, 420 U.S. 251 (1975); *Sears, Roebuck & Co.*, 118 LRRM 1329 (1985).

31. *Taracorp Industries*, 117 LRRM 1497 (1984).

32. The three lead cases are called the "Steelworkers Trilogy": *United Steelworkers v. American Mfg. Co.*, 363 U.S. 561 (1960); *United Steelworkers v. Warrior & Gulf Navigation Co.*, 363 U.S. 574 (1960); *United Steelworkers v. Enterprise Wheel & Car Corp.*, 363 U.S. 593 (1960).

33. Peter Rachleff, "Activism After Last Year's Railroad Defeats Had an Effect on This Year's Bargaining," *Labor Notes* (Oct. 1992), p. 7.

34. See Freeman, "Unionism Comes to the Public Sector," and Michael D. Yates, *Labor Law Handbook* (Boston: South End Press, 1987), pp. 44-51.

35. See Pennsylvania School Boards Association, *Act 195*, pp. 111-146 for references to many such cases.

36. See Feldacker, *Labor Guide to Labor Law*, pp. 146-147.

37. Martin J. Levitt, *Confessions of a Union Buster* (New York: Crown Publishers, Inc., 1993), pp. 163-225.

38. Ibid., p. 224.

39. See, for an example, *NLRB v. Local 13, Longshoremen*, 549 F.2d 1346 (9th Cir. 1977).

40. *Wilson v. NLRB*, 135 LRRM 3177 (1990).

41. *Ellis v. Brotherhood of Railway Clerks*, 466 U.S. 435 (1984).

42. See, for example, William H. Volz and David Costa, "A Public Employee's 'Fair Share' of Union Dues," *Labor Law Journal* 40 (March 1989), pp. 131-137.

43. *National Woodwork Manufacturers Assn. v. NLRB*, 386 U.S. 612 (1967).

44. See footnote 18 above.

45. *Gateway Coal Co. v. United Mine Workers*, 414 U.S. 368 (1974).

46. *IBEW Local 1212, 128 LRRM 1219 (1988)*, affirmed *WPIX, Inc. v. NLRB*, 870 F. 2d 858 (2nd Cir. 1989).

47. *Coca-Cola Bottling Co.*, 227 NLRB 1276 (1977).

48. See *Industrial Union of Marine Workers v. NLRB*, 320 F.2d 615 (3d Cir. 1963); *Nolde Brothers v. Bakery Workers Local 358*, 430 U.S. 243 (1977).

49. *Alexander v. Gardner-Denver Co.*, 415 U.S. 36 (1974).

50. See Chapter Two, footnote 34.

51. On ESOP, see Corey Rosen and Karen M. Young, *Understanding Employee Ownership* (Ithaca, N.Y.: ILR Press, 1991). On WARN, see Wilson McLeod, "Judicial Devitalization of the WARN Act," *Labor Law Journal* 44 (April 1993), pp. 221-229.

CHAPTER SIX: THE WEAPONS OF WAR: STRIKES, PICKETS, BOYCOTTS, AND INJUNCTIONS

1. See Melvyn Dubofsky and Warren Van Tine, *John L. Lewis* (New York: Quadrangle/The New York Times Book Co., 1977); Paul F. Clark, *The Miners' Fight for Democracy: Arnold Miller and the Reform of the United Mine Workers* (Ithaca, N.Y.: ILR Press, 1981).

2. Much of this account of the strike relies on Michael D. Yates, "From the Coal Wars to the Pittston Strike," *Monthly Review* 42 (June 1990), pp. 25-39 and references therein, and upon conversations with my friend, John Duray, special assistant to Richard Trumka, president of the UMW.

3. Yates, "From the Coal Wars to the Pittston Strike," p. 28.

4. *Thornhill v. Alabama*, 310 U.S. 88 (1940).

5. See Chapter Five, footnote 25.

6. *San Diego Building Trades v. Garmon*, 359 U.S. 236 (1959).

7. Perritt, *Labor Injunctions*, pp. 413-439.

8. Ibid., p. 420.

9. Ibid., pp. 433-434.

10. Yates, "From the Coal Wars to the Pittston Strike," p. 29.

11. Ibid., p. 29.

12. See James Gray Pope, "Labor and the Constitution: From Abolition to Deindustrialization," *Texas Law Review* 65 (May   1987), pp. 1071-1136.

13. *County Sanitation District No. 2 of Los Angeles County v. Local 660, SEIU*, 38 Cal. 564 (1985).

14. See Perritt, *Labor Injunctions*, pp. 226-228.

15. *Ashley, Drew & N. Ry. v. UTU*, 625 F.2d 1357 (8th Cir. 1980).

16. This is true under New York's public employee law. See Ronald Donovan, *Administering the Taylor Law* (Ithaca, N.Y.: ILR Press, 1990), pp. 200-229.

17. *Carbon Fuel Co. v. Mine Workers*, 444 U.S. 212 (1979); *Complete Auto Transit, Inc. v. Reis*, 451 U.S. 401 (1981).

18. *Teamster Local 174 v, Lucas Flour Co.*, 369 U.S. 95 (1962).

19. *Boys Markets Inc. v. Retail Clerks, Local 770*, 398 U.S. 235 (1970).

20. *Mastro Plastics Corp. v. NLRB*, 350 U.S. 270 (1956); *Dow Chemical Co.*, 244 NLRB 1060 (1979).

21. *NLRB v. Mackay Radio and Telegraph Co.*, 304 U.S. 333 (1938).

22. *NLRB v. Erie Resistor Corp.*, 373 U.S. 221 (1963); *NLRB v. Great Dane Trailers Inc., 388 U.S. 26 (1967)*.

23. Belknap v. Hale, 463 U.S. 491 (1983).

24. American Shipbuilding Co. v. NLRB, 380 U.S. 300 (1965); *NLRB v. Brown*, 380 U.S. 278 (1965).

25. See Brecher, *Strike*, pp. 101-114.

26. *NLRB v. Local 3, IBEW*, 477 F.2d 260 (2nd Cir. 1973).

27. *Graphic Arts Union, Local 277*, 93 LRRM 1113 (1976).

28. Feldacker has a good discussion of this issue. See Feldacker, *Labor Guide to Labor Law*, pp. 194-196.

29. *Butterworth-Manning-Ashmore Mortuary*, 270 NLRB No. 148 (1984).

30. *Indianapolis Power & Light Co.*, 291 NLRB No. 145 (1988).
31. *Teamsters Local 83*, 96 LRRM 1165 (1977).
32. *Vegelahn v. Guntner*, 167 Mass. 92 (1896).
33. See footnote 4 above.
34. *Carpenters and Joiners Union v. Ritter's Cafe*, 315 U.S. 722 (1942); *Giboney v. Empire Storage and Ice Co.*, 335 U.S. 490 (1949); *Building and Service Employees v. Gazzam*, 339 U.S. 532 (1950); *Plumbers' Union v. Graham*, 345 U.S. 192 (1953).
35. *Lechmere, Inc. v. NLRB*, 112 S.Ct. 841 (1992).
36. *Hudgens v. NLRB*, 424 U.S. 507 (1976).
37. See Feldacker, *Labor Guide to Labor Law*, p. 235.
38. *Elevator Constructors Union Local 3*, 129 LRRM 1066 (1988).
39. *Barker Brothers*, 328 F.2d 431 (9th Cir. 1964).
40. *Claude Everett Construction Co.*, 136 NLRB 321 (1962).
41. *DeBartolo Corp. v. Florida Gulf Coast Building and Construction Trades Council*, 108 S. Ct. 1392 (1988). See also J. Patrick Tielborg, "Handbilling and the First Amendment: The Impact of *DeBartolo v. Florida Building Trades Council*," *Labor Law Journal* 41 (April 1990), pp. 235-248.
42. *NLRB v. Denver and Construction Trade Council*, 341 U.S. 675 (1951).
43. *Sailor's Union of the Pacific (Moore Dry Dock)*, 92 NLRB No. 93, (1950).
44. *Electrical Workers Local 501 v. NLRB*, 756 F.2d 888 (D.C. Cir. 1985).
45. See Footnote 31 above.
46. *Electrical Workers Local 761 v. NLRB (General Electric)*, 366 U.S. 667 (1961).
47. *United Steelworkers of America v. NLRB & Carrier Corp.*, 376 U.S. 492 (1964).
48. See the long discussion in Perritt, *Labor Injunctions*, Chapter 6.
49. Ibid., Chapter 10.
50. *Black's Law Dictionary*, p. 169.
51. See Richard W. Hurd, "Organizing the Poor: The California Grape Strike Experience," *The Review of Radical Political Economics* 6 (Spring 1974), pp. 50-75.
52. *Duplex Printing Press Co. v. Deering*, 254 U.S. 443 (1921).
53. *NLRB v. Fruit and Vegetable Packers and Warehousemen, Local 760 (Tree Fruits Inc.)*, 377 U.S. 58 (1964).
54. *NLRB v. Retail Clerks, Local 1001 (Safeco Title Insurance Co.)*, 447 U.S. 607 (1980).
55. See Perritt, *Labor Injunctions*.
56. See footnote 49 above.
57. See footnote 48 above.
58. See footnote 6 above.
59. *Allis-Chalmers Corp. v. Lueck*, 471 U.S. 202 (1985).
60. *Golden State Transit Corp. v. Los Angeles*, 459 U.S. 1105 (1986).
61. *Lingle v. Norge Div. of Magic Chef*, 108 S.Ct. 1877 (1988).
62. *Sears, Roebuck & Co. v. Carpenters*, 436 U.S. 180 (1978).
63. B.V.H. Schneider, "Public Sector Labor Legislation—An Evolutionary Analysis," in Benjamin Aaron et. al., editors, *Public Sector Bargaining* (Washington, D.C.: BNA, 1988). p. 201.
64. *Buffalo Forge v. Steelworkers*, 428 U.S 397 (1976); *Jacksonville Bulk Terminals, Inc. v. International Longshoremen's Association*, 457 U.S. 702 (1982).

65. *NLRB v. Great Dane Trailers, Inc.*, 388 U.S. 26 (1967).

66. See footnote 54 above.

67. See footnote 52 above.

68. *United States v. Hutcheson*, 312 U.S. 219 (1941).

69. *Allen Bradley Co. v. Local Union No. 3, IBEW*, 325 U.S. 797 (1945).

CHAPTER SEVEN: THE DEMOCRATIC RIGHTS OF UNION MEMBERS

1. This section relies upon Steven Brill, *The Teamsters* (New York: Simon & Schuster, 1978); Kenneth C. Crowe, *Collision: How the Rank and File Took Back the Teamsters* (New York: Charles Scribner's Sons, 1993); Michael J. Goldberg, "Cleaning Labor's House: Institutional Reform Litigation in the Labor Movement," *Duke Law Journal* 1989 (Sept. 1989), pp. 904-1011.

2. Goldberg, "Cleaning Labor's House," p. 909.

3. Crowe, *Collision*, p. 150.

4. *Vaca v. Sipes*, 386 U.S. 171 (1967).

5. *Ford Motor Co. v. Huffman*, 345 U.S. 330 (1953); *Humphrey v. Moore*, 375 U.S. 335 (1964); *Alpa v. O'Neill*, 111 S.Ct. 1127 (1991).

6. *BASF Wyandotte v. ICWU Local 327*, 791 F.2d 1046 (2d Cir. 1987).

7. See H.W. Benson, *Democratic Rights for Union Members* (New York: Association for Union Democracy, 1979).

8. *United Steelworkers of America v. Edward Sadlowski*, 457 U.S. 102 (1982).

9. Goldberg, "Cleaning Labor's House," pp. 927-937.

10. Ibid., p. 986.

11. Ibid., p. 948.

12. Ibid., p. 949.

13. *Steele v. Louisville and Nashville Railroad*, 323 U.S. 92 (1944).

14. *Miranda Fuel Co.*, 140 NLRB 181 (1962).

15. Ibid.

16. See footnote 4 above and Jean T. McKelvey, editor, *The Changing Law of Fair Representation* (Ithaca, N.Y.: ILR Press, 1985). See also Elvis C. Stephens, "The Union's Duty of Fair Representation: Current Examination and Interpretation of Standards," *Labor Law Journal* 44 (Nov. 1993), pp. 685-696.

17. *DelCostello v. Teamsters*, 462 U.S. 151 (1987).

18. See footnote 4 above.

19. *Bowen v. United States Postal Service*, 459 U.S. 212 (1983).

20. *Hines v. Anchor Motor Freight, Inc.*, 424 U.S. 554 (1976).

21. *Riley v. Letter Carriers' Local 380*, 668 F.2d 224 (3d Cir. 1981). See also James E. Jones, Jr., "Time for a Midcourse Correction?," in McKelvey, *The Changing Law Of Fair Representation*, pp. 223-268.

22. *Alpa v. O'Neill*, see footnote 5 above.

23. *Castelli v. Douglas Aircraft Co.*, 752 F.2d 1480 (9th Cir. 1985); see also Robert J. Rabin, "Fair Representation in Arbitration," in McKelvey, *The Changing Law of Fair Representation*, pp. 173-207.

24. *Hellums v. Quaker Oats Co.*, 760 F.2d 202 (8th Cir. 1985).

25. See Feldacker, *Labor Guide to Labor Law*, pp. 334-336; *Tawas Tube Products, Inc.*, 58 LRRM 1330 (1965).

26. *Finnegan v. Leu*, 456 U.S. 431 (1982).

27. See Chapter Four, footnote 25.

28. *H.C. Macaulay Foundry Co. v. NLRB*, 543 F.2d 1198 (9th Cir. 1977).

29. Ibid.

30. Goldberg, "Cleaning Labor's House," pp. 923-925.

31. Clark, *The Miners' Fight for Democracy*.

32. See Levitt, *Confessions of a Union Buster*, pp. 40-43.

33. See Association for Union Democracy, *$50+ Club News*, No. 41 (March 1994), pp. 1-2.

34. See, for example, "U.S. Court Orders New Election in UAW Region 5," *Union Democracy Review* (May 1988), p. 3.

35. Goldberg, "Cleaning Labor's House," pp. 943-946. On ERISA, see Barbara J. Coleman, *Primer on Employee Retirement Income Security Act* (Washington, D.C.: Bureau of National Affairs, 1985).

36. See John C. Truesdale, "The NLRB and the Duty," in McKelvey, *The Changing Law of Fair Representation*, pp. 208-222.

37. See Feldacker, *Labor Guide to Labor Law*, p. 332.

38. See footnote 25 above.

CHAPTER EIGHT: THE CONSTITUTION

1. *Pickering v. Board of Education*, 20 L Ed. 2d 811 (1968).

2. See Jerry Fresia, *Toward an American Revolution: Exposing the Constitution and Other Illusions* (Boston: South End Press, 1988); Jules Lobel, editor, *A Less Than Perfect Union: Alternative Perspectives on the U.S. Constitution* (New York: Monthly Review Press, 1988).

3. See Brecher, *Strike*, pp. 101-143; Goldstein, *Political Repression in Modern America*.

4. Goldstein, *Political Repression in Modern America*, p. 10.

5. *Pickering v. Board of Education*, p. 817.

6. *Givhan v. Western Line Consolidated School District*, 439 U.S. 410 (1979).

7. *Rankin v. McPherson*, 483 U.S. 378 (1987).

8. *Connick v. Myers*, 461 U.S. 138 (1983). Public employee speech rights have been further restricted in *Waters v. Churchill*, 62 USLW 4397 (1994).

9. *Skinner v. Railway Labor Executives' Association*, 109 S.Ct. 1402 (1989).

10. See Augustus Abbey and Charles Redel, "Drug Testing in the Workplace: Public and Private Sector Employers and the Courts," *Labor Law Journal* 42 (April 1991), pp. 239-245.

11. *Black's Law Dictionary*, p. 1081.

12. See Justice Marshall's dissent in *Skinner v. Railway Labor Executives' Association*. The quote is on page 1114 of this   decision.

13. *O'Connor v. Ortega*, 108 S.Ct. 1492 (1987).

14. See footnote 9 above.

15. *National Treasury Employees Union v. Von Raab*, 109 S.Ct. 1384 (1989).
16. See Footnote 10 above and Stephen A. Liem, "The Fourth Amendment and Drug Testing in the Workplace: Current U.S. Court Decisions," *Labor Law Journal* 43 (Jan. 1992), pp. 50-57.
17. *Black's Law Dictionary*, p. 481.
18. See Francisco Hernandez, "Homosexuals in Public Service: A New Suspect Class?," *Labor Law Journal* 42 (Dec. 1991), pp. 800-806.
19. *Watkins v. U.S. Army*, 847 F.2d 1329 (9th Cir. 1988).
20. See Chapter Six, footnote 12.
21. See Chapter Six, footnote 4.
22. See Chapter Six, footnote 34.
23. See Chapter Three, footnote 29.
24. See Chapter Six, footnote 41.
25. *NLRB v. Jones & Laughlin Steel Corporation*, 301 U.S. 1 (1937). See also Richard C. Cortner, *The Jones & Laughlin Case* (New York: Alfred A. Knopf, 1970).
26. See Forbath, "The Shaping of the American Labor Movement," Appendix A.
27. Cortner, *The Jones & Laughlin Case*.

CHAPTER NINE: AT-WILL EMPLOYMENT

1. See William E. Hartsfield, "Polygraphs," *Labor Law Journal* 36 (Nov. 1985), pp. 817-834; Daniel P. Westman, *Whistleblowing: The Law of Retaliatory Discharge* (Washington, D.C.: BNA Books, 1991), pp. 93-95.
2. Isaac Shapiro and Marion Nichols, *Far from Fixed* (Washington, D.C.: Center on Budget and Policy Priorities, 1992).
3. *Black's Law Dictionary*, pp. 250-251.
4. See Brian Hershizer, "The New Common Law of Employment: Changes in the Concept of Employment at Will," *Labor Law Journal* 36 (Feb. 1985), pp. 95-107; Lewis L. Maltby, "The Decline of Employment at Will—A Quantitative Analysis," *Labor Law Journal* 41 (Jan. 1990), pp. 51-54; Marvin J. Levine, "The Erosion of the Employment-at-Will Doctrine: Recent Developments," *Labor Law Journal* 45 (Feb. 1994), pp. 79-89.
5. *Payne v. Western and A.R.R.*, 81 Tenn. 507 (1884).
6. Jack Stieber, "Recent Developments in Employment-at-Will," *Labor Law Journal* 36 (Aug. 1985), p. 557.
7. *Petermann v. Teamsters*, 174 Cal. App. 2d 184 (1959).
8. *Tameny v. Atlantic Richfield Co.*, 27 Cal. 3d 167 (1980).
9. See the many cases cited in Daniel P. Westman, *Whistleblowing: The Law of Retaliatory Discharge*, pp. 81-118.
10. Weiler, *Governing the Workplace*, p. 81.
11. *Monge v. Beebe Rubber Co.*, 114 N.H. 130 (1974).
12. See references in footnotes 1, 4, and 6 above.
13. *Duldulao v. St. Mary Nazareth Hospital Center*, 115 Ill.2d 482 (1987).
14. Weiler, *Governing the Workplace*, p. 54.
15. Ibid., p. 81.

16. See Westman, *Whistleblowing: The Law of Retaliatory Discharge*, pp. 61-80.

17. See Geoffrey Aronson, "Buying Silence," *The Progressive* 56 (Aug. 1992), pp. 25-27.

CHAPTER TEN: HEALTH, SAFETY, WAGES, AND HOURS

1. Laurie Udesky, "Sweatshops Behind the Labels," *The Nation* 258 (May 16, 1994), p. 665.

2. Elizabeth Martinez, "Levi's, Button Your Fly: Your Greed Is Showing," *Z Magazine* 6 (Jan. 1993), p. 25.

3. Ibid., p. 27.

4. JoAnn Wypijewski, "Profits of Pain," *The Nation* 258 (April 11, 1994), p. 472.

5. Udesky, "Sweatshops Behind the Labels," p. 667.

6. Wypijewski, "Profits of Pain," p. 471.

7. Ibid., p. 472.

8. Ibid.

9. Elaine Dodge and Terri Shuck, "Two Years After the North Carolina Poultry Fire, What's Changed?," *Labor Notes* (February 1994), p. 11.

10. David Levin, "Seven-Month Lockout Ends in Victory for Restaurant Workers in New York's Chinatown," *Labor Notes* (May 1994), p. 16.

11. Glenn Omatsu, "How Prejudice Against Asian Workers is Hurting Unions in the United States," *Labor Notes* (May 1992), p. 8.

12. Most of the information on the Fair Labor Standards Act is taken from Joseph E. Kalet, *Primer on Wage & Hour Laws* (Washington, D.C.: The Bureau of National Affairs, Inc., 1990).

13. Ibid., Appendix C.

14. Ibid., pp. 39-40.

15. Ibid., p. 33.

16. Ibid., 34.

17. Ibid., Appendix C.

18. Ibid., pp. 41-42.

19. Yates, *Labor Law Handbook*, pp. 84-85.

20. Wypijewski, "Profits of Pain," p. 472.

21. Barbara Ellen Smith, "History and Politics of the Black Lung Movement," *Radical America* 17 (March-June 1983), pp. 89-109.

22. Much of the information on the OSH Act is taken from Don J. Lofgren, *Dangerous Premises: An Insider's View of OSHA Enforcement* (Ithaca, N.Y.: ILR Press, 1989).

23. Ibid., p. 1.

24. *Marshall v. Barlow's, Inc.*, 436 U.S. 307 (1978).

25. *Martin v. OSHRC*, 111 S.Ct. 1171 (1991).

26. Lofgren, *Dangerous Premises*, p. 205.

27. *Industrial Union Department v. American Petroleum Institute*, 448 U.S. 607 (1980).

28. *American Textile Manufacturers Institute v. Donovan*, 452 U.S. 490 (1981).

29. *UAW v. General Dynamics Land Systems Division*, 815 F.2d 1570 (D.C. Cir. 1987).

30. Lofgren, *Dangerous Premises*, pp. 2-4.

31. Ibid., p. 4.

32. Ibid., pp. 201-203.

33. Ibid., pp. 212-221.

34. Loretta Samenga, "Workers' Compensation: The Exclusivity Doctrine," *Labor Law Journal* 41 (Jan. 1990), pp. 13-21.

INDEX

About South End Press

South End Press is a nonprofit, collectively-run book publisher with over 180 titles in print. Since our founding in 1977, we have tried to meet the needs of readers who are exploring, or are already committed to, the politics of radical social change.

Our goal is to publish books that encourage critical thinking and constructive action on the key political, cultural, social, economic, and ecological issues shaping life in the United States and in the world. In this way, we hope to give expression to a wide diversity of democratic social movements and to provide an alternative to the products of corporate publishing.

If you would like a free catalog of South End Press books or information about our membership program—which offers two free books and a 40% discount on all titles—please write to us at South End Press, 116 Saint Botolph Street, Boston, MA 02115.

Other titles of interest from South End Press:

Hard-pressed in the Heartland:
The Hormel Strike and the Future of the Labor Movement

Peter Rachleff

Strike!
A History of the American Workers Movement

Jeremy Brecher

Plant Closures: Myth, Realities, and Responses

Gilda Hass

Women in the Global Factory

Annette Fuentes and Barbara Ehrenreich

Toward an American Revolution:
Exposing the Constitution and Other Illusions

Jerry Fresia